THE KOHUT SEMINARS

on Self Psychology and Psychotherapy
With Adolescents and Young Adults

By Heinz Kohut

*The Analysis of the Self: A Systematic Approach
to the Psychoanalytic Treatment of
Narcissistic Personality Disorders* (1971)

The Restoration of the Self (1977)

How Does Analysis Cure? (1984),
Edited by Arnold Goldberg
with the collaboration of Paul E. Stepansky

*The Search for the Self: Selected Writings of
Heinz Kohut 1950–1978,*
Edited by Paul H. Ornstein.
Two Volumes (1978):
Volume III forthcoming

*Self Psychology and the Humanities:
Reflections on a New Psychoanalytic Approach* (Norton, 1985)
Edited by Charles B. Strozier

By Miriam Elson

Self Psychology in Clinical Social Work

A NORTON PROFESSIONAL BOOK

THE KOHUT SEMINARS

on Self Psychology and Psychotherapy

With Adolescents and Young Adults

Edited by

MIRIAM ELSON

W. W. NORTON & COMPANY • *NEW YORK* • LONDON

Published simultaneously in Canada by Penguin Books Canada Ltd.,
2801 John Street, Markham, Ontario L3R 1B4.

Printed in the United States of America.

Library of Congress Cataloging-in-Publication Data

Kohut, Heinz.
    The Kohut seminars.

    Originally published: Self esteem and ideals.
[Chicago?] : M. Elson, c1974.
    "A Norton professional book"—P. facing t.p.
    Includes bibliographical references.
    1. Adolescent psychotherapy. 2. Self. 3. Kohut,
Heinz. I. Elson, Miriam. II. Kohut, Heinz. Self
esteem and ideals. III. Title
RJ503.K64 1987   616.89′14′088055   87-7724

ISBN   0-393-70041-0

W. W. Norton & Company, Inc., 500 Fifth Avenue, New York, N.Y. 10110
W. W. Norton & Company Ltd., 37 Great Russell Street, London WC1B 3NU

                1 2 3 4 5 6 7 8 9 0

Foreword

THOSE WHO ARE trying to help people via psychotherapy will be grateful to Miriam Elson for having taped and carefully edited my husband's ensuing lectures and discussions. I believe that they are unique in that they clearly illustrate how he taught, how he viewed psychotherapy, and what contributions he believed psychoanalysis can make to psychotherapy. His empathic approach to the students described in the case vignettes, his ability to see and explain the subtle nuances of feeling and their influence on the relationships between the students and their families, and his ability to see a variety of explanations for the way in which the students functioned are clearly spelled out.

What one learns from these chapters is not only theory but, perhaps more importantly, a way of seeing our patients or clients. We learn to see, or try to see, their core selves and how those selves are struggling to maintain and fulfill themselves. It is because of Mrs. Elson's patient persistence and scholarship that these lectures have been made available. I, for one, am very grateful to her.

Elizabeth Kohut

Contents

Introduction

A N EDITOR OF A SERIES of seminars by a distinguished and gifted teacher remains under the spell of his spoken word. One seeks to master his characteristic style in order to render a faithful account to the reader. But what is spoken may have to be stated in a variety of ways so that the listener can absorb nuances of reasoning. To the reader who needs only to look again at a phrase or sentence, this may become a needless intrusion. Working from tapes, I have tried to retain and present in these pages the experience of those who participated in the seminars: the sense of discovery, the spirited exchange, the process of mastering complex theoretical considerations, or the hope of further study which would lead to such mastery in the future.

For three-fourths of a year, Dr. Heinz Kohut shared with the staff of the Student Mental Health Clinic of the University of Chicago the rich gleanings of his psychoanalytic practice and research in the study of narcissism. He was completing a monograph, later published under the title of *The Analysis of the Self: A Systematic Approach to the Psychoanalytic Treatment of Narcissistic Personality Disorders*. The clinical application of his theories to our work with university students seemed particularly relevant.

Many young people achieve university admission with a background of substantial achievement in some field. Their promise of future greatness is fueled by the approval of parents, mentors, and friends. In the new social environment to which they have come, they expect a continuity of this approval, fulfillment of that destiny for which they have been prepared. Competition with other well-prepared students comes as a sudden disruption of what has appeared to be a continuous course, well laid out, and they are forced to reorganize their feelings and thoughts about themselves and their destiny. This occurs both in the lives of students whose grades continue at a very high level and those for whom

ix

grades indicate less preparation, less promise, or less interest in pursuing a course of study than anticipated. These students suffer painful loss of confidence; they question their own worth and the value of long-cherished goals. They complain of emptiness, of feeling unloved, of being unable to respond to others. They may experience severe depression, disturbing dreams, immobilization or frenetic activity; they may have painful physical symptoms. In sum, under the impact of transition, their self-system becomes painfully exposed and vulnerable to illness.

Although social forces have shaken loose many of the rigidities which distort human growth, they have at the same time weakened some of the supports which enhance it. Rarely in history has the individual been so visible and his needs so much a matter of massive concern. Yet, simultaneously, an examination of the inner life of the individual has seldom appeared so futile an exercise as now in the face of the profound threat to human survival.

Students are keenly aware of this paradox. A study of the role of narcissism, its states of equilibrium and imbalance in youth, offers another dimension to our understanding of the ways in which we can free young people for the process of forging new ideals and goals for themselves and society. The vicissitudes of individual growth have always had profound and far-reaching consequences for communities and nations. The leaders who emerge become the symbols of the future.

Young men and women are at various stages of transition from the first years of college through attainment of a doctoral degree, contending with internal demands and external forces which severely test their self-esteem and threaten disturbing inroads into their system of ideals, values and goals. Most students accomplish this transition, not without difficulty or suffering, but with increased strength, enhanced self-esteem, an expansion of their values and guiding ideals, a better delineation of their goals. Without becoming engulfed or overwhelmed, they appear to move between highly productive academic work and those additional pleasures which enrich life—a loving relationship, friends, various cultural and physical activities, or simple playful behavior. When they do become deeply upset, they appear to be able to employ measures which restore their equilibrium.

What is it that differentiates these young people from others who suffer a profound loss of gratification in their work, family, friends, or activities? Why is it that some students are unable to modulate internal forces and external demands, instead withdrawing from society or seeking out groups which lead them away from vigorous pursuit of solutions to their problems or to the problems of society?

To consider these questions with us, Kohut first presented his theories about the genesis of narcissism, its lines of development and its vicissitudes in youth. Following this, psychiatrists, social workers, and psychiatric residents presented case vignettes for discussion. Essentially case fragments drawn at random, they represented mild forms of disturbance, for it is in the milder forms of imbalance that a system in transition can be studied.

One may well question how the insights and modes of work in prolonged psychoanalytic treatment of narcissistic personality disorders can be applied to work with students. The special aid in working with these young men and women is that, even for students with lifelong habits of loneliness and isolation, there is a great pressure to confide. Shorn of the customary supports of family and familiar surroundings, and faced by increasing demands to function as adults, they experience a keen sharpening of their senses. Everything they see, read, or experience in waking or dreaming states resonates to earlier stages of their development. There is a certain urgency in the time at which they come for help, and they are eager to avail themselves of this help. The freshness of their experiences, the poignancy of their memories, the richness of their imagery make it possible to work with these students over relatively brief periods of time.

There are, of course, many young students whose emotional difficulties will require a long period of treatment and some for whom leaving school to give this procedure the priority it requires is the only avenue available to them. But in these seminars Kohut never permitted us to feel that because our insights were derived from relatively brief treatment modes they were less valid. Rather, he allowed us to feel included in the breadth and depth of his understanding of the human organism. He shared with us, as colleagues, the difficulties he experienced in working through complex problems of human illness. And he enlarged our view of the potential for health in human strivings, which are often labeled immature personality distortions. As a lecturer, teacher and contributor, his wish was to stimulate certain thought processes. The subject matter studied was open to our experience, as it will be to the reader's, and thus, in communicating, we need only touch on certain experiential configurations in others to evoke the same content or feeling tone.

The contributions of these seminars is in an understanding of the genesis and growth of narcissism, its forms and transformations throughout life as the source of our pride in ourselves and of our guiding ideals and values. The complexities of narcissism in our relations with others, as well as in its relationship to the parallel line of development of object love, is worked out in rich detail. It is illuminated by concrete clinical material drawn from Kohut's research and from cases presented by seminar participants.

A dozen years have elapsed since Heinz Kohut conducted these seminars, which I originally edited under the title of *Self Esteem and Ideals: The Development of Narcissism and Its Vicissitudes in Youth*.[1] Yet their relevance for understanding and working with young people remains unabated. This is true whether they are students seeking to define and professionalize their skills and talents at college and universities or young people not in school but seeking definition and worth in the work world and in society.

Up to the time of his death in 1981, and reflected in his numerous publications, Kohut continued to develop and enlarge the basic concepts of self psychology. Others have traced their development in his work, notably Paul Ornstein in his introductory chapter to *The Search for the Self: Selected Writings of Heinz Kohut: 1950–1978* (1978). The unique value of these seminars, however, is that they provide an opportunity to study the spontaneous workings of Kohut's mind as he moved from clinical experience to theory building and then returned to live clinical experience. The care with which he examined well-established concepts to determine their potential usefulness, or the regret with which he relinquished them when he came to the conclusion that they no longer had the power to illuminate behavior or feeling states, is open to the reader. So, too, is his empathic mode of observation, his ability to view the whole individual and only then to consider symptomatic behavior as part of the individual's striving to regulate self-esteem, to establish relationships, to find and pursue meaningful goals.

One can trace in early form the emergence of Kohut's concept of the self in infancy, its consolidation in early childhood, and the sustenance of the self in adult life. He illustrated the unique function of selfobjects for youth in transition to adult life, demonstrating through clinical examples that the healing power within the self/selfobject matrix lies in the opportunity for a response by a new selfobject to the particular mirroring and idealizing needs the individual exposes. He further illustrated the manner in which these selfobject functions are transmuted into self-

---

[1]Copyright 1974. Copies were made available to seminar members and to Dr. Paul Ornstein for use in a seminar he conducted for the faculty and staff of the department of psychiatry of the University of Cincinnati Medical Center, 1975–76. Additional copies were made available to a number of members of the faculty and staff of the Chicago Institute for Psychoanalysis.

functions as the individual seeks to master new tasks in the pursuit of goals. I have sought through footnotes to alert the reader to relevant material in Kohut's later publications in which he develops and carries forward specific concepts which appear in these seminars in larval form. The footnotes are deliberately brief in order to avoid unnecessary intrusion in the flow of the discussion.

In once more preparing these seminars for publication, I have most recently had the assistance of Elizabeth M. Kohut, a colleague for many years and an old and valued friend. Only minor changes in the original edition of the seminars have been made for the purpose of clarification. In studying Kohut's spoken word and his exceptional gift for describing the process by which he arrived at clinical and theoretical formulations, the reader will have an opportunity to observe a gifted scholar, theoretician and clinician at work.

Miriam Elson
Chicago, 1987

THE KOHUT SEMINARS

on Self Psychology and Psychotherapy

With Adolescents and Young Adults

SECTION I

Theory

1

Value Judgments
Surrounding Narcissism

M Y FAVORITE MODE of teaching, learning, and interacting, perhaps even with patients, but of course much more so with colleagues, is on the level of an appropriate mixture between concrete clinical material and theoretical understanding. There is no such thing as pure clinical observation, regardless of the particular specialty in which we engage. Any clinical observation has in the background of the observer something of ordering principles. One has to be prejudiced in some way to see anything. The person who has been blind all his life and now is led back to sight sees nothing. He sees a confusing array of impressions. His own reality is to learn what to expect. To learn, for example, that certain configurations are called tables and serve specific purposes is necessary so that then he can "see" tables. So prejudice-free, theoretically unencumbered observation exists nowhere, and certainly not in our field. It is not a question of no theory and no prejudice. It is only a question of good theory and/or improvable theory.

Any theory is hypothetical. But there are axiomatic ideas that are not hypothetical. They are simply ordering principles. One can propose to look at people from the point of view of their size and divide them into large, small, and medium-sized. This is indisputable. But to propose then to use this as a means of determining how much they need to eat would have no heuristic value, since large people would not necessarily eat more than small people. Still, the division into size as a way of looking at people would be axiomatic and need not be questioned; it is only to be questioned in terms of its usefulness.

When one develops any kind of theory at all—as, for example, in my deciding to speak of narcissism—there is already a host of theoretical assumptions present. Anybody who wishes to question my basic right to talk about narcissism could easily bring up a good many arguments, and we would have to spend our time defending the topic. So just as Coleridge (1907, p. 6) spoke of "the willing suspension of disbelief," there is also a necessity for the *willing suspension of disbelief* when you listen to a particular mode in which a topic is presented to you. I do not suggest the willing suspension of disbelief forever; I suggest only a suspension of disbelief until you have grasped what the other person has to offer. In other words, one does not object before one has first heard the other person out to some extent.

What I therefore propose is a series of lectures concerning narcissism, and particularly the contributions I hope I have made to this particular field in recent years, encouraging in the course of these initial sessions your active participation in making further contributions drawn from your own thinking and from your theoretical and clinical experience. We will then shift from this type of interaction to other modes in which current clinical material takes on a much more important role than our initial use of it.

At first we will use clinical material to illustrate subsidiary theoretical points in order to make things concrete. But later on our purpose will be to test out such clinical data vis-à-vis the ideas that I have presented to you, and thus to examine their usefulness. Does their explanatory power actually assist you in understanding and therefore in managing, helping, and technically handling the human problem area that you encounter for the specific purpose that we tend to call cure, help, assistance, adaptation or whatever normative or less normative value judgments you may introduce? This can be on the broad spectrum from maturation and growth to the more narrowly conceived initial, immediate, or temporary adaptation.

These are all value judgments that we introduce: The patient seeks help in order to become more mature—or at least that is what he says and this is what we assume we are doing. But in order to achieve this kind of goal—again this is another axiom, another assumption that for our purposes I do not think we need to question—we assume that our understanding of what is going on in the patient will help us to make him more mature, help him to adapt. This may be questioned, but in our circle we assume this to be an axiomatic truth. I do not mean to say it would not be appropriate to make the question of cure the topic of another kind of discussion group, but I like to be clear about what I discuss; otherwise, one goes from X to Y and finds no real answer.

It has been one of the unspoken assumptions in psychiatry of almost any persuasion that the most important dimension of human development and of human activity is best assessed by examining an individual's relationship to others, predominantly of course, to other people, but secondarily in a broader sense to objects. The word *objects* is most frequently used in psychoanalysis, as well as in the fields of psychiatry and of the other anthropological specialties that cluster around dynamic psychiatry, to include not only people but other foci of human interest outside the individual. *Objects* may suffice to describe other people, animals, pets, interests in things one pursues, such as art, music, or whatever it may be. And generally health has been measured by the degree to which people are capable of an unencumbered, rich, variegated, profound, intense interest in objects.

Now man in his object world can be approached in an enormously sophisticated way. The mere use of the word *object* instead of *people*—the richness of such a term, in contrast to *other-directedness*, which relates narrowly to people—the richness, the capacity of broad application, needs hardly any defense. It includes awareness that it is completely compatible with the heights of health for a person to be lonesome. Lonesomeness and even aloofness are not in opposition to object love. As a matter of fact, as you know full well, people who shed objects indiscriminately, who can lose one seemingly beloved person and immediately turn toward another person and replace and substitute, lose one pet and buy another the next day, frequently reflect shallowness of object relationships. We know that people who have been traumatized early in life in their object relationships tend to be just this particular type. They quickly, like stray dogs, attach themselves to anybody who comes along, without discriminating between one or the other and without any real continuity. They cannot stand being alone, and not being able to stand being alone, cannot truly attach themselves to others. The loss of others, if one really attaches himself to these others, if one is really capable of such attachment, is accompanied by the one great sign or proof of object love: the capacity to suffer when an object is lost, the capacity to mourn or to long for an object when it is not present. The individual who quickly passes from attachment to attachment must indeed have an object present, but these are pseudo-objects.

But I do not propose here to talk about object love—this is another developmental line. I simply want to caution you that there must be great sophistication when we deal with the object world.

The wealth of the explanatory power of a system of psychology can to some extent be demonstrated by the variety of ways in which, for example, objects are to be experienced. There has been the unspoken assumption—although in the theoretical sense it has often been denied—that the capacity for object love is *the* sign of emotional maturity. The implication has always been that normal development leads from self-preoccupation to preoccupation with objects, from self-concern to concern with others, and more simply from egoism to altruism. It is my contention that, while a good deal is to be said in favor of this approach, by presenting it to you in this way I may be reproached with caricaturing the meaning or presenting it too extremely in order to make a point. Later on I will present this in a more sophisticated way that I hope will put me beyond this reproach.

Theoretically it has often been said that the term *narcissism* is not a value judgment. Yet, there is no question that in practical application it is, and not only in the psychoanalytic locker-room chitchat: "He is narcissistic" meaning "down with him," as opposed to "He has a full array of object love," so "up with him." It is a value judgment in terms of the much more sophisticated conceptualizations of a developmental or maturational sequence.

There is an unspoken assumption (sometimes not so unspoken) that confuses developmental sequences with value judgments: In other words, that mature is good and immature is bad, that mature is valuable but that immature is not valuable. Such terms, for example, as *fixation* and *regression*, although they describe simply moments in a developmental scale, become subtle value judgments. "He is regressing" or "he has remained fixated on this level" implies that we must help him get unfixated and develop quickly up to where he belongs. Again, having said something averse in a somewhat caricaturing way, I must take it back. To some extent this is true, or at least not entirely wrong. But what are value judgments? In what way is maturity better than fixation at a regressive point? For what purpose is it more valuable to be mature rather than immature?

If you put evaluative judgments in an epigenetic sequence as, for example, Erikson did (1956), and examine them, you find they are really value judgments. It is good to be trusting; it is bad not to be trusting. It is good to be autonomous; it is not good to be symbiotic. Under the guise of description, of fact-reporting, a sequence of value judgments of opposing couples is introduced, of which one is always good and the other always bad. If you define the point of view from which you evaluate things as good or bad, then you are perfectly right. But what are such points of view?

An honest point of view is the one that Heinz Hartmann introduced into psychoanalysis in writing about adaptation. He does not say whether adaptation is good or bad necessarily; he examines phenomena from the point of view of adaptation, and he adds, in a very sophisticated way, adaptation to an average expected environment (Hartmann, 1958, p. 55). From this point of view one can say that in an average expected human environment what is usually called maturity in the sequence tends to be the very best mode of functioning that leads to adaptation. This is not necessarily true in environments that are not of average expected nature. For instance, under extreme political circumstances, certain paranoid characters are the only ones who have the courage to stand up, while the average expected mature person tends to shrink into oblivion and death. Under extreme circumstances—I am just giving some tentative examples—the messianic character who thinks he is invulnerable and is not afraid of his own death will carry the flag high and perhaps encourage some people to follow his leadership and stand up against oppression. This is just to illustrate that what is adaptive depends entirely on the circumstances and what is quite maladaptive may under certain circumstances become the best there is.

Leader figures chosen by nations under normal circumstances are very different from leader figures chosen under extreme circumstances. Under normal circumstances Churchill does not get elected in England for good reasons. Under circumstances, however, on the brink of disaster, when only a person with enormous ideas of invulnerability and enormous conviction of the total righteousness and greatness of his own kind is needed to key people up against despair, then such a person is pushed into the foreground. A person like Churchill is chosen—a person of the utmost maturity, this cigar smoking, chain-smoking man who has to have his staff conferences embedded like a happy baby, who has to drink champagne in the morning for breakfast, who in his teens had fantasies in which he believed that he could jump off a bridge and not be killed. Perhaps you remember the little vignette I wrote in one of the papers (Kohut, 1966) you read in preparation for this seminar; to my mind, Churchill very likely had some kind of grandiose fantasy that he was invulnerable and could fly. And yet, it is just such a person who is needed under certain circumstances in order to aid adaptation.

Now again, all this has to be treated with sophistication. A mere flying fantasy is not adaptive. A fixation on an early phase of development is not adaptive at any time. But development within a fixation point can become highly adaptive. The very fixation on old modes of development, if they become subjugated by a certain rich ramification of the total personality, can lead to results that are vastly superior in our evaluations.

But you have to say, evaluating of what? What am I leading up to? I am leading up to the point that until not so long ago, notwithstanding some sort of detached theoretical statements to the contrary, narcissism was considered to be no good under this particular kind of prejudiced value judgment. Something quite correct entered here into a marriage with something quite incorrect. There are indeed many forms of narcissism, as there are many forms of object love, that are maladaptive and, if you wish, sick. But even these concepts, sickness and health, are value judgments. There is no way in which one can define sickness. It defies definition; one returns to maladaptive. Again, the ideal state of full development and perfect functioning of some abstract organism or some abstract psyche depends only on the average expected environment, not on some other environment.

We will be talking about the pathology of narcissism. We will in many ways show how certain modes of narcissism are indeed a hindrance in adaptation, in well-being, in happiness, in relating to the world, in relating to one's work, in relating to all kinds of things that we justifiably consider to be valuable. Exactly the same thing could be said for certain types of object fixations. I would think that while it is quite justifiable to find out the non-adaptive, non-valuable aspects of certain modes of narcissism, narcissism in and of itself in general cannot be said to be non-adaptive.

Now where does this value judgment come from? As I said, it comes from two sides. The one is the ingrained prejudice that object love develops out of narcissism (in other words, that narcissism disappears as object love appears) and that when object love is at its height, then narcissism is at its lowest ebb. A lovely ramification of this value judgment is that in maturity man is most involved with object love. The second prejudice is that as he gets older and becomes less able to deal with the world, he becomes again more narcissistic—regresses to childhood, as it were, to babyhood. This is all to some extent a truthful observation. And yet, this is not a proof that narcissism is not as good as object love. It only shows that non-adaptive narcissism, pathological narcissism, less valuable narcissism perhaps—I say *perhaps* right away— appears at times like an early childhood in later life. At the height of one's powers, it seems to have receded. But again, even a little reflection will tell you that one has to be more sophisticated.

It is perfectly clear that when one is ill, for example, one has to be narcissistic in order to be healed. When one is in the throes of a severe physical illness, one cannot at this particular time be tremendously preoccupied with people. My value judgment would then be that a person who is ill and who cannot retire to his bed, when his fever is high and he really should concentrate on the healing processes in his own body, reveals something amiss in his psychic economy, even though one might say it is admirable that, despite his illness, he is still preoccupied with others.

Certainly in old age, as one's powers narrow down, one naturally has to husband one's forces and look after oneself. One is naturally more narcissistic, and therefore such narcissism is more adaptive. I have nothing against the value judgment that says, "We like people best at the height of their powers in the middle of their life." Why not? But it reveals nothing about narcissism per se.

The mere fact that there has been an ingrained idea that object love develops out of narcissism, that any return to narcissism is a valueless, or value-decreased regression, is one of the ways that has caused us to push narcissism aside, as something to be put out of the way, to be replaced by the capacity to relate to others. Do not underestimate, however, the total cultural setting in which we are living. For nearly 2,000 years we have lived in a culture, particularly the Western culture, in which altruism is the height of all virtue. To love one's neighbor more than oneself, essentially not to be concerned with oneself, that is obviously a value of the highest degree. It has tended to become the only basic value. And even though some people might not subscribe to organized religious beliefs, even though they might be professed atheists, it is much easier to be an atheist than to withdraw from such a broad cultural outlook as the one concerning the overriding value of altruism.

There has been a cultural overvaluation or unique valuation of altruism. It has buttressed a particular type of prejudice, and, I believe, narrowed our vision concerning the evaluation of psychological phenomena in a very important aspect of the human mind. It may take the form of a true religious belief or a vague general feeling of the way people ought to live; it may become a sociopolitical translation of religious belief or socialism. Regardless of what form it takes, the marriage of this type of cultural ideal with the ideal of development and maturation has its own evaluated judgment. This is true particularly since Darwin: the higher form of development is considered better than the lower one. These two attitudes have combined to narrow our view on narcissism, and in particular on the one basic tenet that I would like to submit to you as I have done in the past. Namely, not only do primitive forms of object relatedness develop into higher forms of object relatedness, but narcissism in and of itself has its own developmental sequence, its own mode of development, its own series of developmental steps. Narcissism has its own epigenetic sequence, as does object love, but this has to be looked upon in a sophisticated fashion.

We will try to investigate lower and earlier forms of narcissism, and see how, in the various phases of development throughout life, up and down, these may develop, describing in sequence how one follows the other. We may in general say that we like certain forms of narcissism more than others. For example, if somebody were to say that in motherhood the child is included in the mother's narcissism, the flag goes up.

That is good narcissism. But if somebody watches his bank account and feels connected with the height of the numbers, this is around the anal possessions and is bad narcissism. We have to be sophisticated and not immediately place a value judgement on the term narcissism; rather, we have to examine how it develops. We should be equally sophisticated in terms of the various phases of the development of narcissism—or, to speak with Anna Freud (1963), the developmental line of narcissism—and evaluate the various way stations within this developmental line.

We must question the prejudice that what comes later is necessarily better; we must say only that perhaps in an average expected environment what comes later is probably better. Occasionally in specific circumstances what comes earlier may cluster out and develop in such an unusual way that it becomes culturally (value judgments tend to be within the cultural framework) more valuable than, let us say, later modes of development.

I would like to make one other very crucial basic point of understanding or definition concerning the topic that we will be dealing with. Narcissism is by definition the investment of the self, the instinctual libidinal investment of the self. (I use psychoanalytic terminology because it happens to be the one I am familiar with.) In psychoanalytic language when we say instinctual investment of an object we use the word cathexis as another word to describe the phenomenon. The degree of attention, the degree of appetite, the degree of wanting to get to it, of having it, that is drive-connected and that is clustered around the image of an object—this we call the cathexis or investment of an object. The contrast to the investment of objects, or to use the broadest and easiest of terms, object love, is narcissism, that is, the love of the self, the investment of the self with all the things that one does to something that is being loved. One wants to maintain it; one wants to show it off; one wants to have it close. Narcissus was in love with himself. Of course, this is a gross symbolic representation of a much more subtle set of circumstances; so is mythology in general.

But how about objects as narcissism? It is an old error that is extremely important to be clear about: narcissism does not exclude object relations. Object relations are not the same thing as object love. There are many relationships to other people that have nothing to do with loving other people but that are in the service of narcissistic aims. As a matter of fact, some of the most intense relationships to objects serve narcissistic purposes.

There is a theoretical zero point in development—and it really is only a theoretical point—that is often called primary narcissism (S. Freud, 1914c). I will not bother you much with that concept, only mentioning that it has a certain usefulness. It is not something that exists, but, like a zero point in the infinite at one side of a mathematical or geometrical equation, serves some usefulness. It is an ordering principle to the type of observations that we can indeed make with babies (unless you are an extreme environmentalist) that there are innate propensities by which a baby can be more or less easily stimulated. Let us say with X numbers of stimulations from a particular type of good mother, so-and-so many babies will respond. But there will be a number of babies who will need more stimulation than that, and some babies will not respond to the finest stimulation. Others will respond to the very minimum of stimulation from the environment without retiring and retreating upon themselves. In extreme examples of lack of stimulation in hospitals, some (not all) babies will wall themselves off (Spitz, 1945, 1946); here life itself seems to retreat.

So primary narcissism is not a clinical phenomenon, but a kind of directional force. The concept is perhaps most sensibly employed when we talk about such unknown factors as the innate propensity toward narcissistic fixations versus the capacity to develop narcissism into higher forms or to develop a rich and variegated object life. What we experience and what we can observe as narcissism is very much involved in a setting of object relations from the outset of life. The object, however, is first of all not loved under these circumstances, not cognitively recognized as something separate from the primitive self. It is either experienced as a part of the self or used for the maintenance of self-love, self-cathexis, self-investment—narcissism.[1]

In a simpler form, when an exhibitionist, sexual or nonsexual, shows his penis off in a park, or in a subway or a bus, to a woman with glasses, he does not love that person. He needs her tremendously, but there is no love involved. There is nothing that this person has that another person does not have. Perhaps the fact that glasses are necessary for this—I'm using a particular clinical example—defines at least some beginning rudimentary differentiation of a particular narcissistically invested object. This is not, however, a loved object, but an object that he uses for the reaffirmation of the powerful impression of his penis, of how frightening his penis can be, how much blushing and embarrassment it can produce in the person to whom he shows it. He needs this prop in the environment, but it is a narcissistic prop. It is a prop in the service of something that has reference only to a specific mode of heightening his self-esteem, in terms of the powerfulness of his penis. Regardless of whether there is

---

[1]This forecasts the evolution of the concept of selfobject (see Kohut, 1978, Vol. II, p. 554)

a fixation of an old fantasy of power or an identification with a powerful penis he saw early in his life, exposing himself serves the purpose of self-aggrandizement. It has nothing to do with love of the person to whom the penis is shown.

Yet my feeling would be, if such a person comes into analysis with me, not, "I hope I will be able to make this person love other people." My feeling would be, "Wait a moment! This man has already some refinement in the way in which he sees the environment. This girl that he exposes himself to has glasses. There is a little hope there. He is not totally preoccupied with himself." Maybe there will be some leverage, some time, not to make him love these people to whom he exposes himself, but some leverage in seeing that the narcissistic world in which he lives can be a richer world than just this very crude and simple one of taking out his penis and in some way becoming reassured when the woman looks away and blushes and is obviously flustered and frightened.

So you can see that the background of one's attitude, one's recognition of the complexity of psychological material, immediately and very subtly influences one's attitude toward one's patient, one's therapeutic strategy, therapeutic goals and tack, and the particular mode of leverage that one begins to exert with the patient.

The clinical material we will be talking about is predominantly centered around a very significant change in life, a very significant transitional phase.[2] And since transitional phases shape not only one's capacity for detaching oneself from one set of objects—for example, the parental ones—and reinvesting in new objects—for example, the marriage partner—the step from adolescence into adulthood also shakes up a particular image of oneself, a particular mode in which one sees oneself. It echoes, therefore, old trauma about the self, old modes in which self-esteem is shaken. Such popular and in many ways significant and helpful terms as "identity crisis" or "identity diffusion" can become much richer and more meaningful when seen in terms of the way in which responses develop. But this must be seen not simply as something that happens at a particular given moment, a particular task of the step from adolescence into adulthood, but also, to some extent, a repetition of some point at which the person failed earlier, when in earlier stages of the forming of the self and being secure there was a failure.

As the young student passes through this transitional phase, one

---

[2]See Kohut, 1966, "Forms and Transformations of Narcissism."

sometimes unsuspectingly begins to apply value judgments to the description of acute distress which he communicates and portrays. We apply value judgments when we use seemingly non-evaluative terms as if we were talking about objective facts. Further, certain phases of development are taken to represent immaturity or illness. But, for instance, health and disease are also value judgments. They do not refer to any objectively circumscribed assessment of reality. And when we speak about a developmental sequence from chronologically early to chronologically late, or from a beginning rudimentary function to a fully developed function, we describe sequences of events, of psychological or psychophysiological events, but we ought not necessarily imply value judgments.

In other words, a developed function is not always better than an undeveloped function. One can define this only if one knows the kind of task and under what sort of circumstances the function is considered better. It is particularly naive to use—Freud in his own descriptions never did this—developmental schemata in this pseudo-evaluative sense. It is the kind of thing that is sometimes referred to as "health morality." In other words, the healthy is also the good, because it is healthy, which is not true by any measure.

We have noted that many of the greatest achievements, as seen by the usual evaluative scale of cultural value, are by no means dependent on mature functions; rather, very frequently they depend on the higher development of somewhat immature functions, of part functions. Such an idea as the "genital man," then, the fully developed psychosocial and psychophysiological specimen, is not necessarily the most valuable one. It may be that in a certain average developmental scale this stage may be reached last. Before it is reached, any half-point can undergo its own clustering and its own tremendous development, and then lead to enormously valuable cultural results.

There is, for example, an oral sadistic fixation point in Michelangelo that later led to the urge to hammer forms out of this white marble because he was furious at the white breast of his mother. I have not analyzed Michelangelo. There are some reasonably good supports for just such a theory, but the actual veracity of the theory is beside the point. The main issue is that the fixation point at a comparatively primitive level of psychosexual development and its further development led to a result which is highly valuable within the framework of cultural achievement.

To say, then, that genital is better than anal, and anal is a little bit better than oral, and they are all much better than primary narcissism, is nonsense. These concepts should not be value judgments. I have, in other words, tried to make clear that one must not confuse evaluation of psychological functions with what should be approached in simple descriptive terms—in terms of how it works and how it fits in with other parts of the personality, and how adequate it is to what kind of task.[3] The capacity for a person to regress in sleep, for example, is obviously a highly adaptive one. The incapacity for a person to do this—that is, the need to remain at a higher level of consciousness, which is obviously a much more mature balance of psychological powers—during periods when this type of regression is permissible and necessary, is not adaptive.

The person with insomnia, for example, may be anxious that he may never emerge again from this regression, or he may be unable to relax watchfulness because of some primitive kind of impulses which might then become untamed, or he may equate sleeping with death, or whatever the problem may be. But the capacity for what one calls regression in sleep is the capacity to be healthy, and health, of course, is a value judgment. It is appropriate to the maintenance of oneself and one's psychophysiological equilibrium over the long period. The same is true of the capacity in parenthood to regress and to play with a small child. The person who is incapable of doing this fails—and here we have a value judgment—in his regressive capacity to go down and crawl on the floor and play with the child and to be empathic with the child's capacity to enjoy himself with blocks, with balls, and with simple kinds of things. This ability is an adaptive one.

I stressed earlier that narcissism should not at any time become subtly nor covertly, let along overtly, a value judgment. There is good narcissism, and there is not such good narcissism, depending on the task at hand. To be capable of adapting to the unexpected, as well as to the expected, may under some circumstances separate the wheat from the chaff. A person with normal adaptive span might do well in a normal adaptive environment, but only people who under normal circumstances would seem to be pathological might survive the unusual.

There is an implicit value judgment in Freud's work that he made explicit, I believe, only once: Where id was there shall ego be (Freud, 1933, p. 80). Put in other ways, the highest degree of consciousness, the highest degree of awareness, the greatest expansion of the realm of the ego (they are not totally synonymous, but for our purposes at this moment let's assume they are), this is also the good, the desirable. Freud (E. Jones, 1965, III, p. 144) did not tolerate any lack of veracity, whether this

---

[3]This represents the beginning of evolution of Kohut's relinquishment of clinical drive theory.

was in terms of denial or in terms of conscious lying. All his life's work was devoted to the expansion of consciousness. What is not known should become known, in the depth of the person and in the scientific attitude in the investigation of the environment, whether pleasant or unpleasant. You may say, for a great scientist, this can be the motto on his flag. But there are obvious circumstances when such an attitude is by no means so certain. Is it, for instance, correct to say that it is always adaptive to know exactly what is going on? If one is dying in the Sahara, is it adaptive, once one has lost all powers, to realize to the last dying breath that one is dying in the Sahara? Is it not more adaptive to have the capacity under such circumstances to hallucinate that one drinks and dies comparatively peacefully?

As a less extreme kind of example, there was an interesting study reported at one time about the influence of prolonged solitary confinement on individuals. Those individuals who survived really prolonged and very narrowed solitary confinement, who never hallucinated during that period, who always remained aware of the fact that they were alone and of how psychologically deprived they were, these people, after they were discharged, had permanent personality defects that seemed to be irreversible. There was a blunting in the personality, an inability to respond again to people in the full richness of interpersonal feelings, that was apparently not reversible. It is the kind of thing we see sometimes in survivors of European concentration camps; there is an absolutely irreversible personality defect (Krystal, 1969). They marry, they have children; they imitate and live as other people do. But they have no clearcut feeling about their new families. Essentially, when left to themselves, they always want to drift back to the company of former concentration camp inmates who also survived, because they are the only ones with at least a little touch of the old relationships. I am not altogether sure that I can subscribe to that particular example, but it rings very true to me.

A more common experience occurs with individuals who are senile or disorganized post-operatively. When they are in a dark room at night they are absolutely convinced that long-dead people to whom they have been close are there. This type of hallucinatory experience makes them grossly psychotic for long periods, as though in solitary confinement. By contrast, in the study mentioned above, those people who during their solitary confinement were by all criteria that we employ grossly psychotic, those who hallucinated being surrounded by their family, not just in imagination but really hallucinated and talked with them, lost all their hallucinatory activity as soon as they were discharged from solitary confinement. It seemed clear that people who hallucinated healed with much less defect than those who did not, and they returned to a much more normal adaptability toward their environment than those who had rigidly held on to the assessment of reality as it was.

I am using these examples to bring out the paradox that what for all of us is the height of illness, namely, the incapacity of the ego to maintain its ties to reality, even the abrogation of reality-testing, may, given certain circumstances, become an asset to the personality, and its absence may be a defect. Freud's attitude of facing up to the truth whether it was pleasant or unpleasant obviously inspires us all, and it is a fine attitude for a scientist. But not everybody is able to go through with it. It was Freud's way to his dying day. When Freud heard, I think it was a few days before he died, that he had only a few more days to live, he heard also that for a moment his physician had discussed with the family whether he should be informed. He became furious that it was even considered. "With what right would people keep something important like that from me? What right do they have to protect me?" (E. Jones, 1965, III, pp. 144–145).

In other words, this was Freud's personality. He could face truth of this particular kind, which is nothing to be amazed about when one thinks of the type of discovery he made unsupported and unaided. So there must be an unusual capacity to tolerate realistically unpleasant truths. This is again an individual matter, and I think everybody has times when even such tolerance is not feasible anymore. He did, indeed, finally agree to a pact with his physician, who died recently in New York, that when things were completely hopeless, and nothing left but pain, and he no longer had working capacity, he would receive a bigger dose of morphine. But he was to be told and he was to give his consent. And so this was done consciously and intentionally, and he died (E. Jones, 1965, III, p. 246).

First then, seen by itself, narcissism must not be confused as something that is evaluatively less good than object love. Secondly, narcissism is not the opposite of object relations; it is the opposite of object love; some of the most intense object relationships are in essence narcissistic ones. I will not go into details at this time. If you have any questions about this very general topic, put them aside, because we will come back to it. Thirdly, narcissism has to be evaluated in the same way developmentally and maturationally as *parallel* to object love. In other words, it has a developmental scale from early to late, from primitive to developed, from immature to mature. But I must again caution you that one must not confuse these with value judgments. Primitive narcissism may have its place, too. But first of all we have to say that narcissism in and of itself is not evaluatively bad, and then we must emphasize that there is a developmental line or a developmental scale of narcissism which one can see only when one has made the first step. So long as you consider narcissism as bad you do not think of a developmental scale. It must always be the primitive precursor of object love. But once you have made the step and said, "No, it is not a primitive precursor of object love, it has value of its own," then you can begin to see that narcissism too has a developmental line. There is a primitive kind of narcissism that relates to earlier situations of the small baby, and there are healthy forms of narcissism, developed forms of narcissism, mature forms of narcissism. In this sense neither *health* nor *mature* nor *developed* have value or evaluative meanings; the term health perhaps should be avoided altogether, but at any rate, forms of narcissism are adaptive in the mature sense of a developed person and have their own place (see Kohut, 1966). One can then see how these forms develop in the same way as one can see how object relations and object love develop.

Having made these three points then, we are ready to go from the most general discussion to the more specific, namely, the development and growth of narcissism in the individual.

2

The Separate Developmental Lines
of Narcissism and Object Love

T HE DEFINITION OF narcissism presupposes, at least from a certain moment in the developmental concept of the self, a psychological structure that corresponds to the concept of an object. At one time or another a child realizes that he is a limited unit with some cohesion in a spatially oriented universe. A body, with its limitations, its functions, and its internal processes that one is aware of—thinking processes and feeling processes—has within a moment of time some kind of cohesion. This self, this I, also has cohesion along a time axis. These are our two major orientations in the world. What exists now is *I*, although it may be somewhat different later on. During a life span this is often very taxing for us to realize. One looks into the mirror and sees one has white hair, and this is the same young boy that down deep one still thinks one is. "How can it be! This must be somebody else." But no, we know it is not somebody else. There is some continuum. And even if we do not know that there is a continuum—we cannot remember every moment of it— there is the knowledge, the feeling that there is.

So, together, the continuity of sameness in time and cohesion in space of something that we call *I* and that is recognized by others as such form the self. And just as objects—anything outside ourselves, such as a book, pet, friend, husband, wife, children—can be desired, important to us, or (to use the ugliest analytic word in the psychoanalytic lingo) imbued with libidinal cathexis, so the self can also be more or less highly cathected.

It has been an old and, to some extent, correct observation, but only within a certain set of limits, that the cathexis of the self, that is, the importance to us of ourselves, and the importance to us of objects are in an antithetical relationship to one another. Up to a point, and within certain limits, as a theory that covers a comparatively large field of observable data, this is a correct hypothesis. An old, oft cited example is that it is almost unthinkable to be in love when one has a severe toothache. In other words, a high degree of self-preoccupation, the increased narcissism that normally and adaptively begins to cluster around a disease of part of the self, precludes in general the extension of object cathexis. One cannot be in love when one has severe, ongoing physical pain. Conversely, one can say that the person devoted totally to something outside himself will ignore the demands of the self; for example, the man who is meeting the beloved and goes through sleet, hail, and rain hardly notices the discomfort because he is totally concentrated on reunion with the beloved object. And as so frequently is true, it is the cathexis of the inner representation of the object at the point before it is reached which is always the highest degree of object love. At the moment of reunion itself, a balance is reached and total investment in the object subsides to a degree.

That this involves not just objects in the usual sense bears emphasis. The total involvement in an external task is tantamount to the devotion to an object. Soldiers buoyed up for an attack and totally devoted to the goal of storming a particular fortress, for example, are known to have suffered intensely severe injuries, including the loss of a limb, without noticing it. In other words, when one is totally devoted to a particular goal, that too would correspond to the man in love who does not notice the rain, the hail, or the sleet.

Like so many theories, this theory of the antithetical deployment of object libido and narcissistic libido correctly explains a broad area of observable data. It has served to support an old developmental theory, namely, that narcissism is more primitive and object love more developed, and that object love develops out of narcissism. And there are hidden value judgments; we start out as egotistical babies, but we end up as social workers, as people with social concerns. We end up in our professions, devoting ourselves to others. While this theory is in error—it is incomplete—there are again a great many areas that it does indeed explain in a satisfactory manner. There is a certain truthfulness in the fact that a small child is and should be preoccupied with himself. As time goes on, and as we live in a complex social environment, we adapt ourselves more and more to the need to be concerned with the feelings of others, with the wishes of others. And since parenthood, in the realm of usual sociocultural development and maintenance of the race, becomes something that is achieved in maturity, parents, too, are required to put the well-being of their offspring above their own.

It has been known for a long time that people with low self-esteem are not the ones who are the greatest lovers or who are the most capable of devoting themselves to other people. On the other hand, we know that a well-developed capacity for object love, a strong involvement with other people, heightens self-esteem and does not drain us. So in some ways, our descriptions of the antithesis between certain types of narcissism is correct; it can be healthy in physical illness or pathological in psychotic hypochondriasis.

I believe there are some schizophrenics with a highly intact capacity for very refined, sincere, and profound object love (even though it may be circumscribed). And yet they are severely narcissistically fixated, with a high degree of primitivization of narcissism. I have a different explanation for what is going on: It is not that there is a *regression* from object love to narcissism, but a *breakdown* of higher forms of narcissism and a regression, sometimes independent of their capacity for object love, toward more primitive forms of narcissism. We will come to that when we move from general discussions to clinical data.

Until recently, the idea was generally accepted that there was a developmental scale from narcissism to object love. Even those who could accept, at least in a theoretical framework, the fact that narcissism did not necessarily imply a value judgment would see it as a regression from object love, not necessarily to be called evil, or bad, or disgusting, or ill, yet a regression, just as one regresses, let us say, in sleep. Even the lovely term, "regression in the service of the ego,"[1] that Hartmann (1958, p. 37) devised covered over the various inconsistencies. In other words, one could say that regression is not necessarily evil or bad or ill, but that sometimes it can serve adaptive purposes. That is all it really means. So narcissism was in that sense acceptable. Yet the basic conceptualization of the developmental scale from narcissism to object love was not abandoned.

My suggestion is that it behooves us to think of two independent lines of development. We must think of a line of development of object love from very primitive modes of object perception and object investment to very highly developed, very sophisticated and nuanced ones, both in the cognitive sphere, namely, now the object is recognized, and also in the degree and kind of emotions that are directed toward it. But the same thing is also true in the realm of narcissism. In and of itself, narcissism has just as much right to be investigated in terms of its own developmental scale as object love.

On the other hand, I have no particular axe to grind about the question of a unitary or dual theory of instincts. It does not make a great deal of

---

[1]Hartmann attributes this term to Kris (1934) and quotes him.

sense to fight battles over the question of whether there may be very early in life a kind of cohesion between these two developmental lines, narcissism and object love. We may say there is some primary narcissism or some primary object love that is beyond empathy, as far as I am concerned, something out of which both of these lines of development may finally separate themselves. Once we get into areas as primitive as this, I think modes of psychological assessments are inadequate means of study. I think there are, rather, modes of psychophysiological correlation that should be studied. And I think we are some distance from any real leverage into this type of problem. But I mention this to you as open to any theoretical mind. To argue one way or another, even though there are good points to be made, is not at this moment what I am particularly interested in. It really does not belong to our psychological field.

Next I would like to draw your attention to the fact that, in assessing the development of narcissism as having its own developmental line, a particular moment in psychological development has forced itself upon me as of greatest importance. As you know, my field of inquiry, my experimental setup, my realm of observation, is the individual over prolonged periods under the specific observational circumstances which are called the psychoanalytic situation. The advantages and disadvantages of this particular observational setup we cannot discuss here. They have been comparatively well defined. The psychoanalytic situation has the great advantage of allowing one individual for a lifetime to refine his skills under a certain set of circumstances. It is in that sense like the experience of a great microscopist. I do not know whether you have had years, as I have myself, of microscopic study. Gradually, over hours and hours of looking at slides—and years and years—one develops skills. To the uninitiated there appears to be a set of blobs that nobody can make sense out of. But a microscopist will see that what up to now has been considered an artifact is really a new discovery. This is the way in which science moves. And I think this is the way in which our science, the science on which I rely, moves too.

What I need to stress here is that the clues to the results that I will present to you concerning narcissism were not given to me by the direct observation of very small infants, who may indeed at a particular moment live through the kind of phasal change or phase of development that I am reconstructing; rather, I am extrapolating early experiences from regressive swings and progressive movements after the swing is over in my analytic patients.

This has many disadvantages, and it has many advantages. The inestimable advantages (to my mind, particularly when they are supported by analytically sophisticated and applied direct child observation) are that the patient is enlisted with his own self-observation in describing the regressive experience. In other words, he has the verbal facility to communicate to you something that is going on at any given time. As in microscopy, there must be certain expected notions. Unless you have some idea of what you may see you will never see anything. You will also not be capable of discarding an erroneous expectation if the facts indeed will not consistently lead you to the same result. It is this particular kind of method of observing progressive and regressive swings of a particular kind, the reestablishment of early situations, that allows us to tentatively reconstruct early normal developmental phases. That there are possibilities for error in such a reconstruction goes without saying. These are the same error possibilities that we have in archeology, although I think the archeologist is in a much more difficult situation than we are. We are dealing with still existing, still living ancient times, while the archeologist digs out relics only.

Our assumption is that the child in the grownup is somewhere still alive, and that its total potential can still be to some extent observed, although it is covered over and refracted through intermediary media that have in the meantime clustered around it. The living original tribe is still there somewhere. It is not only that you find its pottery pieces. It is not only that you see the historical results of early events. Those are the ways in which history reconstructs. One can see the actual end results of historical developments and can therefore conclude by describing the language of a particular people.

In a small valley in Switzerland a language is discovered, let us say, like *Romanche*, which has strong Latin admixtures to it. You obviously can conclude from the fact that there are some Latin admixtures that, at one time or another, the ancestors of this particular group of people must have been in touch with the Latin culture. It would be impossible to deny it. But how they were in touch is another story. If you also find relics in these Alpine villages or in the larger cities in the area that show you that indeed Romans had a camp there at an earlier time, then you are permitted to make certain reconstructions about the ancestors of these people who now speak *Romanche*. And you can, perhaps by analyzing these, obtain certain data or confirm pieces of information that come from different sources. This historical method, however, is very limited. The historical method is also used in analysis, but it is not a specifically analytic tool.

Any dynamic psychiatrist or developmentally oriented psychologist will indeed use the historical method and will assess the present functions in terms of what an individual says about the past. The psychoanalytic method, however, goes one step in addition to this particular one. It says, and I think it has a good deal to offer as proof, that not only has the old tribe once met the ancestors of the present one, not only was there once a child whose experiences have influenced adult functioning (to put it in straightforward non-analogizing terms), but that the old child is still somewhere there and still somewhere alive. Given the right circumstances this child will act very much the same, perhaps only slightly overlaid by adult attitudes which are called the defensive function of the adult mind and which cannot be completely eliminated. This particular child can at least be seen without the abrogation of the adult.

I am simply justifying to some extent that one can indeed reach reconstructions of a rather high degree of probability from careful and consistent observation of psychological behavior over long periods of time under circumstances to which I believe the psychoanalytic situation allows us access. That the findings should be investigated by applying them to direct child observation goes without saying. But one cannot expect too much from direct child observation. One can observe a child's behavior, but empathizing with what the child feels and how he experiences his environment is very difficult unless one has clues from regressive behavior of adults that channel one's expectations and allow one to ask: How is this compatible with what the child really feels at a given moment?

It is an old insight that the best access to the study of the human mind (probably true also for physiological functions) is the observation of systems in transition. The rigid, established, leveled-out, well-functioning unit teaches you, in general, less than a unit that is a bit out of balance. On the other hand, the system that is totally out of balance is equally difficult to study in terms of an assessment. In other words, mild forms of transitional imbalance tend to be the ones that are most likely to give you access to insight. This may not always be true, but I think in general it is.

Let me again use an analogy. The study of normal cell behavior is unlikely to be as interesting to the observer of abnormal cell development as the cell that is just in the transition of becoming pathological under the influence of a chronic irritant. These are the cells that a sophisticated histologist or histo-pathologist would most likely study. I do not mean to say that this is necessarily true, but certainly in psychology it very frequently is.

Therefore, it is neither the total destruction of the cohesive self to which I would like to draw your attention, nor the self that is so firmly and so securely established that it functions silently. One is aware of the self most when there is some illness in it, when there is some degree of uncertainty about it, not when it is either totally destroyed or under such severe regression that the communicative and observing faculties are also destroyed along with it. The patient then cannot really tell you what his experiences are, and these are what we are interested in. Nor is it likely that the person who is so fully and firmly established as an individual, as a permanent self as it were, will notice himself at all. He just lives naively. So it is the mild disturbance, the self in the moment it begins to reassemble itself, that is most likely to tell you something. And it is most likely to tell you something about that particular developmental phase in which the self or that particular part of the self was first formed.

Freud's original theoretical contribution to our topic was related to observations on psychotics. He was particularly interested in the observation of individuals who become hypochondriacal. The normal body-feeling, the sense of well-being, of having a cohesive body with which we are pleased, is so important to our well-being and our self-concept.

In contrast, I remember a patient many, many years ago who in his early dreams dreamed of himself as a head and only something very schematic underneath the head. He presented it as very like Giacometti's sculpture of a thin body with a well-developed head. And he, as I now know in retrospect, tried early to tell me something about the disturbance of his body-self—that he could view himself only as a thinking individual, that he was alive in *self* only so far as his intelligence was at play. He could not conceive of himself, and for very good reasons, as a well-delimited, total, body-mind-self unit on the basis of which he could act, relate, and see himself in the world. Freud (1914c) discussed the hypochondria, the pathological version of this kind of rounded body self-esteem that we continuously have whether we know it or not. He said that under certain circumstances a regression takes place in which individual body parts become intensely hypercathected with narcissistic libido, to use the language of psychoanalytic metapsychology. These parts are experienced by the patient as producing some kind of uncomfortable pressure very different from body parts that become the leading parts of our personality.

It is very true, let us say, that a great boxer might have a tremendous feeling about "me and my biceps, me and my musculature, my leg work, my marvelous upper-cut with a left," or whatever he is particularly proud of. But this is only seen as the leading zone of a totally cathected self. This is only, as it were, the convergence of a cohesive self-feeling. And when we speak, for example, of the phases of libido development, of the meaning of the penis for the five-year-old or of the total coquettish body of an oedipal little girl, then we know that this is not a hypochondriacal hypercathexis of this part or that part. But it is the very part that has become the leading convergence of a totally compact sense of self.

When this is in danger, then the total self-feeling is in danger of breaking up.

The nuances of diagnostic criteria sometimes are refined when you have some theoretical background to what you are feeling. Let us say you are confronted with a physiological complaint in a patient and you are puzzled as to whether it is a hysterical episode or a psychotic regression. How can you differentiate? Well, there are many ways of differentiating. It makes a great deal of difference if you know what is behind the two structures. It makes a great deal of difference if you know when a hysterical woman, on the basis of some kind of regression toward oral impregnation, fantasies that something is wrong with the swallowing apparatus, that she is disgusted and does not want to swallow anything . It is very different when a schizophrenic person in regression says, "My lips are different."

"What's wrong with them?"

"Well, they're bigger."

"No, they're not really bigger."

"I can't really describe it to you. They're so big; they're so full."

Then you gradually get the feeling there is something that this poor woman is trying to describe, something that has detached itself from the rest of the body scheme and has taken on a meaning and a libidinization all its own. It is very different from the lips or the swallowing apparatus that become involved in a hysterical fantasy in which the total little girl's incestuous wish may be involved and rejected. It is bizarre; it may be embarrassing; it may be something very rejected; it may lead to a very severe dysfunction. But it is not as bizarre, as strange, as separated from the total body-self as, let us say, the schizophrenic regression that leads to a particular hypercathexis of the lips, or of the body, or of the thought when functions that should belong together begin to separate themselves out.

So what do we see? Freud (1915a) postulated that there was a phase in earliest life, which he called the phase of autoerotism, which preceded the phase of narcissism. We see, in Freudian terms, a phase of autoerotism in which the normally healthy child feels every one of his functions at any given moment singly, totally and isolatedly. It is revived in the later regressive state, in psychotic disintegration.

In the early child, if he is normal and healthy, there is a normal developmental phase in which each individual moment, each cooing, each swallowing, each precursor of a thought process, each little recognition is there all by itself, intensely enjoyable, but not yet integrated into a total concept: "This is only a part of me." But gradually, the influx of maturational pressures (repeated ontogenetically, phylogenetically, over millions of years) has contributed to the development of the race. This repeats itself today as a forward move toward the unification of single, as yet isolated, fragmentary separate experiences; they become subsumed under the experience of total self. It is this particular development, this movement from isolated functions, from isolated body parts, toward a total cathexis of a total self, which is the phase of the development from autoerotism to narcissism. I think this is somewhat restricted terminology simply on the basis of a libido theory, but quite appropriate to Freud's findings at the turn of the century when he formed this theory. As we would say now, this is a development from a phase of a fragmented self or of single experiences to a phase of a cohesive, nonfragmented, unitary self.

When we speak about the unitary self, however, we do not mean that the unitary self precludes the experience of divisions of the self. As I said, pride in one's physique, pride even in one's capacity to love objects, and enjoyment of an intellectual task completed are not only compatible with a feeling of a cohesive self but support it. But the parts are always seen as areas of an undestroyed total self. It is extremely instructive, on the other hand, to observe people who in the course of prolonged treatment begin to reconstitute a sense of self and feel themselves whole and on the basis of that wholeness to engage in activities they formerly could not engage in.

I remember, for instance, a particular patient, somebody that I have not treated myself, but somebody that a colleague in another city has been treating and still is treating. This was a very disturbed man, an adopted child who had a highly unresponsive adoptive mother and a very cold father. This man was left with a great sense of pervasive unreality about himself and a peculiar set of complaints. People struggle for words to explain to you what the tensions are that they are suffering. This man, over the course of some years of sophisticated treatment, not only began to be able to pinpoint where his pathology lay and to be empathic with himself, which is a very important preliminary step in the cure, but also gradually reconstituted himself. He began to show the cohesion of his personality and of himself and to engage in enthusiastic activities.

One day he described how he was taking lessons in folk singing with an accordion and he repeated some of the phases that he early in life had missed so much: exhibiting to an admiring environment and getting the applause that was appropriate for a small child. He got himself lost one day in the accordion playing, and he became terribly frightened. The therapist did not understand what happened until we discussed it in some detail. Our understanding of his fright was confirmed many times afterward, and the patient felt totally understood when the therapist explained it to him. What happened was that in devoting himself to a function, namely, the enthusiastic playing of the accordion, his as yet fragile, reconstituted self was in danger of being drained into the activity and of breaking up again. So that the very thing that for a healthy self is confirmation of a well-functioning self may become very frightening to a fragile self. Thus, even success sometimes becomes frightening, not because of the guilt, not because of what one often calls the negative therapeutic reaction—in other words, that it is guilt-laden to be success-ful—but because *even the success drains the self* when it is not yet firmly established. We need a constitution of a cohesive self in addition to the capacity to realize that there are single functions in single parts.

How does the environment relate to this transitional phase, the forma-tion of a cohesive self? What in the attitude of the mother, for better or worse, can contribute to the firming of the total self-concept in the inter-action with the mother? What can she contribute in preventing or in hampering this normal phase in the development of narcissism? This we will develop in succeeding seminars.

The theoretical concepts I am presenting to you (and I think it is very much in the tradition in which my whole thinking has developed) are not derived inductively. They are derived empirically. They are not de-duced from purely theoretical concepts. It is on the basis of a variety of clinical observations that concepts gradually peel themselves out. They are not deduced from some basic axioms. So when I talk about the contrast between object love and object relations—this is really the main point that I have tried to make—I wanted to say that narcissism is highly compatible with intense object relationships.

Many object relationships are used for narcissistic purposes.[2] There are objects in the child's surroundings, and in the surroundings of all of us, that are highly important to us, but that serve narcissistic purposes. When the child begins, for example, to get a sense of his own value, of his own cohesiveness, of being somebody, he needs other people to confirm this. This is an intense need. But these other people are not loved for their sake. They are not important as centers of their own volition or initiative or as independent human beings with their own goal-directedness. They are important only insofar as they serve the heightening or the maintenance of the self-esteem, let us say, of the baby or of us. It makes a great deal of sense to differentiate between object relations that serve narcissistic purposes and the love of an object when

---

[2]Kohut here spells out further his empirical discovery of the selfobject and its functions.

the other person is longed for, but is recognized and is imbued with interest, love, libido, or whatever you want to call it, as a human being with his or her own purposes, independent of oneself—independent of the heightening of one's self-esteem.

Let me illustrate this point by the giving and the receiving of gifts: If you choose a gift primarily for the purpose of gaining the gratitude of the other person, you may say that the emphasis of this particular activity was a narcissistic one. If you give it, however, for the purpose of the enjoyment of the other person who is an independent person, then the emphasis is on object love in this particular transaction.

It is true that there is always some degree of narcissistic enhancement in any kind of object love. But to ascribe a continuum between narcissism and object love is a logical fallacy. One can never do that. One can always prove that dark and light are the same because there are only degrees of grayness in between. So the fact remains that there are relationships to others in which the self is almost forgotten and the enjoyment that one gains is in the recognition of the other.

There are other relationships, however, in which the point of gravity lies in the self. The extremes are the easiest ones to recognize. When one is in love one does not think of oneself. If we examine the imagery that goes on in an individual in love, it is totally about the other person— what she looks like, what she wishes, how she smiles. In other words, one is not particularly involved with oneself. This is true not only for human objects, but also for cherished tasks. We have talked about that before. I gave you the example of somebody so involved in a national goal or an idealistic goal that, in the process of aiming at it, he totally disregards himself, to the point that he does not feel injuries, which would obviously be the experience that would most call forth a narcissistic investment. On the other hand, when you are very much concerned with yourself, either with your own body or with your personality, whatever aspect of the self that is most invested, then very frequently you disregard others.

I think there is a difference between a mature being in love and the kind of primitive merger fantasies that are really an extension of the self or a merging into the self. The fact is that in the condition of being in love very frequently all kinds of narcissistic fantasies are also activated simultaneously. When we talk about the separation of concepts on this explicit level, it is usually not helpful to look at the complexity of the actual empirical occurrence. I think that in a normal love relationship there are some narcissistic factors involved that are subordinated to the essential relationship to the other person. I think any kind of love relationship one encounters, particularly among younger people, has a good many narcissistic elements. Paradoxically, in the state of being in love, the overestimation of the object, if one examines it in detail, is not due to the heightened investment of object love or object libido. It is due, rather, to the narcissistic element in the love, in other words, to an old self-imagery that is projected onto the other individual. These are details that one can only analyze when one examines such relationships clinically or in detail.

The major point that I would like to stress is that the mere presence or absence of object relationships does not tell you anything about the *narcissistic state* of the individual. People may, for example, be alone, but their aloneness does not mean any narcissistic regression, or any narcissistic retreat, or even, without value judgment, any narcissism. It may simply be a longing for somebody whom one loves very much. The person, for example, who is deprived of somebody whom he loves, or of a whole group of people whom he loves—the person who is displaced, for example, and loses his home, his family, everything that was of value to him—such a person may in new surroundings be alone for a long time.

A second kind of person, however, placed in new surroundings will make the transition to the new set of objects with the greatest of ease. Put that way, chances are, sight unseen, that the second person's relationships are much shallower and much more narcissistic than those of the first person. The person who is incapable of attaching himself to a variety of totally new objects remains internally connected to the old ones. He is alone, but not narcissistic. The other one is surrounded with many people, but they mean nothing to him except in terms of his self, or as relief of loneliness, or as confirming his presence. The main point is that the mere presence or absence of relationships to other people does not tell you anything about the nature of the relationships.

These are complex points. I do not think they have an enormously important bearing on the material with which we are dealing here, but I do not want to avoid theoretical formulations where there are difficulties. We ask ourselves, for example, about the cognitive investment or the cognitive ability to recognize other people's independence—in other words, to love somebody who is different from ourselves. Freud (1914c) spoke about the fact that homosexuality takes an intermediary step between object love and narcissism, one loves somebody more like oneself. This has to be taken with a grain of salt. I can draw a diagram and say this is homosexuality, and this is heterosexuality, and this is narcissism, and this is object love. There are types of heterosexual relationships that are highly narcissistic, and there are some very developed homosexual relationships in which the partner is very much recognized as an individual in his own right. There are stable long-term relationships among homosexuals in which the partner is recognized and loved very much as an independent human being who is permitted a certain degree of being different from oneself. And there is no love relationship in which the partner is totally permitted to be different. I think the degree of difference that is permitted within a love relationship depends on the empathic capacity of the partners.

Empathy has, at least historically, narcissistic roots. Empathy does develop originally out of a narcissistic relationship to another human being. The likeness of the mother-child relationship, their feeling the same thing at the same time—this is how empathy originates. But the historical development—this is an old rule that one also must not forget—the fact that one can prove that something develops out of a common root does not mean that it is still the same that it was originally. We speak of a change of function (Hartmann, 1958), of the historical fallacy or the genetic fallacy. The fact remains that empathy subserves object love goals. On the whole one can differentiate, at least in terms of direction, objects who are recognized and permitted to be different, permitted to have their own wishes, their own interests. They are loved not only despite differences but because of differences complementing one's interest. In contrast, narcissistically invested objects are interesting to the person only insofar as they serve to maintain his own narcissistic goals.

There is, of course, no human relationship that does not contain features of both object love and narcissistic love. On theoretical levels one should differentiate the two components. In clinical instances, either one or the other is crucial to the understanding of the personality. The capacity to help a love partner maintain his self-esteem by showing interest in him when he needs it, for example by listening to him when he needs to be listened to, is subordinated to the higher capacity for love and to the kind of mutuality that arises from knowledge that the partner will respond when you are in need of this kind of service. So a variety of detailed activities on both sides enters into any kind of complex human relationship.

In other words, to give explanations to somebody who is suffering from a fragmented sense of self and from a shaky self-esteem—in terms of the disturbances in his object love is fallacious. It does not lead anywhere. He would not feel understood.

As is so frequently the case with these complex topics, clinical material will make meaningful what we are discussing here theoretically, but one should know the theory in order to make the clinical material meaningful.

3

Early Stages in the Formation of Self-Esteem

WHY THEN DO WE talk about early childhood experiences? Why do we talk about the fact that there is a normal phase of development which children experience—individual physical and mental processes— each at a given moment, without having yet the sense that these processes all belong to them as one person? Why do we talk about how the interaction between mother and child enables the child gradually to subsume all these individual functions in body parts under one cohesive self-experience? Why is this all so important? Why do we spend so much time and thought on all this? To me it is important to realize what an enormous role disturbances in this area play in human behavior.

Years ago, when I first became interested in this topic, strangely enough, my interest was not primarily motivated by clinical material. I became interested at a time when I had the least opportunity to do any clinical or theoretical thinking. It was at the time of my most intense involvement, of all things, in administrative affairs. As some of you know, several years ago I was involved in high administrative positions in psychoanalytic organizations. I think it was at that time that the intensity of the narcissistic involvement of people really came home to me. I learned, for example, to think in such terms when somebody who had formerly been a friend of psychoanalysis became inimical and would write critiques with the most fantastic armamentarium of reasoning. I learned to look back to the time in his life when he suddenly discovered that everything that psychoanalysis had found was wrong. More likely than not one would learn that it had occurred when he had been running for an office and was defeated, or submitted a paper that was not accepted, or was not appointed to a chairmanship of a committee, or some comparably stupid kind of an event occurred to hurt his feelings. Over and over again we find this among highly sophisticated people who supposedly know a great deal about themselves, yet who completely lost track of themselves following a narcissistic wound—and I have found I am no exception to this rule.

Although one learns to some extent to control and take hold of oneself by greater insights, narcissistic sensitivities of people enormously influence their actual behavior and thinking, even in seemingly very distant areas. Once one's eyes are opened one can hardly believe that one had overlooked the importance of these features among patients. The degree to which people suffer under the fluctuations of their self-esteem, the undue hurts to their self-esteem, is extreme; the intensity or the lengths to which people will go in order to balance a shaky self-esteem is enormous.

It is this kind of an experience which makes the investigation of the growth of the self-image, of the disturbances of self-esteem, of the historical facts that make a person more or less vulnerable in these areas, becomes so important. It is with this knowledge that clinical material, particularly among young people in the transitional phase from youth to adulthood, can be so illuminating. One more or less formed self-image has to give way and to be replaced by another. In other words, it is in late adolescence and early adulthood that problems of the cohesiveness of the self and fear of the breakdown of the self occur. Attempts are made in one form or another, either by submitting to the culture or by forming a counterculture to balance a shaky self-esteem. It is my conviction that a real understanding of this self-esteem problem can only be achieved if the genetic dimension, the history of the development of self-esteem and its early vicissitudes, as well as the weak spots in the personality, is taken into account.

There are many people who, in going from adolescence into adulthood, make tremendous steps of adaptation. But they do not all break down; they do not all become depressed; they do not all turn to security measures like drugs, or touch therapy, or whatever may be involved in order to confirm the fact that they are alive, real, and worthwhile. There are many people who can suffer through the normal process and pain of making the change from one system of the self to another one. Why do some break down? Why is it that some people with very shaky early experiences do not break down? What luck in the supporting environment later on prevents a breakdown, even though everything that we have learned about them may seem to have predisposed them to a break in their later self-configuration and in the maintenance of their later self-esteem? There are many answers to these questions. It is not to be forgotten, however, that gross early factors are not necessarily the most influential ones. Sometimes very subtle ones constitute the critical determinant in the personality development.

I stressed last time that the transitional phase of the formation of the most archaic forms of the cohesive self is crucial for our study and assessment. The normal developmental phase of narcissism is an enormous maturational advance over the preceding, also normal phase of the still-fragmented self.

When we speak of the fragmented self, there is a sound of pathology and I think rightfully so. From the clinical point of view, in the adult, indeed in general, we can speak about fragmentation experiences in one's own personality; that is, feeling that one is not real, that one is not cohesive, that one has no continuity in time, that one is not a whole. The social role, for instance, is a support in feeling whole. Knowing that one is a physician, knowing that one has some kind of specialty, allows people with very shaky self-esteem to find a niche, something special that only they themselves have; they use it not so much because it is so terribly interesting (certain hobbies, for instance, perform that function) but because it becomes a crutch to their self-esteem.

I once had a patient who had nothing in the world, but he was a Kurt Vonnegut specialist. He read every book and every biography of Kurt Vonnegut. He was known as a Vonnegut specialist. Knowing how very shaky this person was, I had the feeling this gave him some kind of hold over himself. His greatest vulnerability was not what most people would fear—not having much money, failing in a basic career, or losing a job. This particular person experienced all these adversities but took them in his stride. But if somebody belittled his Vonnegut hobby, then he became depressed.

When we speak about the fragmentation of the self, it has a connotation of psychopathology. However, the fact that disintegration products of mature organizations correspond to early phases in development does not make the early phases of development a pathology. What was once a perfectly appropriate developmental step becomes a disintegration product when it occurs anachronistically late in life. This is one of the basic points in the understanding of a genetically oriented or developmentally oriented psychology. So that while it is perfectly appropriate, we assume, for a small baby to have experiences that would correspond with the hypochondriacal disintegrations of the schizophrenic regression, this kind of parallel does not make the original phase a pathological one. I think, for example, that Melanie Klein (1932), who had some very interesting theories, made the error of comparing what is a normal phase, with healthy aspects, of the child's development, with adult psychopathology. In other words, modes of thinking and feeling that may be replicas of early stages in adult pathology are assumed to be somehow pathological in the baby. This goes against the grain of any kind of developmental thought.

So it would seem to me that, in the capacity to think oneself into early developmental phases (which is very difficult, with many grave dangers, and always incomplete), one must safeguard the fact that these are normal and healthy developmental phases.

The capacity of a child to feel that he is totally *the hand* at the moment that he grasps, that he is totally *the mouth* and *the tongue* sucking at a particular moment, is not pathology; this is health. It becomes pathology if later a cohesive self begins to disintegrate under the influence of trauma. In the schizophrenic regression, when the healthy part of the person observes the disintegration as a fragmentation of the rest of his personality and tries by hook or crook to integrate what is going on by trying to describe it as a kind of disease, that still makes sense. When we have a physical disease, when a boil hurts before it bursts, we still have a sense of "I," even though our mind is concentrated around the boil. We still remain cohesive. The schizophrenic, in his regression to this fragmentation of the formerly cohesive self, attempts to interpret the already fragmented aspects of his experience as if there were a physical disease, as if there were something strange happening, and as if the self were still holding together. He can only try to bring a theoretical mantle around it, but he cannot truly feel anything.

The forward movement of normal development is quite different. First of all, there is the stage of the baby experiencing separate processes in mental and physical body parts. In this developmental phase it is enormously important for the maternal environment to respond according to the baby's needs. I do not mean necessarily the biological mother, but whoever the mothering adult may be. This may be a man, for maternal feelings are common to both. The maternal environment responds to the individual body part without yet seeing the whole, but at each particular moment relating to the presenting part of the body, to the presenting new achievement, whether it is now lifting the head, the first moving over, the first cooing noise, or whatever it may be. Gradually, however, and in tune with the maturational pressures that bring the baby forward, the maternal environment becomes ready not only to enjoy each individual moment, and each individual rudimentary thought process or discovery of the world, which is not yet separated from the self, but also, having responded to each part in tune with the baby's needs, to respond now to the whole: calling the child's name—the higher cathexis of the response to the name. In other words, this is not only the hand of little Dickie, but this is Dickie's little hand. Not only is each individual body part then important and accepted by the environment, and confirmed as it is accepted, but it is also part and parcel of the total unity of self.

These are the rudimentary aspects of the self experience. The environment can thus in many ways support, hinder, or distort this development of the self. The most basic of all the activities of the environment, and an enormously important one, is the capacity to respond to what I insist on calling the baby's exhibitionism. It is as if the wish of the baby could be verbalized, "Look, I am here. I am I." And the environment should then, usually visually, respond with the gleam in the mother's eye, the smile of the mother, the responsiveness of the mother's activity vis-à-vis the exhibitionism of the child. This is very different from, let us say, other needs of the child: for example, the response to the child's need to be fed.

If you asked me at this point to distinguish where rudimentary object love begins and how it separates itself from rudimentary narcissism, I would be unable to make such distinction. It is sometimes very difficult to separate these, and in the earliest phases I would be very willing to say they form a unit and that we should not worry about separating them. But out of the mother's response, let us say to the hunger needs of the baby, there emerges an interplay of development which in the long run does lead to recognition of the independent needs of two independent individuals. The showing off of the child, the wish to produce pleasure in the mother, the lowering of self-esteem when there is no response—these certainly lead to the confirming or the lack of confirming of the narcissistic needs of the child. Confirmation of these needs is just as important for survival as satisfaction of the caloric or feeding needs of the child. It is the lack of responsiveness to the individual child, the deprivation of the child's narcissistic requirements, that leads to so many of these states that are described, for example, in the hospitalism babies seen by Spitz (1945, 1946) long ago.

Severe narcissistic defects may occur as late as the beginning of latency, but what I am talking about now are the rudimentary beginnings of an early developmental phase. The height of the exhibitionistic responses for the baby would probably be within the first year of life. Later on, particularly after weaning, I would think it is the narcissism that is already involved in certain of his functions, his products, for example, around toilet training, and things of that particular type—the pride in the visible urination of the little boy—that may meet with a crucial lack of responsiveness.

Certainly the narcissistic aspects in the oedipal phase are enormously important: the phallic narcissism of the little boy and the narcissism of the total body configuration of the coquettish little girl. All of these are now side by side with object passions. The enormous object passions of the oedipal complex[1] are, of course, very well-known. At the same time, there are still very great narcissistic needs. So the blow that the oedipal defeat constitutes, and how it is suffered, is to be understood not only in terms of the disappointed object love, but also in the disappointment of fantasy of unfathomable greatness, of being a conqueror. How this is suffered, the degree, the fractionation—this is the riddle. No infantile narcissism can remain in anybody who grows up. But what happens to it? Later we will talk at great length about the transformations of this narcissism, the traumatic way in which it is defeated, thus making the difference between future vulnerability or future fitness.

One of the most important issues, then, is the response of the environment. This is something in which you can, I believe, see most clearly the methodology by which one can extrapolate early developmental phases from adult pathology. Why are some people insatiable in their needs for acclaim while others are less so? There is, of course, pathology of a totally different nature in which people do not seem to have any need at all, but this is extreme illness of another kind. Take, as an example, the grandiosity of the messianic paranoid leader who seems to be totally without need for the confirmation of others. His belief is unshaken by the disbelief of the rest of the world. He can either be a crank, or he can finally, by dint of his enormous conviction, convince others to become his followers. In essence his narcissism seems to be well-balanced, but of course this is pathology. You may say pathology, under certain circumstances, becomes socially a highly important phenomenon. We talked about this in our first session, and how tricky all this is. When one speaks in terms of value judgment, one has to see the total environment in which a term is used. We know that a paranoid is ill by any kind of value scale that we subscribe to. We will not go into sophistry now, in which somebody may try to prove that such an individual is not ill and that everybody else is, although from his point of view, from his value scale, this is true.

Under normal circumstances, we all need a steady stream of self-confirmation, and we have it. There are of course ups and downs. Have you ever thought about the narcissistic value of a bull session in which one takes other people apart? It is a contract between people who sit down together and talk about others who are not there, how lacking in

---

[1]Kohut later called this the oedipal stage. He came to view the oedipus complex embedded in drive theory, as a disintegration product arising because of empathic failure on the part of the selfobject milieu.

intelligence and how fallacious they are. Cheeks glow, and everybody has a marvelous time. Why? Self-esteem is heightened by mutual confirmation of the lowness of others. Similarly, prejudice against an outgroup always has the effect of heightening self-esteem. Is it good or is it bad? Is this health or is this disease? Obviously, knowing the socially disastrous effects of prejudice, the suffering that it produces, it is social pathology. And yet, as with my fellow with the Vonnegut hobby, there are some people who are held together only by dint of their prejudice. If they were to give this up, they would fall apart. It is almost impossible to convince somebody that his prejudice is just what it is. It is always imbricated, as is true for any delusion with some realistic factors. No delusion is generally made out of whole cloth; there is always something to it. But what is the purpose that it serves?

I am emphasizing all this because all that we see in our observations of adults—from the normal to the abnormal, from our patients to ourselves—is indirectly caused in early development. We need a steady influx of the confirmation of ourselves. Nobody exists, again with the exception of some paranoid-like messianic characters, who does not suffer when he is totally unknown in some place. Many a person has made a comparatively reasonable adjustment in a small town or village where everybody knows that he is the son of the English teacher or the grocer, for example. Suddenly, at a big university where nobody knows him, the question "Who am I?" looms large. Previously his self-concept was kept in balance by steady confirmation from morning till night of the surrounding small village or town, where everyone knows who he is, where he hears each day, "Hi, Dick," or "Tom," or whatever his name may be. Suddenly, here he is in an anonymous environment. He goes to class where the teacher does not know him, to classes where there are so many students that he will never be known. Then there comes the yearning, and finally a tremendous attachment to somebody who gives him a personalized response.

Now there are other people who come from small towns who may suffer a bit, but do not need to make these tremendous attachments. In the anonymous environment of a huge university, they do not become deeply depressed, reaching for drugs, suddenly feeling that their whole existence is unreal in a schizoid-like phenomenology or symptomatology.

Why does this occur to some and not others? There again, life is not so simple. One has to examine what weak spots in the individual environment converged upon the particular precipitating factor, and these have to be weighed. It is obvious that one usually begins by showing the person understanding for the present task that has precipitated his sense of unreality. But first of all, one has to pinpoint, "It's the way you feel."

The mere fact that one shows him that this is the way he feels now makes him *somebody*, because there is someone else in this world who has been capable of reaching out enough for him to know what is going on. So very frequently, the mere *understanding* is a step toward feeling better.

I go through developmental precursors of the problems we are discussing here, and veer back and forth between glimpses of child and adult, not only to prove to you that it is important to investigate these early experiences because they have significance in terms of what we find in our everyday life and in our functions as healers, but also to give you an idea of the many nuances of the disturbances in the self experience, of disturbances in self-esteem, and the various interactions both in terms of maintenance and breakdown of self-esteem.

For example, the mirroring of the mother is gross behavior that one can certainly see. Perhaps one can be led to recognize it more sharply when one has lived with patients and has seen their eternal wish, "Please tell me that what I say is right. Say it again. Say it was good. Say it was fine. Say it was the finest thing you ever heard. Say this was progress. Don't just sit there." And so when there is a patient in whom the need to have a response fills hour after hour, you can gradually recognize there must be some kind of lack early in life which makes him still cling to and want such reassurance when he should have had his fill. The sophisticated child observer, recognizing this need, may see things he would perhaps otherwise not have paid much attention to, or he can see some things now in their fullest significance.

You can see what this kind of behavior and interaction in childhood will finally lead to in terms of either satisfaction and balance or still persisting needs and imbalance. It may make you aware of something that I was very proud to have seen: that it is the gleam in the mother's eye that the child misses.

In Copenhagen I saw a movie which was probably shown here at one time or another. It was a movie that Dorothy Burlingham made of her treatment of blind children (Burlingham and Robertson, 1966). The movie portrayed the interactions among these congenitally blind children, the nurse, and the therapist. It occurred to me that these children lack the response par excellence that other children have. They cannot see the responsive gleam in the mother's eye to their beauty. Let us assume the mother is narcissistically hurt because her child is defective. A normal mother will still respond, in fact overrespond in a healing fashion, to the defective child. The movie demonstrated how the sophisticated and empathic nurses and teachers would respond in other ways. The therapist and the nurse would communicate their feelings by their voices or by hugging the child. There are phases, of course, in the growing up of any child in which the mirror per se begins to play a certain role. The vanity of children sometimes is aggravating to us, because we envy them, and we say, "Don't look in the mirror all the time." This is what the blind children are deprived of.

There was a beautiful scene in which one of the children, with some musical talent, played the piano and received acclaim, the normal mirroring of adults' saying it was beautiful or applauding. But the height of the experience came when the playing, which was tape recorded, was replayed. The child suddenly recognized, "That's me!" There was this narcissistic bliss that you could suddenly see in this blind child. It was a very moving experience.

In many ways, our patients need just this kind of thing. What one does for the patient is really not giving him what he has missed. As a matter of fact, most patients are very sensitive about that and dislike it intensely. If you do that they feel patronized; they feel treated like children, as though you have given to them as to a beggar. I think it is much more sophisticated, and much more a real gift, when one recognizes the need and explains it from one adult to another.[2] Then the person is free to make his own peace in finding out how much it is reasonable to try to get. He can occasionally say, "Yes, I know that, but really I do need something." Then maybe from time to time one can, recognizing an enormous need, give something that one knows is, for the time being, necessary. I have a nice phrase for it: I call it the "reluctant compliance with the childhood wish."

But it is different once this is done against the background of a nonpatronizing, from-one-adult-to-another-adult attitude of understanding and explaining, so that the person gets greater mastery over his needs, rather than the direct feeding of some kind of expressed wish. Direct gratification in the long run leads to an unbreakable kind of tie, so that therapy really does not become therapy but becomes a relationship which simply postpones the day of reckoning, namely the day when the relationship has to end. In most people it is also actually a humiliating experience. People who want this and have this need find a response generally outside of psychiatry.

While the mirroring relationship of mother and child is one that can be very easily observed, there are other relationships of a narcissistic nature that are even more important but that are unusually difficult to observe because they are not shown by outward behavior. There are silent modes

---

[2]Too often self psychology is thought to gratify needs rather than to rely on interpretation. This passage clearly demonstrates the contrary.

of experiencing in which the environment is considered to be part of the self, in which there is nothing observable present except when this particular favorable balance is disturbed. When a small child is deprived of his parents, he is deprived not only of their response in terms of self-confirmation, but also of part of the self in a way for which it is terribly difficult to find adult words.

It is, however, something that you can repeatedly observe in certain narcissistically fixated patients who feel well, without any need for a mirroring confirmation from the side of the therapist, so long as the regularity of appointments maintains some kind of an unspoken tie with the therapist. But they are left out, feeling themselves more as inhuman, like pieces of wood or pieces of furniture, not quite alive, when the other person with whom they had felt united in this very primitive kind of a bond is absent and has made himself independent. When children do not recognize their parents, after they come back home and remain what one sometimes calls depressed, it is really not a depression. They live on a lower level of life until, if the relationship has not been broken for too long, it is reestablished. Others are recognized in the same way in which a schizophrenic might say, "Yes, I know this is a table."

"Do you know what this is?"

"Yes, it's a table. But you know, it isn't really a table. It isn't the table I used to know."

The "oomph" has gone out of the table for the schizophrenic; the libido with which it is cathected is gone.

So when there has been premature or traumatic separation from parents, or when in our relationships with our adult or adolescent patients a silent kind of merging unit has been interrupted, then we do not have any missing of the other person. There is no point in telling the other person, "You have missed me, that's why you are sad." He has not missed you, and he is not sad. He was not longing, and he is not being spiteful. This is simply not the type of relationship with somebody for whom one longs. The other person, as such, is not important. That person was important only insofar as he was present and *part of the self*. Again, it is only the observation of adults who can talk, who can tell you in detail what they experience, that allows you then to extrapolate developmental phases. And so a merging with an object that I call the idealized object—in other words, where all greatness, all power, all esteem, all worth and value are in the other—the merging with this other as the true believer merges with his God, is perfectly normal.

The child must normally have the conviction that the surroundings which are part of him are unshakable, providing pleasure, bliss, satisfaction, preventing or out-balancing anxiety. When we watch mother and child in their interaction, and the mother empathically responds to the child's needs, we know that we are watching two people, a baby, an independent unit, and a mother, an independent unit; but this tells us nothing about how the child experiences the relationship. To the child the mother is himself. He only knows that when the mother is not here he is much less than he was before. In very much the same way, when somebody who has made the relationship to such a highly overestimated object (by our realistic standards) loses that object, he does not yearn for that somebody but for a part of himself he has lost. His self-esteem is lowered. Again, this is different from the kind of expansion of the self in which one feels great but needs somebody else to be part and parcel and servant to this greatness. Then one does not look up to somebody who is very great and fantastically powerful. One assumes one's self is all powerful and fantastically big, except somebody else is needed to maintain this image of self. The baby, having this kind of conviction, could not maintain it very long unless adults were playing their role and helping him to maintain this. The child does not know that others are doing something out of their good will and out of their maternal and paternal instincts. It is done because he is he, and he wants it, and this is part of his greatness.

So there is a subject-bound narcissism that needs other people to maintain itself, and there is an object-bound narcissism that needs the presence of this other overestimated object to whom one can attach oneself. These developmental lines not only go side by side with the development of object love, but also go side by side with each other; in other words, both of these developments are present at the same time. People who have suffered losses of objects during phases of development in which the object is still experienced as part of the self suffer later on—not from being deprived of somebody they love, but rather, from missing part of their own psychological equipment. They chase all their lives after objects, trying to fill an inner void.

There are people who have lost an idealized parent before the formation of their own idealized superego—in other words, before they have set up a system of their own goals and values that is so highly idealized in all of us. The content of our values may change, but the normal person always idealizes. Ideals always play a special role in the mental setup. They may be different this year than they were ten years ago, but if we are fairly healthy in this particular way, we feel pleased with ourselves when we live up to our ideals. Our self-esteem is high when we live up to our values and goals. There are, however, people who have lost an idealized parent so suddenly that they were unable to transform this external figure into a set of idealized values. These are people who over and over again attach themselves to one idealized figure after another. They seem to be hungry for objects. But they are not hungry for objects;

they are filling the void of something that they themselves do not have. They must look up to somebody. And only when this other somebody then says, "Yes, you are good. Yes, you have lived up to my values," will they have this sense of balanced self-esteem that is prized so highly by everybody.

In principle this occurs before superego formation. However, I have extended it in a practical way to the period including the very beginning of latency, because the newly formed superego is still fragile at that time, and although it has been achieved, it apparently can still be undone. But that does not alter the principle. There is an inner void, a missing function, the lack of an inner capacity to feed one's self-esteem by living up to one's own values, which depends on the idealization of the superego, which is achieved by the gradual detachment from the idealized other. There is one area in my own observation in which I feel a little bit insecure yet. I have no question that the nuclear content of the superego is basically laid down and firmly crystalized at the end of the oedipal period. I believe that the idealization of the superego, more than laying down of content, has another very important firming to go through in puberty. So the detachment from the idealized figures of puberty has a genetic kind of meaning that the repetition of the oedipus complex at puberty no longer has. I am still in doubt about that.

Anybody can imagine how it feels to feel good about oneself—you have done some active work and you feel all warmed up physically, or you have done some good thinking and you feel satisfied with yourself. You feel as a cohesive whole, as it were. This is in contrast to the kind of disheveled experience about oneself that one sometimes gets, a feeling of not hanging together well. I know I am talking about this now in very nonpathological analogies, but you can see it in much grosser forms in the type of patient that I am particularly interested in, the patient with the narcissistic personality disturbance. Such patients are not psychotic people. They are not borderline people. They are not necessarily very sick or very ill people. They are people who lend themselves very well to insight therapy. But there are very specific disturbances in their self-esteem. Their problems are not primarily rejected impulses and conflicts about them. Their problems are primarily in the realm of self-esteem, of self-feeling, of hanging together, of feeling real about themselves.

This all seems to have an ominous sound, but it does not deserve such an ominous sound. We will discuss the reason later when I try to differentiate these disorders from the psychoses or from those larval or hidden psychoses that are now frequently called borderline cases.

So one can observe in the clinical situation and in everyday life how a cohesiveness of the self-experience disintegrates under the impact of the threatened loss of a self-esteem-sustaining relationship or a disappointment in anything that one has felt very ambitious about, in which one has proved oneself. One then feels fragmented in time and space. For example, in the course of analysis—and I am sure it is also true in the course of psychotherapy where interviews are less frequent—people will tell you that it seems every time as if they had never been here before. They might say an enormously long time has passed since they had been here, or they have no idea what they had been talking about last time. It turns out very frequently that this is not true, not intellectually correct. They may remember every word that was spoken last time, and yet that feeling remains—that is, they have the feeling of a noncohesiveness of themselves along a time axis.

Let me remind you again of a patient I described in one of my papers (1968). The analyst at one particular time began some interpretation when the patient came in on a Monday, very disheveled and feeling very broken up. As I have said, not taking care of oneself and looking disheveled is an external symptom or indication of an internal state of the lack of cohesiveness. That does not mean that one cannot look very cohesive or intentionally look like a hippie. It is not an abstract kind of way in which one looks disheveled. With a little sensitivity you can grasp, particularly when you know one particular person, whether he is well put together or falling apart.

In this particular instance the patient already knew, and the analyst already knew, that when he was separated from her over the long weekends from Thursday till Monday, he would come back in this disheveled state, feeling unrealistic and falling apart. After she had observed this for part of an hour, the analyst wanted to begin an interpretation about what all this meant. She remembered something that the patient had said earlier about what happened to him in childhood when his mother was gone. But she started her interpretation by saying, "As you told me two weeks ago . . . " And before she had yet begun to give her interpretation, the patient felt wonderful and all the disheveled state disappeared. Why? Because in her mind he had existed as a continuum for two weeks. You see, she could remember something that had happened to him two weeks ago. So he grew together as a whole through being seen as one continuum by a person who still provided this cement that we seemingly do not need anymore, though we always need it to some extent.

What happens to people when they are totally unsupported by any confirming experience, by any mirroring experience, by any capacity to affirm themselves? I have not been interested enough to pursue this in an experimental sense. But I do know that, in personalities with pathology centered in problems of cohesion, you can continuously see the inner swinging back and forth. You can see the breaking up and holding together again under the influence of an external figure who provides the functions originally provided by the sustaining environment. In the process of growth these functions allowed the individual to make out of the individual parts a cohesive self.

We speak of a cohesive self, of a fragmented self. In the clinical situation there are oscillations between these two. Developmentally, the stage of fragmentation is better called the stage of self nuclei, meaning the stage of developmental potential. Then you come to the stage of the cohesive self. In Freudian terminology there were the stages of autoerotism and of narcissism. These are similar terms, but with a little different emphasis. The cohesive self and fragmented self are the best terms for the actual clinical situation. In other words, you see somebody one day, and he is holding together well. Then you say, "I won't be able to see you for two days," and he fragments. There may be oscillations between cohension and fragmentation. You explain what has happened to him, and then he becomes cohesive again. If you see these oscillations, then I think fragmentation is the best term. But if you talk about the child *having self nuclei*, then you speak about the *developmental* potential.

In other words, we assume that a child has experiences early in life in which each individual sensory impression, each individual movement, each individual feeling, is at the moment all of it, and that includes certain things that the observer knows to be external. For example, when the baby sucks, the complex of oral cavity and nipple is one single experience. This complex of oral cavity and nipple is recoverable—can be extrapolated—from schizophrenic experience. The phenomenon can be seen, then, almost in pure culture: a regression takes place to this particular phase—and beyond, as a matter of fact. We will talk about this when we examine the essential differences between the psychotic state, the borderline cases which are larval or hidden psychotic states, and the more labile states.

The point is that, developmentally speaking, the child has experiences which are repeated in cases of narcissistic character disorders—brief oscillations which touch on this childhood base but are quickly overcome. This base is more stably cathected and more permanently reached in the psychoses. They give us marvelous access to the reconstruction of this developmental phase as a positive experience. In other words, when the small child feeds he has not even a rudimentary concept of "All of me also feeds." All there is at the moment is the feeding. It is this particular part of the oral cavity plus the nipple that is experienced; everything else is not there. And later, with another feeding experience, this is something else again; it does not yet hang together bound by memory. The infant does not have the capacity to think, "Formerly I was enjoying myself ecstatically on the nipple. Now I'm gladly falling back to sleep again."

In the initial stages of a schizophrenic regression, when it is still emerging, when it is still new, before it is covered over by secondary maneuvers which really fixate the regressive state, you can observe what happens. In these initial stages of the schizophrenic regression, the healthy part of the patient's personality watches helplessly as a regression takes place. This occurs generally after a hurt to the self-esteem. This regression, however, does not settle down in primitive phases of an archaic cohesive narcissism. In other words, there is not a quick swing back and forth from one position to another, but a massive regression to this particular stage, which then goes on in other directions which we will perhaps discuss in another context. We do not need to go into that now. What happens under such circumstances is that the patient then revives as a *pathological* state what formerly was a *normal* developmental state.

This is one of the crucial issues to be understood if one wants to grasp the nature of sophisticated developmental psychology. What once was a healthy, appropriate developmental state becomes something, or may become something, highly pathological. So the schizophrenic, in the initial stages of the schizophrenic regression, watches with dismay and fright the uncontrollable regression to an archaic mode of experience, in which individual body parts are cathected in an isolated, fragmented way and no longer belong to the total self.

I would like to compare two occurrences one is sometimes confronted with diagnostically which may concern the same organ system and which may on superficial examination look similar. Yet they have totally different prognostic meaning. One is a physical symptom clustering around a hysterical fantasy. The other is a schizophrenic regression. Let me take the hysterical fantasy in a young woman that relates to impregnation through the mouth. This is a ubiquitous childhood fantasy clustered around oedipal experiences. It is elaborated in childhood in the unconscious around seeing the penis of the adult and wanting to swallow it. It may arise also when a child has heard something about impregnation. The child hears that the baby comes out somewhere down there, and the feces come out that way, and the child knows something about eating and defecating. Thus, everything is made cohesive and elaborated into a combined fantasy, as it were. This particular experience then is repressed, and there is a barrier of disgust or ridiculousness. When the average person is confronted with such an idea, he tends to feel some kind of mild disgust reaction or an urge to laugh. In other words, the defensive part of our personality is set into motion. Now, assume such a regression to this oedipal fantasy of impregnation by swallowing the father's penis is activated in a patient. Let us say a young woman marries an older man. The man is impotent and cannot satisfy her, to use a very simple kind of story. Under the impact of the disappointment, she detaches herself from the present and regresses into an unconscious fantasy, which then, being activated, creates a hysterical symptom. The hysterical symptom may now be located around the mouth.

This is very, very different, and will impress us very differently. By the way, if you want to learn psychiatric diagnosis, this is the way, not by a science that makes two and two four. It is through being empathic with the meaning of the symptom, independent of whether a specific, potentially verbalizable fantasy lies behind the physical symptom, even though you may never recover that verbalizable fantasy. This is not as unintelligible as the schizophrenic's sense of body distortion. You will react to it either with disgust or with a sense of the ludicrous. You will never react in that way to the deep concern about body change, particularly that leading part of the lips, that an early schizophrenic undergoes.

What is happening in schizophrenia is that something has become cathected with autoerotic libido, if you wish. It has made itself separate from the rest of the body. There is still a cohesive self somewhere around, but autoerotism has now begun to hold sway. Something is separate from the rest of the self; it is not the leading part of an otherwise healthy self.

The difficulty lies in the following: If we have a person whose self-cohesiveness is tenuous, then a physical disease is not just followed by a healthy shift from object interest to narcissistic interest around an aching tooth, for example. The individual becomes threatened by the possibility of fragmentation. There is, then, a real threat of regression to archaic narcissism in a particularly vulnerable person under the impact of a physical illness that emphasizes a particular body part.

Reacting hypochondriacally to a physical illness is very different from caring for oneself narcissistically, finding a good excuse to go to bed and indulge oneself. Such a tendency is not beyond our empathy. We all know how to react hypochondriacally. It is the quantity which is the issue. But, one has first to understand how to measure quantity. One must know qualitatively what we are measuring before we can identify the quantity.

4

Empathic Environment
and the Grandiose Self

THE GRADUAL DEVELOPMENT of single detached experiences may be viewed as precursors of the self. There follows, then, a gradually increasing awareness of the experience of individual functions, body parts, and mental activities. With the integration and awareness of these experiences the total self emerges and takes form. It is not that the total self replaces former experiences. It is that *in addition* it integrates all former experiences.

The capacity to lose ourselves in a specific single activity is part and parcel of health. We are capable of enjoying an individual activity, a body part to which we are devoted, or pet thoughts that we have, because we know it is not a point of no return. We know full well that the total self experience is easily available to us. In anticipation of what we are now discussing in more detail, I mentioned earlier that there are vulnerable individuals to whom a physical illness with its shift toward narcissism becomes a threat to a shakily achieved balance of cohesiveness. These people, having made progress in the course of intensive analysis, are now capable of devoting themselves to activities formerly avoided because of their need to protect what little self they had. They were hatching themselves, like mother hens sitting on the egg of their own selves all the time. Now they are a little bit freer, and so they involve themselves in something. Suddenly they become frightened because the activity seems to drain the fragile self that has been achieved.

With the adopted child I mentioned earlier, who had enormous self-esteem problems and a great tendency toward experiencing himself as unreal, self-cathexis was poorly established. People of this type very often struggle for words. They cannot describe general tension states or feelings of unreality. Under systematic working-through of deficiencies in his self-esteem, particularly in the vicissitudes of interaction between him and his therapist, a woman, this patient began to devote himself to a new activity, playing the accordion. A fantasy about his adoption emerged in which a mother was walking through a nursery and, suddenly fascinated by the dazzling sight of this baby, namely himself, said, "This is the baby I want."

It was a healthy fantasy he had defensively erected against the feeling that nobody wanted him or cared about him. Do not misunderstand it as something pathological. The capacity to form such fantasies is a great sign of potential health. Later on in childhood, he formed the fantasy that he would be a spellbinder of crowds by being a virtuoso, but he could never quite make it. We can easily see why. It was too exciting, unrealistic, grandiose, and, if he indulged the fantasy, destructive. He could not in fact allow himself any initiative in such a direction. Now, under the impact of systematic work on his self-esteem, he felt capable of doing so and indeed began to play the accordion. And during one such playing session, when he was alone, he began to imagine he was sitting in a huge auditorium surrounded by people. He was taken over by the fantasy. He became terribly frightened; it drained him, and he had to stop playing.

We would think that we need nothing better or want nothing better than an enhancement of self-esteem. But it is not just enjoyable. Even some otherwise beautifully put together people become frightened or embarrassed and tremendously tense under the impact of a sudden stimulation of self-esteem. My favorite proverb in this context is, "Praise to the face is disgrace." The proverb emphasizes that direct praise is embarrassing. It makes an individual feel ashamed, shame being nothing else but an outflux, a sudden onrush of narcissistic exhibitionistic libido that cannot find its proper distribution all at once. So it leads to blushing, to heat, rather than to the normal warmth of self-esteem.[1]

By the way, total body warmth and self-esteem are very closely related. This has a lot to do with the genesis of the common cold. When one is chilled, when one is depressed and does not feel cared for, there are drops in self-esteem which are very frequently followed by the common cold. And a warm bath, for example, restores self-esteem. It is a common measure in hydrotherapy, although we do no know quite why. Other experiences such as physical exercise may also restore self-esteem.

The point I wish to make is that even otherwise very healthy people feel overstimulated, embarrassed, and under tension when they are suddenly overburdened by self-esteem.

---

[1]For further discussion see Kohut, 1978, I:69–71, 441–442; II:628–632.

Perhaps this is a good time to elaborate some vicissitudes of the growth process of self-esteem. The psychic economy of the speed with which the developmental phases are stepped, like the steps of a ladder from one to another, is of the utmost importance. Trauma occurs when the child is held back at a developmental or maturational phase although he is ready to move forward. This occurs if the mother insists on experiencing the child as part of her own body-self at a time when the child wants to exert his own initiative. The child at this point wants to see the mother to some extent as somebody with her own initiative who is not immediately affected by his moods. In other words, an echo must now last longer and must not be as immediate. The mother has to change with the child.

Psychic economy plays a role in the growth process. If a maturational step is imposed on a child too quickly and too suddenly, this is trauma. If the mother demands of the child that he suddenly give her up after having been totally involved with her, then it is traumatic. It is also traumatic if she keeps him too long under her wings. In other words, what is healthy in one developmental phase is traumatic in another.

There are two particularly beautiful childhood games that illustrate paradigmatically the economic issue in important and crucial transitional phases of both the developmental line of object love and object loss and the developmental line of narcissism and self-formation. Let me start first with the crucial game in the developmental line of object love and object loss: the peek-a-boo game. As I have often joked, the most important part of the game is the space between the mother's fingers. Why? The mother covers her face; she is gone. It has to be played at the right moment in life. If I played peek-a-boo with you, you would think me an idiot. If I play peek-a-boo with a very small child, I am still an idiot, but the child does not think so. It has to be played at the time when separation experiences are in gear. Only then is it meaningful. What happens then? The mother covers her face. The child is anxious, "Where is mother?" Mother watches the child's face between her fingers, sees the child become a little bit anxious, and then uncovers her face. An, there she is again! She looks, watches the child's anxiety rise up to a certain level, then reveals herself again, and bliss takes over once more.

And so, an optimal, psychoeconomically decisive, specific level has to be reached. It is different at different stages of development. The important issue is the mother's empathy for gauging just the right moment when the separation from the object has set up enough anxiety to make it blissful to leap to a reunion.

The whole theory of artistic enjoyment is in this capsule. There are endless ramifications in setting up tensions and then relieving them, in setting up attitudes that seem to be real and exciting, followed by the reassurance that it is just play. It illustrates the psychoeconomic factor, and it is in the realm of object love. Art comes to be in the specificity of the point at which such a game must be played.

The corresponding game in terms of self-cohesion and self-fragmentation is "This-little-piggy-went-to-market." Again, if you play this game with an older child, he thinks you are absurd. If you play it with a very small child, again you are absurd, even though the child does not think that. But if you play it at the right time, and if you play it with the right kind of empathy for the child, then what do you do? You take him apart, toe by toe, "This little piggy, this little piggy, this little piggy." Finally, when the child, with excitement and anxiety, has been all taken apart, what comes then? The mother embraces the child and, in a laughing and mutually enjoyable embrace, the child is put back together again, united with himself and with the idealized mother in a blissful experience of being a selfobject all in one.

When I say selfobject,[2] it is *self* which is emphasized. The self-experience at that particular point still includes an object that does things for you. If you only take apart and do not provide reunion, there would be no pleasure. It would be just as in playing a musical theme; one awaits the return to the tonic. Here too, after you take the child apart, you have to restore the sense of unity. At a specific point in the development, fragmentation in the game is set up intentionally, followed by reuniting, making the child whole once more.

Now all this is far from being only an interesting theoretical hypothesis. Fragmentation and restoration, loss and reunion are poignantly and clinically important. Of course, you do not play "this little-piggy-went-to-market" or "peek-a-boo" with your patients, but you do see the self-fragmentations. You do see how the self-fragmentations are healed again, not by embraces, but by an empathic understanding. Some patients, for example, without knowing why, come disheveled to you. After mentioning the experience of being in a new place, as the college setting, you make a few additional fine interpretations and think you are a fine psychiatrist because the patient feels better. But he does not feel better because you have made such marvelous interpretations. He feels better because he has been remembered—he has a continuum of the next appointment. He has somebody toward whom he relates and a specific office in which you see him.

---

[2]Throughout these seminars, Kohut is working toward a formulation of the concept of selfobject. For fuller discussion, see Kohut, 1978, I: 60–62; II:554–557; 1984 throughout.

In this context, it is very important not to shift from one office to another. It is very important not to see a person helter-skelter, here and there. Especially for patients of this particular type, the specific place, not moving the furniture for example, is important. Settled psychiatrists have an asset in the mere fact that they do not shift so much. Some patients experience an affront, as when one has come back from vacation: "Your plant isn't there. It has grown a new leaf. Where was I?" You have to decide whether this is a fantasy that is revived in terms of old object relations, whether there is sibling rivalry (a new "baby" has been born in the meantime), or whether he sees a change in something that should not change. There is a very different import.

The inanimate environment is sometimes given exaggerated importance. Yet one must approach this with sophistication, because some seemingly inanimate environment is really animate environment if it has been placed there by somebody who is animate. It becomes an extension of that individual.

If the bed is warmed and opened for you by somebody, the bed is part and parcel of the person who has prepared it for you. You settle down into it because somebody has warmed your pillows. Myriad acts of this type are continuously done for children.

But the most important issue is that no inanimate object can empathically respond to the child. Before I examine the positive side, let me first show the much more important negative issues here. When a child or particularly vulnerable adult is enormously devoted to environmental issues of the past, the inanimate objects of the past, there is already a depressive equivalent. Things are used to elicit, to replace, what really should have been there in an animated, live way.

What I would like to transmit to you is the role of people in terms of the upkeep of the narcissistic equilibrium[3] of grownups and of children. The child's narcissistic equilibrium in the stage of primary narcissism depends entirely on the upkeep of certain physiological balances. He must not get too cold or too hot, must not stay wet or soiled; he must not be kept unattended when he needs stimulation and he must not be disturbed when he wants to sleep. There are a million and one changing requirements to which the environment must respond. It must respond on the basis of feeling itself into the child, of being attuned to him. These are all functions that later on the older child and the adult fulfill for

---

[3]In these seminars Kohut sometimes uses the expression "narcissistic equilibrium." From 1971 forward, "self-cohesion," the use of selfobjects in the regulation of self-esteem, emerges as the basic concept.

themselves. Just think of the miracle, when walking, of being in a labile balance. If we were not continuously aided by millions of little muscle tensions—we are equilibrating ourselves—we would naturally topple over, because we are top-heavy. But we do not notice this anymore. This has become such second nature to us that we do not even notice this magnificent fear of keeping in balance on a rather narrow surface.

Similarly, with narcissistic equilibrium, we are continuously engaged in a stream of activities, maintaining ourselves warm, keeping ourselves supplied with just the sufficient amount of attention by the environment. If somebody in this seminar gets too fed up, or is not fed, by what I am saying, he will begin to do something with his pencil or will scratch himself to be sure that he is alive. "Nobody else is doing anything for me. At least I'm doing something to myself." There are a variety of things we do when we feel deprived narcissistically, that is, when we sit around and have to listen to somebody else for too long.

The point I am making is that the environment is engaged in the upkeep of the narcissistic balance of the small child in an inordinately demanding way. This is what taxes parenthood so much. There is essentially not a moment of respite. Thank God, parents are fallible, because then the child is encouraged, if the traumata are not too severe, to begin to fend a little on his own and to take over some of the functions that formerly were handled by the caretaking adult.

The caretaking adult, with a radar of empathy for the child, is continuously in tune with his need to be narcissistically put into equilibrium. It is the failures of this equilibrium,[4] if they are appropriately frustrating—in tune with the child's maturation and progress in taking over—which enable the child to grow. It is the traumatic failure in equilibrium and empathy which sets up severe trauma.

When we consider the nonhuman environment, the vital issue is the relationship of this nonhuman environment to the human environment. If it is experienced as a deputy of the human environment, it will gradually take the place of the human environment. If it is in the form of appropriate gifts, as a pet that is given with love by Daddy or Mommy, toys that they have enjoyed with the child, then gradually, as the child plays with these, they become a reassuring part of the environment. They are deputies of what formerly was human environment.

Ultimately, everything in the world is a deputy of what formerly was human environment. As I have said earlier, when a schizophrenic tells

---

[4]Kohut would ultimately settle upon the use of the term "fragmentation" to describe disruptions or failures in self-esteem regulation.

you, "Yes, this is a table. I know it's a table. I know the word for it. I recognize the shape of it. Of course I know it's a table, but it's not a table anymore—the kind of table that it was," what he describes is that the human environment originally leading into his table experience has disappeared. It is the deep loss of self and object that is suffered when this table now looks unreal. It is the connectedness and the depth of which finally everything else has become a deputy or derivative. These connections have been lost in the dim past of the individual existence. But in terms of the child growing up one can certainly see the difference between parents who surround the child with expensive toys because they want to be rid of him and the ones who offer simple meaningful toys. This is the old, touching story, which is very true, that nothing can take the place of simple toys that Daddy or Grandfather made as the child watched. These are the prized possessions that are sometimes taken to new environments.

When somebody takes a doll or some toy into the university or college setting, I would want to ask a lot of sophisticated questions before I evaluate its meaning. The meaning may vary from very positive hanging on to a fine and warm childhood surrounding (one still likes to take the toy along even though one is grown up otherwise) or it may be the crumbling last hold of a person at the brink of schizophrenic disintegration to something that is part of a self that is in some way externalized. The external symbol cannot tell you the whole story. I think this is probably as far as I can go in showing, at least in some depth, what simple things of this particular type may signify.

Our next step will be to discuss the two specific developmental lines of narcissism—namely, the subject-bound and the object-bound lines. is an enormous topic, but nobody is looking over our shoulder at how we are going about it. I hope you feel as I do. I would like to be an empathic responder to your childhood needs. Are there any questions?[5]

I still have difficulty with the way in which primary narcissism and the transitional object fit into your theory of the developmental lines of narcissism.

It would be a conceptual project of the first order to respond to and clarify this question. If one were to pursue the concept of primary narcissism throughout Freud's writings, one would come to different defini-

---

[5]We have sought here to retain the quality of the seminars. In this instance Kohut's response to a question allows us a glimpse into his typical theory-building. Here and elsewhere in the book, questions and comments from the participants are in italic.

tions depending on the different contexts in which he used the term. And if one were to examine the concept of a transitional object in depth, as it has been used in the literature, one would find out that it is not very well defined theoretically. Therefore, the fault is not entirely mine when I cannot cleanly or clearly fit these concepts into my schemes.

One can nevertheless make certain approximations and by making approximations learn more about the facts that we are dealing with; this is really what is important. It is not important to have conceptual clarity in our field all the time, at least certainly not from the beginning. Freud knew that. In his basic paper, "Narcissism, An Introduction," he makes the famous statement about the meaning of metapsychology, that it is the coping of the structure that can be discarded at will (1914c, pp. 74–75). The basis of what we do is always observation, observation only, and the interpretation of it. But the broader conceptualizations come and go. Neither in psychoanalysis nor in any of our related approaches do we deal with a conceptual framework that is simply stated on the basis of definition. We try to approximate it to what we observe.

When we speak about primary narcissism, my attempt would be to work from clinical experience in attempting to reconstruct developmental phases. This is the classical approach of depth psychology.

It seems to me that the concept of primary narcissism is one that is on a more experience-distant level, in other words, a libido distribution which falls into the period before Freud introduced the concept of aggression as a drive. It falls into a libido distribution when there was not yet any reaching out, or what later on would become object libido. But it was all diffusely concentrated on what? The self has not been formed yet either. In other words, it strikes me as a prepsychological concept, referring to a phase not yet psychologically definable. But it is not a useless concept. I can give you an example in which I consider this concept useful.

Children respond to maternal stimulation in a variety of ways. Some children need very little stimulation; others will not respond even when mothers strongly stimulate (and respond empathically to) them. One may say that there is something congenital, inherited, an innate factor that accounts for the very ability of the child to respond to the varieties of environmental stimuli. And one may say that the primary narcissism of the child who does not respond is greater, at one end of a scale, than the narcissism of the child who from the outset responds to comparatively small stimuli.

So a concept of an innate propensity for the libido to remain centripetal, rather than centrifugal, comes close to this zero point in development that Freud at one level called primary narcissism.

When Freud said that the schizophrenic regresses to the level of primary narcissism, he seems to say that what we now call the autoerotic phase—or in my terminology the phase of the fragmented self—is primary narcissism. Indeed, you may say that these particular levels of experience, or of empathized-with experience, may be so archaic, so remote from a self-observing function, from any reflective awareness of the self, that one cannot really define them in terms of psychological concepts that in any way relate to inner experience. We derive abstractions from inner experience even when we speak about drives. For example, we know wishes, we know needs, we know urges, and out of all this we extrapolate something that we call a drive: something that partakes of all these pushing forces that we experience.

What I was trying to show in our earlier discussion was that regression to isolated body feelings after the self has split into individual body parts, in a nonhuman, machine-like, dehumanized, isolated, fragmented fashion, becomes very frightening to the healthy part of the person's awareness. The experience is of something prepsychological, something nonhuman happening, and one empathizes with the strangeness. The schizophrenic's symptoms and experiences described in psychiatric textbooks can be summed up in such sentences as, "No, I don't want to understand. I can't understand; it's bizarre; it's odd; it's different; it's something out of the ordinary." One could call this primary narcissism; it is something beyond the empathizable, beyond the usual reality world in which we live. It is even beyond a narcissistic world in which we want the reflection of ourselves in other people. This is still a world that we all immediately understand or can at least with some effort understand. When this fragments in the schizophrenic experience, we can only say it is bizarre or odd. In other words, it is pre-empathic.

The schizophrenic experiences this regression with horror, with the greatest anxiety. There is a split in the psychosis too. There is a healthy observing part in the psychotic patient which observes that a big sector of his personality has undergone regression. And seeing that part of him regressed to such an extent that it is unintelligible even to himself is a terribly frightening experience. So that from the outset, since our mental apparatus is always defensive, the rest of the personality begins, in Glover's terms (1956), to form theories about what is really no longer intelligible. By the way, the term "defensive" is not a psychiatric swear word; it is a good word which describes psychological homeostasis. The healthy, observing part of the ego then defensively attempts to describe the regression to the individual experience of fragmented body parts in terms of a world that is more realistic. He tries to explain and rationalize it, and then complains of illness, as if it were an illness. Illness has a meaning that is quite apart from the experience.

"Something hurts me." Everybody knows what that means when one remains in the world of experience. However, what happens to the lips, to the arm, to the thinking processes in the schizophrenic is beyond that. The healthy part of the personality, still actively trying to save itself in some way, weaves this now into an as-if-intelligible context, explains it and complains. This is the hypochondria of the early phases of schizophrenia: trying to explain the unexplainable. Even though I still may sound evasive, and properly so, concerning the question of primary narcissism, I think at least I am clarifying where my problems lie and what I am trying to do with them.

As to the question about the transitional object, it was Winnicott (1951) who introduced the term. But the concept was known and used by Freud (1920) in "Beyond the Pleasure Principle." Winnicott views the transitional object, if I understand him correctly, as a point in the development toward object love.

For a long, long time, the empathic adult environment of a child—correctly empathic, if it is a feelingful, understanding environment—will not insist on object love from the child, but will take for granted that the environment is being used in a narcissistic sense by the child,[6] because it fits his developmental capacities. Again, we can only go by approximations. Over what does a grownup person normally have a sense of narcissistic control and mastery? Over his own body. You may imagine the cognitive center, whatever this may be, as located in the eyes, or in the brain, or whatever theory you have formed. I am not talking about anatomy now. I am talking about a psychological experience.

One sometimes feels estranged from a particular body part. In a half-awake state when you are estranged from yourself, you may wake up and see an arm lying there without knowing that it is yours, as it were. It would be a different feeling from that of telling your hand to lift and finding it would not lift, as with a stroke. It makes you angry enough if somebody does not follow your orders—outside of you is a person with his own initiative—but this is a different degree of anger from that which people experience with the loss of function in strokes. Those of you who have had neurological training and neurological experiences will have seen this kind of anger when something as intimate as one's thinking processes does not follow one's commands or when something as close to the center of one's self-feeling as one's language fails. Most of the psychiatrists here have seen, during their neurological training, a particular condition in which people think clearly, but their capacity to trans-

---

[6]In other words, the environment functions as a selfobject.

late what they are thinking into understandable words is organically impaired by a certain type of brain damage. The rage these people experience when they want to say a word and only a silly mumble comes out is terrific. Why? Because something that one has supposedly total possession and control over is now not under one's control.

Why do I go through this? In our empathic experimentation with early phases of development, what we as adults know to be an external object with its own centers of initiative, able to say *yes* or *no* to commands, is for the baby an extension of himself, just as much as the arm or one's own thoughts. When the baby cries, it means that now the nipple should come into mouth. In just the same way, my thought should follow my ideas, and my hand should follow my thought. It is this kind of an intimacy.

Therefore, it is traumatic—and hark that word, because we have to come back to that a number of times—when this early relationship is interrupted, massively and prematurely so. The spaces between the mother's fingers when playing peek-a-boo tell her that the child is not too anxious, but a little anxious. Such little delays are grist for the mill of maturation and of acquiring new modes of mastery. But if the trauma occurs of separation from an object that still is to fulfill the narcissistic functions[7] of the child in the same way as we expect our hand to come up, our thoughts to follow suit, and our speech to come out, if this is suddenly gone—namely the mother is suddenly gone, without preparation, and there is no substitute when the child wants her—then the child asserts mastery by saying, "No. My objects come and go when I want them to." And so it is with the transitional object.

Let us take, for instance, the first description of a transitional object, the description of the spool in Freud's monograph, "Beyond the Pleasure Principle." Freud (1920) described that, under the impact of the separation from his mother, his little grandson played with a spool. He tied the spool to a string that was under the bed. He made it disappear, and then he pulled it back again and said, "Gone, and here it is again." Freud (1920) described, at that particular time, a specific mechanism that relates to a rudimentary stage of object love. A symbol of an object that has made itself independent is mastered by a mechanism called active mastery. "No, mother, you're not going away. This is you, mother. I'll make you go away if I want to. And I'll pull you back again when I want you to come back." Then the spool on the string replaces the mother. In

---

[7]Later Kohut would refer to this as a selfobject function.

order to handle his particular separation anxiety, the child asserts control through his game.

I think you will understand much of the so-called childish behavior of grownups, their insisting on control and their anger when things do not go their way, if you develop gradually the capacity not just to think yourself into single acts, but to recreate a whole world view: the fixation of the whole world view of a young child.

For the child, the whole world is still connected with the self and ought to follow one's commands. The frustrations that we all have to suffer are experienced by such people as narcissistic blows. These are not just the usual frustrations that one mourns about, or things that one cannot have that one desires, but the overwhelming, "My God, how can it happen to me! It must not happen. This is still all mine," even though the mind tells them it is not. To make fun of them, to be harsh with them, or to criticize them for it is unempathic. It is not under their control to feel the world that way. To help them, one has to go a totally different route, which will gradually emerge in the course of our meetings here. I can only repeat that I do not have an easy answer to the question of primary narcissism and the transitional object.[8]

What we are discussing is the development of a self-concept. The archaic objects that are involved with the development of the self concept have nothing to do, necessarily, with the development of object love. That is a separate and independent developmental line. Now if you ask me at what time in the child's development the selfobject plays a role, my speculation would be that it belongs somewhere in this interim phase between autoerotism, or narcissism, and an established self. But it is outside the development of this particular developmental line that we are talking about, at least so far as I can judge. These transitional objects, like this particular spool, or the blankets that children carry about, are way-stations in the development from rudimentary or immature to mature object love. I am quite convinced that it deals with rudimentary object love. It deals with an object that has initiative, an object that has activities of its own. This mother made herself independent. And what this child is struggling with is to allow this mother independence only insofar as he has something to say about it too. He deals with the suddenness of the disappearance of the mother.

As far as primary narcissism is concerned, there are certain levels of

---

[8]For Kohut's last discussion of narcissism and object love as separate lines of development, see 1984, p. 185 and p. 226, n. 2.

development that we can again empathize with or that we can reconstruct dimly in grownup experience. Indeed, one gets the feeling that
very early distributions, very early concepts of self-hood or selfness are
being revived as, for example, sensitivity to temperature regulation. I do
not think that is my fantasy. In general, I think it is true that schizoid
people have a poor regulatory sense of temperature. They tend to be
physically cool; their hands are cold. I read somewhere that their periph-
eral capillary system was found to be rather poorly vascularized. Now
whether this is an outgrowth of innate, congenital, psychophysiological
equipment or of early disturbances that lead to a lack in blood vessel
formation in the skin, the end result is that very frequently they are
chronically cold and cold-skinned people. At the other end of the scale,
all of us, regardless of how welcome we were in this world, and how
reasonably firm our self-experience has been, may catch colds, and may
feel cold, as a result of narcissistic blows of some kind, with feelings of
being deprived of contact with an idealized object.

I think if you are empathic toward people with acute disturbances of
this kind, sometimes a very simple remedy is to offer them a hot drink. I
do not serve meals in sessions with my patients, but I have had some
very ill people to whom I have said, "You're feeling terrible today. Let us
go down and have a cup of coffee." It seemed to be the only thing to do,
because all my verbal approaches did not seem to meet their need. And
the lending of my own body warmth, like putting my arms around
them, as some people do, or touching, seemed too seductive. But one
must be aware of the individual's discomfort: "Is it cold here? I'll turn on
the radiator." People, for example, take hot baths to restore themselves;
the hot bath is used for calming purposes. People who are terribly frustrated and feel they are falling apart find such envelopment in a warm
bath restorative. This is not simply a return to the womb, which is so
often offered as explanation of what makes them feel better. They feel
better because the general warmth is a very intricate way of restoring
narcissistic equilibrium on a very primitive level of body temperature.

I would like now to turn to a more detailed discussion of the early
development of narcissism, namely, the kinds of things that you know
from my papers I call the grandiose self, on the one hand, and the
idealized object, on the other hand. A second direction that I would like
to take is to illustrate the gradual building of psychic structure, the
firming of an internal self-experience, the firming of an internal way of
regulating self-esteem, being pleased with oneself when one has done
well.

One does not always need other people to feed one's self-esteem. I think everyone knows certain things one can do for oneself to boost self-esteem when it has been shattered. For example, an individual can sit down and do good work by himself. Nobody else knows it, but he will feel better. This is one of the best means I have to regulate my self-esteem when I am low. To sit down and work, after some blow to my self-esteem, and then, to come up with something that I consider to be good—this experience makes me feel better. But there are many other ways to regulate self-esteem, from the crude aspects of physical exercise in which one stimulates one's body cohesively, as in a fast run, or a cold shower or hot bath, to some intellectual work.

Freud (1933, p. 101) used to say that intellectual work was one of the best safeguards for mental health. I puzzled for the longest time as to what he meant. He never explained it. It was an aside somewhere, but the question of what he meant lingered in my mind. I think this is what it must mean—the self-confirming effect, the capacity to confirm yourself. Of course, like the stock market, it can rise or fall sharply. There are some regulatory mechanisms even in regressed schizophrenics. This was true of Schreber, who even in very dilapidated phases was able to do things for himself by intensive thinking and by building schemes. Bizarre though they were, they always had some little residue of his former highly intellectual, moral and very impressive personality. You may want to read this fascinating story—not Freud's history (1911a), but the autobiography of Schreber (1903) which Freud analyzed.[9]

In the future program that I am trying to lay out for myself and for you, I will discuss in some detail the development of early narcissistic experiences which, because of fixation points and residuals of these points, allow us ever so much better to understand clinical data. I will also discuss how self-regulatory capacities are acquired.

---

[9]See also Kohut, 1978, I:283–286, 299–300, 305–307; II:833–835.

5

Building Psychic Structure
That Regulates Self-Esteem

How is SELF-REGULATION of esteem acquired? Of course the answer is by the gradual building up of internal structures that take over the functions performed by the narcissistic object. Under what circumstances does the loss of a narcissistic object, then, leave a person with a defect that leads to a lifelong search for a narcissistic object who will perform these functions? And under what other circumstances does the loss of such an object lead to the internal taking over of the functions? Who are the people, and what happens to those people who, having lost the admiring mother in one form or another, run through life looking for mothers to admire them, regardless of the sex or gender—continuously hungry for a verbal *oohing* and *ahing* echo to themselves? And who are those who have lost their admiring others and now do not need mothers anymore because they have taken over the function of admiration when they are pleased with themselves? What are the differences between such losses? This is a problem that goes under the broad heading of internalization of self-esteem and its vicissitudes. I would like now to embark on a discussion of these two related areas.

Let me begin by a very crude presentation, familiar to you since you have read my two papers[1] in which I spelled it out so centrally. In the original prepsychological narcissistic equilibrium, in which there is as yet no frustration (a theoretical zero point in the development called primary narcissism), there are, sooner or later, experiences of narcissistic disequilibrium. They are experienced by the baby as unpleasant. It is cold, it is hungry, it is wet—and there is no immediate regulation. The

---

[1] "Forms and Transformations of Narcissism" (1966) and "The Psychoanalytic Treatment of Narcissistic Personality Disorders: Outline of a Systematic Approach," (1968), in Kohut, 1978, I:Chapters 32 and 34.

body's homeostasis performs some. The baby uses up calories; there is a store of glycogen in the liver that is made available. But then, finally, comes hunger, for these internal regulations are not sufficient. Something that we know to be external is needed: the nipple, the breast, the bottle, the mother who responds as the liver responds.

For the baby, mother is tantamount to the liver. She is an external liver. This is nothing that we need to be aware of. When we are hungry we do not call on the liver to mobilize glycogen. But since the mother is not the liver, and is not as perfectly, homeostatically interconnected with the needs of the child as his physical organs are, there will be a response and the hunger will not be allowed to become too great if she is empathic, responsive, and attentive. But there will be a delay, at night longer, or if the baby is bottle-fed, until the bottles are prepared, or simply because the mother, being the center of her own initiative, is unwilling or angry at the baby for crying. She is not as perfect as the liver.

A beginning of otherness, a rudimentary suspicion of otherness, must somehow arise in the baby. Yet this otherness is only of interest to the baby in terms of regulating what it experiences in this primitive way as well-being, which is indistinguishable from what we call self-esteem. There is no question that it later becomes ramified and branches out into perfection of all kinds—physical, mental, moral, esthetic, and all the different forms perfection may take. Originally, it is all one big package that we may call well-being. This is the narcissistic equilibrium.

In its perfect form, the narcissistic equilibrium of the baby includes all these needs that are being physically cared for—and more. The baby has drives. It not only has drives around sequences of hunger satiation, but also has drives of a kind that, approximating the closest adult experience, for want of a better word, Freud (1905a, 1915a) called sexual drive. From the best known of a series of rather similar experiences, he called all libidinal experiences sexual, not only because they appear in perversions, where they are clearly sexual, but also because even when they are not sexual they have an urgency or pleasure-seeking familiar to everyone. They are alike in intensity. So, in a similar kind of correlation, I suggest that we talk about the exhibitionistic drive and the need of the adult to spin out great fantasies about himself, and that we correlate these with rudimentary beginnings.

In my first paper on narcissism (1966; in 1978, *I*, p. 438). I spoke of "baby worship." I tried to show the social situation in which one might say the baby is at the peak of this kind of narcissistic equilibrium, exhibiting his body. This would probably occur in an autoerotic state, perhaps of delight in the self. "This is me, and isn't it beautiful!" If the baby could speak this is what he would say. And since he cannot say it, the mother responds to him, setting up a baseline of total equilibrium, of total narcissistic bliss, a baseline of perfection. I would think that at such moments there must be a convergence of grandiosity and exhibitionism all in one little bundle. Whatever the baby does is responded to by the gleam in the mother's eyes, by her warmth, by her enthusiasm. Her self-esteem is heightened as she feels at one with the excited and exhibiting baby. It is this kind of an equilibrium, though on a much more silent level, that we are striving for all our lives.

Eventually, it is no longer an ecstatic experience. All our experiences gradually become toned down and lose this initial lustre, but a degree of this lustre exists in every given moment of our lives, even when I talk to you and I want to see how you respond to me. Everybody who has given lectures knows about the person who looks away. How you would love him to look at you and how this sadist will continue to look the other way! He deprives the lecturer of the pleasure of knowing that he is responded to. Someone in the audience will look at the lecturer and nod, and how mean of the lecturer then to look away rather than nod back! We do this millions of times without knowing what we are doing, from morning till night, not just during lectures. I used the example because it happens to be my baby worship at the moment. You are the mothers, as it were.

But all these things go on all the time in a subdued, not excited, not ecstatic, not sexualized manner. I believe, for example, that what is called the fear of death is actually a fear of losing narcissistic responses, since Freud quite cogently and correctly observed that we should not be afraid of death because it has not been an experience (Freud, 1915b, p. 289). How can one be afraid of something one does not know or has never experienced? Freud felt that the fear of death was generally mutilation anxiety. It may very well be that some neurotic fears of death are that. But I think the basic fear of death, the non-neurotic fear of death, is one of losing the narcissistic responses. I think the best dying man's helper is the kind of person who continues to give narcissistic supplies to the dying person.

This is not difficult to do. You may, for instance, congratulate him for his heroism in the way he faces death. You may appreciate how he can tolerate himself in this extreme situation. But you must not abandon him. You must not withdraw from him. You must give him something that confirms him even in his dying. I think people who have this kind of response are likely to die with much more satisfaction and peace than people who feel that someone has withdrawn from them. Now in the final agonizing stages, I think it would be a disturbance to interfere with the dying person's self-achieved equilibrium, when he wants to turn to the other side and look at the wall. He does not at this point want any more to do with the surroundings; he wants to concentrate on himself and die his own death without being disturbed by anybody who still wants to give him something. To be empathic with a dying person is probably very taxing for most of us, because we want to wall ourselves off from an experience that we all will have to face one of these days, though we try to deny that fact.

These are illustrations which, by the way, are not so abstruse, because, once the principles are known to you and understood, I think they can be applied in many ways. In your work, you do not deal with baby worship, and you do not deal with dying patients, but you do work with many people who experience disturbed narcissistic equilibrium. If you know what is at stake, you will at least begin to be attuned to what is needed. You do not have to offer narcissistic supplies. This is not the point. But at least if you understand you can then help your patient to participate in your understanding, which is alone an enormous help. It is much greater help than any ill-advised play therapy with patients. I am using the term "play therapy" in the sense that one gives something that makes them terribly dependent if they accept. Further, if they are not helped, they become angry at you for humiliating them by treating them as babies.

What I am at the moment illustrating here is that I think there is an excellent array of evidence to support the claim that, even when the small child cognitively begins to see that there are objects other than himself, they still serve a narcissistic dimension. They have names; they are selves. They have significance to him as libidinal objects for whom he longs and to whom he wants to give something. They continue to serve also a narcissistic dimension.[2] And what I call the mirror transference in its various phases of development is an expression of the fact that others are experienced and needed in the sense of being *agents for self-confirmation*, for self-approval. You know Freud's famous statement about his own life which he never theoretically elaborated very much, a personal statement made once or twice in his writings, namely, that he was the firstborn son of a young mother. He said the firstborn son of a young mother keeps throughout life the feeling of a conqueror (Jones, 1953, I:5). And then comes the very important afterthought that this created a feeling, irrational though it might be (he does not say that, but obviously this is implied), a feeling which may indeed make him a conqueror, may indeed lead to success in life.

---

[2]They perform selfobject functions.

This is not pathology. The irrational basis of rational behavior is a very important one. Our best deeds and thoughts are not autonomous modes of reacting on the surface of our personalities. They are always, as I like to say, sectorial. They dig deep into our depths. We must not act like babies and require people to admire our toes once our toes have become very ugly creatures indeed. But yet, having once had our toes kissed and counted, we know there may be something about us that remains interesting and acceptable and that maintains us despite external reverses. Some people have an enormous resilience despite external reverses. But nobody has resilience that is foolproof. Deprive a person of the necessary basic physiological equipment severely enough and long enough and his self-esteem will go down. We may retreat to hallucinatory wish fulfillment, as I reported to you the very first time we were here together. An individual may even have a pseudo-pathological, but in essence healthy, mode of reestablishing his equilibrium on the basis of an old narcissistic supply.

You may ask: How does that relate to basic trust, for example? There is a certain kind of relatedness to this concept. But basic trust strikes me as a bit sentimental, a bit less than optimally psychologically refined. And I think it is a value judgment, which I dislike, because one ought to have a basic trust and a basic distrust, too. Both are valuable experiences. It is true that people ought to be capable of trusting other people, but one also ought to be developing the capacity of not trusting them. One would obviously not survive if one had not also learned that a basic trust which is all embracing would be incompatible with life. The richest psychological armamentarium is the best. But this is an aside.

I want to emphasize the importance of the capacity to experience this mirroring from the environment and to be confirmed by an acceptance of what the adult observer knows to be another human being. One needs to experience oneself as having an effect, of receiving a response, of being important. I gave you examples of this kind. What is called the mirror transference is of course very clear. Why do schizophrenics stare into the mirror? What are they trying to do? The answer is obvious. They feel themselves crumbling and disappearing. By vision they are trying to see "No, I'm still there. I can see myself." But a mirror is cold; it is only a mirror visually. The mother is not just such a mirror. She is a responding mirror, which is a very different kind of mirror. If the child is deprived of the visual aspects, then the auditory aspects are put into place, as in Burlingham and Robertson's movie about the blind children (1966).

There are precursors to this mirroring response. The developmental chronology is not clear to me. I am talking about the phases of the merger and of the alter ego experience as preceding the mirror experience. I call all three the mirror transference when it reestablishes itself. It is a misnomer, but I could think of no better label. It was the leading and best known example for a whole group of similar examples.

There is an important issue in all three stages. In the merger with another person that other is experienced as an extension of the self. In the alter ego or twinship experience the other is experienced as just like oneself. Finally, we have the most differentiated other in the true mirror transference. In the narrower sense, the other person is important only insofar as he confirms in enthusiasm and applause.

All these stages have one thing in common. The self-experience is enhanced and confirmed by the response to the exhibitionistic needs of the child and to the grandiosity of the adult so that he feels powerful, perfect, all-knowing. It is the support that the external environment, as we know it to exist, gives to the child in maintaining these delusions, as we may wish to call them. Psychologically speaking they are the deepest truths about the small child, although objectively speaking they are erroneous. He must have this state of mind before he can give it up.

So this is one line of development, and as I said, I do not know how these different phases relate to each other. I know, from the experience of an analyst, that a sequence establishes itself in general that begins with a merger, through twinship and likeness experiences to the mirroring response. One has the impression that it is a sequence toward maturity. Reflection also would support this. Obviously, a mirroring adult, already cognitively clearly recognized, presupposes an older child with cognitive equipment of somewhat greater development. Nevertheless, there are other times when one has the feeling that merger, twinship, and mirroring may go on simultaneously. Sometimes we need to merge into another person. Even an older child will sometimes not want to be approved, but will want to be hugged, to merge in a symbolic way. It would be quite erroneous, for instance, to praise a child or an adult who is totally crestfallen and say, "You have done well." He would feel misunderstood. "This is not what I want now. At this moment I want to be hugged. I want to be included in something." Sometimes the silent presence of another person is the best one can offer. And the tolerance of psychotherapists in the right circumstances can be enormously helpful. To remain silent next to a silent patient is something that I knew long before I knew why I was doing such things.

I remember many years ago, as a matter of fact, in these holy halls, I was treating a schizophrenic novelist. All I was doing was breathing in her breathing rhythm. I observed that when I would breathe in another rhythm than hers, she would become anxious. I would breathe in her rhythm while she was reading her novel. She would bring me some odd gifts . . . I ended up with a whole collection of dried plants from the area where she lived. I accepted them and put them away. I do not know why; perhaps I thought she might someday want to prove that I really kept them, but she never did. But I did understand that I had to listen to her reading, which was interesting. My listening was not artificial, nor was my acceptance of her gifts. The only artificiality was that I kept them so long. But I did observe that my breathing in rhythm with her made her feel very comfortable, and when I did not do so she became anxious. I think there was an early merging that she attempted to achieve by these regressive gifts, in which she gave me part of herself, probably symbolically. When she read these verbally unintelligible, but still fascinating sounding productions to me, then she felt to some extent in equilibrium.

Again, what is the relationship of the merger or mirroring to symbiosis? Symbiosis describes a different frame of reference. Symbiosis describes two separate individuals doing something for one another, a sociobiological framework. But I am talking about a framework of empathy with a psychological state. The merger is not something that really takes place. It is a feeling tone of a relationship. This novelist I am describing had a husband, and they were in this kind of togetherness that must have fulfilled enormous needs in both of them. He was not schizophrenic but a very simple-minded individual, a laborer. He admired her greatly despite the fact that he knew she was obviously bizarre. She had great contempt for him but used him. And between the two of them they made a fantastic couple. He brought her in once a week for my breathing exercises with her, and we maintained her for a long time.

I give you little sidelights. You do not treat such regressed schizophrenics and I do not treat such people anymore. But there are times during almost any form of psychotherapy in which the patient does not particularly feel like talking. This is not a resistance that has to be overcome; you must be capable, with empathic responsiveness, just to sit for a while. Make little noises perhaps, so they know that you are awake and that you are there and that you are tolerant of the silence. It may, for a while, be the most important thing you can do. You may help to nudge the patient into slightly more alert modes of communication simply by being side by side.

This kind of a combined silence can be a very primitive kind of merger, not necessarily an ill one. It may be a curing and wholesome one, or it may simply be, as in twinship, like two people sitting next to each other. I remember Greenson gave a lecture many years ago and spoke about the sighing experience. The patient sits down, very depressed, and after a long silence he sighs deeply. The therapist waits for a while, and then he too sighs deeply. The patient and the doctor feel sort of combined. He felt this was sometimes the best way of initiating contact. He sees this in a totally different frame of reference, building up therapeutic alliances. To me, it is a much more basic and central aspect of the personality that is being activated and responded to, not for the purpose of any real therapy, and yet it is already the beginning of real therapy. It is not a question of twisting an emphasis here and there. This is a different outlook on similar phenomena.

A student reported an experience to me this week which has left me puzzling as to whether it represents merger, whether it represents twinship, whether it is subject-bound or object-bound. The incident was this: A young man is very much at odds with everyone but particularly with his father right now. In the course of looking back to a time when things might have been different between them, he suddenly burst into tears and had a great deal of difficulty in controlling himself. When he could finally master his feelings enough to say anything, he reported that, when he was six, he was about to be taken to the hospital for an operation on his appendix. His father carried him down the stairs because he could not walk. His tears arose when he explained, ''The children could see that, like them, I had a father.'' The importance at one level of his father doing this for him prompts my question of what this all meant: Was it a merger such as you have just described? Was this subject-bound or object-bound narcissism? Was it so intricately combined that I could not possibly have puzzled it through except from the viewpoint of psychoanalysis?

I wish I could answer this but I cannot. I would have to know more about the context in which this moving experience came up and what it meant to him. Being carried means essentially being supported, essentially being enclosed or held by somebody who is strong and vigorous while he at that particular moment was weak and sick. It has certain exhibitionistic elements in it too. What he really felt so moved about apparently at this moment was not only that he was being carried, but also that he was seen being carried. In other words, the other children saw him and admired him: he had this wonderful father as perhaps the others did not.

But one would have to know a great deal more about the meaning of this particular experience. For example, I would immediately think, when I hear such an incident, that this may be in the nature of a screen memory. At this particular moment what he is talking about with such great stress as a positive experience may serve to cover up the fact that he was then separated from the supporting father and was terribly afraid of surgery and of being abandoned, perhaps for the first time, by his parents. In other words, what happens very frequently is that when this particular kind of childhood memory comes up, it covers over in a positive way something negative.

I am allowing myself to fantasy freely. I do not know what this particular individual wanted to communicate and why he was so touched by it. But it offers to us a rich example of the importance of the narcissistic balances and relationships that maintain an inner narcissistic equilibrium. The phase of the grandiose feeling about the self, one's own omnipotence, one's own perfection, one's own acceptedness—all the things for which one can use a million and one words—describes something that is essentially open to everyone's introspective capacities. We all have experiences in that particular realm; we know when we feel good about ourselves and we know what other people can contribute to this feeling.

But there is one thing I would like to recommend to your own thought experimentations, because this is really the best way in which one can learn. As a lecturer, as a teacher and as a contributor, I can only stimulate certain thought processes. There is a great advantage in psychology which makes for a totally different level of scientific explanation despite a supposedly nonscientific methodology. This is why, despite the fact that we do not have the methodology of weighing and measuring, we can be very exact in our communications. The subject matter we study is also open to our own experience, so that, when we communicate from one to another, all we need to touch are certain experiential configurations in others that bring home to us the same kind of content or feeling tone.

We all know what narcissistic equilibrium is, that is, we all know how it feels to feel good about ourselves. But what I would like to recommend to you is that in your own thought experimentations the most useful moments to investigate are minor degrees of disequilibrium, a slight beginning of disequilibrium, not total traumatic disequilibrium, not the depth of depression, not the depth of the fragmentation of a schizophrenic regression.

On the whole what is easily accessible to us are minor degrees of disequilibrium. And when you think about such minor degrees of disequilibrium and what another person can do to help you under such circumstances, then you can recognize that, for each of these states that I call merger, alter ego or twinship, and mirroring, there is replica in a minor key. For instance, if somebody is upset, there is no question that any physical motion that symbolizes merger is sustaining. One picks up a small child; with a grownup person, one puts an arm around his shoulders or sits close and silently next to him. In a nonverbal way this is helpful, while words may not be helpful when such merging is demanded. Why? Because words, in that sense, stress the otherness of the other. They stress a distance. They stress the difference between human beings when what is needed at that particular moment is participation in the security of another person.

In other words, somebody reaches out for another person and must be allowed to be embraced, for example. That you must then in your own feeling tone be empathic means simply that you participate in the upset of the other person and therefore encourage the merger. It is also true that you must do something with the merger so that it does not remain at the degree of anxiety that the other person feels. But you cannot overcome anxiety helpfully by being reassuring.

When somebody is really upset and you tell him, "Cheer up old guy. Forget about it. Let's go out and have a drink," that usually does not work, at least not with sensitive people who are really upset. It usually just stresses the otherness of the other, that the other person does not want to bend down to participate empathically. But neither is it any good to be exactly as excited and upset as the other person.

This is extremely important technical advice in psychotherapy, as well as in certain other situations. To act as if the other person were not upset, when he is upset, is nonsense. To talk him out of it is nonsense. Most of this talking other people out of their upsets is usually correctly understood as rejection, namely, "Don't try to upset me by your upset." When a person talks somebody else out of being upset he really is trying to do something for himself, but not for the other. He does something for the other by being empathically involved and then allowing his own broader absorbing powers, at this particular moment, to diminish slightly what the upset is all about.

This is one way. The alter ego or twinship again has its own everyday kind of replica—"when a fellow needs a friend," that is, when he needs somebody who is like him, with whom he can communicate and who he supposes is in many ways the kind of person he is.[3] Under certain circumstances we are interested in people who are very different from us. It is exciting to meet character types we have not known before, to see personalities that function very differently from ourselves. We will not want to see people who are very different from us when we are upset, when we are narcissistically disturbed, when we have suffered a narcis-

---

[3]Kohut would later describe this as the sense of being human among other human beings. For further discussion of this element in what he later described as the alter ego transference see Kohut, 1984, pp. 194–207. Clinical experience led him to separate the alter ego transference, originally included as an aspect of the mirroring transference, as a transference in its own right.

sistic blow. We will naturally drift to people like ourselves, of our own cultural, emotional makeup. Then one feels enclosed again; one feels reinforced and supported.

I do not need to explain to you in the narrowest sense of the mirror transference that, when one has had a blow to one's self-esteem, one certainly needs nobody to inflict blame. When a child comes home with a poor grade, he is upset and does not want reproaches on how lazy he has been. He may have been lazy, but at that time he is upset about the poor grade. The first thing is not to blame him; insecure parents tend to respond by blaming the child. But at such a time it is important to find assets, including the capacity to tolerate a misfortune. One can say, "I guess it was a bad thing that happened to you, but I know you're a strong person. You'll snap back." You pay attention but you do not intimate, in self-defense, that this is not to be done again. In other words, you can praise another person for his resilience and for positive capacities, but you will not praise something that is not there. You will praise something of which, let us say, there is a trifle there. The child is upset, but at the same time he is trying to absorb the blow, and one tries to help him with that effort. So in that sense he is beginning to display strength. You are a magnifying mirror for an asset at that particular moment.

Mirroring in the usual sense does not relate to a person in disequilibrium. It relates to a person who, under the impact of certain positive things about himself, now wants the participation of others in these good feelings. In other words, when a child comes home with good grades, then you reflect his own joy in the good grades. But I was trying to go on in the sequence of comparatively mild disequilibrium.

The overriding similarity of these three externally so very different attitudes is the *internal configuration* that is being activated in the individual who is in difficulty. This can be understood only if you have grasped the developmental line that I tried to explain to you earlier: namely, that there is a basic degree of self-confidence, of pride in oneself, of self-cohesiveness, a basic degree of ideas of greatness about oneself, of self-acceptance, a basic minimum or optimum of showing off, of exhibiting oneself, which belongs to mental health.

From childhood to adulthood, the character of this changes. But even in adults, there is a nuance of the old baby worship that is still left even in our comparatively subdued demands for attention and approval. These demands are not grandiose, as they are in the child who recognizes nothing apart from himself. We still maintain certain illusions about ourselves, which are indeed not illusional but rather, in a sense, our right, the right for survival, the right for success. They are infringed on by other people's rights. One has to learn gradually how one can make demands for attention for oneself and yet realize that these demands must be limited.

This need for a merger, a mirror image, an alter ego or twin-like creature is asking that other people, even though different, concentrate on oneself and give one attention, echoing and approval. What all these demands have in common is that they arise within the same structure; they arise inside the subject. It is this structure that I call the grandiose self on the basis of its development and its origin.

I think it is quite important that you remember the following basic rule, particularly for your therapeutic assessments of clinical situations in the course of treatment: When higher forms of satisfaction in one's self-esteem are interfered with, generally lower forms appear. Narcissistically vulnerable people, in the course of treatment, may relate to the therapist with a new narcissistic equilibrium if the therapist is sensitive, reasonably calm, responsive, attentive, without any particular plan. I am sure there is not a single person in this room who has not experienced this with patients. You do not know what you have done. The patient had come a few sessions before very disturbed. You have really done nothing in particular except pay attention to him, be friendly with him, put him into the center of this one-hour session. In other words, in that particular little universe of therapy he has been in the center, and he feels better. His work has improved on the basis of the fact that he feels better about himself. This is again one of the rules that I would recommend that you keep in mind.

If self-esteem is enhanced, if the self has become more cohesive, less fragmented, then this kind of self-esteem becomes an organizer of ego activities. Ego functions improve, and this includes learning, studying, talking, thinking, observing.[4]

When narcissistic equilibrium has established itself, then it may happen that something disturbs this equilibrium, again unavoidably. First of all, the therapist makes mistakes. Secondly, the demands may go beyond the capacity of the therapist to fulfill. Thirdly, there are external circumstances that will interrupt the honeymoon, as it were, of the relationship. Not infrequently, then, you find a very open regression to more primitive modes of grandiosity. When the pleasure and warmth of feeling great in the acceptance of another human being who fulfills a narcissistic function he cannot fulfill himself are disturbed, you suddenly find attitudes of cold haughtiness, of superiority, of stilted language. Grandiose features emerge that are much less acceptable to other people than a

---

[4]Kohut would, in his later formulations, refer to these as self-functions. See Kohut, 1984.

demand for attention would be. The demand for attention becomes un-acceptable only in its degree, very frequently in the tyranny of its de-mand, in the need for absoluteness which most of us are hard put to adapt ourselves to, although we should try.

I have the feeling that most therapists are much too eager to curb the patient's demands too quickly, for fear that the patient will become ad-dicted to or spoiled by them or that they themselves will give too much. I think this is an exaggerated fear. The patient demands only as much as he needs. It may be more than you can give him, but you do not have to go out of your way to show him this or to blame the patient for it. The natural limits of your capacity to give will become apparent. And it is much better to show the patient where the natural limits lie than actively to inflict something on the patient. Then the patient feels played with and really treated condescendingly, rather than essentially as an equal who has a specific type of psychological shortcoming that he has to learn to live with or to replace.

What I am trying to show you is that under such circumstances you can bring home to the patient the degrees of narcissistic balance that are achieved in the interaction with another person who has begun to serve an important function in his narcissistic household. The therapist, by paying attention, sees that the patient now has become much less cold, less haughty, much warmer—and he feels better. Then the time comes when you either misunderstand him or have to cancel an appointment. Vacations come up or something interferes. Suddenly the patient be-comes haughty, cold, superior, or uses language in a stilted, grandiose kind of way. He may use many foreign phrases that he would not other-wise use or abstract terms that you feel do not serve the communication but are more undisguised bragging and exhibitionism which make him much less likable. Under these circumstances, instead of rapping his knuckles and telling him he is a terrible person in one form or another, the best thing to do for him is to show him his regression in a dynamic context.

Now what does that mean? It means that you show him he has changed. You show him when the change began, and you show him to what he responded with this particular kind of change. You can say, for instance, "I have the impression, during the last few weeks, that we've been getting along pretty well here. You must have gotten some emo-tional help here from my listening to you." You can do this without any superiority, as a psychological given.

If you can establish for him that being listened to is a basic human need, you can then show the patient that his own attitude has changed. It changed at a point when he was told you would be away for a few weeks, or when he misunderstood, or when he came with some story of improvement for which he wanted approval and did not receive it because the therapist was obtuse. If one can show the patient that following this he became haughty, more overtly bragging, more demanding and cold, then it does not feel like blame. It is showing a human propensity in context. "Here, but for the grace of God, go I." You do not say that; it should go without saying. It is a human way of reacting, except that it happened to him.

Understanding increases a person's mastery over his reactions. It gives him greater control. He can swing forward again into an equilibrium of greater narcissistic self-acceptance as he is accepted and understood by another human being. This is an expansion of his own capacities. The important thing is not so much the theoretical explanation but the human explanation in a human context; this allows the person to expand his own self-understanding. Therefore, the next time he is hurt, and he begins to become a bit haughty, he can catch himself with the recognition of what is happening: "Here we go again." With this recognition there is the first trifle of a transformation[5] of narcissism, a touch of the relativity of the self and its narcissistic swings and demands.

As you know, I prize humor very much when it comes as an outgrowth of real progress in psychotherapy, not if it is preventing progress. There are some people who belittle anything ahead of time to make themselves inaccessible. That kind of humor is usually sarcasm rather than humor. It does not have the warmth of real humor. Real humor is always a degree of self-acceptance, of the relativity of oneself. It includes the capacity to joke about onself, one's race, one's nation, or one's profession, but not the necessity to joke all the time, not an obsession about it. When one is in real straits, the capacity to be humorous can be helpful, as in the great story with which Freud introduced his beautiful essay on humor about the man who was led to the gallows on Monday and said the week was beginning badly (1905b, p. 229). By setting himself above his misery, in that sense, he saved a bit of the otherwise all too destructible self. In Freud's joke, the person is indestructible, even though his body is to be destroyed. If one can have this degree of humor under such circumstances, it is almost a superhuman degree of wisdom or strength.

I have on numerous occasions oriented a patient to the idea that, "You'll learn to catch yourself doing it." The patient then gets to the position where he says,

---

[5]This description forecasts the process of transmuting internalization through which a selfobject function becomes a self-function.

"I know I have a tendency and need to do this, or to get myself into a situation where I want some praise, and now I can catch myself as I am about to do it, but I still do it." This gets into the whole concept that insight does not really cure. How do you conceptualize that position?

The question theoretically centers about the topic of internalization and of structure building. How does one develop a psyche that can perform these functions that formerly were performed by other people, an absorbing structure so that you yourself absorb blows to your self-esteem without the aid of others?

In long-term psychotherapy, the process that leads to structure building is called working-through. But how does the repetition of the same experience lead to the formation of internal structures? I do not want to do more now than to give you a broad outline but to reassure you that later I will talk about it more fully. Obviously you cannot help the patient by giving him these answers, but I think it does help him if you yourself have some knowledge about it. Your total attitude will reveal that you are not expecting him to be all well by a first insight. Insight does not cure. Insight is a trailblazer toward the opening up of certain psychological processes that really change the individual psychologically. In that sense, insight is an important stepping stone, and something not to be neglected. I think it is extremely important.

Freud (1914a) said that the mere repetition of an experience leads to nothing. He said an hysteric can repeat the primal scene experience, witnessing parental intercourse and, psychologically speaking, his participation in it, a thousand times in a lifetime of symbolic reenactments in his hysterical attacks. He can dream about it a thousand times, but he will be completely the same afterward. Nothing has changed.

Mere insight is nothing; but the repetition, with insight, is a great deal. Now why are both necessary? Why is the economic point of view, as it is called in psychoanalytic therapy, important? It is not just what one learns but how one learns it. The degree to which at any given time one faces breaking up an experience into digestible portions makes all the difference in the world, leading finally to some kind of structural change.

I would think, however, that the patient is not right, even when he reproaches you with the comment that insight does not cure. I would think that he has already learned a little, and is not quite the same. I am quite convinced of that. I think he is by no means as far as he would like to be, but I would not doubt that he is a little better. Freud (1910) pointed this out in his paper "On Wild Analysis . . . " Somebody confronts a patient with the whole of the oedipus complex and Freud called it wild analysis. But, even there, he said a little bit may have changed too. One should not be so desperate about it. As bad as it is, even in this kind of silly therapy a little bit of a change may also occur.

As we learn more about the later fate of Freud's early cases, something very interesting emerges. Anyone who has read with any degree of knowledge about what psychoanalysis became in Freud's own later phases, and much beyond Freud, anyone who has any degree of knowledge about the slowness and the carefulness of the working-through process in analysis, can only marvel at the therapeutic results that Freud achieved in a few months. Insights were given with—it makes us shudder—a kind of directness, an id analysis. It seems incredible that these patients got better. But they did, for Freud was a very keen and objective observer who did not falsify records. Almost all of the great cases are now known; their identities have been established. Some have been investigated throughout their whole lifetime and are being reinvestigated. What happened is that most of these patients lost their symptoms; instead most began to act out. They began to have what is nowadays called *fate neuroses*, to enact their former pathology in their real lives, whereas formerly their pathology was expressed in hysterical symptoms. So their mode of pathology at that time changed because of all-too-quick symptom relief. Even though an insight was gained into their pathology, not enough working-through occurred, so that the pressure of the essentially unconscious conflict was still active. What followed was that these people involved themselves in all kinds of deleterious activities. They were unable to experience the careful working-through which leads to structure building and change.

6

The Admiring Selfobject
and the Idealized Selfobject

I WOULD LIKE TO TURN now to the idealizing transference, beginning with an example from my own experience. This was at a time when I began to have dim understandings of the kind of problem area I can now present to you in a more systematic and, I think, deeper and more sophisticated way, before I knew what I had now learned. I now know this case should have been carried further. The issue that was not worked through was an intense narcissistic transference to me, stemming from a severe infantile disappointment in an idealized figure of the past.

I wish I could tell you or write up the details of this marvelous case, but unfortunately I cannot, because it is too identifiable. In general terms it is unidentifiable, but the specifics would be very beautiful to present. I did exactly what I described in my second paper in the section on resistances of analysts to the idealizing transference (1968). I rejected the idealizing transference by making fun of it. In other words, "I'm not so great. Don't think I'm such a great man." I was embarrassed by the idealization.

I rejected the idealizing transference systematically. Over and over again the patient tried to extend "a tendril" of idealization to me and every time I would cut it off. I did so in the way I had been trained. I did so in a way which I thought was beneficial to the patient. I did not do so out of any evil intentions. I thought I was properly modest and realistic about myself. I did not allow her to start again where she had stopped in childhood. She wanted again to experience, in a more moderate way now, the disappointment in the idealized individual. The analysis ended with the patient feeling helped. But I know that afterward she became intensely religious and continued the unresolved idealizing transference in an intense religious experience. I think this was to the detriment of

77

other possibilities that would have been available to her. This was many years ago, but in retrospect I know exactly where things went wrong. I did not know any better.

I think this would not happen now. Not that I would make no errors; not that, under the impact of having my own narcissistic grandiose fantasy stimulated by a patient, I might not too quickly and too traumatically debunk the patient's need rather than let it first unfold. You know, such idealization will die of unreality. After all, I am not that great. The patient sooner or later will recognize my shortcomings. I do not have to go out of my way to tell the patient, "My dear child, I'm not God," which only means, in a sense, "Yes, I am."

Patients forgive your single mistakes. The only thing that patients cannot overcome is a total characterological attitude, buttressed by a whole system of theoretical conceptions, that stands in the way of the unfolding of an attitude that must enter into the therapeutic situation in order to be resolved. Let us now examine more systematically the other developmental line of early narcissism[1], the idealizing transference.

Both lines of the development of narcissism have in common that the original narcissistic equilibrium, whatever it may be, has a perfection for which there is no adult replica. At this point it is not yet split up into perfect beauty, perfect morality, perfect strength, or perfect knowledge. The omni series—omniscience, omnipotence—all this is still one little whole, because cognitively it is not yet elaborated. It is simply a kind of undisturbed narcissistic well-being. Anything that frustrates the physical and mental well-being of the child—any noise, any coldness, any wetness, any hunger, any delay—all this is a narcissistic disturbance. And then the child, recognizing that there are shortcomings in this narcissistic paradise, that it is not limitless, attempts to save it in some way. The child saves it in ways that are difficult to grasp by any direct empathy, but there are replicas in adult experience that at least bring us closer to understanding it. The child saves it in two antithetical ways. Put simply in a verbal formula which is very far from the experience, the child tucks away the feeling, "I am all good, but everything else is bad. I am all great, but there is some badness outside that doesn't belong."

Freud spoke of the purified pleasure ego before the term ego was yet a structural concept (1920). It was not part of the mental apparatus. This came later, when he set up the ego, the superego and the id (1923). This

---

[1]In the previous chapter, Kohut described the development of the grandiose pole of the self. In this chapter he describes the structuralization of the idealizing pole. Together they constitute the bipolar self. See Kohut, 1977, Chapter 4.

early use of the term ego is much closer to what we now call the *self*, the *I*. So a purified pleasure ego is that in which the self, as it were, maintains some degree of this old perfection, clustering around exhibitionism: "Look Mom, I'm wonderful. I'm flying." Flying fantasies become very much the carriers of the old omnipotence: "I know everything. I can do everything. I am perfect in beauty. I am perfect in strength. Everybody loves me." This has, then, to be maintained in its limited sense. And it is maintained in the ways which we have just discussed, by expanding into others—yes, they are acceptable, but they are like oneself—or by having others who simply confirm how great one is. The gradual changes in this direction we will discuss when we recall the subject of internalization, the gradual frustration, the working-through processes in therapy.

However, the other line of narcissism, the idealizing transference, is just the opposite. "I am nothing, but at least there is something great and perfect outside myself that is the carrier of what I formerly experienced. All I can do now is to try to attach myself to it, even though I am nothing, and then I will become as great as it is."

As I said earlier, there are dim little replicas of both these experiences in adult life that we find in the prejudice against anything that is foreign and other. One finds it in national prejudice, national pride, when the nation becomes, as it were, the heir of the old grandiose self. The nation is an expansion of the self. It depends on how one experiences it, of course. Some people may experience the nation as an idealized object, but most of the time not so. The supernations, like the fascist states, were not essentially experienced as ideals with which one united, although ideals were of course formed also. They were essentially experienced as all-powerful expansions of the self. In the same way, the tank, for the tank driver, becomes his power, rather than his merging into an ideal carrier that he admires.

For the religious person, the adult replica for the idealized object is the absolute God, particularly the God of the mystics. The great mystic writers of the Middle Ages, for example, described over and over again this experience of merging into something great, into something perfect, the God life, and feeling themselves to be absolutely nothing. The individual death becomes quite meaningless, because it becomes a reuniting with this super power.

This example is an adult empathizable replica of an early child's experience, which is otherwise difficult to grasp. That both of these experiences, one's own grandiosity or one's own insignificance, may involve merger should not mislead you. The fact that the mere description of the external circumstances may not allow you an immediate answer should not deter you. Sometimes you have to investigate what the feeling tone is, by finding out what it means to the person. It is true there are swings between these two positions. The direction of the swing is very much determined by the specific experiences and disappointments of childhood.

There are highly specific disappointments in idealized objects, while one's own grandiose self and the admiration one had for oneself, let us say from a mother, may be reasonably well maintained. People may have reasonably well-integrated and high degrees of self-esteem in terms of their exhibitionism, ambitions and performance, but may be sorely lacking in capacity to form important idealized values. Therefore, a whole important area of humanness is cut off from them.

With the students you see in the Student Mental Health Clinic, I am sure that the differential diagnosis, whether the error lies in one realm or the other, is of greatest importance. Does this person suffer from an absence of really valued ideals? Does he suffer from the lack of guiding ideals, from meaningful goals, from something around which his life potentials can cluster, on which he can converge to maintain a sense of direction? Is that what ails him? Or is it rather that he has meaningful goals but lacks basic self-esteem? Does he have some incapacity to be ambitious and to strive for success in an area that has nothing to do with ideals, but in an area that has something to do with wanting to be big and strong and recognized? One is very different from the other.

The fact is that very frequently these students have disturbances in both areas. Nevertheless, both do not present at the same time. And to talk to a person about one thing when he is trying to show you another leads to his feeling misunderstood. It interferes with your establishing the sense of a bond with him that is often described as the therapeutic alliance, a term I do not particularly like. It is something akin to basic understanding that is part and parcel of the treatment, not something extraneous to the treatment. This is one of my prejudices, and I do not want to burden you with it. The main thing is that you understand the two lines of thought.

The vicissitudes of both the grandiose self and the idealized parent imago lead us now into the last chapter of our theoretical discussions. After that we will begin with the clinical material. The grandiose self, under the influence of maturational givens and the optimal selection of parental responses finds increasing capacity to manage reality and see oneself realistically. In other words, a three-year-old's mother will no longer respond to the toesies, to the little bellybutton, to the little cooing noises of the child, but will respond to other things that the child performs appropriately, from toilet training, to certain manual skills, to certain language performance. The mother will respond to things selectively, giving approval for certain things but not for others, clearly withdrawing approval in specific situations.

A little example that I used in my first narcissism paper (1966) was that of the mother who shrieks with delight when the baby pulls her hair. Later on, she will not shriek with delight anymore, but she will shriek with anger. And the child will know that this not good and will see that there are limits to one's performance and to one's acceptability.

So in the developmental sequence—the increasing selectivity of the parental responses, the increasing frustration, the increasing loss of the approving object, not by death and sudden disappearance, but by the gradual withholding of approval, which is always part of an object that is lost, if you take the term object in the sophisticated sense—all this leads to the gradual taking over by the psyche of functions that were formerly performed by others. In the case of the idealized object there is also a loss. There is recognition that the ideal is not ideal. But it must be recognized not prematurely and not massively; otherwise it becomes traumatic and indigestible. It becomes useful for the psyche when it occurs at the right moment and at the right speed.[2] Then it leads to the setting up internally of the formerly external ideal, with all the ensuing advantages of having an internal ideal object, namely, one's values, goals and ideals. They then feed one's narcissistic approval if one approaches these goals. One is therefore less in need of an external idealized object.

The strongest and most mature people have strong ideals which are more important to them than external approval. Nobody is limitless in that respect; everyone is capable of being swung around by the threatened loss of ideals or by the approval or disapproval of external leaders. But an individual usually can maintain himself without being affected by external leaders. However, under the influence of an enormous mass movement, almost anybody will fall victim to strong external pressures, regardless of how firm his internal ideals have been. As in the fascist states earlier in our century, as you know, even comparatively healthy people were not capable of maintaining themselves, but were swept up for long periods in the grandiosity of the surrounding environment and in the need to merge with the all-powerful state. This reduced the individual to infancy in many ways, by regimentation, by total thought control, by a variety of infantilizing devices. We strictly avoid this in psycho-

---

[2]Kohut will use the term "transmuting internalization" to describe this process set in motion by optimal frustration throughout his later writings (Kohut, 1971, p. 50; 1977, pp. 30–32, 86, 123, 127; 1978, pp. 63–64; 1984, pp. 100–102).

therapy, because then irreversible regressions would follow. Even though some degree of therapeutic success occurs, it lasts only as long as the irreversible regression is maintained. To return to our example of the fascist state, people immediately see the light as soon as the state loses its power. Then all the masses again see the world realistically.

A workable definition of mental health may be the capacity to choose from a number of psychic mechanisms according to need.

There is an important rule to remember: When higher forms of adaptation fail, then the grandiose self emerges. And when in the treatment you recognize that this is happening, it is helpful to the patient to point out when you think it happened and what brought it on. If you help the patient to recognize that his loss of self esteem, angry sullen behavior, hypochondriacal symptoms, or excessive shame, for example, arose because of separation from the therapist or from an unempathic response, you help him to deal with the blow. You may help him to understand that under states of severe loss of self-esteem his feeling is akin to, "Everything on the inside is bad; everything on the outside is good."

A combination of shifts in the narcissistic object from the grandiose self to the idealized parental imago, according to the vicissitudes of the self-esteem system, would be ideal. However, most people do not operate that way. The most common problem encountered is a lack of internalization; that is, the grown person is constantly seeking applause and approval from the outside. And when you recognize that, it is important to differentiate whether he seeks approval because he wants reaffirmation of his own grandiosity or because he wants approval from the idealized value system.[3]

Another more subtle form of the grandiose self fantasy is the skilled person who is always belittling what he has accomplished, saying, "I have accomplished nothing; everything good has been done by somebody somewhere else, or something on the outside." Competent people, such as analysts, often have this attitude toward Freud, that nothing new has been done since his discoveries. Sometimes this is referred to as success guilt, but it may also represent an illusion that somebody else, all-powerful and God-like, has done everything. In this way he gains strength from merging with his image of the strong other.

In the light of this discussion, can we differentiate narcissistic character disorders from borderline character disorders?

---

[3]In a speech honoring Alexander Mitscherlich, presented in October, 1969, just before these seminars were undertaken, Kohut discussed developmental and pathological forms of structure building derived from the idealized value system (Kohut, 1978, Chapter 37).

To the question of what differentiates borderline character disorders from narcissistic character disorders, it can be said that a borderline person always has a psychotic core, but the psychotic core does not always invade the entire character. Only under regression does it become obvious that a person has a loss of psychic structure and reverts to the pre-object state. Essentially in such people it is only that the symptomatology is not obvious. In contrast, the narcissistic character suffers *temporary* regressions under the sway of the grandiose self, through which the pre-object state emerges.

I suspect that the genetic core of the narcissistic neurosis[4] lies in the pathology of the characters of both parents and in their reason for choosing each other. But this is still in the speculative state. What I can say from observation is that, when the mother has a personality problem, it may lead to diffuse narcissistic vulnerability on the part of the child. In adult life the person engages in an eternal struggle for praise from adults. The mother may have been unable to appreciate the baby's exhibitionism at the appropriate time or prolonged her worship of the baby's exhibitionism beyond the appropriate time. Whatever the origin, when the child gets to be three or so, he turns to the father for the kind of idealized role he has not been able to receive from the mother. And if the father is able to allow the child to idealize him in this way, then the adult does not end up as sick as he might have. However, if the father distances himself, as in some way the mother had in the past, and does not allow the child to mimic, imitate, and follow him around, a shift from wanting to be admired to at least actively admiring cannot take place. If the attempt to look up to the father as a great man is frustrated, then this is a second blow, for here, too, the child is frustrated. If this dual frustration takes place, the core of narcissism develops badly. In analytic treatment of people of this sort, the material at the beginning, and for long periods of time, first concerns the relationship to their father, and one may or may not get to the original problem in the relationship to the mother. If the material is dealt with sufficiently in relation to the father, it may not be necessary to deal with the relationship to the mother.

There are variations in the narcissistic problems of mothers and, as a result, variations in the way infants respond. The cold mechanical mother really lacks empathy and has to operate according to rules. There is also the mother who does respond to the child, but responds according to her own concerns rather than to the child's needs. Sometimes she is

---

[4]For clarification of the self psychological view of neurosis, see Kohut, 1984, pp. 5, 22–26, 101–102, 106–110; 1977, p. 32, and Chapter 2.

overresponsive and hypochondriacally involved in the child's symptoms. Another variation is that of the mother who responds appropriately as long as the state of total immersion exists, the child being an extension of herself. But she cannot appreciate the child when he begins periods of separation and individuation, when he moves on and needs to be appreciated as a separate individual.

Thus mental health cannot be defined by one form of mechanism or another, but, if anything, by the capacity to turn to the full instrumentation of possibilities, depending on one's momentary needs or particular psychological task. Health is thus determined by the variety of possibilities that a person has at his disposal rather than a rigid narrow way of dealing with the world and with inner and outer problems. The capacity to turn toward another under stress and to ask for this other person's protection, to some kind of replica of the merger, also belongs to the armamentarium of mental health and is very compatible with mental health.

I am not presenting this as a prescription, saying that one who does not use this particular mechanism is mentally unhealthy. There are many kinds of helpful mechanisms. Each person has his own favorite ways of dealing with the world. Certainly it is fully compatible with mental health to be, under stress, capable of turning toward another person and confiding in him and, as it were, merging in and with him, allowing his comparative strength temporarily to infuse oneself. It is an irrational or prerational kind of mechanism, but a very important one. As I said earlier, embracing, an arm over the shoulder, physical closeness, or quietly sitting next to one another has its place in certain trying moments in life.

What is the difference, then, between a healthy capacity to merge with another person under stressful need and pathological forms of merging?[5] The answer would be that the initiation of the activity must be by the individual's adult and mature aspect of his personality. It must not become the one and only automatic response to any kind of stress, and it must be something that is controlled and controllable. There must be a choice about it. One must be capable of recognizing that, for example, when one has merger needs of this particular kind, one cannot go simply to the next person who happens to be in the room. One has to choose somebody with whom one has ties of friendship. One must be

---

[5]Here Kohut clearly spells out the difference and the validity of mature selfobject needs from pathological needs. He clarifies the difference between mature selfobject needs and object relationships.

capable of tolerating the delay until one reaches somebody with whom this kind of appeal for prerational support is an appropriate one.

The capacity for the particular kind of regression, necessary in all therapeutic relationships, is part and parcel of a healthy aspect of the personality. It is the minimum of health, as it were, that one must ask of a patient. It does not have to be asked for in the first session, but at least potentially this is what we hope the patient will be capable of. Now what is the opposite? The opposite state arises when merging needs have not been fulfilled to a certain minimum in childhood, and therefore, the archaic intensity of these needs tends to overwhelm the person. Then he is not capable of delay; then he is not capable of discriminating or—and this is all-important—of modulating.

You know, a little bit of a merger is all right; it is symbolic; an arm around the person or an understanding listener should be enough. But if that is not enough, if one expects to be taken in totally by the other person, then it can only lead to tyrannical demands without any regard to the reality situation or to the other person's readiness or capacity to respond. A person with such demands must strictly inhibit himself in this particular area.

The sophisticated approach—and I appeal to your psychological so-phistication here—the sophisticated approach to this kind of problem will lead you to understand that, for the great majority of individuals who have such unmodulated, intense, archaic, primitive merger needs unfulfilled early in life, their actual behavioral, phenomenological re-sponse will be a strict avoidance of situations because of fear of being hurt. They have learned that they would be rebuffed under those cir-cumstances, so that they cannot allow themselves this modicum of re-gression, this nuance of controlled gratification of friendship and merger needs of which other people are capable.

This is true of people in psychotherapy just as much as in analysis. As you make progress in this particular direction, the individual does not become less capable of allowing himself to ask for this kind of support or inclusion but becomes more capable of it, simply because he feels more in control of the situation and his demands are not so very great.

Let me describe a very convincing recent clinical experience of just this particular type. A patient reported a dream in which he felt himself very confused about a particular location. He knew that he was in a particular place with his wife, but his wife was somewhere outside this place; she was there and at the same time she was not there. He walked around in this building, trying to locate himself, to find where he belonged. He felt himself disheveled, his shirt was hanging out, and he felt at sixes and sevens—to use his language. As he reported the dream, the general feeling was of utter confusion about himself and his orientation in space. As I pointed out earlier, when you see your patients arrive looking disheveled, you know this expresses something about their self-state, how they feel about themselves. When they are more neatly put together, then you have the feeling that they know where their borders lie, who they are and what they are. This state of dishevelment occurs now only in dream states, and only tiny replicas of it recur in his waking life. After we had pinpointed the emotional state which the dream portrayed, we could trace this disheveled and disoriented feeling about himself to a very typical situation, namely, a situation in which he was reacting to a particular time when he would see me outside the therapeutic situation. This is something he desired very greatly, and yet he feared tremendously.

Why did he fear me? I am telling you this because I want to show you, in a concrete way, the subtlety with which one has to pursue understanding the emotional state of another person. The general principles that I can teach you and lay out for you here are only guidelines. Not applying guidelines, blueprints, as point-by-point explanation of any given clinical situation separates the expert from the amateur in psychological matters. Guidelines are only orientations, like a map that you generally can follow. But you still must follow the individual meaning; otherwise, even with a great deal of sophisticated understanding of theoretical issues your patients will tend to feel misunderstood. Only when you have followed through the very specific way in which people feel and react will they feel understood.

In this case both the patient and I are working on the basis of a large fund of already investigated past and a real trust that we both have in understanding what makes him tick. He knows I understand, and he has learned a great deal about where his vulnerabilities lie over a long period of treatment with me. The point is that this individual had been a child in a family in which he was truly emotionally neglected. Nobody took time with him. He always waited on the sidelines, attempting to get his parents' attention. He would have it for a moment, but then he would be brushed off. The parents might play with him, but they were looking at the clock to see when they could leave him again. He was allowed to ask some questions, which the parents did answer, but, "That is enough now." He always had the feeling of, "When is 'that is enough' coming?" All children experience this kind of brush-off, finally, because they are insatiable. But his experience was obviously more traumatic in the poignant memories of his particular childhood.

This family ate later than most families in the small town where he was brought up. His family ate at 6:30, and families usually ate at 5:30. So between 5:30 and 6:30, when both parents were still busy, he had to play alone. He was hungry and lonely. It was in this lonely hour when the other children were already in their homes or when he was visiting with other children in their homes in the afternoon, that he would fantasy that he was a member of that other family. That fantasy always broke down when eating time came, because then he was sent home. "Go home now little boy. You were here just visiting." But he had thought himself and felt himself to be a part of this family in the unfulfilled hunger of belonging and yearning to be included in another family.

All his life this man felt he did not quite belong where he was, and yet he fastened with intensity to any situation as if he did belong, always on the verge of overdoing it. He could never integrate himself into groups for the simple reason that his demands were so great.

It took us a long time to understand his particular shyness, the sudden outbursts of faux-pas-like intimacies toward other people for which they were totally unprepared. Out of nowhere, he would suddenly become enormously intimate. And it was all wrong; people sort of shrank back, and then he got the brush-off. "This silent person suddenly talks to me as if he had known me all along." He did not discriminate between the person with whom he had some tie and the one with whom he had none. In certain groups, there were people whom he had known for decades, but he would treat them in the same way as people whom he saw for the first time—some not intimately enough, as it were, and others much too intimately. Thus, he was always in danger.

It was in this context that we came to understand the meaning of this particular anxiety about meeting me on certain occasions. The greatest traumatic moments of his early life arose when he was in between situations, when he was neither with friends with whom he fantasied he was at home nor really at home. These moments occurred when he was somewhere in between—when he did not know whether he belonged to the place he had just left or to the place to which he would go.

There was an early memory that came up; these are the things that are so beautiful in early treatment situations. It is like a mystery story. Here is the puzzle, but what does it mean? Very early in his analysis he told me the story of how, as a child, he once became tremendously anxious. It was a phobic type memory. He was alone, and he was going home. And somewhere, it seemed to him that a train was being shunted onto side tracks. Suddenly he had this terrific fear that he would go somewhere, not home, and that he would be permanently lost. By now we had found out that this was more or less exactly in the midst, at least emotionally, of having been with friends away from home, and then having been shipped back home again alone. It was the emotional state of no longer belonging to the group of people with whom he had been for a few weeks and not yet having returned to his parents. Of course, the background of all this was that really he felt there was no place to which he totally belonged. If one has a sense of belonging, then one can leave one place and go to another.

Now the memory that came to me was that about two or three years earlier he had had an enormous attack of anxiety (but I did not mention this memory to him). After an analytic hour, he was supposed to meet his wife at 5:00, but his analytic hour was over at 2:30. He had two and a half hours to spend between the end of the analytic hour and meeting his wife. It was in this period between leaving me and going to his wife that he became terribly anxious. Interestingly enough, he cured this anxiety in a very specific and important way. He began to walk very fast. He walked and walked, with tremendous emphasis on his body, to the point of panting and sweating. And as he panted and sweated, he felt a bit better. It was a confirmation of himself physically before he had the confirming relationship to his wife, with whom he is in a very good and sustaining marriage. It is this subtlety of understanding in which so many things become clear: the relationship to his wife; how he related to groups; how indiscriminately he related to everybody, as if everybody were his best friend, yet the good friends did not mean any more than the ones he knew superficially. All this comes up now, but as hints in dreams, as echoes of what was formerly a serious illness. It is no longer a serious illness because he knows and masters it now.

It is this nuanced broad understanding by which one understands in depth a person's experience. And by "in depth" I mean as he is now—what everything means, including the footnotes in the history of his life that explain the childhood precursors of these experiences.

What happens to such a person is *not* that he loses his merger needs, it is not that he loses the need to gain that kind of support by belonging to somebody, but just the opposite: he can afford now to *realize* his need. He can afford it because it is under the control of an understanding ego in an adult person who now knows, "These are my needs, and to some extent they can be fulfilled. There is a choice about fulfilling them. I no longer need to be all by myself," namely, he need not be cold, icy, superior in thinking his own thoughts, spinning out his own fantasies, and really not letting anybody get close.

In my attempts at understanding, in the early part of the treatment, he often cold-shouldered me. But there was no effusiveness on my part, trying to persuade him that I was a trustworthy, fine fellow. I did not do anything like that. I thought it was his right to treat me coldly, and there must be a very good need for him to keep me at arm's length. The only thing I wanted to do was to understand why.

And we gradually did learn to understand. I approached him as one might approach a shy child. Skilled child therapists I have watched do not obtrude themselves on children. They wait till the children make little moves and are capable of responding, but they do not overrespond when the child becomes frightened by too much emotion, stimulating more needs than the child can handle and more needs than the adult could fulfill. One must not raise false hopes in people. One cannot fulfill their intense childhood needs.

How, then, does this illustrate the concept of the grandiose and idealizing transferences? As far as I have investigated it, the dream concentrates on the confusional state, but it does not contain what the relationship to me happens to be. For years now, this patient has been looking up to me as he did to his father, except that his father had no tolerance whatever to being idealized. Neither did the father have any capacity for mirroring him and his needs. He was impatient when the little boy wanted to shine, and he was impatient about allowing the little boy to participate in a father's greatness, except in the most primitive kind of way. It was not a total loss. There was something in this relationship that the father could tolerate, but it was a strange kind of relationship. He could tolerate intimate physical contact from the side of the child, but no disturbance by questions. In other words, on very primitive levels, he could tolerate the child's closeness. The father happened to be a passionate chess player, so the child was permitted to merge bodily into the father while the latter would play for hours. But he was never allowed to disturb the father by asking, "What is this? What is that?"

The goal in any kind of therapy, from the briefest to the most extensive and intensive, is the recognition and acceptance that somewhere there is a limit, at some time there will be a reasonable toning down of narcissistic expectations, seeing that one must live with certain shortcomings that cannot be remedied.[6] But, if we are honest about ourselves, this becomes a philosophical extension of the acceptance of life with its shortcomings. It is true for any achievement of ours; it is also true that life itself is limited. I certainly would not put such an acceptance of the limits of the irremediable damage that was done early in life into the center of a treatment success. If this is all that one can achieve, then I would say one

---

[6]Kohut included, in this necessary toning down of grandiosity, that of the therapist as well.

will have occasional failures. There are certain things that cannot be achieved; that are immobile. This type of pessimism I would not have for most cases. For the rest I think the answer is one that bears perhaps more extended discussion.

What are the therapeutic changes that take place? Let us examine further the treatment session I described with this particular patient. Assuming I were a genius, knowing instantly all that took me so many years to learn from this patient, and assuming I had told him in the best possible way why he was so confused, I do not think much would have been achieved. There are so many transformations subtly occurring in which this gross understanding, this verbalizable giving and obtaining of insight, is only a way station. Even so, it is not useless at any time to understand in this gross way and to transmit this knowledge to a patient, as long as it is transmitted in an empathic way, recognizing just how much the other person can grasp.

Although there are different levels in the continuum of therapeutic changes, it makes sense to differentiate the kind of insight that leads to a person's being able to manage himself better. After achieving such insight, the internal change in one's total personality now brings about a different relationship to the external world. Assume, for example, that at a particular time in his analysis, this understanding in a gross verbalizable way, with none of the subtleties I tried to transmit to you earlier, had been available to the patient. At one particular time it might have helped the patient to realize, "Well here I am again in a group. I know now that my demands are enormous. It reminds me of the time when I attached myself to this family where I was really only welcome until 5:30, when they served dinner, and then I was supposed to go home. I should not try to get close to people whom I hardly know." This is not yet a spontaneous reaction. It is a skill in gross management of oneself. Such a person might then come to the next analytic hour and say, "Here I was in a group situation, and I think I handled it a little bit better yesterday. I still felt very uncomfortable. But I did not really get myself into a situation in which I would expose myself by suddenly talking to people and then receiving these amazed looks, cringing into my corner, unable to say another word. I kept more or less to myself, but I saw so-and-so there, and I waved at him. And when so-and-so talked to me, I had a quick conversation with him, for after all I have known him for a long time. I was not as alone as I usually am under those circumstances."

Now he himself had hardly changed. The person who has changed internally does not consciously have to figure out whom he knows or does not know. Now under the domination of his personality, he does not need to figure out what at any given moment is active in him.

What has happened to change this? How has insight, verbalized insight, led to this particular kind of real change? There is no question that there is a real change of a subtle type very different from manipulation. Both have taken place, as I think is true in all intensive kinds of treatment with which I am familiar. In an emergency situation, there is this extra push of, "What am I doing? Why am I getting myself again into this old situation?" One can pull in the reins in this manipulative way. One is not totally overwhelmed anymore, because one's total personality has to some extent become less vulnerable, more able to buffer, more capable of allowing only a modicum of the old demands to intrude.

The parallel between what transpired in this patient's life developmentally and the developmental changes in the long-term treatment situation offers the best way of understanding and realizing why the treatment situation can never completely undo the damage that was done early in life. At the same time, one can also see how treatment can to some extent undo the damage. And this is all that is needed; a little bit of change makes all the difference in the way the scales swing.

I have already intimated to you many times what happens in the process of growth: the principle of optimal frustration. Optimal frustration in development has something to do with age, time, development, the total situation. With the grown person, the economic factor, as it were, is involved. You do not burden a patient by asking too much of him. Again, it resembles the peek-a-boo game. The therapist watches for signs of the patient's unmanageable anxiety. How much can he tolerate? And this is something that I cannot stress often enough.

There is *never* any need—and by never, I mean never—there is never any need to be artificially traumatic. Simply to give the best you can give is traumatic enough, because you cannot fulfill the real needs.[7] Even if you are the most empathic therapist, you always limp behind the patient's needs. This is true. Generally, you realize his hurt or disappointment after the patient is already hurt. Only then do you wake up. "What did I do again? What did I misunderstand again? What did I again not realize?" You are wrong, whatever you do. If you know full well that a patient will react badly to the fact that an appointment will have to be cancelled, and you cancel the appointment and say right away, "I know this is going to hurt you tremendously," you traumatize the patient by telling him right away. How? You offend his dignity. You treat him like a

---

[7]The principle of optimal frustration which stimulates transmuting internalization (structure building) is extensively illustrated through Kohut's writings. For his latest formulation, see Kohut, 1984, pp. 69–72, 77–78, 99–104, 107–109, 206–207.

baby. But if you do not do it, then he will be hurt tomorrow. There is no way out. I suppose there may be some ideal way of finding just the right word for telling him. But who can do that? Nobody can. It would become so complex that you would traumatize him by overburdening him with talking too much. He would feel, "Let me experience something." And he would be right. There is no way out.

You cannot find a nontraumatic relationship toward infantile needs. If you can realize where the patient is and what he feels, that is good enough. There may seem to be no result from it, but you must not be impatient. You must repeatedly treat the same situation as if it had never been there before, ever again subtly searching for the specific nuance that makes this particular event traumatic.

There is an old paper of mine on introspection and empathy (1959). In it I described an individual who was probably the only overtly psychotic patient whom I have ever attempted to analyze. He would call at two, three or four in the morning. I remember one thing I learned from him. It was around the announcement of some absence, Christmas or Thanksgiving vacation.

When do you announce a vacation? What is the optimal distance from the actual time when it occurs? If it is too long it seems that you are asking the patient, "For goodness sake, get upset now for the next two months." Why? Leave him alone. He is working. If you tell him the day before, the impact is too great; he has no more time to work it through. What is the optimal time? You can never be completely right. But you learn over the years, with particular patients, what is about right. One rule of thumb is to give approximately as long as the absence will be. But this does not apply when the time is very short. There is a minimum you always must have—a number of days must always be there, even if the disappointment is only 10 minutes, as when you shift your appointment. Again, you must not be patronizing. If you tell somebody a week ahead of time that a week from now you will see him at 2:00 rather than at 2:10, it is an offense and becomes traumatic. "Who do you think I am, a baby?"

What I learned from this particular patient, when I announced this particular vacation three weeks ahead of time, was that in retrospect it was much too early. I did not know it then. And this patient, from a comparatively warm relationship to me, became an iceberg, paranoid, grossly suspicious. I still remember those horrible dreams where he was standing on a bridge. There were streams underneath, but the streams were all feces, showing the intensity of his anger and his regression. His treatment of me was haughty, cold, suspicious, and frightening. I did everything I could. I interpreted over and over again how disappointed he was in my leaving. He remained the same; nothing seemed to change him. You are completely unaided in understanding what happened in such a situation. You cannot ask the patient, for he is too offended to help you. You can show your despair, and to all this—no response. The attitude of the patient is, "You work now for what you have done to me." Usually, you have a little feeling that there is hope; otherwise you, too, give up.

Apparently hope was the feeling that sustained me. I finally caught on; like magic, I found the key to the keyhole. What the patient had reacted to was not at all the announcement of the vacation; what he had reacted to was the tone in which I made the announcement. I had announced it in a cold and unempathic way, with the feeling tone that was very understandable as, "Here we go again. Night after night my sleep will be disturbed. He will call every night. He will be frightened by being alone." And so to that I had walled myself off, for his calls were a real hardship. I was working a full schedule. My son was a baby at the time. It was an enormous hardship with sleepless nights and the worry about what he might do. He was in danger because, under such circumstances, this patient would cease to eat. He was a giant of a person, and I was always a little bit physically afraid of him. He was unpredictable in his emotional responses. He had not been violent, but there was that uneasy feeling that he might be.

So all this somehow conveyed itself to him. The real empathic readiness potential for his reaction to my absence was lacking; I was thinking of myself and, "Here we go again." And it was this to which he reacted. As soon as I recognized it, the streams in his dream became water again. There were no more feces. And then he could really express his rage.

There is the famous story that Freud (1900, p. 157) tells about the woman who is engaged and cannot wait to get married. They tell her that the husband is so cruel, "You know, he will beat you." She says, "Oh, if he would only beat me already." So, finally, when he really let me have it, I had the feeling, "We are in business again." It was much better to get his overt attacks. "You goddam dog, you are leaving me again." His coldness and paranoid distance were very frightening and much harder to take.

This, then, illustrates the subtleness of what one must understand to bring about the process of real personality change. Over and above the increased self-manipulation through verbalizable insights, these experiences do lead to a person's setting up internal structures. They do lead to some accretion of the capacity, very subtly, to handle tensions by oneself. How does this happen? I think what happens is that it parallels the developmental growth of psychological structure. It means if one gives up something that another person performs for one, in subtle and small enough doses, then one will set up a little bit of that other person in oneself.[8] And it becomes truly part and parcel of one's internal armamentarium, permanently so, as part of the psychological structure. This is a theory; I have no other way of putting it, but I think it is a correct theory since it fits what I know in all respects.

---

[8]Kohut will later refine this concept to describe the manner in which optimal frustration stimulates structure building. But he will clarify that it is not a "bit of the other person" that is acquired as psychic structure. It is the selfobject *function* which is transmuted into a *self* function (Kohut, 1971, 1977, 1980, 1984).

7

The Acquisition of
Internalized Values, Ideals, and Goals

S TRUCTURE MEANS NOTHING more than having a formerly external function permanently in your possession. An external function now becomes an integral function. Let me show you something I prize very much as an insight: namely, an internal change of this particular type takes place when, subtly, a person with unlimited needs to be understood and admired is confronted with a therapist who tries his utmost to understand his needs, is always with him or tries to be, but fails to understand a good many times. If these failures are not too severe, are not permanent, if the therapist is capable of catching himself sooner or later, then gradually, with each of these failures, the person takes over a little bit of this function for himself. "*You* can do it. Well *I* will do it by *myself*," and then he gradually learns to take over, and the structure is his, not the therapist's.

Now one could say, and I have no quarrel with such a statement, that an identification with the therapist's function has taken place. But I would not recommend the use of this particular term except in the broadest sense, because it has to be strictly differentiated from the gross identification with the total personality of another person. Such gross identification, to which people who lack structure are forever prone, does not last. Gross identification is simply an emergency use of another person, discarded again as soon as the nearness to the other person is gone. Gross identifications are in essence a hindrance to little ones. However, they do occur as way stations to subtle transformations.

There are beautiful clinical examples. The specific person with the confusional dream, about whom I spoke to you (see Chapter 5), when he still felt totally cold toward me and had absolutely no feeling that I meant anything to him, bought a suit, a number of years ago, during a vacation from analysis. And suddenly, after he had bought it out of an irresistible urge, he recognized that it looked like one I wore. This kind of gross identification, otherwise meaningless, was a way station toward much subtler identifications with me and a very important way station. Now, finally, what he uses me for are things he is ready for and that fit him but do not fit my personality at all. There is a little bit of me in him too. He sees qualities in me that he then reinforces in himself. But this reinforcement is truly in tune with the particular task his profession, quite different from mine, demands of him. His mind works very differently from mine but what he uses from me to reinforce himself is a kind of identification in which both what I really am and what he really is are much more clearly assessed. He takes what he needs and what fits him. Now he can take something that he likes about me and in tiny doses.

And with all this he has developed a sense of humor, a sense of relativity, a sense of wisdom. He now has the sense of being more capable of managing himself. And he probably already has the sense that this will all be limited, for one day we will say goodbye to one another. He will not be the kind of person he would have been had he had an ideal childhood; but yet, he is ever so much different from what he was when we first met.

Can this be achieved in psychotherapy?

The importance and usefulness of psychotherapy should not be underestimated. Again, a little bit of help can be very sustaining, specifically and very importantly, when the disease and the imbalance occur in people under the impact of a severe transitional life demand.

As in the students you see in transition from adolescence to adulthood, your support and your understanding of what their demands of themselves are, as well as their fears that they are in danger of falling apart, can temporarily prevent them from disintegrating. This support and understanding can lead them onto the right track again by allowing perhaps a medium-sized identification, not the total gross one. You have to differentiate between those students who look schizoid during a particular period because the life task is so great and those in whom there is really such a pervasive hollowness in their personality that only prolonged work will accomplish any healing for them.

This is the great opportunity that people who deal with college students have, for the intensity of the demand creates pictures of a disturbance looking ever so much more serious than it really is. The same clinical picture at the age of 35 would, or may have, a much more serious import than at 19. An empathic understanding in a number of sessions may revive old friendships, may lead people to seek out support where it is available, confirming them in their ability to work. Their capacity to work is then feedback on the positive side. If you only lead them back to their work capacity, for example, through the borrowed strength of your support in extending yourself to them, they may go back again to working, to using their intellectual capacities. This support can accomplish a great deal, so I would by no means belittle either the work that can be done or the usefulness in briefer treatment of the insights and understanding that I hope I have already given you and that I can continue to give you now in greater detail.

Certain types of individuals, lacking internal structure or lacking a sense of the continuity and the cohesiveness of themselves, continuously take on other people's personalities and shift from one person to another. As I mentioned earlier, this gross identification may occur temporarily. One should never respond to it in an inimical fashion: "Do not imitate me." However subtly you say it, it becomes a rebuff. In the course of treatment this may be the first step a person can make—this kind of gross swallowing you or becoming like the idealized other. Helene Deutsch perhaps more specifically defined it in her description of an "as if" personality (1942). It is very common, initially, in almost any form of psychotherapy, for patients to take on these almost grotesque likeness features of their therapists. This is also true with impressive teachers, for many students take on their external features. To reject this is an error. It is the first positive move toward more solid accretion of structure. If it remains that way, then there is something wrong. But I think you do the patient an injustice if you immediately call this a resistance or say, "This is something you do instead of wanting to gain understanding about yourself."

Now the question of the accretion or buildup of structure is a very central one. The principle underlying the concept of identification as a form of internalization is that the loss of an object used for mirroring or for idealizing, the interruption of the emotional relationship to such an object, tends to be followed by setting up aspects of this object internally, endopsychically.[1] Gross examples of this are quite well-known. Perhaps the earliest descriptions are found in the writings of Karl Abraham (1927). He described such incidents as a married couple living together for many years. When one of the partners dies, there is very often a distinct personality change in the survivor, including even physical features that repeat the lost one. But that is a gross example. The important element is that, in the developmental experience, features of the sur-

---

[1] A function performed by a selfobject, when optimally withdrawn, allows for the process of transmuting internalization through which it becomes a self-function.

rounding objects are set up endopsychically when the psyche is ready for incorporating these features. There is a correlated line of development here, namely, the internal readiness for setting up certain features and the environment's cooperation with it.

So we see that functions, formerly supplied by the external world, tend to be withdrawn from the child at about the time that he is maturationally ready to perform such functions himself. Two elements then combine: maturational readiness to perform the function, and withdrawal of supply of function by the external object. They reinforce the setting up of the specific function inside the person himself. The functions best studied, and most easily observed, are inhibiting and prohibiting functions. One can watch the child who is able to inhibit a particular desire only when the caretaking important adult is actually present. Later on, that child is capable of prohibiting a desire by actively imagining the presence of the object as a sort of transitional phase. One can hear children talk to themselves, threateningly in the tone of the father: "Now you must not do that." It is, as it were, an intermediary step between an internalized—or what we nowadays call a superego—function and an external prohibiting agent. In this step the child actively, as it were, still assumes that this person is present. The child is in the process of internalization. The point is that any kind of prohibition is, in a broad sense, an object loss.

Every desire a child has relates to something loved and affectionately wanted on the outside. So the non-supply on the outside is to him tantamount to a loss on the outside. Every such loss, then, is in some way set up, maintained, and perpetuated internally. How or why this happens is not very clear. The fact of it, however, is well-established. For every tie to the outside that the child phase-specifically loses, and this is very important, a parallel internal replica of the former lost object is set up endopsychically.[2]

As I said earlier, the gross internalization best studied and best known is what we call the superego. The superego under normal circumstances is, in essence, the endopsychic replica, predominantly of the parent of the same sex. The superego incorporates the prohibitions that emanate from that particular parent, as well as the approval, the positive values and goals set up by that particular parent. What I stress in addition is the particular aura of prestige, perfection, and importance that this particular parent had for the child. It is the idealized image of the self originally. In its very origins, when the child was very small, this important parent

---

[2]The loss of the function performed by the selfobject is transformed into a self-function.

or parental figure was, if you speak very loosely, a projection of the child's own narcissism. I will come back to explain why this term projection is erroneous, but for the time being this process has certain similarities to projection. The original term would be primary projection, which is something different from projection as usually understood, for the term, in the meaning I attribute to it here, describes a period when there is still no clear separation between inside and outside. One can hardly talk about projection for that reason. The adult observer knows there is an object outside, but it is perceived by the child still as part of himself. It is to this part of himself that the high degree of prestige, power and perfection is given over. It cannot be maintained in other parts of the self, namely, what the observer knows to be the child himself.

This is a complex point: something that later becomes an archaic object starts out as a somewhat differentiated part of the self, and is then taken back into the self under the impact of a disappointment[3] in this particular individual.

I will be satisfied at this point with giving you only a first crude outline. What happens is the following: let us say this powerful idealized object for the boy is the father. (It is not so simple, because the mother in her nurturing functions is also idealized, but since the superego formation deals particularly with the parent of the same sex, let us continue with the father and the boy.) The father is idealized as powerful and perfect, all knowing. Let us start out with the end of this development, what we call the end of the oedipal period, in which phase-specifically the child withdraws the essentials of his infantile emotions from both parents under the impact of the great disappointment of knowing about parental sex life, parental imperfections, parental lack of omniscience and omnipotence. In other words, there is a maturational readiness to withdraw infantile emotions from parents at that particular time. The competitive situation and the heightened emotional ties which lead to this great disappointment—the whole drama that we call the oedipus complex[4]—play a decisive role for that particular age period.

Be that as it may, and for whatever reasons, whether we know them or not, the fact remains that at the end of the oedipal period the parents are treated differently. They are more separate from the self. They are seen more as educators. They are seen more as people in their own right, with their own shortcomings, their own initiative. All of this leads to two

---

[3]This is an early formulation of the concept of transmuting internalization.

[4]Kohut, 1984, later calls this the oedipal *phase*, which is universal, and reserves oedipal *complex* for those with pathological development. See pp. 14, 22–27, 29, 125–126; 1977, Chapter 5, particularly p. 230 for oedipal *phase*.

results. One is that the ego of the child is no longer predominantly an executor of communication with drive-laden objects. The scale swings away from the ego's being mainly or predominantly the executor of the infantile aspirations of the child, wanting things from the parents, being in fantasy involved with the parents, or with the brothers and sisters who belong in the family structure. The ego is then freed.

Why is it freed? Because the conflicts and the desires—or should I say the frustrations—which were played out predominantly with the child and the surrounding family structure of adults and siblings are shifted to the internal realm. Since the replicas of these external objects have been set up internally, the dominance is now an internal one. An internal desire is responded to by an internal prohibition, no longer by "I want something," and "No, you cannot have it," on the outside.

The ego, no longer in the harness of the drives[5], which demand supplies from the surroundings, no longer being a pleading and arguing ego, as it were, becomes free for other tasks, tasks that it has performed before. But again, as the scale swings, that extra little surge now allows the child to learn. It is therefore an outgrowth of the fact that this swing internally has taken place that school age begins at the end of the oedipal period. Culturalists may say it is the other way around. Be that as it may, there is certainly a concordance between cultural institutions and maturational readiness.

The ego now has an increased freedom for autonomous functions, that is, autonomous from the direct infantile desires and its infantile objects. The child will continue occasionally to run whining and crying to the mother and the father, but normally in this period we call latency the ego is comparatively free from being mostly or predominantly beset by infantile demands and appeal to the objects of the incestuous family. It is free for greater aim-inhibited affection, for learning, for mastery of skills. In other words, it has many other realms at its disposal; of course, it had these before, but only in a subordinate way. Learning does not begin then, but the capacity at the age of five or six to turn toward abstractions in a systematic way (that is, reading and dealing with numbers) is a very important consequence for the now freed ego.

Structure building, then, is best understood when one observes the gross internalized structure, namely, the superego. The child who becomes disappointed in the father, or the child whose father, by his mere

---

[5]Kohut at this point still adheres to the tripartite structure of the mind, to drive and conflict theory. He will gradually move toward theoretical formulations which regard drive-dominated behavior and thought as disintegration products resulting from empathic failures of the selfobject milieu (Kohut, 1984).

presence, actively has interfered at the most intense peak of mobilized infantile drives—namely, the incestuous drive for the mother, and the angry drive, hand in hand with tremendous admiration, for the father— experiences a lack of integration of these various attitudes. A very strong conflict is set up in the child, which leads to an abandonment of the strong infantile emotional tie to this parent. Secondarily, then, this parental figure is set up as an internal structure, and this internal structure we call the superego.

It is important to emphasize that this internal replica of the father is not the father or his representation. Assume that this process is interrupted when, for instance, the father disappears, dies, leaves for the armed services, becomes mentally or physically ill, distant and unreachable. There is an internal representation of the father present in such instances. We call it an imago or a representation. It is a complex of memories which are highly cathected, highly desired.

To elaborate the concept of an imago: if any one of us, as an adult, has to be absent from somebody he cherishes, needs or wants, or to whom we are very close, the memory image of this person remains in us. It becomes an object of longing, and we will think about this person. In the mourning process, by the way, this is also true. The memory process is there also. As a matter of fact, thinking about the dead individual and gradually withdrawing from the representation of that individual is one of the counterforces against identification. The individual becomes an internal object of affection, a memory from which one gradually withdraws. Therefore, one does not have to set the individual up in oneself as a part of oneself. In other words, mourning and identification are two separate ends of the scale, but not quite. I will refine this later.

What I am seeking to clarify at this moment is this: a child who does not have the opportunity to separate himself from the oedipal father at the correct time in life—when he is ready for this separation and when internal separation is still within his span of capabilities—will forever, in the course of his life, search for such a father. In other words, the father image will remain an archaic object which has not been internalized.

You may say that memories are internalizations. This is acceptable, but it is quibbling with terms. Such a memory is an image of a person whom one actually still wants. The experience is different, however, if one finishes with the oedipal father, phase-specifically. One has the chance to give him up either by disappointment or, finally, by tolerating and accepting the prohibitions. It becomes a thing of the past. But there is a residue of this particular process; that residue is a setting up on the inside of those functions which one gave up on the outside. There is a decisive difference between the memory of the archaic father and the superego. When I say decisive, it must be qualified to include the fact that, in each person, the superego has certain actual features of the parent.

One can say, for instance, that some parents work more with threats to the child, some with seduction, and others with promises. It is their superegos that do that. There are some people whose inner set of standards, as it were, offer little bribes. There is the promise that, if one is good, one will allow oneself a reward. There are others with very puritanical superegos. They will say, "Yes, you must do this, but the reward must be simply that you do it, and no extra candy."

These attitudes that people have taught themselves are very frequently replicas of how the significant parent actually worked with the child when that parent was yet an archaic, prestructural object. But they are, as it were, the little insufficiencies of the internalization process. The ideal of the internalization process leads to an integration with the total personality. It leads to something that is perhaps akin to the assimilation of food. In other words, when one eats an ox one does not become an ox. That protein becomes transformed into one's own protein, from beef protein not only to human protein, but one's own specific protein.

So the correct internalization processes, the perfect processes are, as it were, fractionated. The child selects from the personality of the father what he specifically needs in his own personality. He may be a chip off the old block, but he is not an exact mirror image of the old block. Sometimes we are rather different, with our diverse genetic inheritances from a variety of backgrounds that unify themselves in the parents. The son may be more aggressive than the father; therefore, he will need in his superego certain safeguards against aggressions which the father did not need. Yet, since the father had aggressions, too, and since he responded to the child's aggressions selectively, this particular aspect of the father will take on a more specific role in this particular boy's superego at the age of five and a half and six. The superego is not a mirror image of the father but it is a selective, chosen aspect that becomes integrated.

Yet the superego, so far as I can judge, has never, in any individual I have ever encountered, achieved the total integration that ego functions achieve. It will always be a little bit like something from the outside that happens to be on the inside.[6] One relates to one's own values and prohibitions a little as if they were still coming from the outside. Perfection is

---

[6]For further discussion of "the foreign object," see Kohut, 1984, p. 100–160; 1971, p. 49, and Kohut and Wolf, 1978, p. 416.

hardly achieveable. One argues with one's superego. One has pangs of conscience as if something from the outside were forcing one. One cringes under the threat of how one will feel if one transgresses. The superego is not totally integrated.

In these guidelines concerning the formation of the superego, one must also remember that it is not only the prohibitive functions, but also the approving functions, the positive goals incorporated in the parent, that serve as the forerunner of the superego. Keep in mind that the values incorporated in our superegos have this special kind of meaning that we defend to the utmost.

In terms of our own lives, the capacity to imbue our central values within the superego with such high prestige is an enormous safeguard to mental health, but the content of the values may change. It changes gradually, but it changes. It matures in most people, and particularly in thoughtful people. They are capable of changing the content of their values. They cannot do without values. Something will always be their value; even the relativity of values may finally become a cherished value, as it does in some very sophisticated people. It then becomes part and parcel of an attitude of tolerance toward other values and other people's value systems.

Now it is grossly true that at the end of the oedipal period, in the formation of the superego, such an enormously important internalization product or structure, something permanently alters the personality and remains as part of the personality. All this goes on in minute doses from the earliest time to the oedipal period. However, instead of building up the structure of the superego, it builds up, I believe, the basic structure of the ego. For each little "no," an internal "no" is set up. For each little "not this, but that," a little goal is set up in the ego. For each little prestige loss of the parents, an extra little prestige accretion of one of those nos and values is set up within the ego. So that from innumerable moments of experience, every day, with every denial from the parents, with every delay, which is a kind of denial, something is set up internally. The ego performs internally something that formerly was performed externally by the mother or father. Here again, as later on, if the loss is traumatic, beyond what the psyche at a specific developmental moment can actually perform, or if it is done in too great a measure, then there will be a gross identification with the lost parent or withdrawal from the past; thus there will be lack of structure.

What happens in treatment is that these same formerly abandoned areas of development are again allowed to be reactivated in a setting that promises to be comparatively nontraumatic. And under the influence of this particular therapeutic situation old desires are remobilized. The old frustrations are again experienced, but not now in an overwhelming way, from which the psyche must withdraw or toward which the psyche can respond only with gross identification. If it is now done gradually, nontraumatically, the processes that earlier were not finished, that were left with frayed edges, can be woven together. In my experience and understanding, this tiny change has great behavioral and experiential advantages. It is not that you rebuild a person's personality, but the little extra that you can do makes a difference.

In our next sessions we will address clinical material. Let us pause today for questions about areas that were unclear to you.

Returning for a moment to your discussion of phase appropriate learning of abstract symbols, as in reading or math which normally occurs in the latency period. Is there not in gifted children a much earlier interest, let us say at the time of toilet training?

It may be that a gifted child is quite capable of mastering elementary reading or math skills at the age of two and a half or three; the mother is very proud, and all that. But the specific conflicts of the toilet training period, that is the conflict between being active or passive, usually suggest that the kind of mother who prematurely wants the child to read and write is also the kind of mother who is very strict and very proud about the child's cleanliness, the child's early toilet training. This is likely to set up a kind of autonomy conflict in the child:

"I control it."

"No, I control it."

"You put it there."

"No, I will not put it there."

"Now is the time for a bowel movement."

"No, now is not the time for a bowel movement."

To some extent these conflicts between mother and child are part and parcel of the growing-up process, and finding the right degree of firmness and lenience, the right degree of curbing the child's autonomy for the purpose of acculturation, is always a problem.

There is no child in the western culture who does not have his long-term adult personality to some extent influenced by the specific educational methods that are prevalent in our culture and our society. The mild degree of compulsiveness, the mild degree of balking at the passive role, as well as rebellious attitudes, are certainly very frequent. But the point I made was that, when early intellectual pursuits are taught during the time when conflicts about sphincter morality and training are the leading ones, when the ego should devote itself to this, then conflicts around intellectual pursuits will take on anal or urethral attributes. Such individuals will have intellectual inhibitions in the same way as other people have constipation. In other words, they will clamp down on understanding and will for nothing in the world be moved to understand. They will have blocks in reading or in writing and productivity, which can then be traced to the particular period around which these early strivings or early skills were already foisted on the child when the dominant struggle should have been around the anal area. What belongs to the sphincter belongs to the sphincter, and if it is given to the mind, then the mind behaves like a sphincter and rebels.

I hasten to balance my statements. I think almost anything in psychology, when it is made into an ironclad rule, tends toward error. I think, as a principle, what I said is certainly correct. Yet there may be brilliant children who quite spontaneously take to early learning and have not been forced. I am talking about learning as a degree of work—not about learning when it is still playful. One can learn early in life to read as a kind of game. Then it is not a question of having to learn despite tiredness or despite resistance, as one must in work learning.

This is where the crux of the matter comes: I am talking about those in whom language skills, reading skills, abstract thinking, become predominantly enmeshed in inhibitions. Intellectual blocks, reading blocks emerge so that people with supposedly early great promise later become rather sterile and struggle against enormous inhibitions. They exhaust themselves in never ending struggles about being productive and not being productive.

I think, in particular, of a professional woman with a very severe intellectual disturbance of this kind, whom I have now analyzed for years. It was a very difficult analysis. She was an older sister to whom premature responsibilities were given with regard to the younger ones. She was supposed to be able to control herself unaided by the parents. There was a degree of intolerance from the parents; they forgot that she was just a little girl who had problems.

It happens that the majority of instances I know of in which premature intellectual demands were made that led to inhibitions are of men and boys. It may also simply be that this type of intellectual inhibition is more destructive to the career of a man than it is to the career of a woman. I think a compulsive woman more often than not makes the family suffer, and makes her children suffer, but does not suffer quite as much herself. A man with severe intellectual inhibitions and blockings, particularly in a profession, would suffer himself much more, and would much more likely feel himself ill than a woman perhaps with a similar characterological makeup.[7]

Behind the overt symptomatology of inhibition in intellectual perceptiveness, in productivity, periods of blockage in which nothing can be moved so that an individual feels intellectually constipated, one finds very frequently close to the surface struggles with authority figures. It is very much a repetition of the toilet training struggles with the mother in terms of who says when, what, and the deadline that always is fought against. The real point I want to make is simply that when phase-nonspecific skills are being acquired, then the wrong kind of problem is amalgamated with the pursuit of these skills.

Just this afternoon I saw a fairly ill young man. He is under a lot of pressure to finish his Ph.D., and he almost hears a conversation about what he should do or not do.

In himself, a back-and-forth struggle, as if it were? Ask about it at all, and he will speak both halves of the dialogue? And without being capable of deciding one way or the other, remaining hung up in the middle?

He is in quite a tangle. The more he is under pressure, the more he cannot decide what to do. But I was struck with the conversation that is there all the time.

I understand that, for example, as with the woman who is an eternal procrastinator, who can never actually finish her work. She is a very gifted person with splendid ideas, but incapable of finally writing things up properly for publication. She is never quite ready. There is this internal conversation, one side allowing her to be self-fulfilling in achieving the skills for her own fame and claim of success versus the other, feeling resentful that she has to do something for the younger ones and saying that she should really take care of the younger ones. There is this internal conflict. She can neither do one thing and fully enjoy it nor do the other and fully enjoy it. She is still too mad at her mother who, instead of taking care of the younger ones and giving her as much autonomy as she

---

[7]In response to questions from colleagues and students, Kohut later expanded his theoretical formulations from that of classical psychoanalysis to a view of gender based on self psychology. See Kohut, 1978, pp. 776–779 and 782–792; Kohut, 1984.

At the time of these seminars, 1969–1970, the rapidly escalating presence of women in the work force, and in the professions, was just emerging. Kohut's references should not be interpreted here as his dominant view even at that time. His reference to compulsive women whose discontent would more likely make their children suffer, unlike men who would themselves suffer, referred to women whose impoverished selves found no goal-directed purpose beyond childrearing.

needed, let her take the responsibility for the younger ones. And so there is this eternal procrastination.

So far, the discussion on this point has been to relate a work inhibition with a structural conflict. But in some of the narcissistic fixations, we can see work inhibitions as well.

The mere symptomatology or phenomenology of the illness, the mere clinical picture in and of itself, unless it is looked at in a very sophisticated and subtle way, does not give the answer. One has to look behind the symptom and see what causes it dynamically. One of the leading symptom pictures people nowadays present when they come into psychotherapy, and particularly in a student clinic, is work inhibition. A majority of them do not relate predominantly to the type of internalized conflict we were talking about but to ego disturbances in self-esteem and therefore a lack of background for enjoyable work initiative.

People with such inhibition work like automatons but they do not work with a sense of originality and a sense of spontaneous involvement, which must rest on an expansive feeling that "I am I, and I am good; I want to have success, and I want to express myself." In other words, they lack the capacity to work in a manner a bit more related to play. I hope we will talk at some time in the future about this very important differentiation. Any good work begins, in a sense, as play, but in order to finish it there must also be the ability to work. One must be capable of going on with it, even though it is no longer directly enjoyable or gratifying. Creative and positive work, regardless of whether it is in science, building or administration, can all be creative in the sense that one feels pleasure in planning, has new ideas, and is devoted to what one is doing. This is enjoyable; this is fun. But it cannot always be that way. The idea of a game or fun will only assist one in taking the first step, not in carrying such work to conclusion against resistances and the pressures of reality.

Mothers will tell you that the child taught himself how to read or to add by asking, "What letters or numbers are these?" and then putting them together. Do some children, by virtue of their ability, prematurely get curious about these things—or is there always a subtle message? In other words, the mother who might let the child toilet train at his own pace would somehow interest the child in the premature learning process. Having been told, or having read in magazines, that it is not good to force a child to toilet train too early, she will instead transfer this kind of ambitious control to the learning process.

I think all this happens. I think there are children who respond to subtle messages. I imagine, however, there are also some children with bright and outreaching minds who want to know. But between wanting to know what this or that letter is and the kind of persistent work that creates reading skill, there is still a great deal of difference. For a bright child to pick out a number of words almost spontaneously and playfully does not make a reading child. The important issue is whether reading is part and parcel of an educational process. To inhibit or prohibit a child from reaching out and doing what he or she wants to do, I think, would be wrong. An educational process always concerns some pain, some conflict, a little bit more than the child still wants to do, a little overcoming of tiredness, a little persisting with things that are not easily done; otherwise, it is not an educational process. It is just a playful process. I think that, even for a very gifted child, such early abstract intellectual pursuits are not likely to be phase-adequate.

Certain things are phase-adequate that are obviously not directly related to but are in tune with sphincter control. For a child to learn building skills, while it is so involved, seems to me much more appropriate to that particular developmental phase. There is still something physically enjoyable in building with blocks or in fitting things together. This is related at least to the clamping down and letting go of the sphincter, as with the general muscle expansion in walking and the gymnastic skills that a child might learn in climbing. It is all in tune with a particular developmental phase. But the type of quietness that is demanded for persistence in mathematics or reading, where one just works with eye and mind for any length of time, obviously is not phase-appropriate in most pre-oedipal or early childhood. There may be exceptions in which it would be frustrating to a gifted child not to be able to learn something he wants to learn; this is a different story. What I am trying to say is that almost any principle if you make it extreme, becomes poor rather than good.

One cannot ask of a child's ego to devote itself to aim-inhibited tasks when it is, as it were, fully involved in handling skills that relate directly to the dominant drive of a particular period, as the anal period. I think that is important. It is not that a child cannot learn something apart from the dominant drive area, but that, on the whole, such early learning is directly related to his drive tensions.[8]

The point that I am also making is that, if errors occur at this particular phase, then later the specific work inhibitions relate to the particular

---

[8]See Kohut, 1977, pp. 120–121, 171–173, for a description of the process through which empathic failure of the selfobject milieu to respond appropriately to the particular ascendant drive results in a disintegration product.

drive area. Later on, the grownup will react to demands in the intellectu-al sphere with the same kind of inner rebellion that really belongs to the sphincter sphere. This is the one point I wanted to make. The other point I wanted to make is that work inhibitions concerning such specific inter-nal conflicts are, in principle, different from work inhibitions that con-cern the total constitution of the self and the self-esteem. For example, there are individuals in whom the work difficulty has to be analyzed. I do not mean analyzed in terms of psychoanalysis—I mean analyzed in terms of diagnosing dynamically and correctly.

When somebody complains that he cannot work, this can have many meanings. But when you investigate the details of his work inhibition or difficulty, you will see whether rebellious attitudes against authority are involved, whether he is afraid of becoming overstimulated, or whether it is a question of not having this self-propagating or self-propelling initia-tive that is part and parcel of an independent personality. An individual who is secure is free to experiment by forays into the environment. Although all of us have our ups and downs in this respect, when initia-tive is well established, curiosity and the wish to learn are among the most autonomous attributes that people have. They may be restricted to certain areas at the sacrifice of others. Still this sense of wanting to learn more and to branch out will last into high age, despite serious mental and physical impairments.

In other words, I want to emphasize the importance of a more exact diagnosis. It is nonsense to try to relieve somebody's inhibition when there is no inhibition at work. And it is nonsense to encourage some-body by lending him your own enthusiasm temporarily, when it is not a question at all of lacking enthusiasm, but when it is a question of a specific inhibition about a specific thing. Work inhibition has to be diag-nosed and pinpointed before one can do something sensible about it. It is the exact mode in which one then relates to the problem, depending on the more or less correct dynamic diagnosis, that will be helpful. Otherwise, it is a blind attempt without significant direction. It is the need for exact and sensitive diagnosis of the presenting difficulty which you face in your work with students whom you see in your clinic. And it is from an examination of clinical data that I can now help you to under-stand more clearly some of the subtle vicissitudes in the accretion of psychic structure in the developmental lines of narcissism.

SECTION II

Case Illustrations

8

Addictive Need for an Admiring Other in Regulation of Self-Esteem

Tᴏᴅᴀʏ ᴡᴇ ᴀᴛ least symbolically start a new era: the oedipus complex is now over; we are entering latency with this first case presentation.

Editor's note: In the following chapters, cases are presented by members of the staff of the student mental health clinic and of the department of psychiatry at a large university. Each case presentation, as well as comments by the presenter, is in **bold** type. Questions from the seminar members are in *italic*, as elsewhere in the book.

The following case reflects a variety of similar kinds of cases in our clinic. Whether male or female, the student realizes that he is destroying a relationship by the severe, early demands he makes of it. Though he may know that if he continues the behavior he will bring about termination of the relationship, he cannot interrupt the behavior.

A 22-year-old second-year graduate student in teaching was deeply distressed over a breakup with a boyfriend. She noted a pattern over the past several years: she formed an intense relationship and then placed the young man under heavy demands for support, thus alienating him. She was concerned because of her bad after-reactions—namely, depression, very low self-esteem and guilt—and about the future prospect of repeating this same type of relationship. She noted that a relationship with a fellow student, when she was in college elsewhere, seemed to have been a turning point in her life. Prior to that she had had a boyfriend for about five years, from age 14 to 19, whom everyone assumed she would marry. She felt on a "conveyer-belt to suburbia," and the relationship terminated. There followed a very intense six-month period with the boy in college, and her first sexual experience. Her

family, with whom she had always gotten along exceedingly well, became incensed with this particular boy and did everything they could to break up the relationship, despite the fact that they had never met him. She has never felt quite the same about her family since that time.

She noted that she did "crazy things" following the breakup of these relationships, calling the boy at odd hours after it was over, importuning him to return to her. She would then become very upset, saying she knew better, but she just could not control the urge to call.

Currently she works with children. She feels some obligation to straighten out her own "hangups" in order to work better with them. I think it was the pain of repeating this pattern with boyfriends that brought her to us.

Most of her first hour she talked about her many romances and the depressed periods after their termination. At 22, she feels old, fears that she will never be able to marry successfully. She talked about her interest in committing herself to a relationship without stint, and the reluctance of her boyfriends to accept these terms reciprocally. "I will do anything for these guys. I will pay all the attention they want. I want to be with them all the time. I am looking for a guy who will just accept that and return a good portion of it. That is all I want out of life."

Her parents are intelligent people in their mid fifties. Her father is a teacher and her mother a housewife. She describes them as sensitive, intelligent people for whom it was out of character to criticize her previous boyfriend. Since then, they have been their usual accepting, understanding selves. She envies an older sister, 30, who is happily married and the mother of two children. She has a 17-year-old brother who is a high school senior. Her childhood was a happy one; even though, in her work with children, she has recently scrutinized her own childhood and adolescence, she cannot come up with much pathology.

I think it is obvious why I chose this case. She showed some insight into comments by her friends, the nature of which was that she sets herself up for these heartaches; the outcome is inevitable. She commented at first about feelings of guilt with respect to the sexual activity that takes place during the relationships. This guilt does not occur while the relationship is still going on; only afterward does she feel guilty and like a used product, used both in the sense that the boy used her and that the next perfect boy will not want her because she has had previous relationships. Another reason I am bringing up the case is because I think, traditionally, we tend to think of these people as hysterical personalities. In view of the content of the seminar, there is certainly another way to think about them. I have seen her five or six times. I can elaborate or we can pause at this point for comments or questions.

All we know at the moment is that she complains that she apparently wants some kind of an enormously comprehensive and extensive type of relationship with the boyfriend. Then the boyfriend withdraws under the pressure of such enormous demands. And, despite the fact that she views her behavior as shameful, she apparently feels so needy that she keeps begging for a return. This is about the extent of the story. We know that she comes from a certain kind of family, and that she has a brother and sister.

I will elaborate first on the quality of her talking to me. This is a relatively attractive girl who repeatedly acts very embarrassed when talking about her feelings. She says, "I hesitate to say this," or actually hesitates saying it, and with great shame adds, "I want a handsome boy who is not just an ordinary boy." She often calls him a boy. "And I should not be like this. This is school-girlish. But I want someone whom I can really admire, who is very special, and whom other people will see as very handsome. I do not want someone ordinary. My mature self says that it is better to find someone who will be thoughtful, a good provider, with a good education, but I catch myself being attracted to guys because they are good looking, have a good sense of humor, and are too much like what a school girl would want." She describes her feelings of dejection, which in part come from the shame over having made a fool of herself once again—this has happened about five times—and part of it is that she is starving, to use a trite word, when this boy is not around.

This is not her word; this is your word.

It is my word. When there is no one on the scene, life is gray in all its dimensions. She said, "What good is an A on a paper? If he is not there to say 'good' . . . a B or a C is better if he says, 'That's a good job.' I cannot feel pretty unless he is there to see me as pretty." Accomplishments of any kind have no meaning, unshared with this boy who fills this role.

In elaborating on her family, she presents her father, at 59, as still very much in love with her mother, who returns his love. It was very nice to be in this family, because there they glowed at each other. Her sister and her husband also have such a relationship. Both her mother and sister were 18 years of age when they were married. As a child, and right on to the present, she felt this was the natural course; at about age 18 one meets a romanticized figure with whom one is very much in love

and whose hand one holds through life literally and figuratively. For her family, at 22 she is old, four years past when this should have happened. She mentioned that this happened repeatedly with several of her school friends in the suburb in which she lived.

We talked for the first time about the idea that all these marriages may not be idyllic. Maybe all these people who were getting married at age 18 did not go off to a lifetime of happily-ever-after. She had never thought about this before. This was her expectation, because that is all she had ever seen, or chosen to see; in her own family and among her peers, this sort of thing happened.

During the course of one interview she described a boy in whom she is very much interested. She enjoys being with him, but he clearly does not fit into her marriage plans; he really does not fit into the image for he has no plans of getting married. Still she enjoys being with him. He is a neighbor who has taken her out, and to parties. This is a very pleasurable thing, but will not even develop, as she sees it, to one of these three- or four-month type relationships.

She has commented also about how ashamed she is to use my time and to come in with a problem like this. She rebuked herself for not having better control. It was immature of her not to have gotten this thing in hand, and she may be displacing someone who really needs it. She talks about this as a problem of weakness rather than in terms of health or pain, although she readily acknowledges the pain she has. As she discussed her family further, she presented their orientation as a very service-oriented family who think of others. Father, by profession, is in the business of helping other people. Mother is involved in various organizations. Even as a small child she sensed this premium on doing for the group rather than for oneself.

She cited as an example one time when the family was going on a trip; the other kids had brought their stuff downstairs but she had left hers upstairs. Her mother said, ''Do you expect us to bring your stuff down?'' She felt overwhelmed with shame at the attempt to get other people to do her job or not to do her share for the group. The people in the university area are quite different from her family background in their way of life. She finds herself quite aware of a conflict between the goals and aims of her peers and the way her parents feel about things. We have been working to identify times when she feels, so to speak, like herself.

She said she has an urge to tell her mother that she has experimented with smoking marijuana, which would shock and upset her a great deal. We talked about it and came to some understanding. Why would she tell her this when it would upset her? What she is looking for is her mother's approval. That would combine the suburb's set of values with some of the values of her peers and there would be no conflict between the two. We talked about the idea that, somehow, when the boy was on the scene he could extend enough approval so that the conflict seemed to subside, that his approval and his reflection of, "What you are doing is right," or, "I believe in you," were all she really needed. Then somehow whether her parents believed in or approved of what she was doing certainly lost intensity. The boy provided this. He was necessary and sufficient, and certainly that was one of the functions he filled.

We also identified that relationships have two stages. The very needy self did not appear until things began to jell in the relationship. She was not so demanding at first, but as she really got to know the boy and he really got to know her, then she upped her demands, to the point that several of these fellows said, "I did not think this was what we were getting ourselves into when we got together. I just cannot do all the things you want me to do or be with you all the time you want me to be with you. We ought to stop seeing each other." This would come as a crushing blow to her, and then would follow a period of attempting to bring the boy back after he had resigned.

That is a good stopping point. How many times have you seen her?

Seven.

You see her how often?

Once a week.

In other words, you started about two months ago, and the treatment continues. Why don't we just hear some discussion of this case?

Is she primarily operating at the level of object love and hate, or narcissistic object love and hate? Which kinds of clues can we use from this material to go one way or the other in our own minds?

You would like to know the nature of her love demands. We want to assess her personality as it manifests itself in what seems to be the chief complaint, the particular demands she makes on her boyfriends, which then, secondarily, lead to the breakup. We seem to have an avenue directly from the presenting symptom to some crucial question about her personality organization. And you would like to know what the behavioral or phenomenological criteria are that make us now decide whether this is, as you say, a narcissistic demand that she exerts, or whether this is just an intense form of object love, or whether this is perhaps a kind of internal conflict that leads her into setting up relationships that cannot work because of some unconscious guilt. I am just describing a variety of directions in which one's mind might wander. Let us concentrate for the time being on what you suggested, that we discuss in greater detail the peculiar, specific nature, of her demands.

I have only one sense of where an important clue lies, and I cannot evaluate it. Can this be an expression of her feelings toward the therapist when she describes the episode of mother saying, ''How can you expect us to go back and get your things for you?'' I have the sense that in that way it is an initial transference fear and expectation.

This is at the moment really not important to us. The vicissitudes of the treatment situation are not what we are discussing. We are at the moment trying to assess the central issue in her personality, which may relate to her therapist, to her lovers, or to her parents, but we want, in depth, *to investigate it.*[1] As you asked at first, what is the nature of her particular love demands?

Let us think about it. In what way do they seem to be unusual? In what way do they seem to stand in her way? How can we characterize them?

She seems to want total merging and mirrored approval—using the words that we use—because she said she wants the man all the time, under all circumstances, and she can only see herself in reference to him. An "A," in itself, does not mean anything. A "B" is better if the boy she is going with says, "Isn't that nice that you have a B? Aren't you a nice little girl? Aren't you pretty? Aren't you looking good?" She cannot feel good-looking unless somebody is looking at her and says so.

Although what you say is quite correct, my initial empathic response was a little different. I had the feeling there was a certain addictive quality to her relationship. The nature of her love or of her desire is less differentiated than one generally expects from a mature 22-year-old: fondness and love or passion for another person. It has a nondescript urgency to it that is more encountered in the addictions, whether addiction to a drug, to people, to food, to alcohol, to masturbation, or to perverse pursuits. One finds a variety of features, but there is an unnameable quality that an addiction has, a quality of urgency, a no-delay-tolerating quality, wiping out all differentiations. For example, for an alcoholic alcohol is the important thing. It does not matter whether it is good or bad bourbon, good or bad wine; it is what is behind it. This

---

[1]It is characteristic of Kohut's response to a case presentation that he responds to the total individual and not to specific parts or specific symptoms. It is to the whole striving individual that he directs his attention.

means that it is not determined by the elaboration of the object, but by *the needs of the self*. This is why the supply that is striven for becomes less important. It is the urgency of the aim, the urgency of the fulfillment, as if some void had to be filled.

That term has come up. That is the term I have used with her. It is as if she is an addict looking around for something.

So you have had a similar type of feeling. These are tentative guesses, although by now, on the basis of seven interviews by somebody who is experienced in such matters, it is less tentative. This is not just a single intake interview on which we base wild guesses, but we already have some background. The question is whether this desire for objects has an addictive wish or narcissistic aspect to it. Is it filling an internal void? Can we say any more about it? Can we make any further guesses?

I always tend to go in two directions when I hear clinical material. I like to deepen my understanding of the presenting symptom, in which I generally find a most important clue, but in depth, empathic depth. What does that patient really feel when she says that she cannot let go of the boyfriend? Can I understand that—feel with her—as deeply as possible? And then I look for original clues. Is there something in the childhood past that fits with this particular type of feeling or behavior? Usually, one does not learn too much but sometimes one initially gets rather good clues that tell a story which in the end, after many doubts, proves to be rather correct. These are the two ways in which I tend to pursue such initial material.

But can we say more on the basis of what we have learned so far about this hunger, this starvation, this addiction, this need to fill a void, this need to hold onto the other person as if it were a piece of herself in order to give her a good feeling about herself? You know, the emphasis is all on herself. She has particular conditions: the object should be good looking, it should have certain other qualities. This is almost like the question of what kind of drug sends one the most. Perhaps I am exaggerating a bit, but this is my first impression.

At least as a tentative hypothesis, she has not really internalized the narcissistic regulating quality[2] that you spoke of. There is a constant disequilibrium or threat of disequilibrium. I was wondering in both the present and the early past, what happens when the external supplies are

---

[2]Kohut would later describe this as the regulation of self-esteem, the restoration of cohesion through the self function of calming and soothing oneself.

not available—in other words, these objects that are necessary to maintain narcissistic equilibrium?

I fully agree with the comment that there is a degree of narcissistic vulnerability in this girl, and there I go back to what was already visible in the early memory of the mistake that she made. Just feel yourself into this little episode. If a patient brings up such a thing, and you remember it out of the many things she told you, then somewhere it must tell a very significant story. Here she made a little mistake—she did not bring her things down. She was reacted to, not harshly really, but in a subtly destructive way by the mother. "Do you think we ought to do it for you?" She just forgot. She could have been told, "Go up and get them. Quick! Hurry up!" But she responded by an enormous drop in self-esteem. This is already a late memory. I do not know if she was four or 10.

She was probably eight or 10.

Even if she had been four, it does not make any difference. This is a late memory, and this is not what caused her disturbance. It is a symbol, a sequela of an early experience that shows how vulnerable she was. She does not respond to the blame with anger. "Why do you blame me for that? I just forgot." She does not respond with, "Okay Mom, I'll go up and get it. Do not overdo it." But there is a terrific sinking feeling and a loss of self-esteem. She said she felt dreadfully ashamed. There is a deep sense of shame and a loss of self-esteem. Severe degrees of shame usually arise just at moments when one wants to shine and then experiences the opposite. We do not know whether she had just come down with an attractive dress wishing to be admired. They were on an outing?

They were about to go on a trip.

They were going on a trip to which she was looking forward, and at that very moment she was debunked. Maybe this expectation, and suddenly having the rug pulled out from under her, tells you something typical about the parents. Our task now is to solve this strange puzzle, which probably is not quite so strange when we examine it in depth.

How does it occur in such a warm family, with such goodness, so much glow, so much friendliness, and in which so many ideals seem to abound? This is a family in which the sister also has achieved this kind of glow about her life, and feels so warm, so involved, and with such a sense of service toward other people. How, in such a family, does this lowered self-esteem occur in the middle child? Is this something specific for the middle child's position? Is it something about a hypocritical attitude in the family? Is it a family who can give warmth in social issues but not in intimate family relationships? Has it something to do with a second girl in the family in which a boy was wanted? We do not know. These are the questions which begin to open up and which become important for us to investigate in some detail.

Is there any discussion? Do you have a feeling for the case so far? Do you feel that our initial theories are likely to be true? And what do these initial theories mean?

There is a lot to be said before we go on with the clinical material, even on the basis of the little that we have so far. For instance, the two major points. What is there in the nature of her relationship to her friends that makes the boys seek escape? I speculated that it was like an addiction to other people. What does that mean? This is a nice sounding word that immediately creates some feeling of evidence and seems to cut through all sorts of ambiguities. It sounds familiar. But what does it mean when one says that her relationship to another person is like an addiction? Is it a narcissistic relationship or is it a love relationship? This is another way of putting the same question. And if all this is relevant, even from the very little that we have so far heard, how does that relate to our first guess of a sort of shaky girl, so easily crushed by criticism that she gets a sinking feeling right away, and yet abandons all shame and rushes after the men, trying to hold them as if her life were at stake even though they have declared their independence? Can we elaborate a little more about this? With thought experimentation of this kind, one acquires some skills. I find that this kind of freedom, thought experimentation, is fully compatible with the greatest caution and the greatest reverence for clinical evidence. One learns in this particular way to differentiate between evidence which supports a hypothesis and evidence that contradicts it. But unless you have some moving out in response even to early material presented to you, you have nothing against which to measure the future flow of material. You cannot match it and see whether or not it fits.

Again, one has to be careful. There are some people who, once they have a pet theory, see everything fall into place. Since human behavior, symptomatology, and communications are complex, one can always find something that fits. But this is amateurish, and one has to learn the skill not to do that. But I do not think, with what we have done so far, we can be accused of having gone out of our way. I think she really tells us how seemingly addicted she is, how she cannot let go. We know that these men run away from her. We would like to know about that in more detail. Can you make some guesses and then see whether our guesses are way off?

Can we raise the issue of how the picture has not really changed, because it has to be part of her anyway, but that it is skewed by the time at which she comes in, by the fact that the narcissistic blow is so fresh that she presents herself as looking even more vulnerable, chasing these men away even more? We are not going to hear at this point about the qualities of the particular person she has just lost. She is going to lump all losses together. It does not necessarily mean that, if we saw her when she was freshly involved with someone, that she was not capable of more interest in the person.

This is a perfectly appropriate remark to make. I do not think it is likely to fit, but it is a very important cautionary remark. This is more true in depressed people, by the way. When you hear a person who is acutely depressed talk about the past, he sees everything in dark colors. All the childhood memories are dark. One has the feeling life has always been dark, which is by no means true. When this same person is not depressed, he talks about the past in a much more rosy and optimistic way. This does not quite fit this particular story. We do not think she has invented things. After all, this has happened a number of times. Is she at the moment really in the depths of a particular reaction, or is it that a certain repetitive pattern has occurred? It is not that she is at this moment at the low ebb of being crushed, but that she says, "This has happened too many times. I had better see what is behind it. Something crazy is going on with me. I would like to do something about it." This is very different from being in the depths, you know, "Help me," when everything looks the way it happens to feel at the moment.

Both are present. There is a certain control that she exerts in saying, "If I would let myself go, that is the way I would feel, but I am not going to allow it to happen." She can talk about being with the person, and still remembers it as very un-gray, as very nice. All her experience is not colored badly.

I have learned over many years of clinical experience, and not easily, that you will always do best if you believe your patients. It is much more likely that what they say is true than that they want to pull the wool over your eyes. Things will be balanced out. Even if a depressed person paints his past too dark a color, I would not worry even then about believing him. He may talk about the significant aspects of his past as they relate to the depression more meaningfully than if he were capable of giving you a totally balanced picture of all the pluses and minuses of his past. So, in a psychologically valid way, I would be willing to believe the patient and to take seriously what he tells you about his past. Things will balance out. But I would not, from the beginning, take what he tells you predominantly as defensive, as a way of denying things or escaping from the truth. This is a misunderstanding—and I think a somewhat amateurish misunderstanding—of the dynamic point of view in which defenses tend to counterbalance drives.

Under the pressure of a new therapeutic situation, and under the impact of first impressions about other people generally, you are likely to learn more by trusting these first impressions than by trying to look behind them.

In the first few years of psychiatric experience, there is always the feeling that the patient wants to mislead you. This is very unlikely. In general, the patient does not want to mislead you, particularly in the early sessions and generally not in the long run, unless you begin to suspect him, treat him like an enemy, and act as if he were going to withhold things from you. Pretty soon, he begins to behave like an enemy. But on the whole I think this is not so. Anyway, if you make a naive mistake in that way, I do not think there is any particular harm to it. It will balance out in the long run. As I said, my feeling here is that this first hypothesis, the addiction-like quality of her relationship to a man, is worth pursuing in this kind of thought experimentation I mentioned.

When we think about it now, what do we mean when we say this patient is addicted to other people? What do we mean when we say that she is very vulnerable and easily crushed? How do those two things combine, her addictiveness to other people and her vulnerability, the fact that she is easily crushed? Is this a common feature of people who are inclined toward being addictive personalities?

The answer is yes, but I mean how? In what way? How does it fit that the boyfriends run away? What makes people run away from people who are addicted?

I think one of the qualities that is sometimes seen in an addictive personality centers about the need to have pleasure or relief of pain without a serious commitment to effort on their part. I have no sense from this girl's past.

I think what you say is undoubtedly correct. But to my mind this is part and parcel of secondary ego changes, secondary personality changes in established addictions. It is to some extent also a secondary feature of the addictive or potentially addictive personality.

What I am talking about is the potentially addictive personality, not addiction as a mode of life. What is the nature of the personality that tends toward addiction? What is an addiction? What is the difference between loving another person and being addicted to another person?

Magic.

In what way?

That the patient has held onto certain childlike magical ideas that most of us abandon as we go through adolescence and earlier. I think this relates partly to the comment about effort. I think the pre-addictive sort of person has beliefs that long-range pleasures can occur easily, in the way this girl talks about living happily ever after. She has never really thought out the problems of marriage or noticed that some marriages do not do well. Her experience is limited to her mother, her sister, and a few of her close friends.

The impression I have is that both comments describe the features of a childlike and infantile personality. It is true that the two may go hand-in-hand, but it is not the essence of addiction. At least let me say what I think the issue is, though I do not even know if this fits here. I am now talking in a general way.

An addictive person needs the object of his addiction with an absolute intensity which is not the same as the comparative relativity even of passionate love. It does not have anything to do with the total maturity of the surrounding personality. It is not to be denied that in general the infantile features are present, particularly in long-term addictions, and that a certain maturity is needed for the capacity to love. These are secondary features. In the addictive personality I think there is something intrinsically different. The way in which I formulated it once is that addiction tends to relate, so far as I can judge, to just this type of setup that I have talked about so much here—namely, that functions which the reasonably mature individual can perform for himself cannot be performed for themselves by some people. There is some missing aspect of their own psychological structure for which external supplies are needed, while other people do not need that external supply.

The example that is the easiest to understand is the self-soothing capacity. The capacity to calm oneself is not something that grows by itself. It is, like any other internal structuralization, based on the fact that originally there was an external environment present that did that for one.

In other words, there was someone who not only covered you to keep you warm, dried you to keep you dry, and fed you to keep you from being hungry, but that also, when you were anxious, picked you up and included you in her larger calmness so that you could attach yourself and become calm in the process.[3] It is on the basis of first having had this from

---

[3]This is the basis for what Kohut called transmuting internalization.

the outside, and then very gradually losing it, that you gradually acquired the ability to take it over yourself, like any other skill. First, you begin by being included in the adult environment that does it for you[4]; then gradually, not suddenly,[5] you take it over yourself.[6] In either case, never having had such support (which is almost impossible if one survives physically, biologically; for biological survival one has to have a modicum of support) or being suddenly or phase-inappropriately deprived of it will prevent you from developing the capacity to internalize these functions.

This is true for such simple skills as building with blocks. A child who builds with blocks is not born, so far as I can judge, with the knowledge of how one builds with blocks. He watches the parent do it with him, the biggest ones down below and the little ones on top. A skillful father or mother will do it for him, but will let him imitate and will gradually let him do it by himself. If the father or the mother is impatient and says, "Come on now, that takes too long," and does it himself, then the child will not do it, but will remain connected with this image of the omnipotent block-building parent and will in fantasy always want to be connected with an omnipotent block-building parent. Of course, you can translate this into much more complex things, but the issue is that he will not himself create and learn this skill.[7]

For instance, take the skill of going to sleep; sleep disturbances are the childhood neuroses of the 20th century. The way in which one goes to sleep, whether one finds it crazy at first hearing or not, is a learned skill. What is the learned skill about falling asleep? This is ridiculous. This is a drive, obviously. You are tired—you want to sleep. You do not have to learn it. It almost sounds like learning to be hungry and wanting to eat. If it is simplified in this way, then it is ludicrous. But where is the skill? The skill is as always in suppressing something. In order to go to sleep one has to suppress wanting to stay awake, which is a drive too. It is drive-connected to want to be awake with all the wonderful things that are still in the world. There is a mother whom one likes. There is a daddy who has come home with whom one wants to play. One is stimulated, one has had a good time. How many of us have difficulty going to sleep at night? We will talk about that perhaps a little bit in order to clarify this very important point in some detail.

---

[4]Selfobject function.
[5]Optimal frustration.
[6]Transmuting internalization.
[7]He will not be able to transmute a function performed by a selfobject into a self-function through the process of optimal frustration and transmuting internalization.

The ego skill that is acquired is a particular technique: the technique of gradually decathecting the external world, and gradually and increasingly cathecting, turning toward, that regression which is the psychological precondition for the state of sleep. How does the skillful sleeper's helper do that for a child? By giving enough object cathexis to the child so that it does not suddenly miss the world altogether. In other words, out of an excited moment of a marvelous time, bang! "Now you go to bed." Bang! The light is out. Bang! "You go to sleep." One cannot expect that of a child. Very few of us can do that. Somebody has to be so dead-tired that it is no longer a skill. He has learned the trick of going to sleep despite lacking the ego structure that has taught him the skill of going to sleep. A skillful mother will sing a little bit, but she will not sing too loudly. She will read, but not a very exciting story, a going-to-sleep kind of story that is a little bit monotonous. She will provide him with a little physical contact, but not so much that it is physically stimulating, so that he wants to stay awake.

So being given a modicum of that world that one has to relinquish and allowed yet enough peacefulness, quiet, calm, and darkness to encourage going to sleep, the ego learns this particular skill of relinquishing the environment and turning toward the internal world in that particular kind of narcissistic regression which is the state of sleep. It is clear that if a child has had a good mother to do that, the child will gradually take over himself. The child will learn to read a little bit, to listen a little to the radio and gradually turn away from the world with all its attractions. He will be capable of it even at the time when he is not thoroughly tired. In other words, one does not have to exhaust oneself first.

Now assume that a person has not acquired this particular self-soothing structure. Of course you know now that I am not just talking about this specific circumscribed skill of going to sleep but about many other times when one has to learn to turn away from the excitements and anxieties of daily living and has to be capable of relaxing. If somebody has not acquired this particular structure, then he becomes addicted to outside help, not because he loves that outside help as a person in his own right, but because it is a particular function that he cannot fulfill for himself. Such people then become addicted to drugs in order to go to sleep. The same kind of people, when they go into psychotherapy, become addicted to the psychotherapist or to the psychotherapeutic procedure. There is nothing wrong with it. This is the way it should be, because they lack necessary structure at this point. You can say you cannot give them what they need from you. You can give drugs instead of yourself, but then you will not set up the type of situation that in a way repeats the childhood situation by fulfilling for them the functions that they cannot fulfill for themselves. Then you gradually allow them to do it on their own. In other words, you allow them to build up structure.

This has nothing to do, by the way, with the actual clinical treatment of confirmed drug addicts in whom there are profound psychological defects. The complexity of the secondary personality changes in the drug addict or in the alcoholic is a totally different dimension of the problem, because in such addicts not even transferring the need toward another person can take place. As stated earlier, the intolerance of tension, even of this minute degree, any kind of reliance on another person, even though he stands for an archaic prestructural object, cannot be tolerated. In the true addictions, one must go about an attempt to cure with the muscular approach of removing the addictive agent and providing a variety of incarcerative procedures that build up some kind of a force to do away with the poison. But this has nothing to do with the principle that we are talking about.

What I am talking about here is that one gets the feeling, whether rightly or wrongly—these are preliminary fantasies and imaginings—that this particular girl needs these men. She fastens onto them, independent of her morals, or esthetics, or of her pride, because she swallows her pride in many ways. Again, this may not be a correct hypothesis, but it is a possible one. I think it fits well with one other thing: why others run away from her. It is very difficult to be the object of an addiction, because in order to be such an object one is depersonalized. One is not oneself. All that counts is what one is used for.[8]

Again, any principle can go only so far. It always contains elements of the best and the worst meaning. In the most mature relationships, sometimes, the object of one's love is asked to fulfill functions that one cannot fulfill oneself, and the object of one's love will do so temporarily. But if it becomes the only feature in the relationship, just as in perversions, this then becomes such a narrow kind of an approach to the variety of stimulations, fun, experience and experimentation that two intimate people may dare to have with one another that the relationship becomes impoverished. It seems to me that any sophisticated human being can have a sex life that is varied, variegated, and can include anything from A to Z. This is not a perversion. I think it is a perversion if one can do nothing but A. If a relationship consists of nothing but one specific form of an aberrant sexual behavior, that is a different story.

I think this is true also for such things as the addictions. Of course when one is terribly upset and overburdened, then one does not particu-

---

[8]The selfobject function.

larly think of the other person. One thinks only in terms of one's own needs and wants the other person to respond to those needs. In a relationship that two people have it is important that only one person be down at one time. The trouble usually comes when both persons are down, and they both look for some help from the other, and both want more than the other can give. With this particular girl for whom relationship after relationship is so urgent, that she is blind to who the other person might be, then that person feels overburdened and extricates himself.

There was a movie called "The Collector." I have never seen the movie, but I have been told about it by some of my patients so much that I have almost seen it. I have always felt it was a very good example of this kind of relationship, the total possession of another person, like the collector of his butterflies. This same collector then catches a girl and puts her in a kind of cage.

To back up a minute . . .

To back me up, or to back up by going back? I like the first, but I do not like the second. Still, I will tolerate the second.

In making a differential diagnosis between two major lines, it may be interesting to approach it with the question of whether this represents a narcissistic problem or a structural problem.

An internal conflict problem. Right. For example, you could say, when we first began to hear this case, that all we know of this girl is that she has a series of relationships with men. They gradually become more and more intense, and the fellow backs away. Now if we do not know a lot more than that, we could speculate on the internal conflict model. How do we know that these men do not represent for her a father figure that she is intensely attracted to, and these kids get scared and back off?

That is why I presented the case.

This is absolutely correct. I have no quarrel with that at all. I am not saying that this may not turn out to be so. All I am saying is that when I go through clinical material, I allow myself my speculations on the basis of my clinical experience but leave them open to later correction. You were very careful, by the way, in saying "if we had heard nothing more." We learned more things. We learned, for instance, that these people ran away from her. Why did they withdraw from her? The internal conflict would more likely make her withdraw from them rather than overburden them with demands. It may be that she is a teaser, but these are things we have not learned. All I can say, on the basis of what we have learned, is that here is a girl who seems to be a vulnerable creature, who seems to fasten, despite her pride, onto her relationships, and then the men extricate themselves. And over and over again this happens. It may very well turn out that our initial hypothesis is the wrong one. I played it for what it was worth, always saying, "Let us make as complete a picture in this thought experimentation as far as we want it to go; then let us watch for further material." But your hypothesis is absolutely acceptable, appropriate, and we will watch for material to confirm it or to evaluate it. I wonder whether you could give us a little more material.

I chose some things from today's hour, because they are fresh, and because they happen to be, I think by chance, highly relevant to the lines of discussion we are pursuing.

She started the hour by telling me that during the day things are fine. Her work is going very well. She does not feel depressed except that her supervisor mentioned she seems unaware of how much she means to the children she works with. She minimizes her own importance to the children. Then she told me about an incident.

The nights are always bad, but last night was particularly bad. "I came home with three women in a car, and they were talking about income tax and one said, "I do not have to worry about that. My husband always figures out the income tax." She felt extremely resentful that the three women had husbands to do the income tax, but she had to do her own. It had a weird kind of quality since she has no income. She felt unreasonable in her anger at those women.

Were they fellow students?

I think older women, supervisors. Then she had dinner with her roommate. They were doing the dishes afterward and as fast as she could wash, the roommate was putting more dishes in; she just blew up, threw the dish towel across the room, and strode out of the kitchen, into her bedroom, and slammed the door. The roommate came in and said, "What is the matter?"

I went through the whole thing again about how I think I will never get married. I will never have the kind of life I want. Then I said to her, voicing her concern, "I do not want to come home to you. I want to come home to a man." Then she said, "I know we are supposed to be talking about the here-and-now," and this was her reference to her feeling that this is a short-term clinic, "but do you mind if I play my own shrink for a while and tell you about some things from my past?" I said, "Of course." There had been no active discouragement to bringing up things from her past.

"There is this thing in my family. My grandmother died two months before I was born, and yet I have grown up with my grandmother, because she is constantly being mentioned as the saintly person who did all these wonderful things mentioned by my mother. I feel I know her, even though she died before I was born." Among other things, she cited the fact that grandmother was subjected to tremendous dependency needs by many of her relatives and never complained once in years and years. The example of grandmother was being held up by mother to the patient. She said, "I will bet that has had some effect on me, hearing this for years and years."

She went on to say that she herself was in the hospital the first six weeks of her life, hovering between life and death. Throughout the family, occasionally times will come up when the relatives will say, "Aren't we lucky that she is alive! She almost died." During the late part of the pregnancy mother was alternating between a southern city and a northern city by plane to nurse grandmother who was dying of cancer.

She talked about her mother having this tremendous capacity to be strong, stressing the need to be strong when the going is rough. For example, sister wanted to join her fiancé every other weekend while she was engaged. Mother said, "That is an unnecessary expense. Your father was away in the war for three years, and I got along painfully without him. You can get along for a few months without seeing your fiancé." Mother is the type of person who always told her when she was sick, "Put on a fresh nightgown, fix your hair, get a new book, prop up the pillows, and for God's sake, do not look like you are weak, or that you need people. Be strong, like grandmother." Mother always did things and never complained. The message was: Always serve— never be served.

I made some reference to the fact that it sounded as if mother had kept alive the very nice feelings about grandmother and that any other feelings she had about the hardship of nursing her dying mother were all squashed under. She said that that was indeed the way she could conceptualize it. Grandmother could not possibly have been this perfect. She has never thought about it though. This is an accepted belief in the family, that this perfect woman existed.

All right. We will not be able to do too much with this case today. We cannot go beyond a certain point now unless we have more information about what kind of a personality this is. We have wildly speculated as an exercise on the basis of some very thinly investigated presenting symptoms. If we want to know this case a little better, we have to grasp what the flavor of this personality is. Something tells me, on the basis of a few words that you said now, that this is a stronger person than met the eye, that she is aggressive and capable of asserting herself. She talks very freely, you know, "I'll be my own shrink." This is not a fearful kind of person. So I would be very doubtful about some of our early speculations, but we will wait and see.

Let us briefly review the personality structure of an individual predisposed to develop an addiction either to a chemical or to another person. This is not to be confused with the personality changes which arise later, and secondarily, in those people who go on to live out the lifestyle of drug addiction.

A person needs the object of his addiction in a way that is essentially different from the way he needs an object of his love. The difference is that the object of an addiction is needed to perform an important psychological function ordinarily performed by oneself; as in this case, a self-soothing, self-esteem maintaining function that ordinarily in the course of development is internalized as part of one's own psychic structure. In contrast, a love object can be viewed as a person in his own right, with his own needs, as an independent center of initiative who is loved as the uniquely different individual that he is. Unlike the addictive relationship, such a love relationship is not dependent for its very existence on the love object meeting the other's narcissistic needs. While a love object may at times be used to help maintain one's self-esteem, the need is only temporary, and greatly less in frequency, duration and intensity, than is the case with the need of the object in addiction. Viewed in this light, the addictive quality of the patient's object relationships goes hand-in-hand with self-esteem being easily crushed each time one of her boyfriends breaks away.

This patient's need for an admiring other to help maintain self-esteem reflects her failure in having adequately internalized this function. From the perspective of development, a function which was ordinarily performed for a child when he was incapable of doing so for himself is internalized and taken over by the child because the caregiving adult phases out her performance in a gradual way at the appropriate time. It is through this process of phase-adequate, nontraumatic, gradual loss of an outside supply that one comes to take over performing a function for oneself.[9] However, when internalization does not occur, an individual

---

[9]Transmuting internalization.

may then heavily rely on other people or chemicals to carry out this function.

Since this is not a continuous case seminar, we shall use a number of cases to reflect our way of approaching an understanding of the individual through insights stimulated by our consideration of narcissism as a developmental line. Next session we will address another case.

9

Physical Symptom as a Reverberation of Self-Esteem Needs

The distinctive features in the following case are of less importance than the use of the developmental line of narcissism in understanding the student's symptom of sexual dysfunction.

This young man will soon be 23. He was graduated from an Eastern college and has just come to the university. He was transferred to the Mental Health Clinic by Medical Student Health when physical examination for problems with erection proved negative.

Students are asked to fill in a brief form before their appointment and these are the questions and his answers.

(1) Would you fill out in detail what brought you here?

"Over the past six months I have had difficulty achieving a firm erection during intercourse. The doctor examined me, and found me physiologically fit, and referred me to MHC. In addition, I have experienced difficulties of late with a neurotic girlfriend. I have also been troubled by feelings of frustration in attempting to order my life. Principally, I blame this inability to order my life on the draft and financial problems."

(2) Which of these problems do you feel would be most important for you to deal with here?

"At present I am most concerned with the erection difficulty, as I believe it signifies important underlying doubts and so forth."

(3) What were the recent events in your life that led to your coming here at this time?

"I happened to come here this morning because the doctor referred me. I intended to come in the near future anyway.

This was prompted by a girl I care very much for having taken an overdose of barbiturates."
(4) What kind of help have you received for your problems before you came here?
   "None."
(5) Have you considered other sources of help? What were they?
   "I originally went to Student Health with my problem and was referred here."

I have seen him twice so far. His appearance is unusual. He has kind of a rough face, as if he had bad acne, a flat face, an aquiline nose and a wide neck. He was dressed as an establishment college man of 10 or 15 years ago, without a tie. One other bit of information—I gave him an appointment that was fairly close to the time he applied, but he turned it down because of a class, so he came in later than the time I originally offered him. I used that as an indication that his problem was not as urgent as it sounded.

When he sat down, I said I had read what he had written and asked him to tell me some more about it. In essence, he repeated the details, but wanted to make clear to me that he could perform sexually, but there was something about his penis that was bothering him; it was not as big and as firm as it had been. He then went on to assure me that he had been a bon vivant in the past, an experienced man, so that this experience was different. With this he gave me a diffident, embarrassed grin. I think it was about here that I had some sense that he had just dropped his problem in my lap. I rather quickly said, "What do you think it is about?"

There were three things he had thought about. One was that during a physical examination at his previous college last spring a doctor had asked if he had trouble having intercourse. He apparently has some developmental anomaly of his penis. He thought another factor was that maybe his difficulties were related to the fact that he had been going with two girls. One girl was much more involved with him than he with her, and somehow he did not want to take advantage of her. His concern about others tends to be a recurring theme. His relationship with the second girl who had taken an overdose of barbiturates has been very difficult. They have ups and downs, fights, and he has some sense that she is not good for him, but he feels strongly attracted to her.

I told him that this certainly sounded unsettling, but I did not really see what specifically was bothering him about it. At this point, he went back to the summer and a girlfriend he had at home. This was apparently a sustained relationship over a period of years. They had a confrontation about whether they would get married or not. For some reason, which was not clear, he felt he could not marry her while he was going to be here for two years in school. I do not think she told him to get lost, but he somehow instigated breaking up the relationship with some overtones that he did not want to pin her down. Toward the end of summer he was very upset that he could not get back into a relationship with her. She had accepted the break, but he had not. Finally he said he had a great deal of difficulty settling down here; he felt he had not been working as hard as he might in his graduate course. He was also mightily preoccupied with the draft. He had signed up with the army reserve while at college, and this has been taking a certain amount of his time, but this should not be influencing his work. At this point he wonders if he did not make a mistake, and that it would have been better if he had taken his chances with the draft.

In the way he presented these things, I had the sense that they are not real issues to him, and that even he thinks they are only symptomatic.

I commented, ''Well, it sounds like kind of an unsettling time since you have been here. Is this like any other time?''

At this point he said his mother died between his first and second year at college when he was 17 or 18. She was a severe arthritic, and her incapacity had really developed when he was about 12. She was in a wheelchair, and at night both he and his father were involved with her physical care. For his mother to be in a wheelchair, and to be seen by his peers when he was out with her, was embarrassing. He said he has never been very close to his father, and sketched an impression that the mother was a real buffer with father. Mother gave him his money. Mother did everything with him. There was an impression that father was away some, but not that much. He was at loose ends when mother died, and has never been able to get close to father. Father gives him a hard time about money and acts as if he is somewhat of a spendthrift. The patient allows this is true, but does not really view himself as a spendthrift; he needs lots of money, and father is not willing to give him that much. Apparently this has no basis in reality. I gather, but do not know as a fact, that mother's family must have been fairly wealthy, and that father has always made lots of money. A recent example was that he called father for money to buy snow tires for his car. Father said he was hard up but gave him the money. He called up a week or so later and said, ''I need some money for tuition,'' and father says, ''Right away,'' and sends him a check. At this point he goes into a kind of self-justification and says, ''I really could not make money last summer because I was involved with the reserve training, and my father should understand that.''

I have the impression that he was an impulse-ridden kid. He said he was running around, drinking with the boys, and so on. Then, as he talked about his relationship with his mother, I began to wonder about the kind of overindulgence and infantilizing business that seemed to have gone on with her. He stressed how intensely close they had been, as opposed to how distant he had been from his father. Mother was somewhat older than father and had three children by a former marriage. Sister is the significant one; she is 20 years older than he and has a son who is his age. Later he points out that it is this sister he has turned to recently to comfort and support him.

But for all practical and emotional purposes he is an only child?

Yes. That is, she was out of the home all this time. At this point I got interested in piecing his life together. He was born in the east and they were there for about a year, moving to another city when he was about six. From six until twelve they were living in still another eastern city.

Apparently this was the glowing period of his life. He was a great success. He was elected president of student government, went in for athletics, was very popular, and so on. It was a small school, and it sounded like a fairly wealthy suburb because he talked about ponds on the estate, etc. When he was twelve they moved to the west because of mother's arthritis. As far as he remembers, she had had no disability from the arthritis before that. When he was a kid, she could pick him up and play with him. The only thing he remembers is that she did not go swimming. So there was nothing startling about her incapacity until twelve. He apparently had a terrible time making friends, getting along in school, and so on. Along with this, mother was sick.

There is some impression that father was pretty grouchy about having to give up his position in the east where he had been a chemist for a large company. He apparently was kept on the books as a research chemist, but did not have the status he had previously. With mother's increasing disability there were nurses during the day, but he and father took care of mother at night.

When he was a junior in high school, he had some kind of operation on his penis for a congenital defect so he could urinate better. He told me later that he sits to urinate, on occasion, because he has some trouble with his stream. He also said he has trouble initiating urinating in public, and this has always been embarrassing for him. After he had a meatotomy, he started trying to please father by doing better in school. Up to that point, apparently, he had been a poor student, at least from the time they were in the west.

The first year at college was fine, as far as he was concerned; he was one of the boys, doing a lot of drinking, running around. In the second year he latched on to a classmate the same age, quieter and more studious. It sounded as if they had a very intense kind of relationship. I think that fact emerged when I asked about repercussions from his mother's death. In the last two years of college he and his friend drifted apart. The implication was that our student really did not need him that much anymore and that he had gone back to his old ways.

At this point I felt I had a lot of information, but somehow did not have the sense of why he was coming to the clinic now, or what was churning in him, so I said, "Let us go back to that." What he emphasized was his sense of being at loose ends, his unsettledness. I think it was here, when he started talking about his penis being big and strong, that he was really talking about himself, and that he somehow felt not as focused as he once was. Apparently the trouble now in his sexual life is not so much that he is not performing, but it is his inability to get involved in the performance or to enjoy it, as if he were going through the motions. That is roughly the trend of that first hour.

I think the real tone of the first hour was that I was puzzled or did not understand; there was a vagueness about it. When he came in the second time I asked, "What would you like to talk about today?" He said he had not thought of much. He felt better when he left here, and he had been all right until the weekend, when he was again at loose ends and disgusted with himself. He found himself watching television, but he pulled himself up by his bootstraps and went out with another guy and a girl. Still, he was disgusted that he had not made more of the weekend, particularly since his roommate had been away. He thought he could have done all sorts of things, which he had not done. He added, "By the way, on Tuesday that girl I was telling you about made a suicidal attempt but she is going to be all right."

He knew this girl was not good for him, and he was steeling himself to give her up, but somehow deep in him there were fires of longing for her. She had tried to commit suicide before he saw me the first time by taking drugs, and this was now a second attempt. The first time he had taken her home and had talked with her family. Her family sort of dismissed it. He knew she was neurotic. The emphasis was on the idea that this was not good for him; therefore, he should get out of it, but now is having trouble doing so. He had no reaction to the second attempt. His concern was all in terms of others. He hoped her roommates were not upset and so on. He had spent the night before coming to see me with the girl's roommate and had the following dream:

In the dream he did not have a penis. He had a leg from the knee down, and somehow this leg became a hand, and the fingers were like the tentacles of a sea anemone. This was terrifying to him.

I asked, "What do you make of that?" He could only say that the guys kid around about the penis and a third leg. I tried to piece together some kind of chronology, whom he was talking about, and so on. Two things struck me as parallels: he used practically the same words in the predictability of this girl's doing what she did and of his mother's death. It was all settled in his head that his girl was going to do something to herself. In both there was an emphasis on his lack of engagement. He does the proper things, but he is always uninvolved.

For the rest of our hour together he stressed settling down now to face this rather than running back home. He also explained he had been interested in psychological things for some time. He had friends at college who had gone to the health service there, but that had not been particularly helpful. If he had the money he would see somebody privately. He felt that help somehow was being able to talk about the things which he felt he could not tell to friends.

In general, I think that is the way our second hour went. But the sense of confusion, of discouragement and self-concern, was more on the surface than it had been.

This is an interesting individual who, in many ways, presents a typical problem encountered in this age group and this environment. One finds this everywhere, but I think the particular form it takes must be quite characteristic for the student clinic. If we forget about all the details of this case and sort of step back and let the image jell, as it were, what kind of an overall impression would you get?[1]

I get a sense of vagueness about a lot of things, a sense of being lost or looking for something. I do not know if that is what he is feeling.

What kind of vagueness? Do you have the feeling that this is a vaguely delimited person, or a person who sees the world in a vague and confused way, or who sees himself in a vague and confused way, or all of that?

I think he sees himself in a vague way and a confused way.

Is this something new that he is suffering from? Something new and acute? Something chronic? Or something recurring?

---

[1]This is typical of Kohut's initial response to an individual case.

I get the feeling that it is chronic. I do not get the feeling that it is something new.

I think it is neither new or chronic. I think it is recurrent. But it is significant. I want you to learn to pay attention when, on first hearing, one gets the impression there is something basically related to the long-term personality, and I think we all have the feeling this is true here. One perks up when one hears that there was a period when this was not so. Between six and twelve it was different. And it is quite characteristic that what he said was different. He had friends, he was accepted, he was socially engaged and had a social place. For six important years apparently he had a significant position in school, in student organizations; he was a good athlete, he had athletic success. Whether this is falsified is really not important. It is a means of communication; whether it is historically exactly right is not particularly important. For him it is right, and he tells us something when he informs us that at that time he felt particularly better. We also know there were times when he tended to feel worse. But many times in his life he has felt as he does now.

He said what he feels now is almost the way he felt when his mother died, and again when he moved west.

In short, he feels this way when there are changes. This is very frequently the case with people whose personality makeup, whose self-cohesiveness, whose secure outlook on the world is shaky; such people are particularly sensitive to any kind of change. He said that between six and twelve he was in good form, but then they moved to the west and he never made it. I think he tells you that he was shaken out of a comparatively supportive web of social school situations and, in addition, I suspect that father felt good about himself too before the move. This was probably important. Although this student says his relationship with the father is not good, he may very well be influenced by how the father feels about himself. At that time, the father, too, had a prestigious job which he lost. As he talks about himself, in a somewhat minor key he talks about his father. While his father made money in the west and did reasonably well, it was not at the level of the large concern in the east.

So there is a kind of parallel between the father's secure self-esteem and the son's secure self-esteem. I do not know what that parallel means. It may simply have something to do with feeling great to have a father who is secure. It may also have something to do with how the father reacts to the son when he himself feels secure. He may react much more acceptingly toward the son, and this may boost the son's self-esteem. When he himself, perhaps with his own uncertain self-esteem, feels less accepted, less successful, he becomes critical and belittling of his son, which in turn makes his son feel belittled and uncertain in his self-esteem. He married a woman much older than himself. The woman had a lot of money. I gather the father has a good income, but it is not the type of money or background that mother comes from. I do not know what that all means.

What is the significance of the surgery on his penis when he was a junior in high school, and how long had he been having symptoms? For a boy this age, I think that is an important aspect.

This is certainly another important area. I do not know about this particular incident. It may or may not play a role. But his body concept and the disturbance of it obviously plays some kind of role, I would imagine, not just as a symbol, but as an actual fact. The concern about the genitals and the penis must be of significance; it is something that one needs to understand and investigate. What does he look like in general? Is he a good looking man, tall, well-built?

One gets an impression of somebody who looks reasonably well, who is apparently attractive to girls, from what one can judge. There is no glandular disturbance of any kind—he has a deep voice and beard? So in that sense he is all right, but it is the feeling about his body-self that troubles him. As I said, he made a special point that between six and twelve he was athletic and was accepted in terms of his participation with the boys. Of course, twelve is puberty; that signifies a different attitude toward the genitals than before, not only in terms of himself, but also in terms of what the peer group sees, does, and how it reacts. I have no idea what the effect of the genital anomaly is. You know, a narrow meatus is perfectly harmless.

It is something that can be seen. The doctor asked him if he has trouble having intercourse, in terms of his erection. But he said, in the gym locker room, and so on, earlier, this was no problem.

But the motivating symptom he wrote down in his application was that his penis was not big enough, firm enough, and anything else?

He dated this explicitly to six months ago.

In other words, when moving from the east to Chicago. Now what do you think of that? He makes the point that this is something that is not always present. He has been around. He is a man of the world, as it were. He is proud of that. He usually performs better, but now he does not perform well. Now where is the cart and where is the horse? Is he upset because of his poor sexual performance, or is the sexual performance an indicator of his generally less secure mental and emotional state? We do not know, but we can guess, and we can discuss it.

I have the sense that the impotence problem is sort of a leading symptom, but that the major problem relates to another change, presumably coming to Chicago. Change is generally a disequilibrating experience for him, and the leading part of his disequilibrium is the impotence problem.

But the question remains, what does this poor sexual performance at present signify? I do not know the answer. I can go along with your theory, and it may be right. The sexual performance may be interfered with, not because it is a particular conflict that is aroused in him, but because there is a general lack of self-esteem, and there is less initiative, less feeling about himself, a peculiar detachment. This may be a symptom of general personality regression and of being at loose ends. He is at loose ends sexually, too, as it were.

The sexual performance is a very sensitive indicator, at least more overtly in a man, of the general emotional state. In a woman there is not as clear-cut an indication of the emotional state as the penis erection. It may be easier to hide. The poor sexual performance, then, may be part and parcel of his being at loose ends, of being detached, of trying, but not being in it, or with it, not being able to put himself into the act, sexually, and therefore the penis does not perform.

On the other hand, one should not forget that, at least within limits, sexuality is somewhat autonomous. There are many people who are capable, because of their adequate sexual performance, of regaining their self-esteem when they started out with low self-esteem. I get the feeling that here there is a little bit of each. This is already a sensitive organ, and a central part of his earlier disturbance, so it converges with this current disturbance. As I said, one's self-esteem may be low, one may feel out of initiative, but one can do something for one's self-esteem. Among the things that one will do for oneself is to perform adequately sexually. Then one suddenly feels better about oneself and can return to work in a more adequate fashion. It is a mutually influencing episode. But in his case, with a lifelong history of uncertainty about the penis, and having had operations, I would wonder.

You know, I am only speculating on the basis of other experiences. I would not be surprised that the essential connection with the self-esteem is not so much the sexual performance as the urinary performance. Grown men usually are not aware of the connection anymore—this has become subdued and suppressed—but the pride of the big and visible urinary stream in the boy is an important factor in bodily self-esteem.

Likewise, it becomes an important factor in what is often referred to as penis envy or the inferiority feelings of women, not so much that they do not have an erectile organ, or a visible genital, but because of this inability, not only visibly and in a curve to urinate, but to have the capacity to be in control of the direction of the urination. These are important psychosexual differences between the male and the female sex to which one often does not pay enough attention.

This man has to sit. I think his emphasis on his difficulty in urinating in public, at least consciously, seems to be somewhat more troubling than this mysterious business about his penis not working as well as it once did. The problem with erection, which is occasional, appeared to me to be really showing up his ambivalence about his involvement with these two girls, so that his penis kind of half works. Is the difficulty with urinating in public a structural problem, or is it perhaps more of a conflictual problem?

I have the feeling that this man, when he does have some lowering of mood, as with the change to Chicago, may focus on his penis because of previous experiences. But what we do not have an understanding of is his concentration on perhaps slightly inadequate sexual performance as measured by previous standards in regard to this girlfriend. This is the elephant in the room that we have not talked about yet. I am trying to picture what it must be like, going with a girl who has made two attempts on her life.

If he expresses some difficult feelings toward her in their relationship by slightly less adequate penile performance, then he would have another reason to focus on the penis as a displacement for not focusing on what is going on between the two of them. I feel that is a source of data that should be considered.

Did he pick a specific girl at this particular time? What kind of girl did he pick? Why did he pick somebody who is so disturbed? And what, in this specific relationship may contribute to making a sexual performance inadequate? I cannot go beyond that, because I do not know anything about this girl. We ought to know more, and you will probably learn more about her later, as the treatment goes on.

He has this other girl, too, at the same time, but the one he focuses on is the suicidal girl.

Do you know whether his performance is the same with both girls?

Yes. He has the rationalization that he does not like the one girl, and

that the other is not good for him. She is in other ways a pretty girl, who is intellectual, and they can share lots of talk, and so forth.

We will have to wait and see. My impression is that his detachment is more important than anything else, as far as the relationship to the girl is concerned. I first thought that perhaps he is detached defensively against all the excitement and anxiety about these attempts at suicide. But my hunch is that he is just picking a couple of girls who are not very meaningful to him. I cannot prove it; this is the feeling tone I have.

Being at loose ends is the first order of the day; in it all he is floundering about how he handles the draft, he is floundering about girls, he is floundering about his work habits, and he is not really involved with anything. This is the impression I have about the girls—he has two at the same time. What he is complaining about is not the girls. He is complaining about himself and his penis, that they do not perform so well. I think this is probably right.

Is it appropriate to bring up the character in the *Stranger* by Camus, who is the on-looker of events on the surface, which may be turbulent but which do not really move him?

It is perfectly appropriate to compare this, except that here we have psychologically more specific hints concerning the nature of his disengagement with the world, the uncertainty of his own constitution, the insecure base from which he operates.

We do know that given specific types of secure and lasting environments, given specific types of support, he does perform better and feel better about himself. This is very important to know, prognostically, as far as treatment is concerned. If you know that certain things have helped him in the past—not just by rote, but in terms of what they meant in the past—one can at least institute some degree of help for him on that basis. He has a sister who offered a secure base of operations. We have speculated that perhaps the father's good feeling about himself in his work in the east was a positive thing. The supportive peer group and his participation in that were important to him, not sexual performance. And we know, on the other hand, that changes in environment, losses, such as the mother's loss, the loss of the girlfriend, unbalance him. His self-esteem goes down; he flounders and then comes for help.

It is of interest that during the Christmas vacation apparently his sister got him propped up, and he came back early, sort of gung-ho to get going. Then the girl took the pills during the first week he was back.

What do you think the role of the mother is in all that? We do not know, but we can speculate. He stressed that there was no indication that the mere physical existence of the arthritis in the earliest years had already had an effect. He was properly picked up and cuddled, and properly taken care of. That sounds good; and yet here is a man with uncertainties about his performance. Of course, one might say that if he had not had the early nurturing he could be worse off. This is quite possible.

Perhaps her sudden withdrawal, if she got ill suddenly, is a factor.

The mother became ill when he was about twelve—you know, that was the time when they had to move to the west for a change of climate.

The caretaking of the mother—the physical caretaking—that must have been a very strong element in the young man's experience.

I am glad you bring this up. I think it is a fine observation. But one wants to make sure what went on there. Was that the important thing or was the teamwork with the father the important thing? This was one of the few times when these two men were doing something together.

The impression he gives was that mother was the buffer to father. He was the center of mother's universe, and mother was the center of his.

Father was sort of an outsider then? How old was the mother when he was born?

She was 45, I think.

She was 45 when he was a baby, and whether she had arthritis or not, you know, there may be something that was lacking in the responsiveness of a 45-year-old mother to a baby that would have been present in the response of a much younger mother.

There is one thing nobody has mentioned yet. He had a dream. What did he dream, or have you all suppressed it? If I understood it correctly, the dream had sort of an empty space in the middle. Something was not dreamt about, as it were. Instead, he dreamt of his leg, which became his hand, as something grasping, a sea anemone, with all these tentacles, soft and grasping. Didn't you say the dream started with his seeing there was no penis where there should have been a penis? And with a leg from the knee down? Now what does your imagination tell you?

The most impressive thing is that something is missing. The upper part of the leg is missing, and instead of a penis, he has half a leg. In the dream he was frightened. This was the night after the girl attempted

suicide and he was spending it with the girl's roommate, with the rationalization that it would somehow bolster her.

So what would you guess? Of course, we do not know any associations to the dream, and we should not really allow ourselves to speculate, but how can one help it?

His association was, "It's Freudian."

What are your fantasies about it?

This fellow was concerned about the loss of this girl, which returns to the theme of something missing. Half of something is gone with this leg. We speculate that he is focused on the penis, and that if something were missing, and the fear over this girl dying or whatever, that might represent what is gone for him.

This fellow reminds me of a male patient whose prevailing mood of detachment and fear of involvement turns out to be a literal narcissistic loss of substance when he has intercourse. From that recollection of my patient, my thought about the dream is that the girl might be experienced as a mirror, or a twinning, and that having to go to stay with the roommate is for the sake of feeling whole— granted, only half whole, if he does not have the satisfactory experience in his body with her. That is my fantasy.

It is close to what I think, but I would put it a little differently. There is no harm if one allows oneself to speculate in a totally tentative way and it fits so well with many other things we have speculated about. This dream may not be a useful entry, as far as treatment is concerned, to help him with his impotence, but it may give one a first hint of why he is partially impotent.

I think in the dream, if I translate it crudely and literally, he says, "My penis does not serve the usual purpose in intercourse. It has other meanings to me. It has meanings like the tentacles of a sea anemone. It sucks itself on, it takes something in, it grabs something, and it wants to get something. It has a tentacle-like quality, a grasping quality, wanting something. This is not the essential thing in the male part of intercourse, freely giving of something." It is the wish to grab, and it may very well be, if one wants to use the word self-esteem, to grab just that. What does he want from the girls? To come back again to what we have said so many times, he does not love a girl because she is her unique self. But he is proud of being a man of the world. He uses intercourse for raising self-esteem. Because the penis is used for this particular purpose, when his self-esteem is low, it cannot become hard, because it is a grasping, wanting-to-get-something, holding-on kind of an instrument.

Whether this is right or not I do not know. But I think it fits well into his depressed feeling after the girl in the west abandoned him. It fits well with his general outlook about himself at the present time. It fits well with the leading symptom. He says his penis is not hard, it is not strong, and then he dreams about it as if it were not there. Instead, there is the grasping hand with tentacles like a sea anemone. What is a sea anemone? If you have ever stuck your finger at a sea anemone, then you know it sucks you in. He must know it, because he lives in an area where a sea anemone can be readily found.

The leading symptom of this individual seems to be that he uses his penis emotionally, for a purpose that is not intrinsically meant to be performed by the penis. It is a soft grasping hand, like a sea anemone. In addition, it is not firmly attached to his trunk, as it were. Obviously, I am playing a bit with the manifest content of the dream, but it fits so well with so many other things that I think it is permissible to allow this speculation.

One of Freud's early theories (1910a, pp. 217–218; 1914c, pp. 83–84), which in many ways became the basis for much of later psychosomatic medicine, was that organs become diseased when chronically used for emotional purposes for which they are not designed. He differentiated between hysterically determined physical dysfunctions and patho-neuroses, now often called organ neuroses, which are the chronic result of such an emotional use of an organ.

As you know, in the early emotional history of the child, the penis is the last of the several leading organ zones, as it were, a leading aspect of the body-mind-self, which becomes the carrier of pride, the major narcissistic investment, a symbol of the self. Of course, one must not see this in isolation. If you think back, you will discover that quite early in our sessions here, when I talked to you about the two early phases in the formation of the self, I described the self-nuclei, the autoerotic state in which individual functions and body parts become important as they are used or stimulated at any given moment, as if they were not just parts of a total self that has a name.

When I speak about the leading zone of the personality or of the self, I do not mean this in a detached way. I mean this as the convergence, as the focal point of all that is good, right, healthy, progressive, forward looking and active about the self. The pride of a well-functioning, let us say, lip-nipple unit, whatever that early self may be from what one can rediscover in regressive experiences and from empathically watching a baby when he is sucking and enjoying himself in a healthy way in the hunger and satiation experience—this is the leading part of an early self.

To this early self, however, there is firmly attached a cohesive set of experiences that belong to it.

The same is true for the later experiences in the muscular zone when the child begins to walk. The same is true in the babbling-talking zone when the child begins to take delight in the noises he makes and is phase-appropriately responded to by the admiring audience of his parents. What to a nonhuman visitor to our planet might look awfully strange—these admiring sessions of grownups around babies—are really perfectly appropriate and life-sustaining responses that support and fit into the needs of the growing child. The important issue is that it be phase-appropriate.

In the dream of this patient, there is no gap between the mouth-leg experience and the rest of the body-mind experience; it is only the leading part. The important issue is that phallic narcissism is not only a phase appropriate narcissism. It is also the narcissism that in both sexes deals with a straightening out of the total body musculature. The sense of conquering space which the boy has in the urinary stream and by the erection of his penis because it is visible, and the envy of the girl in whom the stream does not traverse space, as it were, make the important differences in the way a healthy boy and a healthy girl look upon themselves, and in their character formation (Greenacre, 1957, 1960). The importance of phallic narcissism and its reverberations is not only that it is one of many other leading zones, but also that it is the last one of all those that still need optimal parental responsiveness. It still refers to that period of life in which childhood sexuality is the dominant theme in the personality. After that there is, as it were, a curtain drawn, and ego autonomous learning and activities take over what formerly was libidinally oriented or childhood aggressively oriented activity and pride. This happens in both sexes.[2]

It is the tragedy of many individuals that they have not experienced this particular phase-appropriate sense of their limitations. To understand this one has to know more than that there is a penis or phallus, in the boy, or even a phallically predominant zone in the female. One has to krow that there is a set of cohesive fantasies that relate to the family situation. And this particular set of fantasies to some extent has to be disappointed, so that the major next step is also supported through this

---

[2]Kohut later modified this view to reflect his belief that if such experiences are responded to phase-appropriately and empathically, the child's grandiosity is modified. The oedipal phase is successfully managed.

particular disappointment. Phase-appropriately the child is then ready to give up these aspirations and to turn toward much less exciting, much less immediate pleasure-giving activities, such as preoccupation with abstract symbols, the preoccupation with learning tasks. All things that in psychoanalysis we call the secondary process, thought processes or psychological processes, come later. The primary ones are those that are directly under the domination of the drives. In secondary processes, it is the delay and refinement of the task performance, as in logical and abstract thinking, that gives one the type of pride which is specifically human.

Human beings are proud, essentially, and rightfully so, because the tasks they can perform, with the aid of the secondary processes, are ever so much greater than the tasks they can perform under the influence of the thrust of a direct drive. Of course, the integration of both is important, too, but this is another story.

A shift thus takes place that is to some extent aided by a particular set of disappointing experiences around the last infantile libido-oriented aspirations of the phallic pride and the phallic performance with the phallic organ.

What I am stressing here, however, is the word phallic. It is an organ meant to serve still exhibitionistic attitudes. The pride in the tumescence of the organ, the urinary stream through space, and of course the sensations, so intense, that are tied up with feelings of conquest and feelings of pride are shifted to pride in the whole body. The blows to the expectations of the child immediately evoke in everybody, nowadays, a reasonably correct meaning of the terms oedipus complex, oedipal disappointment, oedipal defects. However, what I am stressing here is that it is on the basis of the abandonment of phallic narcissism that the important shift takes place in a variety of ways. That same type of pride toward this expanding organ is now shifted toward expansion of ego activities. Then general attitudes toward the exploration and conquest of the world, toward exerting power and asserting oneself socially in the peer group, take over what is abandoned in the direct unmitigated concentrated pride around the last leading organ of the early zones. There may be particular aberrations, for example infantile fantasies remaining too highly cathected because the mother praises the child more than she praises the father, making the child feel he is more important to her than the father. Then he does not see the father as the great victor with whom he clearly knows he cannot compete in the direct physical sphere, but rather sees himself, a little boy, as greater than the father. Any particular shortcomings experienced at this time fixate the child on an original phallic narcissism and then do not allow him this shift in pride toward more ego autonomous and more inhibited performances, which, after all, form the basis for real success later in life.

I am now talking about the end of the oedipal period, not about the beginning of the oedipal period. Obviously, interferences of a mother who is afraid of the penis of the little boy, who cannot let the little boy have his independence in terms of his own sensations, who is envious because she had a little brother, or whatever it may be that does not allow her, at the beginning of this period, to accept the child's pride in his penis and in his general small male body, creates a more basic disturbance in his pride even before it needs to be shifted. Disturbances early in that phase have a totally different meaning from later disturbances. First, the pride has to become firm, but later the child has to be helped to abandon it. This is a rather long period from around four to six. The subdivision of that period needs to be understood and studied in detail.

At this moment I do not think I need to go into specifics of female psychology since the patient we are dealing with is a man and his disturbances are in male development. All I want to say here is that in both sexes normal development leads from the phallic pride to a shift from direct preoccupation with the genital zone. In other words, in the typical male development, there is a shift to the development of a total image of his own mind and body that has certain traces of the particular male phallic exhibitionistic performance, forward moving, conquering of space, moving outward into new directions. There is no need to excuse myself or to describe what I am saying as male prejudice toward female psychology. Many easy analyses are made of this, but I see no evidence to the contrary that this particular genital development does indeed tend to make use of the male intellect, in general, somewhat different from the use of the woman's intellect. I think in male psychology, on the basis of these early experiences of the body, there is more of a conquest of space, this reaching toward new insights or toward the not-yet-reached. It is interesting that nowhere have I found better descriptions of this than in the writing of a woman, Phyllis Greenacre (1952), in her descriptions of the phallic phase.

Even before this final shift takes place, that is, the decathexis, the abandonment of the prideful importance in that leading zone, even before the shift is toward the general use of the body-mind as a unit in learning, conquering, maintaining, and in internalized image, there is an imbrication between later use in pregnancy, for example, of one's body and mind that is predetermined already in the young girl toward the end of the oedipal period. In the little girl, as you know, the absence, by comparison with the little boy, of the visible phallus and the visible urinary stream results in a shift, even before the final shift toward autonomous use of the mind and the body, toward a total use of body that reflects pleasure in self-containedness, in preservation.

In general, I think girls are the better learners. They are the better hoarders of knowledge, the better containers of knowledge, and derive greater pleasure in the collection of knowledge in books and in proper notes. I am talking about smaller children now. Boys, with their urge toward new things, may not have that patience or that pleasure in the containment of the already known which is the early phase of learning. It is my impression, and I think it is generally correct, that if you examine learning successes of the sexes, girls are ahead of boys in the early years of learning and the boys get ahead when the conquest of unusual concepts is demanded. These are only general trends, of course, and have nothing to do with individual girls or individual boys, but I think there is a certain validity when one thinks of it in general terms.

What I am talking about now is a general psychology determined by the male phallic phase versus a general psychology determined by the female phallic phase, and the early shift during the oedipal phase toward the total body configuration as a contained prideful self. In the use of the body, there is no question that the coquettishness of the late oedipal girl is very different from the attitude of the boy. I doubt very much indeed that these are simply reflections of the predominant parental expectations because of the cultural dominance of such expectations. There is a give and take between culture and biopsychology; peculiarities of specific cultural developments may hide underlying psychobiological trends. I think it is particularly difficult for outsiders to penetrate what seems to be the surface behavior in another culture. One first has to learn the total emotional language of that culture. I would imagine, at least to some extent, that this is psychologically determined.

But then, in both sexes, after this still directly body-performance-bound psychological attitude, a further shift is made away from all the drive dominance of the early phase. With the end of the oedipal fantasy—with the end of the fantasy of the little girl that she will be capable of being penetrated, and get the baby, that great gift from daddy, and give it back to him, and of the little boy, that he will be the one that does away with the father, and will give that great forward-moving, penetrating, and aggressive gift to the mother—after this has been shattered, then in the further healthy development, self-confidence is not broken. It is simply shifted. It is then shifted to the autonomous activity of the latency boy and the latency girl in learning and in the aim-inhibited skills that are then supported in their particular way, sex-appropriately or gender-appropriately, by an understanding environment.

I would imagine that even the teacher behaves, whether he knows it or not, in a somewhat different way toward girls and toward boys. He expects different excellence. He takes for granted different excellence. He has more patience with the boys' impatience about learning and less patience with the girls' impatience, if it is there. In other words, there is an expectation that fits the specific development.

Why is all this important? You obviously are not treating latency children. You are not even treating puberty children in general. Maybe one or another of you has had experiences with very young adolescents. On the whole, however, you are treating people in the last of the great early transitional phases, namely, the changeover from adolescence to early adulthood, generally under the impact of a change in environment. The external change, leaving home, leaving the peer group that one has gone with through high school to come into a new environment or at least to face tasks of a totally different nature, which are now geared toward a professional career or toward the adult establishment of adult goals which will be permanently away from the home, usually sets up reverberations. Any transitional phase later in life sets up reverberations of the earlier ones. And the shortcomings in the transitions of the early phases tend to be revived again when later analogous steps have to be undertaken.

So when we consider this young adult of 22, who has undertaken a significant career step and is in his first year of graduate work, who is now with a group of people all of whom are potential competitors for important positions later in life, he experiences a replica of all the previous transitional phases, including the one from the end of the oedipal period to the beginning of latency. Therefore, it is by no means strange that old conflicts about these leading zones of the self should become the symbolic carriers of conflicts that deal broadly now with the personality and how it will assert itself. The use of his penis to obtain some degree of self-confidence, to hang onto the girl, although she is really important to him only as a source of increased self-esteem, is not generally characteristic for a 22-year-old. It may yet be totally characteristic for a young adolescent.

For a young adolescent the early sexual experiences do not tend to be love experiences. They tend to be experiences that are self-confirming of one's masculinity. They are boasted about and talked about. They are generally clearly not additions to a love experience. I am not drawing hyper-idealistic pictures. For individuals at any age there is an accrual of self-esteem from the capacity to have a successful love experience both in the sexual and the psychological sense. To be capable of commanding another person's love, or to give another person the pleasure with one's adequate sexual performance, is a bonus; it is in addition to a much broader kind of relationship.

But the point of gravity in a young adolescent is very different. There may be some early adolescents in whom the love experience plays a great role. But I think most of us would think of this as puppy love.

This is only a background to the significance of sexual symptomatology not only when the broad adjustment to a new psychosocial situation is involved, but also when there are no leading sexual symptoms, as a background to the assessment of the type of problem in transition from any one phase to another.

10

Further Understanding of the Emergence and Subsiding of a Physical Symptom at a Time of Transition

TRANSITIONS DO NOT have to be age-specific and typical, such as one encounters on entering college or graduate school, but they can be brought about by any major change in life. In the case we are discussing (presented first in Chapter 9), one has the feeling that almost any kind of shift in permanent residence will create old anxieties about having to start afresh, because this student seems to depend so much for his self-esteem on a stable environment that knows him, confirms who he is, and responds to him. The experience of this man, with his improvement after seeing the therapist twice, is quite in line with the feeling that there is some kind of center now to which he can relate, which takes him seriously, knows him by name, pays specific and undivided attention to him for an hour. His therapist is somebody who is dignified and an important member of the university community.

I think for that reason a student mental health center plays a particular kind of role. I would imagine that many a youngster going on his own to somebody who is on the faculty, who is also directly connected with the prestige hierarchy of the university, finds in that a different meaning from going to somebody who has an office somewhere for people with problems. Independent of all other qualifications, even comparing an enormously experienced psychotherapist downtown with a comparative novice who is taking his first steps as a psychotherapist at the university, there is an immediate impact on the student seeking help from a person connected with the university hierarchy. This may be much more therapeutic than having to seek help outside the web of the university environment. This would be particularly true for brief therapy, where no deeper engagement of the psychopathology in the transference relationship is to be fostered. Let us now go on with the case.

In this third interview there seemed to be more of a spring in his step, and a little more life in his eyes. The first thing he told me was that he felt better after he left last time. He called his sister's family for the phone number of a girl cousin who has been a very good friend of his in the past. They have drifted apart, because she apparently became more liberal then he. That night he went out to dinner with the roommate of the girl who made the suicidal attempt. Her parents were also there and he was jumpy, could not eat, and was kind of silent. By the time he got himself home he was on the verge of crying. He said he was kind of choked up, and his face was wet, and he was kind of sniffling, but it did not sound as if he ever really cried. He called his sister. He could not let on to her how bad he felt. If he really let his sister know how he felt, somehow he would be flawed in her eyes. He is something special to her. On the other hand, he also called her daughter, who is his niece and peer, and somehow it was safe to let her know his real feelings. So he called both of them that night.

He also felt guilty after leaving me. There were two things—one, that he got out alive, and the other that he didn't come clean. Then, after talking to his niece, he called the sister back to reassure her that he was all right. He did not want to add to her upset because she had her hands full. The issues about guilt were sprinkled through this hour. From then until the next time he came, he had trouble getting to sleep. On going to bed, he ruminates over the day; it has more often to do with how he's behind in school, and he has early morning awakenings.

I asked him if there was any dreaming connected with this, and he said, "No. There is nothing like what I told you last time," but went on to indicate that he thought he was sleeping much more lightly than he usually does, and is aroused by external noises. That is the way the week went.

Then he and his roommate decided to have a party on Saturday. He had a date, but the date instead set him up with a blind date. This blind date and he then went off to another party, and somehow out of that, he felt rejuvenated. On Sunday he took himself in hand in relation to his academic work and decided he was going to drop a course and concentrate on the other two courses. On Monday he saw the dean and accomplished the change. He also called his father and told him not that he has been feeling bad, that he is behind, but that what he has done is a good move. I gather that since then he has been feeling relatively well.

Some of the other information that came out in this interview is that he got involved with this girl the first quarter here. I think there was a kind of ripening in it, and a lot of expectations on both their parts. Just before Christmas vacation she was much more forward and serious about their becoming engaged. He was having his reservations, holding back because she was ''neurotic.'' He felt that he was on guard. He went home with her, and on to his own, and then returned to campus. When she returned, she made her first suicidal attempt. That was that, as far as he was concerned; it was too dangerous a business to be in. He wanted out, but he had to be a good guy.

After several flights from the hospital, she made another attempt on her life. Through all this turmoil he was sure that he should get out. His concern for himself was that he would get hurt if he became involved with her; it sounded as if this hurt would then make it impossible in the future to become involved with somebody else, that his guard would go up totally, and that would be the end. If his mother were alive he could show her how he felt, because somehow his mother had seen him with a child's emotion. But the sister, who was really the ''mother,'' has not seen him so; therefore, he has to be the strong guy.

In part, some of his earlier upset about himself seems related to what you were talking about. At his previous college he would really cram for exams. They were set up so that it was possible. There was a two-week reading period, and the exams were spaced. He would make arrangements to go with a friend to the library and would spend from 9 to 12 there, go back to the fraternity house for lunch, horse around some, then go back to the library for the afternoon, and again at night. He was proud of the amount of investment of energy that would go into his work.

Here, he was not able to perform in that way. In part, he thought it was related to finding it easier if he had a buddy to do it with, and that here he had to do it alone. Another thing is that he does not have a buddy here to share anything with; all he had were these girls. With them he really has to be the strong man rather than the man who is upset. And he got quite upset earlier this summer when it somehow became clear that he was the needy one to the girl rather than the strong one.

In describing his tearfulness, in response to my asking him when that had happened before, he went back to the time when he and an aunt were going through some of mother's possessions after she died. He was all choked up, and went out and got himself a shot of bourbon; that seemed to calm him down. I think that's the substance of that hour.

Of course, a lot is still in the air, but I think there are a number of general issues that one can see very clearly in this individual. Does anybody wish to make any comments?

The most striking thing to me about this person's improvement is that he is consolidating his scholastic debt. He looked over his course load and decided actively to drop one course and concentrate on the others.

What does that mean? To me it means a reassertion of ego dominance and initiative. He actively does something to plan his future. He faces reality—what is bygone is bygone. One cannot cry over spilled milk. This is the situation as it is now; as of now, it is a new beginning.

There is an active taking hold of the situation, which means a kind of resurgence of ego autonomous attitudes. As you remember, I have talked about this many times before. Whenever you see this, it is the opposite of a vicious cycle; having done this, he also feels better because he has taken hold. The question is, what has allowed the initial rise in self-esteem which then secondarily accounts for his becoming active and taking hold of a difficult reality situation?

There is something very interesting and very important about his rise in self-esteem which should give you food for thought. He first calls his sister who is 20 years older. He then calls his niece, emotionally speaking a sister to him. He gets no help from the first, but he seems to get a great deal of help from the second. Why is that? I think that is very easy to understand. This is a person who as a child and youngster was faced with the problems of parents a great deal older than he. They were more like grandparents. At least the age gap was quite significant. When he was 15, mother had severe late arthritis. When she was in her middle sixties she was already close to death. This was a grandparental kind of gap in attitude. These were parents who did not have—again, I can only guess, but everything seems to fit and hold together—the freedom, the capacity to concentrate on the child's problems.

The opposite was true; the child had to put his own developmental problems second and had to live in the predominant terms of the older generation's needs and difficulties. He and the father took care of the arthritic mother. He had to face the death of a mother during the time when everything in him was concentrated on his own developmental tasks. This is very important. Children seem so heartless, and yet you know that is the way it should be. They do not participate in the tragedies of the family when they are small. It is amazing how autonomous their developmental tasks are. You can read heart-breaking stories about concentration camps, where the children go right on with their developmental tasks while generations of adults are being murdered next to them. There are great and moving papers of some of these events, like the paper on group upbringing, by A. Freud and Dann (1951).

The important thing they describe is the autonomous capacity of the psychobiological organism to turn to its own task and to disregard even the enormous catastrophes that go on around it. As with a young plant growing in an area where there is an earthquake, it goes right on with its own task. It does not pay attention to the earthquake. However, children are not quite as lucky as these little plant shoots that I am talking about. They are more influenced by the tasks of the environment. They are made guilty. They feel awful; in a sense, "My mother is dying but I don't care about this. It is not my business that my mother is dying. At this particular time I'm much more interested in how I'll relate to girls and how I'll move on to college." And there is a kind of guilt about the fact that one really should care, because everybody is crying about mother dying.

I think such feelings were probably quite characteristic for a boy who was such a late comer in a family with parents who did not have the give to allow the child to have this kind of developmental autonomy. There is a sense of guilt-ladenness about it. He seeks out a girl for his own needs of security, but the girl turns out to be like his old mother: she is problem-laden. She is deeply disturbed; she buys knives and takes suicidal pills. His reaction is not, "I love you, and I want to protect you," but rather, "I want to get rid of you. This is not what I need." In the same way he must have felt, "For goodness sake, mother, die already."

I have seen this a number of times. There is a vague guilt feeling, and then tremendous relief when the therapist understands and says, "I can understand why you felt that way. It is sort of your right at 16 to feel that way about it. It is a terrible thing to have to face—that your mother whom you loved and whom you also didn't want to die was suffering a terminal illness. And yet, at that time, everything in you cried out, "For goodness sake, if she were only done with dying so that I could go on without guilt and without preoccupation with these extraneous things, and be interested in girls and school tasks." Such states are particularly noticeable in individuals who have chronically ill parents.

There is a beautiful case that I have studied well. It is not a case I am treating myself, but that I have described through the eyes of somebody whom I have supervised. This is the man who paints the analyst without the eyes and the nose when he separates from him. This man had a mother with chronic malignant hypertension. This mother could not respond to him because she was preoccupied with her own slow death. She had kidney disease and strokes. She had a worsening of malignant hypertension right after the boy was born. He was a premature baby, and he was in an incubator, so he did not have the kind of maternal responsiveness he should have had. He had these terrible feelings of wishing his mother dead. She died at approximately the age he wanted the mother dead; and yet the mother was useless to him. This was the man who had for the first time the severe symptom of perverse voyeurism in male bathrooms after the mother did not respond to him when he wanted to go on a ferris wheel. He wanted to have his mother admire him, and the mother was too tired and too ill and said, "I can't. I'm too tired." Then his whole pride and exhibitionism dropped, and he walked off for the first time to a male restroom and began to look for the big male genital with which he then wanted to identify. If he himself could not be the proud phallus substitute, as it were, and have his mother's admiration that way, he got it in this merger through looking. But this is a side issue.

The main point of analogy here is that he felt terribly guilty later on when he wanted his mother to die. And he had near delusional feelings. There was a very early delusional state that this particular patient had—it sounds much more serious than it was—during the time of his mother's death. He ate fish at one time, and he thought the fish was looking at him, that it was alive as he ate it. It had something to do with his relationship to his mother: killing through eating, and all the depressive, regressive feelings that were revived at that particular period.

All these things receded beautifully when the patient was understood, when one could tell him that this was a perfectly acceptable state, and that one could understand both his tremendous guilt as well as his need to withdraw.

It is so beautifully delineated in the case we are discussing here. When the girl friend turns out to be another mother who drives him away rather than giving him what he needs, who is preoccupied with her own hysterical conflicts and suicidal behavior, he loses interest and says, "That's not for me." Yet he feels terribly guilty. He feels a kind of coldness. He should be feeling something for the poor dying mother, but he cannot, because he is in the relationship for himself, to make the next developmental step. And nobody in the older generation can understand him. It is only when a peer finally talks to him that he feels relief.

I am certain this sister figure, this niece of his, did not have to say anything special. It was just her directly understanding attitude, "That's the way our kind feels." This is what gives him relief. There is a twin of some kind, somebody who confirms him by feeling like him. Then he can use his therapist. He can come back with a bounce. There may also be something in the way you respond to him. You are not an authoritarian father figure. You are still at the university. I would not doubt at all that there is probably something brotherly in your attitude that is much more helpful to such a person, an understanding that of course he felt an increase of guilt and a gap between his sister's generation and his own.

The seeming coldness, the seeming egotism while one has to perform an internal task of development or growth, can arouse terrific conflicts in people. From nobody, then, can one get as much support or as much permission to be one's own self in one's own developmental tasks as from somebody who appears to be in the same boat. Therefore, as thera-pist, one must not be an authority at that particular time, but something like a playful older brother who is not as involved as the student is in this kind of difficulty.

That is why some individuals are particularly good with adolescents. I think this is more personality specific, the gift of treating adolescents or young adults; otherwise, I think the personality of the therapist is specif-ic only in negatives. That is, there are certain types of cases with which certain therapists cannot deal very well. They may have overcome earlier traumata but in so doing they have been taxed so deeply that they cannot allow the necessary regression which would enable them to be in tune with their patient. If the patient is a direct replica of some of the most traumatic experiences of such a therapist, then this is not a case for him. But when the specifics of the personality of the therapist are positive, the situation is somewhat different.

I think, on the whole, one should be capable of treating all kinds of personalities and personality disturbances, give and take, a little better or a little less well. This is the pleasure of our work, being capable of relating to many different kinds of people. One cannot live many differ-ent kinds of lives, but one can be empathic with different types of per-sonalities. I think the capacity to set up an immediately workable bond with adolescents or with young adults is much facilitated if one has this freedom to be particularly empathic with this age group. One has re-tained some of the positive enjoyment of this developmental phase. Although one has made a commitment to one's career and to one's life, one still has retained some of that playfulness, some of the tentativeness, which other people, who have become so dignified as adults, have per-haps abandoned.

I think people who tend to like to remain in an academic atmosphere may have some of that freedom and some of that capacity. Again, one cannot generalize. There are a variety of things which may account for the therapist's choice of setting, but I would not doubt that this quality is to some extent there. I do not count myself out. I do not work in an academic atmosphere, but I have a great deal of feeling for it.

How is the concept of neutralization related to your description of the way in which activities turn from being libidinally dominated to more drive independent activities?

Neutralization is a mechanism, and I am not talking about specific mechanisms. I was trying to describe a shift in the total personality attitude vis-à-vis the drives and independent external tasks. Neutralization is one of the mechanisms that is gradually acquired, and one which is necessary if one is to become capable of performing these tasks. It is, however, a comparatively narrow mechanism.

Neutralization deals essentially with the concept that drives are originally present in a very crude, direct, primary, sexual and aggressive form. And as psychological structure is built up, neutralization allows the psyche to shift and change the nature of the drive, so that what was originally a directly pleasure-seeking, sexually exciting goal, now becomes an experience. The nature of the drive experience itself changes. The directness of sexual pleasure and the direct expression and experience of aggression disappear. There are only hints of it present, and they are all way stations.

I have very recently been struggling with a way to express this and coined the term *a sieve in depth*. In other words, psychological structure is gradually acquired through various experiential interactions with the environment, so that layer after layer of a yet sieve-like substance is built up. Gradually, as the child grows older, the original, direct, sexual, aggressive experience of the instinct becomes delibidinized, desexualized, de-instinctivized, de-aggressivized.

Would you elaborate on your phrase ''a sieve in depth'' and its relationship to structure?

Structure *is* a sieve in depth. In other words, the final structure is a kind of sieve in depth. Let us say an aggressive drive, originally a clearly instinctual one, a strong raging experience of the baby or young child, is opposed by educational counterforces, whatever they may be, such as deflection from the aggressive aim responded to with love or by prohibition. "Don't do this, but you can do this. You can do it in this way, but not in the originally direct way. You can complain, but you must not bite or scratch."

Each of these countermeasures is, in a way, a tiny loss of an object: this aspect you cannot have. The principle is that for any loss of object in the external world an internal replica is set up. Something is permanently laid down in the psyche that continues internally to fulfill the very function which this outside prohibition performed, this outside countering of one drive with another drive. Let us say a sexual maneuver is countered by an aggression from the side of the parents, and an aggressive impulse is countered with love. These internal replicas of the loss, the frustrating, inhibiting or prohibiting aspect of the external environment, are permanently laid down. And anything that is permanently laid down, even a memory trace, one might call a psychological structure. An external function is now permanently performed endopsychically. We assume that this happens billions of times in all periods during the child's growing up. A structure is formed through which the original drive goes, but as it goes through it is progressively less instinctual. The end result in the psyche, as I said, can be seen in the analogy of a sieve in depth. It is not just a one-layered sieve, but a multi-layered sieve. As it finally emerges, there are still certain elements in common with what it originally was, but it has been neutralized. An aggression becomes less aggressive.

Let us say the firmness with which one is able to devote oneself to a task, the firmness with which one pushes aside disturbances, may still have traces of an instinctually aggressive beginning. But it is not truly aggressive anymore. It has become highly neutralized. When we firmly concentrate on a task, we no longer feel that this is an aggressive action. When we sink our teeth into a new idea and think about it, we no longer really think about biting. Yet there is still a little bit of the original aggression left, a little bit of the moral reaction, the firmness, and there is still something of the original strength or the pushing away. In analyzing the complex act, it may still have a trace of the old tearing apart by the teeth of something that was whole, but it has lost the aggressive, experiential meaning. So neutralization, one line, as it were, on which the original instinct can be handled, is performed by the psyche in depth, and this I compared to the sieve in depth.

How does neutralization, then, fit into the whole concept of sublimation?

The important issue is that neutralization is a mechanism. It is just one aspect of the many changes. First of all, it must be understood that it is not the height of maturity to have *only* desexualized and de-aggressivized experience. It is part and parcel of maturity to be capable *also* of having sexual and aggressive experiences. In other words, infantilism or defect in this particular area will not permit de-aggressivized or desexualized experiences in areas that are not sexual and aggressive. I can give you a very good example.

This is a patient with years of successful analysis behind him. You will recall that I mentioned him in the context of gradually shifting from gross identifications toward very aim-inhibited identifications with me

(p. 85 et seq.). Recently this person mentioned that he was pleased with a certain kind of work he is doing, that he got some reverberations of acceptance. He came in rather buoyantly, after a very important piece of work that we had done in the session before, which had only taken hold after the session. For ten days or two weeks before this he had been more flat than usual, particularly in his relationship to me. In the session yesterday I finally discovered what was causing this flatness. Something I had done had hurt his feelings. It was difficult to get at what the hurt was because I had also done something good for him which covered over something that was bad. Without going into details, it was hard to get at, but I had finally caught on. He could not immediately accept it, but he kept working on it, and then felt relieved. He again had dreams: in other words, he was again very involved in the relationship and work in the analysis. In addition, he could also enjoy himself more generally and he came in with this buoyant feeling. When he had told me all this, about how he enjoyed his work, and how well things were going, he mentioned, as if it had no relationship, that he had a peculiar erotic feeling in the shaft of his penis. And he wondered what this was all about and to whom he was sexualizing.

I said, "I know the relationship which you are sexualizing. You're sexualizing the relationship to yourself." Namely, he was pleased with himself. He still had a little remnant of the old isolated and very abstruse sexual feelings about himself which were present early in life. Then he had felt very isolated and lonesome; sexual fantasies were abstruse and of a bizarre nature; his penis played a fantastic role. It was not the enjoyable penis of a phallic boy, but more a substitute for self. This feeling in the penis was a little echo of this past. Here he was talking about himself.

When we talk about ourselves and our pleasure in ourselves, most of us have an enjoyable feeling, but it is not a self-sexual excitement. He had the beginning of an erection. He had the beginning of an erotic feeling in his penis as he was talking about what good work he was doing. So there is just a trace left, late in the analysis, just enough to understand better now what had happened before, and to bring the past and the present in the course of these years of analytic work into some cohesive integration. He understood immediately and there was no question about the correctness of this understanding. Now here was a lack of the *neutralization* of the self enjoyment. It was still sexual, even though isolated.

Sexualization does not relate only to one's love relationships to others. Resexualization is an important issue in the transference neurosis where the inner conflict about others is at stake. For instance, Freud described the symptom of writer's cramp in hysteria, when there are fantasies in which the writing takes on the oedipal fantasy of the penis penetrating into an incestuous object. When this happens because of the strong sexualization of the nonsexual activity, an inhibition takes place or a symptom develops. All I am adding here is that the same is true, not only in terms of instincts or fantasies that are directed toward other people, not only as a reversion to an infantile experience in which the incestuous interfamilial object produces the conflict when there would be no conflict if it were a mature relationship to a present-day object, but also with instincts that do not refer to others but to the self.

In the case I described, instead of pleasurable, nonsexual self-esteem, there were still traces of the original crudely sexual exhibitionism now no longer phase-appropriate. A little boy may phase-appropriately still get a terrific sexualized kick out of the way he urinates the first few times when he sees himself perform or becomes aware of his performance. But this gradually becomes channeled into an interest in, for example, fire engines, into excitement when one hears the sirens, and it later becomes channeled into playing with fire equipment. It becomes more or less crudely translated into more aim-inhibited and deflected behavior. Then these various activities finally become secondarily autonomous. They sever all connections with the original source of sexual enjoyment.

In this tiny vignette, for one second, there was a resexualization of something that should have been smoothly integrated as a nonsexual self enjoyment. Therefore, the danger is still of overexcitement, overstimulation, less than optimal enjoyment, less than smoothly integrated pleasure in oneself in the usual experience. If one's exhibitionistic pleasure in talking becomes very great, then some people become tongue-tied; they become embarrassed, they blush, and are obviously ill at ease. Why are they ill at ease? Because something uncomfortable of the old, still crude, sexual aspect of their enjoyment in themselves begins to interfere with the present situation.

As a personal example, I went to several parties the other night. At the first party I played a couple of pieces. There weren't many people around, and I knew the pieces completely. I went to a second party, and there was a group of ten or fifteen people intensely listening. And when I became aware of that, my memory failed completely. There was a piece that I had not played for a while, but at the previous party I went right through it—that same evening.

You, as the center of attention, being stared at and listened to—whatever fantasy it stirred up in you, led to inhibiting you. That is a perfectly good example. From my own practice, I have similar examples of a pianist whom I analyzed at one time. These sudden memory defects, which almost all pianists dread, are very common, because of the closeness to the original drive. This is very important, particularly among performing artists. I would think that sieve I described is not very deep in performing artists. Contrary to what one might think, their performance has not become a highly autonomous and totally nonsexualized activity, at least not in a good many of these artists.

This also leads us into the whole realm of high-level creativity in which also the sieve is not very deep. There may be sudden intrusions of sexualized or disturbed thinking which alternate with thinking of very high caliber, particularly in a passionate artistic production, which sometimes takes place in a kind of frenzied way. The disturbance potential is therefore very great. The nearness to the primary process, to the original instinctual mode of experiencing, creates a kind of intensity that must be matched by an ego's capacity to handle this in a very high-level performance, and not everyone can do this. Most of us can work only when our tensions are well-neutralized and well-sieved. Only then can we perform well within the realm of our limitations. Crude exhibitionism is very close to the surface. I have had interesting glimpses of this with patients in whose dreams there was a breakthrough of crudely exhibitionistic behavior in childhood which was matched in the performance and then began to paralyze the performer. In individual instances, one cannot tell from the surface behavior that performance is being inhibited but there is an interrelationship between the depth, as it were, of the instinctual source of the activity and the actual performance. Performance can become inhibited when the instinctual urge is too great. When the ego is asked to perform, the original instinctual aim suddenly intrudes. "I don't want to play anymore. I really want to be naked and be admired by a crowd." All this then becomes immediately inhibited and the performance, too, is inhibited.

Is it possible to make any generalization about what effect analysis itself has on that process?

I do not know how to answer this. It is too great a generality. I have never known of an example of a very, very great artist. Good artists, I believe, are clearly helped by analysis. The interferences are mastered and are better understood. I would have a hard time differentiating between the effect of analysis on a creative genius, and what you probably have more in mind, a performing artist. I would speculate that it depends a little on the kind of analysis. Freud was very cautious about it. He generally did not undertake the analysis of great artists. He saw them a few times, gave them some advice, provided them with a few wildly given, deep insights—something he never did with anyone else. He did this clearly with some great artists, as with Gustav Mahler, who consulted him and with whom he had one or two sessions (Reik, 1953). He gave him interpretations of really great depth, something that he would clearly otherwise judge to be a wild analysis and not desirable. It would seem to me that in these instances he would allow himself to follow one lead into the depth. He had a poetic kind of description of his interviews with Mahler. He said, "It was as if I was able to dig one single shaft into the depth of a very deep and complicated mind, going through all kinds of surprising vistas, but really never knowing exactly how they hang together." He was not able to see things at various depths. It is a very nice description. Freud apparently helped Mahler tremendously. He unblocked a creative impasse in one or two sessions which kept Mahler going. But he did not offer to analyze him.

It seems that analysis would be deepening the sieve. You talk about the correlation between a shallow sieve and the creative or performing process, and I wonder if analysis would neutralize the energy.

I understand fully what you are saying, but the real success of analysis in general is not the deepening of the sieve alone (Kohut, 1984). The success of an analysis is to have a deep sieve available, but also to have the option of discarding it under the control of the ego. In other words, the success of analysis is not to create people who cannot have strong feelings, who cannot be passionate, who cannot fly off in a rage or be violent, but to enable them to choose when, where and how to express their strong feelings.

There is a difference between an impulse-ridden character and a person who is capable of having deep feelings, passions. They are not the same. There are certain tasks in certain areas in which one should be capable of being dispassionate. But there are certain other areas in which one should be capable of drawing on the deepest instincts, undisguised, that are at one's disposal. It is not so simple. Since ideal analytic results are not easily come by, there is a certain doubt about interfering with a top-level performing genius. One might say, perhaps after so many years of analysis, his performance might be even better, but who knows? It might get stuck somewhere before one got to this optimal result. Can one help a person of this type—including his persistent psychopathology? As I said, I have treated very good artists and high-level scientists, but not on the genius level, or what I would consider to be. But then, how many are there?

Neutralization, however, is only part and parcel of this broader mechanism of sublimation. Neutralization alone is not sublimation. A scientific investigator in his libidinal history might have infantile sexual curiosity as the zero point of this developmental line. But neutralization alone does not lead from the excitement about the primal scene in the next room to the lesser excitement of being fascinated with a new idea, a new chapter in psychology or a new chapter of biology, chemistry, or whatever idea the investigator has. Neutralization is only one aspect of it. There are other things that are needed. There must be a shift away from the content. In other words, there is also displacement. Secondly, there is aim inhibition, which is also not neutralization. The aim is no longer what it once was in the infantile curiosity of wanting to see and to participate in the sexually stimulating goings-on, to identify with both partners when one watches the excitement of intercourse or hears something in the next room. It is not only that in the original situation there was unneutralized libidinal excitement, but also that there is a shift now from the sexual scene to something totally different. This can be the wish to investigate a new country, a new art form, a new chapter of chemistry or psychology. It is a deflection—it is a shifting away. So it is (a) neutralization, (b) a shift away in content, (c) aim-inhibited. One does not now behave with the immediacy of wanting to be involved. One can wait, one can do all kinds of in-between preparatory work. All these three together make for sublimation.

Thus when you talk about neutralization you are really speaking about a specific part-mechanism which may be, and sometimes is, specifically disturbed.

In the patient I have just described, there was a specific defect in his neutralizing capacity. What he was doing was aim-inhibited—it was deflected from the original aim. He was fully sublimating except for the trace of a lack of this fully reestablished neutralizing capacity, the *sieve in depth*. For a moment the original sexual feelings still came up. And I think self-observation may well teach you that this can occasionally occur in everyone. Certainly I never feel, if I have a patient with severe regressive beginnings that this particular person had, that there is in any way a failure if he knows what happened. It is good to know it; one has a sense of greater mastery because one knows why it happens. I think he felt very much that way, too. I do not know what will happen tomorrow, but today, when I caught on to what happened, he felt an increase in his mastery and broadened in his understanding of himself.

Under certain external and internal stress this young man again will reinvest with more unneutralized narcissistic libido, the leading zone, the leading part of an earlier phase. How did he happen to pick this one? What is the mechanism that allows this?

The word is simple: it is called fixation. In other words, you speak about a latent or potential fixation, not just on a particular zone but also in terms of old interpersonal love-and-hate relationships to a particular object. The examination of Freud's analogies can be helpful even though these pictorial analogies are sometimes attacked as unscientific—that he was analogizing too much or that he was too much a poet and not enough a scientist. Yet I think his analogies are extremely impressive. He very rarely used mechanistic analogies. He almost always used analogies of people in motion, of social groups standing for specific endopsychic arrangements. I am translating your question into the usual metapsychological terms.

You asked about the relationship between the predisposing fixation and regression. Why does the regression come back to this particular point and not to another? Freud used this beautiful example: If an army moves forward, wherever it stays it leaves a few people behind to form a garrison, to provide for supplies and retreats. The army advances, and finally suffers a terrific defeat. The army then floods backward. How far will it flood back? It will flood back to that point that is most fortified from the past, and in which the most remaining groups have been left. That is where it will be comparatively safe. That is where enough fresh people will be present, who can say, "Let's make a stand here." It is on that basis that there is a flooding back to a particular part of the past that was most important and in which most of the libidinal forces have been retained.

The situation is more complex than this very simple kind of an answer will give you. It depends a lot on the external event, the intertwining of factors. The mere fact that there is a fixation does not yet make for a regression. Fixations may deprive the individual of the energy for forward movement if there is a variety of unconscious fixations and if there is a very strong tie to infantile figures. Yet development may take place around it, and the fixation is sort of shoved into the background. An individual with many old fixations will perhaps be emotionally somewhat deprived later on and will not experience the full richness of his later relationships.

Therefore, the greater the fixation, the greater the ease with which comparatively minor frustrations of later life will bring about regressions. This is what Freud called the complementary series of factors (1933a). In other words, there are fixations of such a degree that almost anything, the slightest frustration, will send the army reeling backward to the point of the major garrison. But if the fixations are comparatively small, then only severe blows later in life will affect the individual. There are extremes on either side; there may be blows severe enough in adult life so that even a comparatively healthy individual will regress. Every night's dream, in that sense, is a regression. Given the right kind of circumstances, there will be a regression. However, in detail, a particular situation or zone is very difficult to ascertain unless one knows the person very well.

I believe that the student who had the vivid dream of the unattached penis-like organ, like a grasping hand, was fixated at a stage which is composed of phallic and early prephallic oral elements. This is where the complexities come in. The regression point itself is led up to by the child's history. The whole pre-oedipal and oedipal history very frequently combines in the choice of a vulnerable spot to which the regression then takes place. And it becomes the great skill and the great difficulty of many forms of treatment to understand the person correctly, namely, whether the early or the later aspects of this same fixation point are predominantly in play. It is not necessarily, as one would think, that originally the later ones are at play, and then, as the patient gets better, the earlier ones. Very frequently there is oscillation, even at the very moment, from one point to another.

One has to be with the patient at every given moment. One has to be open to understanding the total flavor of the personality. When I think about the case which was presented, what I would do is try to learn whether this is mostly an oral phallus at this particular moment. Is this man in need of sustenance of self-esteem, of caretaking environments, or, even though there is an oral weakness in his history, is he at this moment more interested in the expanding, grasping aspects? In other words, I would attempt a sort of broad empathy to the feeling tone of the particular leading regresssive zone.

The history of these particular points is sometimes very fascinating. Very frequently it teaches one something about the capacity for substitute gratifications in childhood. I would give you direct practical advice: always from the outset and for a long time, try to see the positive value of what the patient is doing. Do not look upon it negatively; do not evaluate it in terms of abstract maturity.

For example, a very frequently occurring symptom is voyeuristic preoccupation. I am certain this is true among your patients. Whether they admit it to you or not, perverse voyeuristic pursuits under the impact of emotional deprivation, of feeling unsupported in the new environment, of feeling alone, this kind of melancholy, depressive sexual gratification through looking is an extremely frequent occurrence. It is true that people will feel bad, guilty and ashamed about such activity. They feel this is not mature, they may be caught, they can be seen, and yet they are gripped by this enormous urge to go through with it.

Behind the enormous attraction of pornography which channels these feelings, and the enormous attraction of some of the movies, I think with a reasonable degree of certainty you can almost expect that these were children who were contact hungry, were not cuddled or held enough, not responded to warmly enough in their physical bodily contact needs. But in addition, what should have been a small, subordinated extra enjoyment of the interplay between mother and child—seeing and look-ing—was missing. As one embraces one also sees the happy face of the mother, and as one is being embraced one sees the smile of the mother who looks at one and enjoys one.

The voyeuristic issues come up in individuals who have felt deeply deprived in this more comprehensive interaction with others. The long-ing looking becomes the carrier. As Freud said in his paper on "Psycho-genic Visual Disturbances," one organ is abused when it carries on the functions of the others (1910b).

Thus, the visual contact becomes abused. It becomes the carrier of what should have been muscular contact, skin contact, voice contact, and all the other channels of pleasure. It is as if one thing had to carry everything, bringing about regression into its old sexual meanings. The patient I spoke of, who drew the picture of the analyst with himself instead of the eyes, is a voyeur. His mother had malignant hypertension. He was an incubator baby, and he was not even touched for six or eight months while he was lying in the crib because he was supposed to be so fragile. But it is never just this simple kind of thing. If the baby is not touched, then mothers will talk and sing and be around without touch-ing. There is still a lot to be offered, and not everything channels itself into touching. Even if the child has only the experience of looking, if the looking is responded to, it can then gradually be desexualized. There can be early means by which in the mutual interplay, even within one organ system, as it were, a sieve in depth can be acquired. This is not to be done in brief psychotherapy, obviously, but on the other hand, these insights will stand anybody in good stead who does therapy of any kind, simply because you understand more broadly, you are more empathic with the patient. You naturally do the right thing if you understand.

It is beautiful to see, in the cohesive revival of the early relationship in the transference of an ongoing analysis, how in small doses these regres-sions are revived again. At what times does the patient who has given up voyeuristic pursuits suddenly return to them when he feels hurt and rejected by you? Gradually he will recognize when the impulse arises, but he will not need to satisfy it anymore, because he knows what happens to bring about this urge. An ever broadening empathic relation-ship then begins to replace this isolated pleasure-hunting through the eyes, or through whatever other kind of perversion.

There are many perversions and addictions which ought to be under-stood on this particular level. Of course perversions and addictions can also build up on original zones. Freud in his early formulations, under the aegis only of the libido theory, spoke about genital dominance in his "Three Essays on the Theory of Sexuality" (1905a). This was still all expressed in the terms of a libido theory. It is all there, except still in the comparatively narrow theoretical framework which was the only one Freud then had at his disposal, before ego psychology was introduced at the end of the second decade of this century and the beginning of the third.

11

Separation From Family
and the Struggle to Potentiate
Ideals and Goals

M ANY UNDERGRADUATES experience acute anxiety as they try to find direction in their studies toward a goal which will confirm their worth. They cling to and yet seek escape from the familiar shelter of family and old associates.

This is a 19-year-old second year student whose family lives within 100 miles of Chicago. He is a young boy of Greek parentage, round-faced, dark-eyed, dark-haired, who was wearing a little red sweater such as one knits for a latency-aged boy. It was totally inappropriate for a college setting. His shirt did not quite cover him so that his midriff was bare.

He wrote, "I am scarred" (meaning 'scared' a word which he consistently misspelled). "I am scarred and nervous about school and my future. I worry constantly about grades, and possibly getting into medical school. However, I have no clear-cut goals in my life. I'm wishy-washy, indecisive, and have little motivation. My future doesn't look like it's going to be much fun. I feel stupid. I feel I shouldn't be at this school sometimes. I lack self-confidence. I worry excessively, and when I worry I can't work. I feel I must work all the time to get through school. I want to try to be the best at what I can do. I'm in general not having a good time. And unless I can get all great marks I don't enjoy myself. Smart people bother me. I'd like to get a feeling of self-confidence and get rid of my worrying, because I can't work at all when I'm worried."

Then he tells what brought him to the clinic. "During the first few weeks last quarter I felt very scarred and alone because lots of people left the dorm. I had a single, and I feared my studies. However, I worked hard, and I got good grades. I expected better grades, however, because I worked hard. This quarter I've got fears that I would not do as well. I don't know my career plans. I lack motivation, I thought of rearranging my courses and changing my schedule. I was very indecisive. I worried much, and was nervous. I couldn't eat or sleep. I went to Student Health, and they referred me here."

The help he has received before has been through talking with friends and parents. His college board scores are verbal 660, average for his entering class and math 780, only 20 points from the top.

He waited only a day for his first appointment and I have now seen him five times. He talked about his fear of the future; he had gone home for the weekend but was so afraid he would not get his studying done that he had his parents drive him back to school early. He wonders if he really wants to be a doctor. He points out that one of his problems is that he just feels out of competition with a lot of students here because, for example, though he's Greek, he doesn't know Plato, and a lot of students who are not Greek know Plato.

He is an only child; his parents are 66 and 56, and he is 19. He went into a long discourse on his family. He has three maternal uncles and one paternal uncle. They are so involved in his life that I felt my office was knee deep in uncles. Mother feels cheated because all the brothers are wealthy—they own a hotel, they have material things, and she does not. Father never made much money, and the constant refrain to this student was, "Don't be like your father." This was not only Mother's message—this was everybody's message to him. The parents separated when he was 10 or 11, but they were reunited after a year. He states that the last time he felt good about himself was at age 11. For the first 11 years of his life he lived with his parents in a northern state where father was a practicing attorney. Then something occurred which resulted in father's being demoted. Father had to leave his job. That may have been a factor in the parents' separation, but he is not sure. But while the family was intact he remembers with great happiness standing in the doorway and hearing the sound of father's whistle down the street. This was a great joy to him, and he felt very good, very complete. He and father used to do things together. Father would take him places in his car. When father worked in his office, he would sharpen father's pencils, and would feel very good about himself. With mother he had problems, although in the first interview he gave me the impression that mother and he were inseparable and father was out on the periphery—a man who never amounted to much, and of whom all his uncles warned him, "Don't be like your father. He doesn't work hard enough," and so on.

Did that kind of message begin before he was 11 or only after the father got into difficulty?

It's very hard for him to differentiate, but you'll see that he does so later on. He described these big, strong, successful uncles as owning a hotel. They tell him to go out and cut the grass, and then, for example, reward him by vastly overpaying him.

He returned to his memory of feeling good, hearing father whistling as he came down the street. By contrast he described an incident in which he was in a store with mother. He was always shopping with mother, and he groaned when he said this. He used to shop for dresses with her, and when she scraped the hangers on the bar he would sit there and cringe. In one of these experiences, he threw his arms around the legs of a man who passed by and said, "Daddy!" But it was a different pair of legs, and daddy was nowhere around.

I saw this student for the second time a day later, because I thought it might be effective in modifying his anxiety and because he had not experienced a sense of relief from the first hour. He said that mother used to dress him up in all kinds of things. There was a cowboy outfit, and a Snow White outfit; she would have liked him to become a model. And he would have "made it," except that he cried, and did not want to. He described this as failure but what came through to me was that the boy had been exploited, a plaything.

In describing parents' separation, he cannot recall the circumstances. He was sent to an aunt and uncle over a summer, and that part was good. But when mother came to pick him up there was something different about him and about her which he cannot describe. For about a year they lived in grandparents' home alone with his uncles who were still young and unmarried. At the end of the year the parents reunited. Father now has a relatively less important job at which he earns a moderate income.

When he returned a week later for the third interview he looked good, more integrated, and his clothes were appropriate. He said he was studying marvelously. He brought out his flash cards and told me all about his mechanisms for handling the work, and that everything is great.

He returned again to all the memories of his father—what a good guy he was. Father not only helped him build a house for a pet cat he had as a child, but also fixed some cement for the cat to put his paw print in. Father did everything to facilitate the boy's ownership and relationship to this pet. One day the cat was gone. Mother said she was very sorry but the cat had run off. A year or two later he "caught her in a total lie."

She apparently had forgotten what she had told him and said she had the cat put away. He could not get over that she had lied to him. And he kept asking himself in the interview, "What is so terrible about my father? He's a great guy. He lets me do what I want to do. He doesn't tell me what to do or order my life the way mother does. Mother uses me. She has the idea than when I get to be a great doctor she'll live with me and have all kinds of good things." He looks at father and father's family—not only father, but grandfather went to college. This uncle is a hard working internist well thought of in the community.

At home mother continues to boss him around. If relatives come over he has to clean his room, and so on. He can't have his room the way he wants it. He complained that his parents were always dropping in at the dorm. He described standing at the window and hearing a whistle. He jumped up, and sure enough it was father. He felt glad father was coming, except that in tow was mother. She had dyed her hair. He didn't know how to get out of seeing her. She brought him a shirt, a gift from his aunt and wanted him to call his aunt and thank her right away for it. She brought a box of crackers, and wanted him to take them to his room, but he didn't want to. In fact, he said, "I want to go to the library," but he couldn't get rid of her. He had begun to grow a beard. Mother said he looked terrible, and to cut it off. Father said, "You look grubby, but if you like it, okay."

He continues to feel much better. When he came the next time he said father had called to say they were going out to dinner—the two of them and his uncle, the internist—and he felt great. But they did not go to dinner. Instead the uncle gave him a thorough physical examination, and then a "long song and dance" of how he had made it in medical school. He too had felt anxious; that was to be expected and only a sign that the adrenalin was pumping, and so on. But the student felt indignation that father had lied to him.

I said he must have felt very disappointed. His response was, "I'd like to have a girl. I'd like to be able to date a girl." Then he told me he had begun to date a girl in high school. He liked her very much and told his mother about her. But when mother happened to see the girl at school, she didn't like her. Mother wanted him to go out with somebody she would choose. So his dating stopped until his first year here in college when he began to date a girl he liked. He remembered taking her out to dinner, and as they were sitting across the table, she said, "I like your eyebrows." Then he said, "My eyebrows! What about my mind?" He felt she wanted to get too close to him and so he cut off the relationship. All her friends have been down on him.

What do you mean by "cut off the relationship"? I'm interested in how this came out. Did he report this to you with a kind of humor?

No. He found that as he grew to know her more, he didn't like her. She couldn't talk about the things he wanted to talk about, and so on.

She got on his nerves.

Right. All her friends were down on him, so he didn't have a link to other girls. Now he would like to go out again. There is a particular girl in the dorm at whom he looks longingly; he wonders whether she would like him or whether she wouldn't like him, whether she would accept him or not. Maybe she's just as scared as he is, and so on.

That's about where we are; except that he came back this week, feeling nervous again and apprehensive. He's doing all right in his courses. He got two A's and a B, and mother said, "Well maybe you can work harder." I said it was awfully hard to go to school with four uncles *and* a father and mother. What did he want for himself? This is about where we are.

You see him regularly once a week?

I saw him five times in four weeks.

The first two times you saw him close together because you felt he was depressed. He is not nearly as depressed as he was in the beginning, I take it. He sleeps well, eats well, and is not so depressed.

What continues to trouble him is his indecisiveness. He can always indulge himself in work. He can work long hours in his lab, where he's an assistant. When he goes to the bookshop and buys a set of index cards, he would also like to buy a candy bar or a cigar. He can't make up his mind between the candy bar and the cigar, so he walks out with the index cards.

You told us something about his original appearance and how inappropriately dressed he was. A great deal of the flavor of the personality comes through, but I'd like a little more of that. He's a man who is enormously conscientious in many ways, to the point of this caricature that you mentioned at the end, where he agonizes over two pleasure possibilities; he gives up the pleasure and walks out with the duty. As you said, he indulges in work forever, but has a hard time with enjoyments.

I have the impression of a youngster who is darting and dodging all the time—offering bits of information about himself, as he must have

done with mother and father, trying to get some kind of feed-in to resolve the anxiety; but he is never really prepared to stay with that lest the person to whom he tells it will approve, correct, guide, or direct. I wondered how much he was really taking in of me, the kind of person I was, and who I was. If he saw me on the street would he really know me? Whereas I could not forget him.

That would probably be true of many people who are upset. They think of themselves. They don't scrutinize the person. You are an institution, for him, I would imagine. One might speculate that he might assume that you're this kind of person, as you said, that would correct him and steer him, and judge him and evaluate him—you know, from the history one would assume this might likely be so. But is there any evidence that he really sees you that way? I haven't yet had any feeling tone of what really went on. How does he talk? What kind of an impression does he make? At first, was he depressed?

Very anxious, but that subsided. Then, for example, when I said it must have been very disappointing when he was given a physical examination instead of going out to dinner, his response, without even a momentary contemplation as usually occurs with other students, was an immediate, ''I'd like to have a girl.'' It seemed to me that he was saying he felt somewhat better and felt the permission to move ahead. This is one of the areas he wants to work on, but was afraid, initially, of saying this directly. Many other students his age come and say directly what it is they want.

This is a specific episode you're describing. I'm not sure I understand this episode. It's an interesting one. It bears a lot of reflection. Why do the father and uncle do that? He talks about it, and you respond to it, in terms of a falsehood. It's true that it's a falsehood; but what strikes me much more than the falsehood is something else. It is a complex business this family has to go through to get him a physical examination. They don't dare tell him, "We're worried about you, and we'd like you to be examined." They have to sort of sneak it to him. In other words, what is his role in all this? Why are they so scared to tell him directly, "We're worried about you. You haven't been eating properly, and you're working so hard. We'd like your uncle to look you over." Instead, a long diplomatic family council must have taken place as if to plan how one can channel him. What is his contribution, that he's considered to be that breakable or that much of a tyrant, to have to go through this?

I get the same feeling from two aspects of the presentation. One is that he was seen 24 hours after his first appointment which must have been a response to a similar kind of communication—not the tyrant, but the fragility. The other is the way in which he gives the signal at home that he has to go back in the middle of the weekend because he's got to study. He gives me the impression of somebody who is in perpetual agony. But I think the people in this family respond to statements about agony. There is a quality almost of caricature—this I'm not so sure about. It's not play-acting, but the capacity for this almost histrionic shifting about strikes me as a mode that they all must indulge in with each other.

It has not jelled for me yet, to come to this kind of personality diagnosis, even on a superficial level. As I said, my wish is to move into a little deeper understanding of the personality. There is this puzzling shift that you caught where he suddenly says, "I want a girl," after you had said how disappointed he must have been. That's open to all kinds of interpretations. Maybe he felt embarrassed about your empathy and wanted to shift quickly to something else.

There is this kind of strange communication. You're right about this maneuver to get the doctor. For example, he feels better after he leaves me. Then he calls his mother and says he's having real problems about growing up. He calls it the Peter Pan syndrome—that he hates to grow up. Mother says, "Maybe you ought to join the army and grow up that way. Maybe you ought to go to Vietnam." Is she angered by his confiding his problems so that she replies with an essentially hostile comment?

I think it's an interesting case. We want to go on with it and study it in depth. This seems to me a family in which people are enormously involved with each other, and in which the child becomes terribly stimulated by the closeness of so many people. My feeling, as a therapist, would be to be a bit distant, so that he doesn't have the feeling right away, "Ah, here is another member of the family."

It's his second year in college. He's of Greek parentage on both sides of the family. Father occupies a dull job. What does he do now?

He works with the uncles in the hotel, at a lesser job. Whether it's actually legal, or in some way related, I'm not sure.

At any rate, according to the student's description, the father seems to be a somewhat down-trodden figure; certainly by comparison with his brother, and even more so by comparison with the mother's brothers. He's a kind of negative ideal for the boy—"You mustn't be like your father." What were the symptoms he came in with—learning difficulties and depressed feelings?

Constant anxiety about not being able to make top grades, indecisive-

ness—just a feeling of being scared and anxious all the time, and not liking people who are smart. He doesn't go on to say that they're competitors, but they somehow diminish his rewards.

When did these symptoms begin?

He has had them continuously.

Ever since he started college? Does he live at home, or does he live here?

He lives in the dorm. Last year he had a roommate. This year he's in a single, and he tells us something about this.

But the chief complaint is of anxiety.

He worries about his future. He has fears of failure if he isn't able to make the grade as a pre-med student.

Depressed?

I would say it's an anxious kind of depression.

But he works. His grades are actually reasonably good?

Yes, a strong B, if not an A-minus.

The parents apparently were worried about him. That's why they got him to take this medical examination. What caused their great worry?

He tells us in this hour that when he's uncomfortable he calls them. It's not that they alone are intrusive, but they take over when he confides his discomfort.

He calls them—he's helpless. He's an only child and his parents are quite along in years. Father was 47 and mother was 37 when this child was born. The parents got married late in life?

That I don't know.

At any rate, he was born rather late in their lives. He's a student who lives in the metropolitan area of Chicago, but the family was up north during the first 11 years of his life until parents separated? Did the separation occur because mother was disappointed in the father's failure, disbarment, or whatever it was? That doesn't come out. But there is evidence of this boy's yearning for the father in this memory of the department store, where he embraced the leg of a man and was disappointed.

That occurred when he was a young boy and the father was still part of the family.

That occurred then, but it expressed some kind of disappointment; that somebody is there who is not his father.

I had more the feeling that it was a desperate effort to escape from the mother, who was taking him shopping and looking for clothes. There was this male figure; I saw it as a desperate move to get away from mother.

We don't know. It's quite possible. Your fantasy is as good as mine. These are all possibilities.

He stresses that father makes him feel good. Father allows him autonomy. He does nice things with father. In any case, he selected this to remember.

The point at stake is not so much a particular episode, but to get the flavor of the whole family influence on the boy. One gets the impression that the pressure and the demands come from the mother. The mother is forever not satisfied. It is the mother who wants higher grades. It is the mother who is dissatisfied with the father, and so on. In many such instances, then, father becomes kind of an older brother and pal. In that sense, he represents a kind of relief from these pressures. So there is more love and comradeship toward the father than toward the mother. Whether that is a fact or not I don't know. It's just something that happens frequently in such families. But as I said, I do also have the impression that this is an enormously involved family; and that there is a kind of openness toward each other that is hard on a child.

One of the things that is striking is that he has difficulty being alone. On the one hand, he is trying to extricate himself from this terrific family involvement; on the other hand, when he is alone, he feels incomplete and anxious and turns toward the family for support. He is hung up on this and comes for help. He knows he should no longer be clinging to his mother and father. He needs somebody, however, to fulfill some of these functions for him—calming him, telling him what to do, and so forth. Is there any further material?

This is the sixth session. He came up the stairs as I went into my room. The secretary must have sent him up without notifying me. There were several other people in the hall. He looked above, beyond, below, behind, but never at me or anybody else until he got into the room and the door was closed. Then he just launched in. He looked at me directly all the time, except when there was a kind of interruption in

the flow of his thought—not necessarily any interruption that I made. He looked well-groomed and very well put together. He was carrying a dashing sweater and a dark blue beret, and in his left hand he had his flash cards. He had just come from an organic chemistry exam. He said he felt good all week and described it as "gliding." Last night, for the first time, he felt apprehensive; and took a Compoz, studied as hard as he could, for he felt the important thing was for him to be fresh and rested. Then he would be able to make use of his knowledge. He went to bed at 8:00 but awoke, studied again, and fell asleep again. He thinks he probably slept about six hours, but he felt he handled the exam well.

Without interruption he launched into a discussion of the girl he has not as yet been able to sit next to. She is a pretty girl who sits in the lounge. He hasn't the nerve to walk up to her and just sit down and make conversation. He thinks about his future, the fantasy that he's going to be Joe Doctor, that he's going to have a family and kids. And it's a good feeling that he has. But even before he thinks about making the first step, of going up and sitting down and saying hello to her, he already feels sad, because they're going to break up. The breaking up has to do with the feeling that somehow he'll be incompetent—he won't know what to talk about.

He says that sometimes he just sits down and doesn't know what to say to people. At other times he talks a lot, but he doesn't know whether what he's saying is the right thing. He feels he has trouble expressing himself verbally. He recalls a sonnet he wrote for humanities last spring that was so beautiful! He wanted to show it to me, but he couldn't find it. He worked hard on it and read it to one or two other people. He was also supposed to write one page of explanation, to tell the instructor what he had in mind. But he thought the metaphors were so easy to understand that he did not need to turn in the page of explanation. He got only a C-plus, with the comment, "I don't know what you mean. You should have had the other paper." He felt terrible. Then he proceeded to describe the sonnet in great detail. He was in the dorm and he was looking out on the street. He describes himself as a boat; there was the water and the sky was dark. There was no wind. As he looks into the water he sees currents of all kinds.

This is the content of the sonnet?

This is the content of the sonnet. There are schools of fish darting around in the currents, and he has no way of knowing anything more about himself than that he is the boat in this particular sonnet. He went on to vent his displeasure at the grade. He said others talked about hacking it in the dorm, about being jocks, or gave explanations of the rhythm. But his was really poetic. There was a change of rhythm to reflect the waves, and so on. Then there was a slight pause, and I said, "You must have wanted the instructor to know, without the explanation, what it all meant." He nodded his head in agreement, and then went on to say that he had bought a record. I neglected to say that last time, in describing his indecisiveness, the difficulty in making a choice between the candy and the cigar, going out with the index cards, I said, "It looks as if you have no problem deciding on work, but you have a problem making up your mind about simple pleasure. it could have been either, and it wouldn't have mattered." He went on to say that he had bought a record, and he looked rather triumphant. He said it was a terrific record because it expressed feeling. He can't sing, but wishes he could. He put earphones on his ears so that he could hear the music, and not hear his voice. He had a great time. For the first time he had some freedom of body movement. "I walked around the room sort of keeping rhythm with the music."

On Sunday he began to work again. He recalled how hard he had worked during the last quarter, studying nine hours a day. He only got a B, and he should have gotten an A. A friend of his didn't study at all but copies his notes. I don't know whether that student got a good grade or not. But for himself working on schedule is terribly important.

His mother and father came on Sunday, and he was wearing the same outfit I have just described, along with the sweater and beret. He felt good. Mother said, "Look how you're dressing," criticizing his whole approach. I could not hold my tongue, and said, "I think it looks kind of dashing." It really did look that way. He went on to say that he slept late on the day they were going to come. When the telephone rang, he knew it was for him, but he didn't answer the bell. They usually come by the dorm at 5:00 on Sunday if he doesn't come home. This time he was late, and they were almost ready to leave when he walked in. He talks about wanting to get away from them, staying in the university area during the spring and over the summer, working in the lab, and that he's "feeling a dichotomy," as he expresses it. He'll have to begin to make things on his own. He does call home, it's true, when he's upset. That's what happened with the physical exam by uncle—he had been upset, and cried, and so on.

He rehearsed for me what he thinks takes place in situations like this. Mother will become upset, and she'll urge father to do something about it. Father will say, "Leave the boy alone." Mother will say, "Maybe he's ill." Father kids the boy along, and so on. That's probably why the medical visit took place. Then he turns to the question of whether he will fail. He wishes he could be a janitor. When he was in the library studying he could see the janitor; the janitor has only one problem—how to gather the dirt up and how to dispose of it. He wishes that was the only decision he had to make, where to put the dirt. At his uncles' hotel he worked as a janitor for a number of years while he was still in grammar and high school. He used to work out special ways of cleaning up the place, stacking supplies. One day he told mother he'd really like to work as a busboy in a hotel restaurant. Mother told father about this, and father said, "No, the waitresses tend to get fresh, and they would get fresh with him." So instead, his uncle sent him to a westside hotel, which could only use him late at night, and so he couldn't go.

I wondered how he felt when father said the waitresses would get fresh. He said, very indignantly, "Didn't he think I knew how to handle myself?" He recalled walking with mother and seeing a young couple—the boy with his arm around the girl—and mother saying, "Look at that! I don't want to see you doing anything like that!" I asked him how he felt about this. He didn't answer but went on to say that he also asked mother how babies were born. Mother said, "They put in a pill." Then he asked, "How does it get out?" Mother did not answer. Then he asked, "Does the doctor cut you open?" And here mother agreed.

How old was he?

I don't know, but that was his association to mother's response about seeing the boy and girl walking through town. There is this kind of association without any kind of intermediary step. He goes on about the girl in the lounge. He and his boyfriend have seen her sitting and talking with a girlfriend, but when they're ready to go up and talk to the girls they have left. He has been trying to do this for two weeks. He has the fantasy that they'll graduate and they'll separate. I asked him, "What about all the in-between steps?" Why does he fantasy breaking up before he starts?

He said he feels incompetent, and that he will fail. I suggest that I can understand why he would feel this way. Mother says, "I wouldn't want you to put your arm around a girl." Father says, "Girls might get fresh with you."

Then he said, "I'm beginning to titrate in." It appears to be a question of can he handle both studying and a girl. Last year his identity was clear. He was a student, and he studied all the time. His roommate never studied. He goes on to say that he enjoys working and feels best when he is working. I raised the question of whether he did not feel up to handling both and said, "You know, all work and no play." He talked about his feeling of incompetence and I related this to the old pattern of parents being concerned and perhaps overdirecting and guiding him. But as I heard what he said, he also brings them in. It's understandable why he should have some feeling of incompetence—the special circumstances of their all being so closely involved with each other. But now, school is for him.

He said, "I can see I'll have to do things for myself now, and that it's important to have balance; maybe I'll buy another record." I'm sorry to say I couldn't hold my tongue and I said, "Maybe even talk to the girl." As he gets up to go he leaves his chemistry cards on my desk. Before he got to the door, I picked them up and handed them to him. Many other young men have done this and have made many different responses with which all of you are familiar. But he explained to me what the flash cards were for in a rather pedantic manner. That was the end of the hour.

That was certainly an interesting hour. What do you have to say about that? What is your impression? I noticed all kinds of emotional reactions to the material. Does some general feeling emerge about this fellow and his mode of living with the world?

Just for a word, he sounds very boyish. When he told the story of the question about where babies come from—I assume he was in the ninth grade—everyone sort of believed it for a moment, at 14 years of age he'd still be asking questions of this sort. I get the feeling of a very youthful boy, not a man. Perhaps this will launch the discussion.

By "boy, not a man," what do you mainly have in mind? I think that's true, there is a certain immaturity. But could you be a bit more specific about the nature of the personality that emerges?

Those of you who have been with me in case seminars know that when I listen to material, I always notice myself being at odds with the rest of the audience. When they laugh, it always strikes me as strange. I don't listen to the material in that way. I try to understand, how does this mind work? How does this personality feel? Can I in some way grasp what the major pattern is in which this man handles his problems and experiences the world? These are all just examples for me. I do not react to them as if they were directed at me. Therefore, I have much less impulse to say anything. You all keep saying, "I'm sorry I said that," as if you felt you shouldn't have. In all honesty, it would never occur to me to react, because I'm all ears, as it were. I'm trying to grasp what makes this man tick. I have no interest at this particular moment to help him to tick differently. I don't even know yet how he ticks. This is my general attitude.

We do have a great deal of interesting, although to me not yet understandable, material. So how does this man tick? You described a kind of immaturity. There is something lacking in this man that does not make him masculine or a grown man. Even though he is only 19, still he could be more of a firm man, with firm action potentials, knowing approximately what he wants, and so on.

I was struck by how he depicted himself as so helpless. The one thing that didn't coincide was when you asked him how he felt about the waitress business. He was indignant, but I thought that was almost because perhaps he thought that is what you expected. Another aspect troubled me. For somebody whose parents are putting up the mode of doing something very intellectual, he's not worrying about getting a chemistry set or getting to work around anything scientific or intellectual. Instead, what came across to me was his pleasure in cleaning things up.

That had a different meaning to me. At that time, he still felt sheltered in the sense that he was part of the family environment, and he was pleasing to the uncles. That's what the meaning of the janitor job had to me.

At this particular point I can see better what became of him than why. He has an interesting mind. He has a very differentiated mind. He has a mind that has fascination, it seems to me, for other people to listen to his products. For example, when he described his sonnet, a truly poetic childlike thought—that he's a boat, seeing the avenue as a stream with schools of fish going by—such thinking shows a rich and interesting mind in the realm of fantasy. This is a man with a tremendous amount of fantasy, and I think perhaps confusing fantasies. You were bothered by it a number of times, when he sort of projected into the future, and he left out all the in-betweens, and you said, "Where are the in-betweens?" He hasn't even talked to the girl, but already he goes through a whole novel of a relationship, including the final jilting. He hasn't even approached her yet. But the important and interesting thing about it is . . .

If I may interrupt, he did not fantasy the in-between steps with her. He fantasied, and the first thing he told me was of breaking up.

The point is he is involved in something that is so removed from any reality as yet. These are fantasies which are really nothing else but spinning plans about action—how one could approach the girl, and the next steps that would happen with her—that would still be near reality. Here, he is already far into the relationship, beyond it, at the tragic end of it. He removes it totally from the present reality. It is as related to this girl as the sonnet is to the street.

I get the impression that this is a boy with very rich fantasy life, of a sort of poetic bent, but a bit confused about the real world in which he lives—not psychotically confused, but just removed from it. His difficulty lies in translating fantasies into plans and plans into actions; this is where he falls short. At the same time, he yearns for something simple. If he could only be a janitor—that is, if he could have a very clear-cut task in front of him, without bothersome and confusing choices.

Now to go back to what we know about his surroundings, and what made him the way he is. It obviously has something to do with his parents. I am not saying this simply because it is what the books always say. This is clear from the way he reacts. He likes to avoid his parents but must relate to them. He knows they are coming at 5:00, but he doesn't answer the bell. Why? What did they do to account for his inability to deal with real things, and at the same time, for this highly differentiated inner life that seems to be bubbling in him all the time? For one thing, it seems to me, he was apparently cut down whenever he translated fantasies into actions. The idea of being a busboy is not anything great, as far as we are concerned, but for him it was a significant step. It meant to do something real. But right away, the adults introduced negatives—the girls will be fresh, and it is not a good enough job.

As for the girls being fresh—whether I am right or wrong, I do not know, but my own empathic response is that it was not primarily a question of cutting him down about sex. I do not believe anything is contained in the girls being fresh that really tells you the story.

I have the impression this is a roundabout family—that they will make a negative comment when they really have something totally different in mind. I do not know why they did not want him to do this kind of work, but this was a convenient way of saying no, the first thing that occurred to the father. He used the same oblique method in getting around to his medical examination.

If this is indeed the way this family interacts—and I do not know why they interact that way, but I think they do—one can see how a child would withdraw from this confusion—from this ever present, never direct, never action potentiating, never accepting something that is real. He would withdraw more and more into fantasy. He sort of locks the door, and keeps spinning fantasies where he, at least, is in control. As far as my instinct as a therapist is concerned, I would not criticize him— even when he is not geared to action; even when he is floundering between decisions; even when he wants to retreat; even when he cannot approach this girl. This is how he is.

Let us start out with what he is and not try immediately to make him something that he is not. I have no doubt that he can conform to your pushes. But he has been pushed all his life, and it seems to me the end result has been that he really has withdrawn more and more, so that when he is faced with real situations, then he gets confused and anxious. I do not know much about his background, but I have the feeling that this is a family overly involved with him in a way that did not lead to constructive results, but rather to his attempt to withdraw from the family, their stimulations, and their confusing outlook on him.

What are the real values? What is he really to do? Nobody knows for sure. I have the impression that nothing clear-cut and modest was ever accepted—and more so by the mother, I think, than by the father. I think the father would be more likely to support him, from that one little memory that we have when he embraced the man's leg. That was something solid. He wants to escape from the confusing mother and at least have a father who is not quite so ambitious, not so mixed up, and does not have such crazy ideas. I do not know what crazy ideas mother has, but one gets the feeling they are a bit overstimulating and yet removed from reality. This young man's assets are in the richness of his fantasies— in the poetic bent—in the mode in which he spins out things by himself. This is an asset. The shortcomings are when he has to relate to a real world—when he has to make real decisions, succeed in real tasks, like talking to the girl instead of doing so in fantasy.

I think this is the kind of communication that would be an early one, listening a great deal to him. I would say, "You know, you have an interesting and a poetic mind, which some people probably have difficulty in understanding. I can understand perfectly well how much was in your sonnet, but you probably gave too much credit to your college instructor. I would not blame him; people are not that much in tune with you. Your sonnet may be very poetic, and maybe he should have understood it, but he didn't. Let bygones be bygones."

I would not tell him to approach this girl without so many fantasies. I would say, "You're a person with a very rich inner life and a good many fantasies, but I think you have some problems with actions and decisions and with concrete tasks, and perhaps that is where you lack self-confidence. You may very well have been belittled, cut down, and questioned a great deal early in your life. But when you are with your own thoughts, you feel in control, and there you have achieved a great deal."

In other words, I would not take sides. I would show him where his difficulties lie, and I would show him where his assets lie, and I would give him the first bit of insight into how this may be connected. And even if you make a mistake in your early speculations, you teach him that is not so bad, because you give these speculations not with iron-clad certainty, and you encourage him to think a bit more about it. He will probably think, "This is quite right. If you really knew my mother, then you would know." Then he will tell you what his mother has contributed.

You must not forget that this family probably comes from a rich cultural heritage that is totally unintegrated in the Anglo-Saxon American culture that is so action-oriented. This is a possibility and may be part of the confusion. Under such circumstances, the male who has kept more of the traditional values is less successful in the new environment, while the quickly Americanized hotel owners are the successes. So he is confronted with confusing issues.

Are the old cultural values important, or is the new monetary success important? Then there is the yearning for the simple kind of life, the simple kind of task—to be a busboy or a janitor—to know clearly what one is doing, and then spin out one's fantasies quietly while one is carrying the dishes. As I said earlier, I think you should not be a person who gives him instructions as to what he should do—a person who disapproves of his lack of action potential and clarity in practical matters—but let him see it is there. This is in his way many times and probably accounts for his anxiety.

You are appreciative of what has become of him, but it can be explained and probably better understood in terms of his parents. I do not mean that you should carry out a deep analysis with him from then on, which would last for years, and go into great detail about his development, but I think with this understanding the battle of breaking away from the parents will take on feasible proportions. With this background of support and understanding, and your nonjudgmental attitude in terms of what he should and should not do, he may see more clearly how and why he needs to break away from his parents. He will see also what the anxiety is when he is away from them.

I think it is an interesting and very subtle kind of problem that you are facing with this student, and not easily formulated. But I think it conveys a little flavor of what I believe are the crucial issues in the treatment of this case.

12

Extending Empathic Understanding, Sharing an Attitude

H ERE KOHUT CONTINUES the discussion of issues raised in Chapter 11, beginning with a question from one of the seminar participants.

From your discussion it would seem that assessing the situation in the first couple of sessions, and sharing this with the patient at the beginning, would foster an intellectual rather than an emotionally experienced understanding. Is it necessary to begin early by showing a patient how you think in formulative terms?

This cannot be answered simply. It depends very much on the patient and his difficulties. I think it also depends on your own mastery of a particular attitude, how it feels to show keen intellectual interest, but at the same time not to intellectualize. To be intelligent is not the same thing as intellectualizing. I think this is an old error.

What I attempted to say is that, in a sense by example, I teach the patient an attitude toward himself. I create an atmosphere—not artificially, however, because it truly is mine—in which a broadened understanding for oneself is encouraged. My own interest is in what is going on in the patient—not only in what he experiences, but also in how he experiences and relates to his difficulties. This is in essence an attitude of an expanded self-empathy—an expanded capacity to be empathic with one's own past, with aspects of oneself that one really does not own, or does not own fully, including even aspects of oneself that have not yet expanded—in other words, one's future possibilities.

The question that you raise is whether this is only an intellectual attitude in terms of abstract thoughts. I see nothing in what I said that would go in this direction. Emotions are as much included in self-understanding as anything else. It is true that words can be used as a hindrance to self-understanding in the same way that words can be used as a hindrance to communication. But still, words are a means of communication, and understanding is a means of communication. Understanding can also be used defensively; and one must not begin in this way. If it is abused in this way, then I would include this particular abuse in the general expansion of understanding.

In other words, let us assume you have a student who has been reading psychology texts. He begins by telling you about his oedipus complex, and about certain psychodynamics that are characteristic for him. This is the kind of history he gives. I would certainly not object in the beginning.

My initial advice to anybody who works in this field would be not to pounce on the patient and tell him he is intellectualizing and that these are just words or formulae. I would wait until I could explain to him in a meaningful, positive way why he is doing what he's doing. I might say that I think intellectual understanding is a means of avoiding anxiety—and after all, we all want to avoid anxiety. In struggling to master ourselves and our impulses, and to avoid being pushed around by forces that we do not really understand, it is often a first step to see oneself in a more objective and abstract light. This allows one to be less frightened.

In the same way, when one is in a strange country and a foreign city, if one has a map and a general idea of the layout of the city, one is helped a bit. In other words, I would not object to what such a person is doing, but would expand his understanding about this particular mode of his functioning. To be afraid of the mere fact that one attempts to understand what is going on in a person, to see this as intellectualizing, as necessarily a hindrance rather than a help, is I think, an error. I think it is a confusion between being intelligent and intellectualizing.

Understanding, with its expression in words, is not anything that one should necessarily be afraid of. I have seen just the opposite being an obstacle, that is, people who cannot speak directly, but can only use terrific emotional terms. Why? Because they are afraid of intellectualizing.

If a patient consults a psychiatrist, why should he suddenly drop all the insights of psychiatry? When he talks about himself he will naturally speak in the language he is used to; if he is an intelligent person he will use intelligent terms. That never stands in the way of experiencing deep emotions. I would advise you, at least to begin with, not to be afraid of this kind of dichotomy. And I would advise you not to object even to the defensive use of intellectual communications too soon.

As a matter of fact, I would not object to intellectual communications, but I would weave in an understanding of this kind of communication as a general need to distance oneself from anxiety-provoking inner conflicts. He has a right to protect himself. If you begin there, then you will not make an enemy of the patient.

I have often seen, when psychiatric residents first present their cases to me, that from the beginning the patient is looked at as somebody who is inimical, in a sense, and wants to pull the wool over your eyes. The idea of defense as a psychodynamically important thing, that the major function of the mind is defensive, is good, not bad. In other words, one has a stimulus barrier which is defensive. Then one does not get blown around. One maintains oneself in the structure and in the permanency that one is. For that one has defenses. In the same way as one has skin and nails, so one also has psychological defenses, a right to maintain oneself by defending against traumatic feelings.

If the patient has the feeling that the psychiatrist wants to inflict pain on him, then he will obviously fight the psychiatrist. This is not, or should not be, your intention at all. It is true that you can sometimes show the patient that the means he uses in maintaining himself in balance are not economical and are not necessary. The pain he fights against is not a real one: to look at things is not the same as being exposed to them. If you want to get to the point with the patient in which he will allow himself to face slightly difficult situations more consciously and more openly, then you must have first built up a feeling which allows him to do so.

It is like taking a child to the dentist. If as a first step the dentist pulls his tooth before the child knows what it is about and he experiences terrific pain, he will never trust a dentist again. However, if the dentist very cautiously and carefully first shows the child what the situation is and says, "This is about as much pain as there will be," if the child has not been traumatized before, than he will later on be capable of tolerating some discomfort in the dentist's chair.

And so with intellectualizing. I have not often found that intellectualizing is a serious hindrance in any treatment situation that I have become familiar with over the years. There are individuals who from way back in their lives have learned to live and survive as if they were living next to themselves. They were exposed prematurely when their psyche was ill-equipped with mental machinery for such a task. But to object to this without yet knowing how it grew, or when it first happened, is an error. This is the essence of their pathology. You do not at the outset ask such a person to give up the essence of his pathology so he can begin treatment.

At the present time, I have somebody in analysis who tends to intellectualize. He speaks distantly about himself, in the third person, and generally treats his life and the vicissitudes of his present and past difficulties with a kind of superior miles-away stance. Characteristically, he does the same thing with me. When I tell him something about himself he will hear me out patiently, and then will tell me in a very kindly way that he had heard I was supposed to be a good and experienced analyst. But the way I phrase my interpretations certainly does not bear out my reputation. There is, he says, a kind of vagueness in the way in which I speak. Frankly, I would not say this was just empty talk. There are some very fine perceptions about me involved in all this. He puts his finger on some weak spots in my personality. Nevertheless, nothing would be easier now than to rise up and defend myself, or worse, seemingly not to defend myself, but to tell him immediately that he is turning the treatment topsy-turvy. This is not a good method, because the patient is doing to me what he is doing to himself. By my general faithfulness to my particular outlook on such things, we have made a great deal of headway.

When this patient was three and a half years old, he was abandoned by both his parents, and for about a year and a half he had to adapt to a very strange and a very frightening environment, not knowing whether he would ever see his parents again or how he would survive. It was during that time that he began to live next to himself in order to survive.

He learned in a very primitive way, a precursor of what is now an ingrained characterological attitude, to handle difficulties as if he were observing himself. I think in essence that was indeed what enabled him to survive. I think that had he not been capable of distancing himself from himself at this particular time, the traumatic impact of the situation would have had much more deleterious results than it did have. My impulse is not to react to the patient, but to understand him. That does not mean that one does not have reactions, but one has trial reactions.

When this person in his detached way hurts my feelings, I am aware of the fact that my feelings are hurt. I do not, however, rise to my defense, but my reaction becomes a tiny aspect of that whole set of communications or that whole complex of information that I try to understand. I ask myself why he wants to hurt me when I am quite sure I did not want to hurt him. It is quite clear that everything about this situation is designed to hurt him. I cannot do anything but hurt him. The mere fact that I am looking at him and trying to understand him hurts. It hurts him because he has spun out this early attitude of living next to himself into something grandiose, and secondarily, enormously valuable. In this way he defends himself against being tossed around or shifted around without being asked anything, against the most important people in his life suddenly disappearing for a year and a half. These experiences are tremendous narcissistic blows of his early life. So he formed against this an enormously effective attitude in which he lives a life superior to himself, like God looking upon himself and at other people. And when anything occurs that might possibly develop into a traumatic situation—for instance, attaching himself to me and then again being abandoned when he is most vulnerable, as he was at the age of three and a half—he defends himself against it. He says, "You're not judging me only; I'm judging you." Now to tell him, "Don't be arrogant. This is an analysis, and you'd better cooperate, and don't intellectualize," would be a grave error. It might lead somewhere, but not where I want it to go.

To point out intellectualization does lead to a kind of cooperation, but not to the kind of a gradual sharing of an attitude that is the essence of analysis. I know you are not conducting analyses here, but I do not think this attitude is in any way at variance with the attitude of the general psychotherapist. What you might do, and how deep you want to go with it is another story. But I think to attack a person's attitude immediately because essentially it usually interferes with the kind of fantasy you have of what the situation should be like is an injustice to the patient. It is not conducive to the best advances that are possible with him.

It is comparatively easy to talk about handling intellectualization, but it is not so easy without some experience in all this to live it in therapy. You can very easily become condescending in this kindness, and such condescension may be almost as bad as, or perhaps even worse than, an honest attack on the patient. You have to be able to do all this without being condescending. In other words, it really has to become part and parcel of yourself, and this does not happen without some inner struggle. I think my patients usually know when they have gotten under my skin, and I have to struggle a bit not to let myself lash out in response to that. I do not give them speeches about it, but I think it must shine through in some way. I am not pretending anything that I am not. But I think sooner or later people become convinced that to the best of my knowledge and ability I am trying to understand them. If I have reactions, I will even regret them, and then do better next time. They know I, too, am a human being.

That is a long answer to your question, but I think it gives you the answer to how I feel about it. To summarize, if somebody begins by intellectualizing I will not object. I will assess this as probably a necessary defense; the more ingrained it is the less likely will I be in any way to try to undermine it. It is a necessary aspect of the character of the personality and has its own meaning. I think the first thing that one can do is to explain this meaning to the patient. The patient will then very likely understand that this is not an attack. Then you have firm ground on which to stand. You have done it in the conviction and the overall knowledge that you were not attacking him—that you were explaining something to him. If he then becomes defensive, you can show that the defensiveness has something to do with anxiety, that he cannot yet see himself living without it, and that he naturally attacks the person who is in any way beginning to interfere with such a reliable lifelong balance.

I want to introduce a little different aspect of the same situation. There are some students whom we see who are too lacking in defenses. They are too undefended. They come in under the impact of a severe loss of self-esteem, but as they talk about themselves they reveal periods when they have functioned very well, perhaps even with grandiosity, as long as they are in contact with a person who ''feels for'' and supports them. It seems that with such students a first step might be to give them this defense and say, ''You tend to feel either very badly about yourself or quite buoyed up.'' In a sense, one is giving them an intellectual or intelligent way of looking at what they're doing and this helps them defend against feelings of real depression. Is it something you can then use as the basis for further work?

I hope you did not see this in any way as in opposition to what we've been talking about, because it is very much in line with what I have been saying.

But the kind of patient I think you're talking about is different from those who come in to see us in this clinic. Many of those we see are in an acute decompensation.

This is a totally different set of problems. I think you're quite right in pointing out that the psychoanalyst sees patients who are more likely to be bogged down in chronic characterological difficulties and will perhaps not come in acute decompensations. They are more likely to fall into the problem area of how one should relate to them. Perhaps in your work in the clinic the acute decompensations, where students are too little defended, more overwhelmed with anxiety, are statistically more frequent. Let me say right away that this is true only for the beginning of treatment. In the long-term treatment of narcissistic personalities I have been working with so much, and have supervised so many people on, and have had so many consultations about, patients often go through periods of severe temporary decompensation and traumatic states of being flooded.

In the course of long-term treatment we are very familiar with what you were describing, except not generally when people come to us initially, although sometimes that occurs too. You know, I see most everything—people from all areas of life, colleagues, and psychiatric residents who come to me in severe acute depressions.

In acute decompensations, what is needed is first an empathic assessment of the particular state in which the individual presents himself. If somebody comes to you who is flooded with anxiety, who is deeply depressed because of some acute decompensation, whether it is that he has just left home and finds himself in a new situation, or he has been jilted, or he is not able to mix with other students, or he has gotten into a terrific funk about an exam, or he has had intercourse and is terribly anxious about having contracted venereal disease—whatever the acute anxiety attacks of adolescence or late adolescence may be—certainly the first reaction will be to express your empathic understanding of the state the patient is in. This is already curative, helpful, therapeutic. This task now is shared and there is a strength that comes from sharing.

You recall the earlier session on the primitive wordless workings of an empathic melting together. It has a history that goes way back to a small child's discomfort, a mother's empathic resonance, a mother's toning down this anxiety in resonating to the child's anxiety but not denying it. The mother then includes the child in her own personality, often with physically embracing and carrying him. This you cannot and do not need to do with your patients, but symbolically you can. If a student comes in a real panic state, you can show a kind of likeness with him, but with a lessened anxiety, a kind of sharing, a showing of how understandable this is. You don't have to say, "I too, when I was your age," or anything like that. There is no need for that. The fact that you understand, and that you elaborate something about the anxiety state before the patient has told you about how he feels, allows him to think, "He knows that too. He must have been through that himself and still lives. He's not so anxious, so I'm not so anxious."

In other words, it is a kind of empathic enclosure that the person finds which is the first defense that you offer. While it may be obviously a defense, at some time or other, for a person to identify wholesale with another person, at this particular moment it is obviously a wholesome defense to share another's personality temporarily. Explanations of the kind that you are bringing should come second. First, you establish this kind of a side-by-side feeling; then, on the basis of having enclosed the patient within your own boundaries, you have allowed him to enclose you within his boundaries (Kohut, 1984). On the basis of that particular new level, and then some intelligent discussion of the situation, some explanation about the ups and downs of his self-esteem would follow, but as a second step. To offer explanation from the beginning would be less effective. In a sense, it would increase the distance between you. It does not mean, and it should not mean, that you are suffering as much as the patient.

I think we talked about this capacity to empathize without taking over the patient's task in the same context many weeks ago here (see Chapter 5, p. 63). I talked about what one does for a dying person. It does not necessarily mean that one pretends that one is dying. I think anybody who is dying and sees healthy people around him must be angry, must envy them, must have the feeling, "You don't know what it means. You will some day, but right now you don't." I think I recommended to you at that time the short story by Tolstoy, "The Death of Ivan Ilich." It is a beautiful description of a man who, as he is dying, becomes more and more aware of the gap between him and all the healthy people whose lives will go on. All the consolation they give him means nothing. But there is one person who helps him. There is an old servant who helps him by allowing physical contact, by being physically helpful to him. These are things, in a nonverbal way, to which people will respond. If one can combine it with an empathically given little gift that enhances the person's self-esteem when he is down, by congratulating the person, then you will help him. I think it is as true for a dying person as for the person who is in the throes of a severe traumatic state.

But to return to our consideration of the student. For the intelligent expansion of his ego, you have to strengthen the ego a little bit by allowing this empathic extension, by lending your own personality. When you have done that, then you can cautiously begin to give insight, something about the dynamics of the ups and downs. You allow the person to distance himself from himself. In other words, you do just the opposite of what we were afraid of at first, telling him that maybe he is too intellectual.

There are certainly times in analysis where the verbal approach to a chronic defensive attitude can be improved upon, in other words, where one can do more than just repeat the same formulae. Sometimes one gets the impression that just to tell the person more about it is not enough. Ferenczi (1950, p. 236), quoting Freud, said that there comes a time in the treatment of phobias when the patient just has to face the phobic situation; unless he has this extra bit of courage the treatment will bog down. Then you can encourage the patient by lending him some of your courage, as it were, to make some steps that seem to be like the muscular approach toward symptoms. It is not because you want to abolish the symptom, but because you want to get to the experience that the patient is avoiding. The phobia is not the true symptom. The phobia is a secondary avoidance reaction.

From the beginning Freud differentiated between anxiety hysteria and phobia (1920). The phobia surrounds the anxiety experience. It protects against the experience. The condition begins with an anxiety attack; then there follows greater and greater spread of all kinds of defensive maneuvers, so that the situation in which the anxiety might occur again is avoided. An elaborate system of defenses protects the phobia. There are people who split off the experience of the analysis by defensively denying that it has any meaning outside the office and the couch. It is as if he says, "It's all valid here," but as soon as he crosses the threshold it doesn't count any more. With such individuals one intuitively learns to do certain things. One gives an interpretation at the end of an hour; the patient gets up, and one says, "Wait a moment," and then one tells him a little more. This is not orthodox technique; what is valid on the couch is valid now too. I have even run after a patient when he was trying to get on the elevator. I have called people up and said, "Listen, I thought about this dream you had last night. It just occurred to me, and I can't wait until tomorrow. It is such a good thought that I want to tell you about it tonight before you go to sleep." One doesn't do this every day, but sometimes one has to be imaginative. It is the kind of thing which, if you do by rote, is absolute nonsense. The technique is perfectly reasonable, and this makes perfectly good sense, but like anything else, it can be abused. It is your job to see to it that it is not abused.

A most important issue raised in the last session was the general internal mental set of the therapist as he sees the case unfold and extends himself empathically to another person. These are preliminary steps only, but they require a particular kind of mental attitude that I think is very important. This is more easily defined in general terms than in specifics, for one can do all kinds of things if one has the right attitude. One can learn by rote what one should say or what one should not say, and treatment will not succeed. We talked about this with reference to the 19-year-old student when I mentioned that I sometimes find myself at variance with the reactivity of people and the kind of questions they ask when a case is being presented. I want to say, "Let me listen." I want something to come to me, and questions disturb me. One wants to know, but the data will fall into place if one listens.

I'm trying to understand the nature of the average expectable response within such a patient when he's responded to in the way you've described. On the surface, it may begin as an identification with your attitude toward him. He becomes interested again, not so much in whether he's right or wrong, or good or bad, but because you're interested in how his mind works. He cannot fail to be impressed with the fact that you explicitly want to understand.

I would hope the result would be a little different. What you are describing may very well be the result of this kind of an attitude if one sees a person several times a week in a very intimate kind of contact. But when one sees a person once a week, I would think that your real understanding of how his mind works, or at least a beginning grasp of why it became the way it is with reference to his parents, would allow the patient, with your help, to solve a specific circumscribed task better than he could alone. He can then say, "Seeing that I have this kind of mind, seeing that this is the way it grew with regard to my parents and the still existing intermeshing with them, grasping this, I know approximately what my anxieties are as I try to extricate myself from my parents and try to face an independent task such as schoolwork or living away from home."

I think this is essentially the problem here. It permits distance and allows one to be less automatic in one's responses. So that with the very circumscribed task for which he comes into treatment, namely that he is so anxiety-ridden vis-à-vis examinations and studies, this approach would help him to diminish his anxiety. There would be greater capacity for seeing the nature of the anxiety.

In other words, I do not envision, as in an analysis, the building up of a complex interpersonal relationship, on the basis of repeating something from the past, and then gradually extricating oneself in the experimental setting of the analysis. But rather, as an auxiliary ego to him, by understanding, you can add insight, giving him greater mastery over present tensions and allowing him greater ease in working himself out of a rather circumscribed problem. That would be my general aim.

The difficulty lies in the following: It is comparatively easy to pinpoint the content of specific internal conflicts. It is much harder, but I think much more important, to pinpoint the mode in which a particular mind works independent of the conflict. That is the focus of my attention in diffuse cases of this particular type.

He might have come in with another symptom at some other time. This happens to be something that drives him at the moment. But he could have come in three months later with something else. He would still be the same person, with the same basic problems, with his particular kind of mind. So with a diffuse problem of this particular type, I try to pinpoint, for my own feeling, how this mind works. Generally one finds out that it is neither positive nor negative, but both. This is an example of my trial identifications or my trial modes of empathy.

In other words, I pointed out his poetry and the way in which he saw himself sitting in the dorm, looking out and seeing the street as a river, the cars as boats, and himself as a boat. His self-esteem is probably shaky, for after all, he sees himself as a boat. It is quite significant that he sees himself as an inanimate thing, as an object that is being driven by waves. But it is poetry. He obviously does not see himself as somebody who takes hold of things, as a man of action who is involved in things. He does not spin out fantasies, as other students might, of being a researcher, a great general, a great football player. He sees himself as a boat somehow driven by the waves, surrounded by other boats; there is very little human life in this imagery. Secondarily, he offers this poetic fantasy to somebody for praise. He then is disappointed. He expected a good grade from his English professor and what he got was a negative grade. So the man did not understand.

To me, this is a good inroad into how a personality works: his sensitivity, his doubts about himself, spinning these out in internally elaborated fantasies, and then offering the fantasy secondarily, to make contact with others, to get, secondarily, some kind of boost to his self-esteem. There are both positives and negatives. The positive is the fine mind, the refinement, the differentiation of his fantasies, of the thinking processes. The negatives are the comparative passivity, the inability to see himself as an initiator of action, and the tremendous dependence on other people's empathic grasp of what is good about his mind. I am using this more as a mode, an example, of how to think when I see such an individual, not that this is a foolproof interpretation of his personality. I would like to hear more and develop further ideas. But having this kind of grasp, then I can tentatively communicate this to the patient.

However, I communicate this not with blame or with praise; rather, I attempt to show the advantages and disadvantages of his particular mode of functioning, so that he gets to know himself better. These are not things that he does not know about himself, but very likely he has never verbalized this to himself. And if he has, if he's very gifted psychologically as some people are, with insights beyond expectation, it does no harm if somebody else can understand too.

A kind of bond, then, is set up, allowing his insights to become even clearer. And this, to my mind, now broadens the basis on which the specific problems of the present situation can be tackled. He has an ally; he has a greater insight into who he is, what he is, and how he functions. One can see that he wants to resist his parents, to extricate himself from them, and one can also recognize that the parents act now exactly in the same way as when what we now consider his mind was formed. In other words, they intrude on him all the time, run his life for him, and very likely they continuously debunk him. After you have made a little inroad that way, then the patient, at least initially and generally, comes forth with a tremendous amount of convincing and, to some extent, confirmatory material.

He will not necessarily confirm you in all things. The most satisfactory responses are those that are basically confirmatory, but with corrections.[1] It is as if the patient were saying, "Yes, you are essentially right, but not quite. Here you are wrong." Then one has the feeling one is understanding him and he feels understood. Knowing this, he will understand that his present task is to extricate himself from his parents and he will also realize that it is difficult. Then he will not blame himself too much for the kind of weakling he is. How could it be otherwise but very difficult since these same parents from whom he wants to separate himself are interfering now?

By the way, let me warn you right from the beginning not to take sides against parents. You do not start out fighting with him against others. This is, at least initially, a very poor policy. You are really doing the same thing the parents did before. You are taking the initiative rather than letting him find the initiative. He will gladly, as it were, fall into line again, but you will not get even the tiny bit of change that you hoped to achieve. Your task is to form some kind of a team with him in which his own base about himself is broadened. Then he will see, to some extent, the difficulty of the task. He will know it in terms of the history and of the present dynamics: that the parents who formerly interfered with his having initiative are now continuing to interfere. They probably make it even harder by being so solicitous. Then you show all the advantages he has from their solicitude but again, without blaming him, "It's not that you're a baby who wants to lean on others and cling. But this is the way your mind is now set, and it could not be otherwise."

You do not try to persuade him to be anything he is not. First let him accept what he is; then, on the basis of this acceptance allow him to see that this task is quite a big one. "Of course you're anxious when this happens. But anxiety is not necessarily a bad thing. This is something we will try to understand together." By such an alliance you are not playing at an empty, flag-waving brotherhood, but real understanding, and modestly so, with the grasp in yourself of how likely you are to make mistakes. It is particularly difficult when the mind of the individual you are helping and his mode of functioning are indeed quite different from your own.

---

[1]The therapist's *approximate* understanding serves as optimal frustration. The individual then transmutes the therapist's selfobject function into a self function. He not only understands what has been interpreted, he enlarges and modifies it or corrects it. It becomes reliable self understanding.

It is difficult to compare my therapy experiences in analysis with what I have gleaned from books. For books will never give you experience. The most well-written, gifted, insightful books will only prepare you for learning from clinical experiences. In other words, without my having studied Freud, as it were, I could not have learned from my patients. Still, what I learned from my patients, I did not learn from Freud essentially. This is only the background which has allowed me over the years to order what I see. As I stated earlier, if you have worked in pathology, you know that one learns from looking through the microscope at innumerable pathology slides. So unless you have studied books that have originally given you the main configurations to search for, you have nothing to build on.

There is a patient that I have often drawn on here for illustrations. This is the same man who at one time made gross identification with me and then gradually subtler ones (Chapter 6, p. 77). This man's mind is actually very different from mine. He lacks many of the good qualities of my own mind, and I lack the very bent and splendid qualities of his mind. He has an enormously exact mind, and he will not let go of definitions in his own field, a very different field from psychiatry, until he has them down to the finest refinement. I have somewhat of a theoretical bent too, but his is a mathematical bent, and mine is not. The following situation arose: In the course of associating to a dream in a preceding session the patient associated in a way that seemed to me to get farther and farther away from the meaning of the dream. He associated, and he had associations to the associations. He took up one word and had a clang association to that word. I finally stopped him and said, "It seems to me that the way you're going about it, you're going farther and farther away from the mood of the dream. At the beginning we knew quite a bit more than where you seem to be going now."

He got furious at me for interrupting him. This was not the time to interrupt. This was his mode of thinking as against my mode of thinking. He thought it was leading somewhere, and my impatience had something to do with the fact that I could not give up the way I was for the way he was, something on that order. I was not in the best condition during that time, and I argued for a while, but I finally stopped. It wasn't easy for me. Sometimes one has days that are better than others.

This is the end of a long analysis in which the person has made tremendous progress. I have no doubt that some of his identifications with me gave me some kind of gratification that I'm probably now beginning to miss as he becomes more and more truly independent. His associations seemed almost like a caricature of independence, and there was kind of a battle between us. I had all kinds of splendid interpretations. I finally took my own advice to my students and supervisees to heart, "Whenever you want to say something, bite your tongue." So I bit my tongue and kept quiet. Even though I was right, it became a battle of who was going to have the last word, and it was obviously he who was supposed to have the last word, not I. So I achieved that tremendous victory over myself.

The reward came in the session afterward in the form of a flood of significant and important memories that I then recognized related to what happened the day before in our tiff about his free association and to what had happened all through his life. We had known this before. This is what one calls working-through, when the same thing comes up over and over again, as you have heard with this patient, and yet with new depth, new meaning and new emotions added to it. The major emotion was that he could do something to me the day before that he was never able to do before. He experienced how furious he was at his father for debunking him and for interfering, and he asserted himself in spite of it. The tiny trifle of newness was that he could, for the first time, feel the resentment fully and could maintain himself in the transference—and this is the important thing—in the actual rebellion against me for having interfered. I had interfered with his free associations in a specific way and that had led to a tiff with me in the previous session. I finally mastered my own reaction, which was a difficult thing for me to do.

In the following session the reward came when he told of an interesting experience. His father was strongly against a particular political party and made fun of it. While the patient was in college he was introduced to a rather liberal professor and began to attend many public functions at which he spoke. This was the first time that strong convictions about government had entered his life. Particular social issues became very important to him. It was sort of like a late adolescent experience for this patient. The parents came to visit him and the patient said he would like to take them to hear this man speak. When they walked out, there was an unforgettable moment when the father said, "The same goddam stuff I've been hearing for 20 years." The patient did not have a feeling of depression, but a typical empty, drained feeling. The self-esteem drained out of his preconscious self-concept that he was beginning to try to acquire in an independent move. The important thing is he felt no anger then at the father whom he had always idealized and in whom he had never seen any shortcomings. He never went back to hear that speaker again, even though he was at that college for a number of years.

So you see the difference between what is happening yesterday and today, as it were, in the analysis. These are not issues that make or break an analysis. This is only a tiny detail among thousands of others. If I had not found my way back yesterday, it would not have destroyed the analysis, for nothing can destroy this analysis anymore. But if one makes nothing but mistakes, that is a different story. This is an example of feeling oneself into another person. And it becomes somewhat more difficult when indeed the kind of mentality is of another type. This person too, as in the patient we were describing, comes to me and tells me about his particular research. He has very interesting research ideas which are very difficult for me to understand. They involve a great deal of mathematics and physics, which are not at my disposal, but it is not so much that. It has something to do with the whole mental setup being different. And yet I have to find my way in allowing him to be different, and not trying to be in his field what I am in my field. It does not fit the field, and it does not fit his personality.

13

Function of Empathy in Building Esteem and Restoring Initiative

THE PROBLEMS POSED by this 18-year-old are common among students in their first years at college. There may be a precipitate engagement, a plan to drop out of school, a sudden loss of interest in a long cherished academic goal. The discomfort and confusion engendered are acute enough to lead the student to the clinic.

This is an 18-year-old girl who is a freshman. She comes from New York. She is a Protestant. There were three things she wanted to discuss. One was her concern about an engagement to a young man. Second was whether she should quit school. Third was whether she should take a job which has been offered her in which she could earn enough money so that she could leave school and travel for a year in Europe. I have seen her four times on a weekly basis except for a week between the third and fourth interviews.

She looks older than 18. She's very attractive, bright, and uses very vivid imagery in her discussions. I have to say very little in order to learn what's on her mind. She was a little hesitant about coming to us because of what she felt were some rather unhappy experiences in the past. In high school, because she was unhappy, she went to see her English teacher a couple of times and he interpreted her difficulties as being an oedipal conflict on the basis of some stories she had written.

Here at the university her unhappiness continued. When she saw an announcement that graduate students in psychology would be glad to interview anybody who felt in need of help, she went for two sessions. She talked about the oedipal conflict, and the interviewer said, "Did it ever occur to you that your father might have these oedipal feelings toward you?" That gave her such terrible nightmares she didn't go back.

So she was a little bit afraid of something like this happening here. She had been home for Christmas and had felt very much left out. As an illustration, at the dining table in the evening she had the feeling that her brother and sisters were talking with her parents and she was sort of an outsider.

She talked immediately about her family. She is the oldest of four. Her father was a hero to her all through her growing-up period. He was the first of his class when he graduated a very prestigious Ivy League school and was voted most likely to succeed. He's big, handsome, and everybody looks up to him.

In the early years of her life, father was teaching at a private New York school; now he teaches in a public high school. He is also the athletic coach. Her first words about her mother were, "Oh, she's so childlike." This student began to have difficulties with her father when the family moved from the community in which she had grown up to a new community where he took a new teaching job. She was in eighth grade then, about 13 years old. He complained bitterly about her lack of responsibility at that time. Instead of helping the family move, she found every excuse possible to stay with her old friends. She didn't want to move in the first place. She was very unhappy about it. Her father's accusations about her irresponsibility continued throughout her adolescence. She found she couldn't communicate with her father, and she finally ran away from home. She didn't go very far, but it was enough to get everybody upset. One of her friends let her family know where she was, and they got her back home again.

When she was 16 she became involved with her present fiancé who is 10 years older than she is. As time has gone on here at the university, she has expressed less and less interest in him and talked more and more about how she wants to break off that relationship. At present this issue of deciding whether she wants to stay engaged or not has faded into the background. Her concern now is about her dating pattern at the university. She knows lots of boys. She doesn't know any girls, except one girlfriend who came from New York with her to this university—an old and good friend with whom she can talk about everything. The dating she has done here has all been on a rather superficial acquaintance level. However, she has fantasies about a man who is somehow involved in the theatre at the university. These are fantasies of a white knight rescuing her. She said, "If I would find a white knight who would listen to me, and understand me, and would hug me when I'm upset, I wouldn't need any therapy." In that way she introduced her doubts about coming into the clinic.

It was my impression in the first three interviews that she was depressed. She was talking in a sort of low key, and she looked unhappy. I remarked on this, and she said she was lonely. She thought she was like her father in that she was keeping herself terribly busy in order to avoid having to be with people. She has either classes or work as a secretary from 10:30 in the morning till 6:00 at night, every day of the week except two; on those days she starts at 11:30. This is a pretty heavy schedule for a student. However, she is doing adequate work and has a good academic record.

She talked about her white knight fantasies. She was very much preoccupied with what she would do with this theatre director in whom she was interested, and he had apparently expressed some interest in her. She felt that what she would do would not be good, no matter what it would be, and she didn't want to get involved with him. She couldn't say how it wouldn't be good, but she had the feeling she wouldn't be herself; rather, she would be playing a role. I think she finally solved that problem by deciding she would write a play. She did so, and as far as I know, she got over her feelings about him. She writes frequently in order to try to deal with things that bother her. She has now found somebody else also interested in the theatre. She has given her play to this man, because he is involved in judging plays for a prize.

Are these autobiographical plays?

No, they have plots—but more than that I don't know. I have the feeling she has a pretty rich fantasy life, much of which she hasn't told me yet. But in the last interview she gave me a few more little hints about what's going on. She looked like a different girl, much younger, and more animated. This was after I missed a week with her—a two-week interval. She began the hour by saying that a lot had happened. She had come to the conclusion that her idea about therapy had not been altogether right. She had thought of therapy as just being oil on the water which would gradually float away. She decided it wasn't quite that, that one could begin to act on what one saw about oneself. That was what she had been trying to do during the last two weeks. She had finished her play. She had met the man who was interested in this competition. She had had some good conversations with him. She had not become very much involved with him, but she had the feeling that he understood her. They had talked in fantasy language with one another, and she had pretended that she was the witch, which is something she frequently thinks about.

I said, "Tell me a little bit more about this witch." In describing this self, she said, "Well, the witch floats through the air and peeks into people's windows, and enjoys what they're doing, but keeps herself detached. This is a very timid witch." I said, "And keeps herself at a distance." She said, "Yes." She went to a costume party dressed as a lascivious witch. The young man with whom she had gotten involved came as a lascivious wizard. Unfortunately, he was with another girl. The man she was with was a very good friend, but in the middle of the party she felt so badly she left. It wasn't that she felt rejected. She just felt out of it; so she went home.

Then she said, "I'm really not as lonely as I was. I've gotten in with a group of girls, and I'm really enjoying them. I've really been feeling good. I've decided to take that job. I think I can handle it by dropping only one course." This is as a secretary to a group that is planning to have a music festival here in the summer, and they say they're going to pay her $5,000 for the work. She thinks she can handle that and school at the same time. That job begins next quarter. There is no more talk of dropping out of school or of going to Europe.

We got back to the business of her leaving the party. She said she has a hard time sometimes feeling feminine. She feels most comfortable in blue jeans and a shirt. She has some nice jewelry, but she can't seem to put it on. Then she talked about her father, how mad she is at him and how he really doesn't like women. He treats her mother in a sort of superior, condescending way, and he treats his daughters in the same way. He wanted her to be all these marvelous things, academically, with broad balance, culture, and so on, but she could never be what he really wanted, which was a boy. She was always a tomboy, but that didn't satisfy him either. She didn't say it in those words, but she implied it.

She talked quite warmly about her mother, in contrast to our earlier discussion. She said, "Mother seems to have finally liberated herself from father's domination." She has become interested in teaching children and is very enthusiastic about her contact with them. And she has finally gotten herself out from under at home. Mother used to do everything father wanted her to do, but she always complained and was angry about doing it. The kids had the feeling that mother was resentful at anything she had to do for them or for anybody at home. But now mother is very different, and she's beginning to feel closer to mother than she did earlier. She's also sort of putting herself in her younger sister's place now. Her first impulse is to treat that sister the way father has treated her, but she's not going to do that. She's going to encourage that younger sister to express herself in her own way and not as other people want her to express herself. That's where we are at the moment.

Let's have a quick review of the salient facts. Her major complaint when she came in was indecision about whether to stay in school and whether to break off with her fiancé who is 10 years older. And she felt depressed, or was that the way you saw it?

That was the way I saw it. There was a conflict about taking this job, which might mean that she'd have to drop out of school.

All right, it's open for discussion. Do you get the flavor of the case? Do you see some major salient point in this complaint, in this personality, and in this history? One picks up different things. One individual fastens on something in the immediate appearance or the immediate complaint, another fastens on something in the background. Is there something that gives you the flavor?

This student comes in and says, "I was told I have an oedipal complex," and she got very upset about that.

You're thinking of the father first—the personality of the father.

Do you think she has an oedipus complex? I don't mean in general, but does that play a role in this?

There is some evidence. She's involved with a man who is 10 years older. It makes one question what's going on. Her father was described as tall, handsome and masculine. It sounds like describing a boyfriend rather than a father.

In other words, you see something central in her relationship to her father. And you would pay attention, specifically, to the personality of a man who was such a good student, such a popular guy, and who ends up as a high school coach. Well, one should not be prejudiced. It may not be so bad. On the face of it, it sounds as if it were not the greatest life career, yet it may be that he fulfills some kind of an ideal life. I'd like to know more before I say he's a failure. He may be in our book, but not in his necessarily.

I wouldn't say so much a failure, but a discrepancy. The other thing she presents in her data is that she became so alarmed by what sounds like an inappropriate interpretation that maybe the father has some interest in her, as well as her having some interest in the father. This led to her having nightmares and then viewing any psychotherapeutic encounter as being a very frightening and threatening situation.

Of course, she has some right, after her experience. That was a bit of wild analysis practiced on her. It's like the person who doesn't like going to a surgeon, because the time before the man took out a knife and stuck it into a boil without any warning or anesthesia.

I think we all agree that her particular knight was her father. The thing that was such wild analysis with her was with respect to her relationship with her father and the suggestion that the father might have what sounds like sexual interest in her.

When she talked about this I'm sure a rather skeptical expression crossed my face.

About what?

About the oedipus complex as being central.

How did she respond to that?

She responded by coming back.

Either you're doubting the oedipus complex, or you were doubting the appropriateness of this vigorous interpretation of it that was flung at her.

I had a response to her description of Christmas at home, and of feeling left out with these siblings, two of whom are close, and the other born when she was 10 years old. There was something she said in a later interview of being a timid witch looking in the window from outside. It was that episode, at age 13, in the eighth grade that struck me. She states that this was the onset of the bitter arguments with her father. She said he was angry because she wasn't pulling her weight when they had to move. Instead, she was talking with the girlfriends she was reluctant to leave. There, I think, she was also expressing the need to belong, and the continuation of wanting to cling to where she belonged. I had one wild fantasy about that same episode. The manifest content I think is the same as at Christmas, that there was the place where she belonged and father was tearing her away from it. My wild fantasy was that if she was 13, and if she was becoming pubescent, it may have been some kind of a threat for him. I'm obviously reasoning backward from her nightmare reaction to the wild interpretation. He might have then dealt with his own response to that by becoming hypercritical, as some fathers do, of a pubertal girl. So I feel the central theme of the material so far is the issue of, ''Where do I belong, and what am I being torn away from?'' As the therapy went on—again it's my fantasy—she got from her therapist some feeling and satisfaction which enabled her to find some girlfriends. To me, this was evidence of seeking to feel at home.

My own feelings parallel these. But I'd like to add another dimension. I think what you're saying about the significance of the particular point in development in which this bitter feeling between her and her father arose, when the father began to reproach her for not taking enough responsibility, very much supports your description. This is a very frequent occurrence. When the breasts begin to swell, and the first physical signs of womanhood or outward femininity come about, the father feels guilty about previous closeness to the girl, and handles it by becoming excessively critical of her. He's critical of her for being what? That's very striking. Of course, one would have to know the father, but let me speculate: for being such a witch, a tempting woman. She becomes an incestuously tempting woman, and he becomes critical of her for being things other than duty-bound, a good solid, non-seductive worker. She can't help it; her body is growing. He displaces the blame and he blames her for it. This is a very typical development in the lives of girls vis-à-vis their fathers. In that sense I would agree, not with the method of telling her that the oedipus complex is the central focus, but in a way this is correct. I would also see that the anger between her and her father is at least to some extent defensive on the father's part.

But this is just the beginning, because what we're really puzzling about is what became of her in all this. Can one already have some kind of theory, or some kind of broader construction that fits the way her personality developed? There is more material. Our theory is not the only one; there must be others. This theory does not explain how empty she felt when she visited at home or why she feels depressed. I have the feeling that the depression and the sense of emptiness have earlier roots that have attached themselves to these comparatively late disturbances. But one begins from the surface and works down.

I think in this particular case, very likely, this is not just from the surface down but rather a crucial moment of her life and in her early adolescence. What happens very frequently is that there is regression to the very point before this kind of emotional disaster has taken place, that is, to the last time when the father was still friendly. Is it a regression to the period when the father was not faced with a tempting witch but with a childlike witch, a charmer who does not yet have breasts or broader hips, who has not yet anything that might be seductive to a grown man, but is still a little girl, and with the mind of a little girl?

It seems to me—now you must confirm it or object to it, because I don't know the girl—this is an attractive person with a pre-adolescent mentality, with poetry and sublimated writing, with an attempt to be a nonsexual charmer. Then there is the lascivious witch, and there is something sort of ghost-like, something on that order that I read between the lines. I may misread it, but this is the first feeling tone that I get. In addition there is another level of the personality which at least hints of a deeper, earlier trauma in her life, earlier, that is, than the oedipal and the revived pubertal oedipal trauma. When we talk about puberty here, it is a tele-scoped replica, for the time being, for what happened at about the age of five. Oedipal material, as it arises in puberty, gives us a glimpse of what happened during the initial oedipal phase.

I think the personality of the father is probably of some importance in all this. I would imagine he is easier with men than with women—you know, athletes and physical culture. Continuing my speculations, there were no girls at his college when he was there. Even if it had been a coeducational institution, the point is that he was a man who was popu-lar among men. Perhaps prostitution occasionally played a role on week-ends and bragging about it, but no emotionally involved relationship with the other sex. He was probably a good athlete, and he became a physical education major. This is his specialty. We do not know yet, but I have a feeling that there must be something about the kind of woman he married. I think this girl was also deprived of basic mothering, not severely, but slightly. At the present time I see her presenting an oedipal problem slightly weighted down by a depressive cast about herself, slightly weighted down; depression is not in the center of things.

We do know that there were two siblings born in very quick succes-sion, so the mother had to be somewhat tied up with taking care of the younger babies and could not have given her as much attention. She also described the mother as being very irritated with having to do things for them up until recently. So, if you put the two together, moth-er must have been pretty burdened down for a few years when she was younger.

These two sets of experiences together are the most important. Mother may have had baby after baby because this was the father's athletic outlook on the world. I don't know what type of person he would marry, perhaps an older sister figure, but under the circumstances she may not have had enough for this little girl. There may be something of this emptiness that is reflected in her visit home. I have the feeling there is another aspect to all this, although it seems, on the face of it, to be essentially an oedipal problem.

Her reason for coming in was that she couldn't make up her mind about her engagement, about staying in school, and about taking a job at which she would earn enough money so that she could travel. She wanted to sort these things out.

She wanted some advisor, counselor, older friend, to help her think over her present life situation. You had the impression that, in general, she was chronically depressed, moody, and couldn't really participate in the fun of the other kids. She felt out of the running. She had been at home and felt out of sorts there, that she wasn't included in the family situation. She didn't really feel included here among her peers, and particularly in heterosexual dating.

She had lots of boyfriends, but nothing meaningful, and no girlfriends, except one from home.

But, if I'm not mistaken, that has changed a little. In other words, as she began to see you and felt more balanced, she felt understood and listened to. She returned to you feeling that she was capable of finding girlfriends, a reaction more consistent with her developmental plan. The frantic search for boyfriends was more imitative and didn't really correspond to the level of her personality development. In general, I think we all agreed that her personality development was a bit fixed on an early adolescent level, and even though she's physically well developed, and even beautiful, psychologically she's suffering a bit from this early rejection of her sexuality by her father. He began to be critical and argumentative when he felt exposed to her growing bosoms. So you had four sessions with her, and now you have had one more.

Before I start with this last one I might say that the kinds of things I commented on with this girl were her loneliness. I remarked that she seemed to feel that her family wanted her to be very grown up and, at the same time, often treated her as if she were a very little girl. I remarked on the fact that she seemed to have such difficulty communicating with her father in words, and sometimes she had to resort to actions, such as running away.
When she came in last week she said she was struggling with the decision as to whether she should go home or not during spring vacation. She wanted to show her independence by staying away from home, but on the other hand she had the need to get across to her father that she is someone in her own right. She wants to explain herself to him. She wants to do this not only because she wants to get on a better footing with him, but also to protect her siblings from having to go through what she has gone through with him. That is, if she can get across to him that one grows up and becomes independent, maybe he'll be easier on the younger siblings. She felt she had made it very hard for them in the past, because she and father got into such arguments when she didn't do what father wanted her to do. She's afraid of going back and trying it, as she did at Christmas, and failing again. She doesn't want to go through the same misery. She can't figure out which is more

mature and what she should do. I said it sounded as if she were trying to decide whether she should act, as she had earlier, or whether she should try talking with her father.

She said, "Yes, that's exactly what I'm trying to say to you; and what I mean by all this business about my younger brother and sisters." Then she dropped that subject and said her fiancé was coming to visit her at the end of that week, and she was looking forward to it. She then told me she had been talking with a professor whom she admires very much. Partly she wanted to see what his attitudes were about what he was teaching, and partly she wanted to talk with him about her future plans and her major. He advised her to go into general studies, because that fits in with her creative abilities. She was enthusiastic but father is going to object. Despite the fact that father always talks with her about her need for a general solid background in the humanities, he also talks with her about the fact that she has to educate herself for a career. He's giving her a double message, and she doesn't know which to listen to. She's afraid that if she goes into the general studies program he's going to be critical of her and she's not going to be able to show him why it's a good idea. She has had a letter from him in which she felt he was telling her she had an unsatisfactory report card because she doesn't write to him the kind of letters that he wants to receive from her. She's too impersonal and talks in generalities about what she's doing; this isn't what he wants to hear. She said she almost called me during the week, because she was being so compulsive in her activities and didn't understand why she was doing what she was doing. She was overeating tremendously, which is something she does when she gets anxious. She was doing things she didn't want to do and thought she had overcome. She went out with a boy, agreed to go to his apartment in the evening and spent the night with him, even though she didn't want to. She felt very annoyed with herself and ashamed. She doesn't understand why she always gets in her own way and seems to spoil her own success.

In this overeating business, she has joined some kind of dance group on campus and she was determined that she would lose weight so she could be in this dance, but instead she went ahead and ate. She sees herself doing this kind of thing repeatedly. She wonders whether she fears succeeding and whether that's why she spoils things for herself, but she says that somehow doesn't feel right. She thought maybe I had suggested that. Then she said, no, somebody else suggested that, and she couldn't remember who. Anyway, it didn't feel right to her.

I said, "Maybe it's something else." She thought about it and said she didn't think it had anything to do with deserving or not deserving to succeed. She thinks it has something to do with being elite. If you succeed you belong to the elite, and she thinks that makes her uncomfortable. She began to talk about June, her good friend from home. June is going to pot; she is in the drug scene, teaching school, and going to New York, where she has become involved with a 50-year-old man. June asks her what she thinks, and this time, in contrast to all other times, the patient told her that she was ruining herself, instead of just listening as she had always done in the past. Now she's beginning to worry about this.

Is she going to lose her friends if she becomes an individual and allows "her core" to develop? She's afraid of allowing her core to develop. "For instance, look at that professor, who has a core," and whom she admires very much. She understands that he has very disturbed children. And what does that mean, as far as core is concerned? If you allow your core to develop, then you can't spend your time on such extraneous things as being feminine, getting dressed up, wearing nice jewelry, and so on. You've got to concentrate on developing yourself. And if you allow your core to develop, then you become an elite. You see the limitations in others, and you become impatient with them; you can't empathize with them, and you set yourself apart.

And what kind of mother would you be? You'd obviously be superior to your children in intelligence. How would you be able to empathize with them, and how will you understand what they feel? This is what her father did to her mother. He never understood her, because mother had limitations and he did not—and he developed a kind of tolerant superior understanding for mother, which meant that they were never together. She feels there can be no real merging of two people if she allows herself to develop this. What she's afraid might develop could be an elite core.

I asked her to enlarge on her understanding of the core, so that I could understand it better. It was my feeling that she was really talking about some kind of grandiosity that she feels within herself. But I didn't say anything about that. The interview ended with her telling me she was looking forward to the visit from her boyfriend. He allowed her to try things out for herself. She felt that his visit would be good, regardless of whether she finally decides to break the engagement. That's where we ended.

That's a very interesting and revealing interview from many sides. It shows how much a patient will reveal of herself if you just let her be.

I'd like you to be a bit more active now. There are a variety of ways in which one could approach this. What do you think of the therapist's attitude? What is her general stance? I think it comes through in the way she describes these sessions. How does this patient react to this? What is it about the therapist's behavior and her interaction with the patient that makes the patient feel better? I think the patient has obviously improved, trusts the therapist and is more able to have friends, and so on. And yet there is this regression; she suddenly becomes unfaithful to something. What is all this business about mobilizing the core and something like being part of an elite. Her professor is an elite; and yet what kind of an elite teacher is it who has children obviously disturbed in serious ways? It seems to me there are a number of inroads to the material.

I think the therapist provided quite a different experience from this very involved, active, and somewhat intrusive father. The patient points this up when she asks, "Why do I get in my own way and tend to spoil things?" She plays around with what other people have told her. Then just the remark, "Well maybe it doesn't mean that." What you didn't say was, "Maybe it means this," but allowed her the experience of what she's coming to more and more, that the fiancé lets her try things out for herself. So she tries out something in the hour, maybe it means belonging to an elite; she ventures. And then, with just a little bit more encouragement, the whole dimension comes out, I think the experience in that hour of trying things on her own finally comes across.

I have the impression that the patient must feel the general sense of respect which I think you have for this girl. You're an older sort of sister. There is a kind of kinship—not the same problems or anything like that, but a kind of kinship and understanding. I think the patient gets this feeling from the way you treat her respectfully; you raise her self-esteem just by being with her, and liking her, and at no time being critical of her, but always respectfully listening and trying to work out what all this might mean. I think there is a general unspoken attitude that must be very helpful to the patient. You said it is in opposition to the way in which the father is intrusive, domineering, manipulating. I think that's true, but I think that's not enough. I think her struggle with the father is a very real one. She's very confused about something. You might call it her values. What is this elite? There is something narcissistic, grandiose perhaps, not in terms of grandiose achievement but in terms of being something very special and different.

Is her father trying to justify what he's done instead of carrying out his early promise, in the sense of being elite? Is there this constant argument within himself: "If I had gone on and done this I would have shown myself to be superior by separating myself from my fellow men." Is there some kind of phony echo back and forth that she has picked up? If she develops her core, she can't be feminine.

The interesting thing that I felt very soon—and I think it's a very hopeful sign—is that she's really not talking about her core, but about something that is almost like a foreign body which she must extricate from herself. There is something very valuable that belongs to the father's personality. She really admires and loves the father to some extent. To be unfaithful to that core means to throw over the father; to love the father means to accept the core.

What is this core? This is one of those peculiar situations, not terribly rare, in which the assessment of another individual's personality becomes extremely important in the treatment of the patient. What is the father like? Even without knowing the father, this is not so difficult because the patient knows him. She's intimately related to him and struggles with this relationship.

My speculation is, on the basis of the life history of the father, and also on the basis of what happened between the father and the patient, that this is a man who, in the same way as the patient, remained fixated in an early adolescent developmental state. He has not made the step into adulthood. There is a collegiate quality about him, a quality of being something superior.

If somebody has a set of generally valid ideals—unreachable, self-sacrificing, political do-gooding, or scientifically ambitious—it may be very hard for an adolescent to live up to such an example. There is a goal set that is very hard to reach, but one does not usually become ill over such a goal. One reaches for it. One may long for it, and one may never be satisfied with oneself, but one does not usually become ill. It is when something is peculiarly idiosyncratic, like this father's eliteness, that the problem arises.

What is that eliteness? This man who was voted most likely to succeed became a coach in prep school and then in high school. It's one thing if somebody has such tremendously strong social ideals that he throws overboard all monetary rewards and sacrifices his life, in a sense, but fulfills his life in socially significant activities. That might put a child into a great conflict. As a student he then might have much more substantial drives for bigger stakes and higher bank accounts than this kind of career would give. He would be struggling with a rarefied goal. But this is not true here, not because the goal is so high, but because it is a little odd. It is something that is really based on some kind of defensive set of fantasies, I believe, in the father. What she is struggling with is a kind of love for a father who strikes me as a death-of-a-salesman type. The analogy is correct and yet it is not correct. This is not a money grubber, but the eternal collegian. It is all that he clings to.

In the case of this girl, however, her father obviously became alarmed at the moment when she became a woman. And I have a hunch he became alarmed in his own life when he was to step beyond the school situation. He develops as an eternal member of schools, as some, not all, teachers do. But in this instance I think this man remained fixated at a particular developmental level, and secondarily imbues it with a sort of ill-defined eliteness. And not knowing exactly what he wants, he probably continuously pushes his children around. Being the oldest one, our student bore the brunt and wants to protect the other ones from suffering the same fate. Her conflicts are then centered about the question of whether she is forever going to remain tied to this kind of ideal, to develop a core eliteness, of no smoking, no drinking, no sex before the ball game. You know that kind of business, the clean attitude, and the school flag uppermost? Is she perhaps instead going to move into something toward which I think her general mode of physical and psychological potentialities thrust her, to make ready to become a woman, a wife and mother, somebody who enjoys life in a deeper way than father could? This is one leverage that she has, which she tries; it is the leverage of the oldest child. She can lift herself away from her father, at the moment, by only one trick: by becoming the protector of the young. Under such circumstances she can oppose the father.

There is a lot of insight that one can give a person here—intelligent insight without intellectualizing—which I think can help her a lot. In theoretical terms, do you understand how communicating to this girl that you realize what she is going through can heal? Does anybody want to tackle that?

You were saying something about toning down the response. I think that's what was meant by an empathic understanding of what the other person is going through. It's a kind of lending her some of your healthy psychic tissue.

But how does that work?

Probably a kind of gross identification with the therapist; at least initially.

I take that as evidence that however alone she has felt with her problem, the therapist is giving signals that it is understandable, which can go a long way. It may reach back to the positives from earlier relationships with the parents, older brothers and sisters. Quite a number of young people in our clinic seem to have a period of improvement after simply having made an appointment. I don't know if that's the same kind of thing or not. The expectation of keeping the appointment has a healing effect.

That's certainly true.

I think it's important to differentiate that this is not necessarily a process dependent on pathological personality structure. I think it's safe to say that the experience of being understood, as a gratifying, warming and uplifting experience, is found in the so-called normal situation.

Yes. It was not meant to be in any other way.

In that respect one could see it as somehow being a dyad that goes back to mother and child, but not in the mirroring sense, or in the sense of a lesion being present.

There is also the notion that if one can be understood without your vibrating with the same panic, it's borrowing the strength from a supportive ego.

It seems to me that everything you said was right, but I had something even more general in mind when I brought up the question. You know, one correctness does not exclude another correctness. It depends on which level one attempts to formulate one's thinking. It is perfectly true that we are talking about a normal phenomenon and not about pathology. But there can be pathology here too, as in too great an ease in being comforted and, at the other extreme, the impossibility of being comforted.

What I have in mind is slightly related to the phenomenon that for a while was popularly called "regression in the service of the ego" (Hartmann, 1958). It was a good term, but it has its shortcomings.

I've mentioned to you a number of times that mental health, if it lends itself to any definition at all, is to my mind best approached by the *variety of positions* that a person has at his disposal—by the variety of possibilities that he has, internally and externally, of adapting. In other words, a person who can adapt only through action, only through changing the external environment, lacks something. There is something missing when a person can adapt only autoplastically. It seems to me it's part of the armamentarium of mental health, depending on the situation, to be capable of using both ways: adapting alloplastically or autoplastically, changing the environment or changing oneself.

There are situations in which an internal change has to be made, and there are situations in which an external change has to be made. When one uses developmental or maturational terms, one must not confuse the direction of development or maturation with the movement from abnormal to normal. The fact that the development proceeds in a certain way includes, to my mind, the possibility of using any of the earlier positions if the situation demands it. In short, it is the *variety* of responses. This is certainly true for the capacity to play, to regress, to let oneself go.

Now when we talk about lending a person in trouble one's own personality, all the mechanisms and all the meanings that you spelled out here are correct. To my mind, however, you must always add that there is a *voluntary* regression in terms of how these two people relate to each other. They voluntarily regress to the stage in which some kind of merging takes place. It is a voluntary, partial, and reversible revival of a rather early developmental stage. A voluntary regression is initiated by *both* individuals involved. The stronger regression is that of the person in need; he is regression-ready because he is anxious and in need.

Anybody who is anxious and in need is in some ways ready to be a child, to submit to some stronger power in order to be relieved. This is true for the helpless patient vis-à-vis the surgeon or the doctor. In general, these are transferences on a regressive level. It is also very gratifying to the narcissistic balance of the helping individual because he's looked up to like a god. The important thing is that the reassurance and the calming effect on a person who is in a traumatic state is initiated by the other person's understanding.

Why is understanding important? In your description you tend to stay, perfectly appropriately, on the phenomenological level. Why does being understood make one feel better? It is not enough to be understood. To be understood is in essence the leverage the other person has to break down the barriers between people, to encourage this further regression, and then to merge. In being understood, a barrier between people is taken away. Empathy, sophisticated though it may become, is highly verbal. But the basic instrumentarium of empathy is still this regressive merging into the other person. And the deepest disturbances in empathy, as I have often discussed with you here, are those that are on the basis of early disappointments, the early empathic failures.

I can see the regressive aspect of the patient, but how is the therapist undergoing a regression?

He is undergoing a regression only insofar as he merges, tentatively, into the other person in order to understand him.

He allows it.

He allows it in the other person. But in order to understand the other person he must tentatively merge with the other person's feeling state, for only in that way can he understand. He must, of course, remain above; he must not allow himself to be flooded by the patient's anxiety. He tastes the patient's anxiety, and then, after savoring it, he says, but without anxiety, "I'm like you, in a sense, because I understand what you feel." The other person, in turn, now becomes part of a unit that understands what is upsetting without being so anxious.

It reminds me that when I was a resident there was a case in which a girl was pouring out her long tragic history to a resident and the resident started to cry. At this point the girl became furious and stormed out of the office because he went too far.

It is not only going too far, but it's not what the patient wants. The patient wants to be understood but not to have it reverberate so that the panic becomes worse. He wants a buffering solution.

How about the earlier comment that some patients get better when they have made the appointment? Is that in contrast to what we've said here? How would you explain that? It is very common. It is a very good sign I would say.

There are a number of things. One is the fact that they have done something about their anxiety. It gives them a feeling of self-confidence, just the fact that they were able to pull themselves together enough to feel like an integrated whole, to make an appointment to see somebody; that has some therapeutic benefit.

That's true. But in the terms that we were discussing here, could that play an important role?

My feeling is that there is a place where people can give you an appointment, where people who understand will offer you an opportunity to talk through these things. It's in preparation for what's going to happen, for the merger.

Of course! These are people who know what's going to happen and feeling better is in anticipation of what's going to happen. This is a perfectly well-known human experience. As a matter of fact, it may very well be that a person diminishes the anxiety in anticipation of being understood and of having another person lend his calming influence to him. He will be disappointed if the person then does not perform as he had anticipated. But I think the anticipatory capacity is a good sign. It simply means he is ready for this kind of an experience and already anticipates it in thought.

There are some patients who never get back to that state of feeling good they had right after making the appointment. From there, it's downhill, because the therapist can never recreate the anticipated merger, the glow that begins to occur around making the appointment. Reality has to disappoint him.

But it is still a good sign. On the whole, I would consider this a favorable sign in anybody who tells me he feels better after he has made the appointment. He may have overexpectations, and you may disappoint him, but you can explain this to the person. At least there is the capacity for this kind of movement.

There are many variants in all this. I think the important thing is to realize there is a certain voluntary regression involved in treatment. An interpersonal situation is created in which some of the barriers that grownups have, that separate people from one another, are diminished, and in this the understanding of the therapist is one leverage. In tune with what you said last, there is undoubtedly an optimum. There are people who are not capable of going even this far. They lack the capacity to regress; they are not trusting or they are afraid to allow the regression.

There are a number of reasons why people will not allow themselves to regress. These reasons each have to be diagnosed for they are not always the same. It may be too much of an addictive seduction. They fear that if they allow themselves to be submerged in such a warm bath of acceptance they will never be able to draw themselves out. Possibly they have had early experiences in which they were seduced into trusting this kind of a gradual diminution of their anxiety only to be deeply disappointed, because of an early death in the family, or some peculiar behavior of the mother, or whatever it may have been.

There are other people who are almost too unreserved—one has the feeling from the beginning, "Now wait a minute; this goes too far." They immediately adore you. They immediately merge, in a sexualized or nonsexualized way, into the therapist. It becomes mushy from the beginning, and you have an unpleasant feeling about it. The empathic therapist will then hold back—not to hurt the patient intentionally, by coldness, but to clarify that such regression may also create an anxious situation. The capacity to extricate onself must also be preserved.

Therefore, the early use of interpretations or insights is a very tricky business and has to be handled with knowledge and care. An experienced psychiatrist or analyst is almost always capable, if he only wants to be, of surprising a patient with a correct and comparatively deep insight after an initial encounter, something he can recognize that the patient never knew about himself. This has to be handled with great care. It is sometimes a very important thing to do, not because the insight in and of itself is so important, but for the leverage it gives you, not by magical means, but by means of understanding. In other words, you set up a feeling, "This person understands me better than I understand myself, after such a short time."

In other words, you are fostering a kind of regression in an individual who otherwise has a hard time allowing himself this initial therapeutic move. It is only a leverage, on the basis of which you now begin your further movements. On the whole, I'm cautious and use this method sparingly. And when I use it, I do so when I am quite clear in my mind that it is necessary in order to mobilize the person for therapy. There are instances in which such a thing is grossly contraindicated—and the more right you are, the better your insight, the greater the harm. In other words, when you have individuals whose self-delimitation is tenuous anyway, who rush in an addictive way toward a permanent merging into others, this kind of deep insight, given too quickly, may set up an irresolvable relationship of adoration and overtrust. The best attitude is one of conflict in the patient—the wish to trust, the wish to have this kind of merger, but against resistance. I will never argue with a patient that he ought to commit himself to the situation. He would not be here if he did not want to be. But I think it's a good sign if he's also in conflict about it. There are all kinds of things that one can do, but insight and understanding, given early, do have a regressive potential, which is good in some instances and in other instances not so good.

There are individuals who trust you from the beginning, but you keep a little distance. There are people who are very reserved; when you find something with a deep insight about them and can offer it to them, not in a superior way, but in a modest and matter-of-fact way, then they feel, "This is the kind of person who can break through and yet will not abuse or overpower me."

It is from that point of an empathic grasp that one then proceeds to gain and communicate to the patient a more insightful and dynamic understanding of why he is experiencing what he is. To attempt such explanations too soon would only be experienced as intellectualized distancing of yourself from him.

14

Emotionally Experienced Understanding of Vulnerability

*W*HEN YOU TALK *about fluctuations in self-esteem and problems in the delimitations of the self, how do you relate this concept to Erikson's (1956) concept of ego identity? He too discusses ego identity as being subject in adolescence to states of diffusion. He describes adolescence as the critical state where identity is resolved in a very critical way.*

Erikson describes something that supposedly arises in late adolescence and early adulthood—in other words, a structure that in essence did not exist before, and that adds something to the personality that never was there before. He speaks of a variety of identifications, a maturational phase in which one finally breaks away from the family of one's origin, chooses a social role, chooses a profession, is ready to get married, and so on, a phase in which one, in an essentially from now on no-more-to-be-changed-way (although there may be variants), forms some kind of an inner configuration of what one is. I have the impression that what Erikson is describing is a specific and perhaps very important preconscious self-representation. Out of the many self-representations and self-configurations that are in existence in us, he describes a leading one, which is conscious or preconscious, which is confirmed, which is the way other people see you, and the way in which you see yourself.

As a descriptive phenomenological step, I have no objection, and I think it is a somewhat enriching concept. In terms of the continuity of development, and in terms of the contrast and conflict between various self-configurations, I have the impression it leaves a good deal to be desired.

The point I am stressing is that the earliest experiences of the self, the earliest experiences of one's own grandiosity, of one's own exhibitionism, of one's own being responded to by the admiring surroundings, set up a nucleus of subject-bound security[1] which gradually has to change and gradually does change. This undoubtedly is a factor in the final preconscious configuration of ego identity that may very well be useful to consider. However, I find that it's much more complex. It is much more useful to see the variety of directions in development, the variety of fixations on earlier phases of self, the multiple ways in which self-concepts develop side-by-side and continue to exist side-by-side. Thus, one should not consider just one preconscious concept of what the self is supposed to be.

To my mind, ego identity is a meaningful construction in terms of a socioculturally oriented psychology in which the preconscious and conscious attitudes of a person to himself are experienced as he delimits himself from others in adolescent and adult life. In other words, within Erikson's own frame of reference, ego identity is a perfectly acceptable concept. However, I would say this concept does not explain the development of narcissistic transferences.[2] Ego identity as a concept is not workable, as far as therapy is concerned, except in terms of conscious persuasion, conscious explanation and conscious adaptation. You can explain to the person what is happening to him on the level at which his preconscious conflict takes place. You can explain to him on the level at which he experiences—that is, the here and now, or the surface level, which is a fine level to begin with. You can explain to him how he has seen himself as an adolescent in such-and-such a way, how he has this-and-this possibility now of seeing himself as an adult in such-and-such a way, and how he is caught between these two.

This may be an educational experience of great significance to the person if a bond that is not further understood forms between the therapist and the individual who feels diffuse or uncertain about himself. He can be helped greatly by an explanation simply on the merging empathic level. A strong figure helps him to explain. But on the basis of Erikson's model, you can never accomplish the deep integration of old fixation points. They are based on the individual's earliest experience of rejections, when there was insistence on getting gratifications of the earliest grandiose fantasies.

Erikson mentions that one has ideals which may be so high that one cannot live up to them. But he does not mention the fact that there may

---

[1]Kohut later described this as the nuclear self.

[2]The term "narcissistic transferences" was later discarded by Kohut (1984). Instead he used the term "selfobject transferences" for mirroring, idealizing and alter ego transferences.

not yet be ideals internalized. There are many people who are still in search of an external ideal because they have never internalized it. In other words, these are again the earlier fixation points that need to be worked through, and that then enrich the personality and produce structural changes. Ego identity is, as it were, a sophisticated configuration on the surface layer of the personality. And this is not a value judgment. One needs a surface psychology.

Erikson has an important insight but it has no relationship to the developmental and maturational descriptions of narcissistic configurations.[3] This is my personal opinion. There are many good things to be said about Erikson. Often, however, his description of the various developmental phases are really value judgments disguised in scientific terms.

I think he has recently tried to be a bit more sophisticated. Instead of his statement of trust vs mistrust, he writes that both are necessary for adaptive purposes. Yet on the whole, these are value judgments. For example, one ought to have an identity. I do not know. There may be external situations in which one has to be able to be fluid about that, in which, for instance, from the point of view of adaptation it would be a question of life or death. Can one or can one not give oneself over to something new?

There are geniuses, so far as I can judge, who are capable of total personality changes late in life. I would say total style change, for example, in an artist, is tantamount to a shift in identity. Many of the greatest artists in phase after phase show that a struggle for ever new forms of such identities goes on. On the other hand, we certainly have great respect for individuals, similar to the Prussian officers' class, who will always be officers; they are marked for life, this is the family tradition. This is a fixed and firm identity—and it may be a very fine one. I am not plugging the Prussian officers, but at their best their style—the gentlemanly attitude, the protective attitude, the kindliness aside from courage in war—was admirable, fitting a particular type of national and cultural development, needed by the state and therefore cultivated.

Such individuals are unchangeable. They have formed an identity at the moment when they graduate from military school, and this is what they remain. The same may be true for the scholar in a family of scholars. This is what he's going to be, and this is the way he lives. Thus, some people have final identities. But there are other people in whom there is a fluidity of identity, what, in Erikson's terms, would be crisis

---

[3]The grandiose and the idealizing poles, the bipolar self.

after crisis, in a state of what would seem like and yet is not pathology. That is why I say there is a hidden value judgment. Ego identity is presented as if the peak of maturity is to achieve this identity. Whether this is so or not is beside the point. The importance of this is that the concept deals with a preconscious configuration both in terms of the ego ideal and in terms of ego identity. It is difficult to oppose one outlook with another. When you ask me what the kind of self that I see is, as compared to ego identity, I can only show you the meaning and the value of the formulations that I have made in understanding a variety of clinical phenomena—and not only clinical phenomena.

How would you explain, in terms of such configurations as the final ego identity, the phenomenon of people who feel enormously exaggerated in their self-esteem at one moment and in the next moment very low. Their old arrogance and childlike fixation breaks through and then again they have to suppress these feelings so that they are left totally deprived of the influx of narcissistic supplies. I do not know if that is a very good example, but there are innumerable others.

Every concept is useful up to a point. The concept of ego identity as a maturational phase is understandable. So also is the tracing of various self and idealized concepts, including those underlying what preconsciously one finally accepts as one's identity.

I do think there is a usefulness in the final configuration that Erikson talks about. In other words, a modicum, a minimum, or an average amount of delimitation of who one is and what one is belongs to the mental health of most individuals. And it is certainly a sign of illness when this is absent, except that this is only a surface explanation. On the basis of what is it absent? On the basis of what is present? Simply to describe it is just the very first step. One needs to investigate how this self grew. What happened to this self in childhood? What of the old self is still there? What of it is buried? Which of it is split off from the main part of the personality? Are there antagonistic self-concepts in a struggle with one another? Are there borrowed ones? When they are borrowed, are they borrowed in defense against others or in order to fill out emptiness? The possibilities are endless and a simple acceptance of a self-identity is not going to be helpful. In that sense, it would narrow me down.

This girl has many positive qualities. She's really a bright girl even though she's not brilliant. She has an attractive mind, and one has the feeling of a background of some solid health, apart from her disturbances. I think that life will educate her that one cannot become an ambassador, or whatever other fantastic ideas she may have. But at this particular moment, to seriously debunk her idea would be a mistake. It is not so much what you say, but what you really feel about it that counts. If you are deeply concerned that such overgrown ambition is a terrible shortcoming in this personality, if you confuse this with unconscious grandiosity that can be a hindrance in certain people, then you deprive her of a direct, forward moving ambition. I think you would do the patient an injustice. If I have any ambition at all for our work here it is to give you a sense at least of *the sophistication of how one listens to people.*

One has to have a feel for "Does it sound healthy or not? Does it sound positive or not?" She may never become an ambassador. It may be crazy for her to have such thoughts. But why shouldn't the girl want to be an ambassador? What's so terrible about that? I have the impression that these "grandiose fantasies" are probably the residuals of intimacy between her and her father, early in life, in which they were carried both by a sense of likeness and by liking each other.

This became a really important nucleus for an inner strength rather than an inner weakness, and it accounts for a good bit of what is so very attractive about this girl. The therapist likes her. One can see that. It is evidenced in the way in which you report the material. You respond to her libidinally in the way in which one responds to an attractive person. She must be an attractive person. Her mind is an attractive mind. When she says, "Just to be on a staff—that doesn't send me. I want to be an ambassador." She wants to have a brilliant mind, not just a bright mind. Father says, "Come on now, you're good enough just being bright." True, but I don't see anything so terrible about her wanting to be brilliant. This is not her sickness. This may give her a few bumps of disappointment in life. But I think its positive driving force betrays its genetic derivation from a positive spinning out of fantasies about her future between father and herself. "Some time, maybe you will be an ambassador, and you will go back to the country I came from, but you will go as the ambassador to Poland," in the way parents and children will sometimes sit together and spin out fantasies. This is done in a setting of love, mutual understanding, fondness for one another and likeness, and the spirit of "you will fulfill some of my ambitions."

One does not protect people from all the bumps that life has to offer— people learn about those bumps and adjust. But this aspect of herself, as is so many times the case, is something positive. The skill of the therapist is not to accept something that is absolutely foolish. Then you must help to protect the person by toning these things down, while simultaneously accepting the positive aspects of it.

What I am trying to say is that for each of the grandiosities of early life there are two sides, as in a coin. It is a life-giving, self-esteem-supporting force which is forward moving—but with the wrong circumstances it is something that becomes a hindrance, a burden, something that from early life on one knew one could never live up to—and one feels bad about it. But if a person at this age still has the capacity for a fantasy life and thinks, "I want to become an ambassador," I would say, "Come now," but I'd say it with an accepting smile. This is the trait of the good psychotherapist—that one can accept the spirit behind it and at the same time say, "Come on now."

The case I have chosen to present could be reviewed in the light of Erikson's identity crisis, but I believe that it will offer greater insight and understanding to review it in the light of our study of self-esteem and ideals, in the developmental line of narcissism.

This is a 20-year-old math major in her second year at the university. She is a large, healthy, wholesome-looking adolescent with freckles on her nose. She was dressed in jeans and a baggy shift and she wrote her complaints in green ink:

"Since my senior year in high school, I've been plagued with a depression, a sense of alienation. I feel completely out of control of my life, incapable of dealing with even the most trivial of daily situations (e.g., balancing a checkbook). I'm not interested in any subject of study. I have become very self-conscious and self-analytical, changing my philosophy of existence every few days. . . . I don't want to get up in the morning anymore; I cry a lot. I wish I could get my emotions under control so at least I could feel functional.

"Recently I decided that I'd been continually escaping reality through my lovers. . . . I couldn't stand myself and so chose to spend time with them. Last week I cut myself off from the lover I had been closest to and resigned myself to being alone. . . . I lapsed into a deep depression and decided I needed help."

She explained that since at least her senior year of high school she has had mounting feelings of depression, along with uncertainty as to what her interests and goals really are. She is the oldest of three girls and describes a much closer relationship to father than to mother. Father is an intelligent man who reads widely but who has not gone beyond high school in formal education. He works as a foreman in an electrical plant.

About her relationship with mother she says little except that when the youngest child was born she was sent away to relatives for a period of time. She has no memory of mother's pregnancy. She remembers only that they were relatives she disliked.

Her own quick mind has long been used for fierce competition in the classroom. In parochial grammar school she was quietly diligent and worked strenuously to please the nuns. Noisier competition emerged in high school, where she delighted in showing off her knowledge in class. It seems most of her self-esteem is tied up in her work.

She felt very different from other high school girls; for one thing, she felt too large and gawky: "I knew I didn't fit." She did not give nearly the attention to her clothes and makeup that other girls did, secretly envying and despising the petite, cute, cheerleader types. She was much more assertive than they. In gym classes, she enjoyed active sports, while most of the other girls just sat around. In academic work, she signed up for the tough "masculine" courses like math, physics, chemistry while peers were doing home economics.

Coming to the university proved a real blow to her strong academic ambitions. No longer the brightest student, as she had been in high school, she looked in dismay at the high achievements of many of her fellow students. In her math and physics courses several people were brighter than she and she felt incapable of matching their attainments, much less surpassing them. She has an image of a really successful college girl as someone who makes unique contributions to her field of study and who in her spare time is a superb artist, with knowledge in many other fields. Measured against this impossible standard, she feels inadequate.

She thus swings between two poles: (1) trying to study strenuously but feeling burdened down with unattainable goals and (2) forgetting all about school work, thinking about dropping out and spending her time with college dropouts whom she does not really like.

One of her chief ways of trying to cope with these feelings is to attach herself to a man, usually brighter than she and whom she uses (1) to reassure herself that she is acceptable by basking in the glow of his accomplishments, (2) to get him to reassure her continually that she is sexually desirable, talented, creative and bright and (3) to just be with her to ease the anxiety which comes with lonely self-preoccupations.

After a while she begins to feel she should be completely self-sufficient and breaks off her affairs, only to start another within a couple of weeks.

The essence of the case is that this 20-year-old girl has been feeling vaguely depressed since she was a senior in high school. Her depression increased when she entered the university. In high school she could maintain her self-esteem by being first in class, by asking very bright questions, and so on. She was more and more at odds in her development with the other girls her age, in whom intellectual brilliance was less important. Being dated, being pretty, being interesting to the boys, and being socially acceptable in the adolescent community became more and more the real giver of prestige and self-esteem. So she had to maintain her own self-esteem more and more by her sense of pride in what she was doing.

We assume that a part of her turning to intellectual pursuits had its root very early in life. It was due perhaps to the position of being the oldest one in the family. Seeing that mother turned to the new children, she had the feeling of being displaced and experienced this as a drop in self-esteem. This is a very important point. One forgets that originally self-esteem depends on what other people do for you and think about you.[4] As we have seen, the libidinization of the early self-concept is related to the fact that what the adult observer knows to be other people is still experienced by the child as being a unit with oneself. So the later capacity to love oneself is the replica of the original narcissistic relationship.

This is not an object libidinal relationship but a narcissistic one, in which the child is experienced by the mother as an extension of herself and in which the child experiences the mother as an enlarged self. So it is that, due to the sudden withdrawal of the external source of acceptance, there is a sudden drop in self-esteem. This leads to a nucleus of non-acceptance of the self in the personality against which many other means are then mobilized, because the pain of self-rejection, the pain of lacking self-acceptance, is most severe.

This is an extremely important point. When confronted with such a situation, the older child tends to make an enormous effort to substitute for the sudden loss in self-esteem by behavior that supplies approval and thus substitutes for the former approval. This belongs to normal development. The pathology we deal with may be one of two kinds. There is perhaps a congenital inborn weakness vis-à-vis even normal withdrawals of approval. This girl may react as some children do, with a traumatic sense of depression, or a precursor of depression, to external events that in other children would not be traumatic. On the other hand, her depression may have more to do with external circumstances, paramount among them being the personality of the important parent. We are only toying with concepts, for the present, to learn something in a particular way.

It would be compatible with her history to find a mother—and this is not unusual or uncommon—who relates very well to one baby at a time

---

[4]Selfobject functions which through optimal frustration via transmuting internalization then become self functions.

but withdraws the love from the older one in anticipation of a new baby or, at any rate, as soon as the new baby is born. The older child is then suddenly faced with a drop in self-esteem. Then comes the next important point, depending very much on the age of the child, but anywhere from three to seven years of age. The child attempts to use already available ego functions or capacities and overburdens them in order to undo this deep feeling of rejection, or self-rejection, which the sudden withdrawal of parental attention brings about. In that sense, it is parallel to what I have already discussed—the ambitious mother who teaches the child how to read and do mathematics at the age of two and a half or three. The exception in this case is that it is not so much an ambition of the mother, but a need of the child. If employed during the age from three to seven in a moderate way, playfully, and then abandoned in oscillation between ego achievement and baby-like regressions, these functions contribute to an appropriate mode of progress. This process constitutes an appropriate means of acquiring new solid functions, new solid sources of self-esteem. However, if there is a sudden withdrawal of parental support, the new function is overburdened. What is most important, also, is that the strivings contain admixtures of earlier wishes.

Let us say there is a six- or seven-year-old child who, up to this time, has been somewhat regressive or immature because she was the only one at home. She was the center of attention, rather immature for her age, and much more a baby than if, from the beginning, she had been one of several children. This has something to do with the particular personality characteristics of the parents. A little sister was born when she was six and a half or seven. It is remarkable that this enormously bright child has absolutely no memory of the mother's pregnancy or any of the circumstances surrounding the birth, except for one detail. She had to go away from home for a while and stay with relatives. It was probably around the time of delivery, either when the mother went to the hospital or, at any rate, was not capable of taking care of her at home, so that she stayed with relatives whom she disliked. This is the top of the iceberg of memories. The only conscious memory is the flavor of being away from home and disliking this family. The crystallizing point for her whole future development was what happened then, namely, that all her self-esteem needs, and they were enormous, began to center around school successes.

In short, when she was ambitiously writing the best paper in class or volunteering to recite, her need had certain qualities of oral jealousy of the young sibling. In other words, her ambition for intellectual pursuits contained some residual oral competition with her newborn sibling. The normal seven-year-old does not have this competitiveness anymore.

Individuals who are so enormously ambitious in the intellectual sphere that they can never say they do not know but always must know may have a similar experience in their background. They can never ask questions but have to think things out by themselves, for it is an offense to them that somebody else knows something that is written in the book. The tricks by which such people learn are remarkable. For those of you who have had medical training, you know that, when people with central visual defects try to read, they always look at the page from the side. The center is blind, so they have to look at the periphery. When they look directly, they don't see. They learn the trick of looking at it some other way, as it were, and learn something in passing. In the same way, people of this particular type always learn in passing. Since they are often very intelligent, they learn a great deal. But how much more easily they could acquire knowledge if they could directly face the fact that, "This I don't know. This I want to learn. He knows it; therefore I'll look, and listen, and read." They can only pretend they know it anyway. They look at it casually, and pick up a little bit, "Of course, I knew that already."

In the early sessions of treatment, you notice, for instance, that the patient will see unimportant things but not the important ones in the office. He will remark on side issues in great detail. He will walk into the office and sit down or lie down and, without looking, will have seen all kinds of things that you did not notice he looked at, but he will have overlooked something very important. This is not without tentative reference to the case we are discussing. This girl is sensitive about her otherwise grownup goals.

Now in such people who respond with enormous drops in self-esteem, you will very frequently find that the ambition, the original wish to succeed, is not far removed from very childlike goals of direct exhibition, of direct feeding. In other words, the oral quality, the exhibitionistic quality, or whatever the drive component happened to be at a particular developmental stage when the original drop in self-esteem occurred, determines, to some extent, the nature of the sensitivity. It also determines the ways in which goals are striven for. Characterologically, the original countermove in terms of setting up goal structures was damaged.

It is obvious, for example, that people who were involved in very strong anal-sadistic conflicts during the time when intellectual pursuits were highly stimulated, because of the birth of a sibling or other reasons, will in their competition be sadistic and sarcastic. They will shame other people, or, when they feel they are not producing something appropriate, they will feel ashamed or sadistically treated. So a variety of the flavor of the drive and the adult urges, as well as the reaction to failures, can be understood in depth only if one knows the historical roots.

To come back then to our speculation about this young woman, we assume that something must have happened early in life.

Her comments clearly support this speculation. She told me in the following hours that her father recently told her that when she was about age two, when her sister was born, something happened to her mother. Mother was acting strangely and became ill, perhaps in an emotional way. She isn't sure whether mother left the home for a long period of time around that year. She didn't question her father about it. So it was more than a sister being born.

I am very grateful for this kind of information. What is unusual is that one learns about it so early in treatment. I usually learn these things after years of treatment. Of course, it's interesting, historically, but in therapy the important matter is how the child experienced whatever happened. In general, the stories are of parental depression.

In a case I wrote about (1971b, Mr. B.), the crucial point was that twins were born when this patient was three and a half. I am sure the twins lived less than a year. The main thing, to us, seemed to be that the mother had turned away from her older son when she was pregnant and continued her lesser involvement with him when the twins were born and later died. She was a very narcissistic mother. We had evidence of this because she was still around and in the picture during the analysis. She was highly unempathic in her interactions with her son who, by that time, was in the academic field. We later learned that during this period his mother had been a barbiturate addict. Her unempathic responses were not only the usual lack of empathy of a narcissistically fixated mother, who was also most likely depressed when her twins died, but also the failure of a woman who was disheveled, unattractive, hated her own body, and did not allow the child to touch her because she was angry with herself. When she came down for breakfast she was drunk on barbiturates. In other words, a much more intense understanding of the later sensitivity of this individual opened up when we learned that he was confronted by an early, unpredictable and, in many ways, revolting maternal response.

In this case, if the mother was away from home, who was the substitute? Was there another person present? Gross historical facts are only arrows to show directions. They do not provide answers. If there is a maid or housekeeper who was there before and who remains after the mother is hospitalized, it makes all the difference in the world. In one instance, the child can be seemingly unscathed, and in the other instance severely disturbed. In talking about congenital factors, it is often difficult to discern them when there are so many unknowns in the environment.

Nevertheless, there is no question but that there are congenital variations. Assuming, for example, that in the present case the father played an inordinate role as the sustaining individual in the household. It is obvious that the father is somewhat unusual. He is a bright man from a simple background, who reads great books and enjoys them. I am playing around with these ideas for pedagogical reasons as well as for therapeutic meaning in this case. Let us assume that the father was the source of the girl's self-esteem. A father who is interested in intellectual betterment and in studying at home at night may very well have taxed the little girl's needs. I am talking about the years from two to six or seven. The bond to the father may very well have been a very strong and mutual one. Why? Because this was a girl, and the father had essentially just lost his wife if the mother was hospitalized. One has to think in terms of the total imbalance of the family. In other words, it is likely that the father, too, is searching for some libidinal gratification; perhaps he finds it in his daughter, whom he then overburdens. Thus, from early on, what should have been a childlike pampering in a triangle, where the mother still plays a great part in gratifying the child, became something that was an overstraining attempt to please her father. The direction of development was set, which led her to become an intellectually achieving and performing girl. Her adaptation to his needs worked well until biological and social requirements suddenly made a change.

What the precipitating circumstances were in senior high school, apart from the fact that the other girls sought different goals, we do not know. It may be that her intellectual equipment is not good enough to compete for, or to secure, the achievements she would like. We may also speculate that, while parents very frequently foster certain attitudes in children, when they see that they have driven the child in a direction that is quite out of keeping with what society usually demands, they become guilty and change their tune: "Why don't you make yourself more feminine?" But for ten or fifteen years the parents have fostered everything but femininity. This brings about another break with the usual sources of self-esteem.

These are educated speculations. I am more interested in trying to show you the imbrication of developmental, maturational, social factors of early and later life with the biological givens, with the biological strivings, with the need for self-esteem that is always there. This causes such painful imbalances that the sufferer will do almost anything to avoid the pain and thus drives the development forward in this inexorable way.

In the case of a boy who uses intellectual achievement as a means of self-esteem, I would think that the problem isn't quite as difficult, because intellectual achievement is more compatible with career than it is with a girl.

It's culturally more acceptable. I would agree with that within limits. I think the career girl nowadays is much more accepted, culturally. I think this is one of the grave developmental tasks that future generations will have to face in terms of overpopulation. Culturally speaking, fewer and fewer women will be able to have children. There will be pressure against this, and perhaps there will be a secondary lessening of the feminine role. In other words, sublimatory channels will have to be found for women that will make careers more and more the standard for women rather than the exception.

Be that as it may, I think the crucial issue is not the difference between the sexes. The crucial issue is the specific individual's history. I have seen plenty of highly unhappy men who were forced prematurely into intellectual pursuits.

I'd like to address a question to what we've touched on at various times, and that is, how malleable is latency? Let us assume that what happened to the girl under discussion does not happen—that the mother is able to tend to the older child adequately and to the younger ones, and the best possible development goes along. You mentioned a patient who had a sibling born at six and a half or seven. By that time, he clearly knows he's different from the mother, and the origins of self-esteem are way down the road. When does the vulnerability to narcissistic injury stop? We're going to experience such injury sooner or later in life. When does the sort of permanence, because of the unconscious determination of the symptoms or the way of dealing with things, occur? There is a connotation of permanence until a major intervention. If the tree bends early in life it's going to be very crooked, but there is a point when it swings back or the bending is just at one of the top little branches. Would you say there is a particular period—I'm certain you can't say ten years old or eight years old—but by puberty (I'm using the concept of the critical period) is it all over with?

The trouble with the question is that it doesn't allow the type of single axis answer that you posit. The parents who suddenly withdraw from children later in life were obviously not ideal parents before that either. There is a gross historical event that seems to be the turning point, but it is an event against a background.

Assuming a reasonably good development through early life—to the age of seven, let's say—and a certain firming of the superego followed by latency, and a reasonable degree of settling down in school, I would think that on the whole, barring traumata of truly excessive proportions, the basic organization of the personality will remain intact. That does not mean that people cannot be unhappy. That is not what you were asking. I think the basic organization of the child will remain intact if the first seven years are lived through appropriately. There may be traumata of such a severe degree later in life, even in adult years, that irreversible damage occurs, as in the case of people who spend years in concentration camps. But barring this, I think the age of seven or eight would probably be a good cutoff point for what you are asking about.

Now this is the grossest and most misleading answer I could possibly give you if I did not say more. When we talk about traumata in reconstructing an early life, we have to take into account a number of very important variables. The most important step is that the traumata of later life are those that the patient remembers and transacts in the treatment. Very frequently they are replicas or focal points for a series of earlier analogous ones. In the treatment situation they are transacted around clusters of memory of later life. In the case of Miss F. (Kohut, 1971b; 1977), I made a decisive step in insight about this. This is the girl who kept pestering me not to interrupt her. When I did not say anything, I was not doing well either. I had to repeat exactly what she had said around the middle of the session. The major memories around which her most intense emotions were experienced, in the analysis, dealt with the early years in grammar school—particularly around the episodes when she came home from school, on an emotional upswing, excited about what she had learned, looking forward to telling her mother. When her mother opened the door, she immediately felt drained because she saw that her mother was depressed. She would try to talk about what she had said in school, and somehow, before long, without knowing how it happened, the mother was talking about her headache and her tiredness. She was talking about herself and her body in a hypochondriacal way, and the patient felt completely lacking in self-esteem—disappointed and enraged, which was even harder for her to see for a long time. And so there was the rage against me. "Why don't you listen to me? Why don't you reflect what I tell you? Don't talk about your brightness. Your interpretations are marvelous, but you give those bright interpretations because you want to enjoy your brain, not because you're listening to me." In essence, this was what she was saying. It took me a while to catch on.

Now as far as the event at age seven or eight is concerned, to treat it as anything less than etiological, in terms of the genetic point of view of psychoanalysis, would have been an injustice to the patient. It was really in this way that she remembered it. I know from historical data—the patient found out about it—that the mother was also depressed during the first year of her life and that she had depressions off and on during the whole period up to that point. Without that preparatory history, the mother's depression when the patient was seven would not have done the great harm it did.

One must take into account the earlier history to understand such comparatively late traumata. Would she have become undisturbed if she had an ideally functioning mother late in life? I don't think so. I think she would have been disturbed. Perhaps she would have been more disturbed in some ways, because this particular cluster of rememberable events would not, in a sense, have given her a chance to work over again something that happened preverbally, which left her with a vague and diffuse feeling of not being wanted and not being any good, as well as a feeling that any effort on her part to display herself would lead nowhere. Once this began to be worked through, she began to exhibit again in a childlike way to the point that she became hypomanically stimulated by her needs for response and very vulnerable in terms of my empathy for her needs. I did not need to applaud, but I had to understand what she was so sensitive about.

To come back to your question, what I call the telescoping of analogous events at the age of six or seven, or even later, does not mean that this is the trauma; the event becomes the focal point in a variety of analogous traumata.

The reason I'm raising this question is that some of us have been thinking about how we can use these concepts in short-term therapy now. I think you're saying that one can work with, in a vastly shorter number of treatment sessions, "Well when I was 14 things happened this way," with the idea that she's giving the top level, and there is probably a stronger, more important, earlier bottom level. We really don't have to know that if we have some grasp of how she experienced it at 14.

Not even 14. The dynamics of the *present* expand the person's mastery over himself, enable him to grasp the particular circumstances to which he's responding. That his vulnerability is understood by somebody else allows him to accept his own vulnerability. He can manage himself better and can anticipate his vulnerability. He realizes, for instance, that his depressions are similar to childlike sulking. This insight can be enormously helpful. It is important to make your point not in terms of a value judgment—"You mustn't sulk"—but in terms of analogies of childhood. Whether this happens to be his childhood in detail or not is beside the point. For instance, in my patient, Miss F., there was no working-through in any specifically verbalized or remembered way of the mother's earliest depression when the patient was only some months old.

This was all worked through around later memories of the relationship with her brother and her father.

I am sure that some degree of vulnerability remained in this patient. I see her once in a great while. She is obviously happy and active and doing very well. She is married, and it is a meaningful marriage. Formerly, her relationships were a sham, and she knew it. She is capable of realizing how much admiration she wants and that she cannot possibly get it. She knows now that this need is childlike, but it is still there to some extent. I imagine she still has some diffuse vulnerability. However, when this first came to the fore she was very threatened by these needs—the need to exhibit, to be admired, loved, and responded to without delay and with total and unfailing empathy, which is obviously not to be bought or had. The psychotherapist must fail. He cannot possibly be there all the time.

To return to your question, it is the personality of the parents that is involved and it is the variety of traumatic periods. The concepts we are discussing here have greater possibilities for brief psychotherapy than do concepts of the infantile object libidinal drives. The infantile object libidinal drives form symptoms or they are repressed. Everybody experiences the active attitudes we are discussing to some extent. The homeostasis of self-esteem is something that plagues everybody, regardless of whether they are unusually vulnerable or not, regardless of whether they are a little miffed when things don't go right or slump down into a depressive spell for some months.

The present case illustrates your point and to some extent answers the question. This girl terminated after the fourth hour, with a complete remission of symptoms and, I think, on a better organizational level, without reverting to her previous way of adjusting. But I don't know why it happened.

Well let's hear about it.

The second hour still has some of the flavor of the first. She again came dressed in jeans and a baggy sweatshirt, with her hair down to her shoulders. She has a way, when talking, of brushing her hair away from one eye, which she does quite often. I was just coming in from outside. I saw her in the waiting room and nodded to her in recognition.

She came in, sat down, and was silent. I said, ''The floor is yours.'' She smiled and said, ''I feel guilty for being here. There are a lot sicker people than me who need help walking around the campus.'' I just waited for her to go on. She said it was exam week; she was feeling low.

Sometimes she thinks she should drop out of school. There is a married couple she goes to visit. She doesn't like them very much. They've dropped out of school, and when visiting she just sits around in their apartment. When she calls, she looks forward to being there. But after getting there she finds that they talk about the same old things. Nothing changes, and she gets discouraged again. She had been feeling especially lonely since she broke up with her previous boyfriend, a graduate student, two or three weeks ago. She was feeling horny, and would like some guy to sleep with. In fact she has gotten very upset lately, because the area around the university is such a small community, it seems like everyone has slept with everyone else. She recently found out that a couple of her former boyfriends are sleeping with girls she knows. She said she relied very heavily on T. and saw him very often. He's a very bright guy, in physics.

Somehow, just being around someone bright and accomplished makes her feel better, because she herself feels so unaccomplished and unattractive. She said, "I really suck a man dry. I get a man and really cling to him. You know, it's funny, after I break up with someone, and I know he's trying hard to forget me, I usually call the next night and say all I want to do is talk with him on the phone. I know that drives him up the wall. I don't know why I do it. Sometimes I feel I ought to stay away from men completely, and just try to manage on my own. That's when I break up with a boy. I try that for a while, and then I find somebody else. In fact, these three weeks have been the longest period since high school that I haven't had a man. T. would often tell me I was attractive and bright. He once taught me to make candles, and I started making them even better than he could. He said, "See, Tony, you are creative." (Her name is Antoinette but people call her Tony, like the oldest son.) She said, "Sometimes I just don't know how much of me is my boyfriend and how much me. For example, I started out in political science, then switched to math because T. was in it, and he encouraged me. I started in an honors class, but after one week I saw the work was beyond me. I was very depressed—crying—and then switched from it to an easier course."

She said, "At the inter-session break I'm going skiing with some people. Why? Because T. skis. He showed me, and I didn't think it was much, but because he seemed to enjoy it I thought I should. I'd really prefer to be home this week and just talk with my mother." I asked her why she had broken up with T. and she said, "He has his problems." She got angry when he took another girl camping and slept with her. T. was married when they met, and it bothered her that he would also sleep with his wife. "He told me that I made him decide to get a divorce. It was because of me." Then she went back to this theme of, "How much is me, and how much is T? Even my coming here was T.'s doing. I told him I was upset. He asked around, and he recommended that I come here. Or like my job in statistics. I got interested in that because he suggested it. I don't even know if I should be in math."

I said, "What are your interests?" She said, "I don't know what my interests are, but I have to find something I can be good at. I read math, for example, and I see a footnote where Newton worked out all his principal formulas by age 30, and then I think I'll never be able to do that."

I said, "When you say you have to find something to be good at, it sounds like you mean you have to find something to be great at, and right away." She smiled and nodded.

I said, "How do you think that came about?" She said, "Somehow, it goes back to sixth grade in parochial school. You know, you really have to please the nuns. It's not just a matter of doing your work well. You have to do it exactly as they want you to do it. Even walking in the hall— they told you how long a step to take. I really enjoyed pleasing them and obeying the rules. I completely memorized my geography lessons. I was very competitive, but in a quiet way. My parents were surprised at that time, after IQ testing, when they discovered I wasn't that bright. They thought my A's were because I was so bright. I guess I'm one of those classic overachievers. Dad still tells me, "Tony, you're not brilliant, only bright,' and he tells me to ease up." When she said "bright" she made a face; it was not good to be bright.

I said, "What was the face about when you said 'bright'?" She said, "Well, to be bright is only second-rate." It was about the end of the hour, and I said, "It seems to me that this state you're in probably had to come—you know, once you find yourself in a place where there are others who can do things better than you can—but I think something very good can come out of your making a more relaxed reappraisal of yourself and what your own interests and limitations are."

Very good. I'm not amazed that she's getting better.

Do you want to hear the next hour?

Sure.

She went on this ski trip during the inter-session break. She said she had a good time skiing. While coming back on the bus she decided she would drop out of math because she really didn't like physics courses or the jobs a math major would get after her B.A. In fact, she had always liked to read philosophy. She told her dad about this when she got home, and he got angry and said, "What are you going to do with a philosophy degree?" She said, "I could go into law," and then he seemed more reconciled to it. His anger puzzled her. She said, "He used to read a lot of philosophy, and attended these great books courses, and seemed always to be in favor of a liberal education. But the two of us had always expected me to do something practical. I'd take my place in society."

"The two of us," meaning her father and she?

Yes. She said, "I sold him on the notion that I'd be a mathematician. Now it seems I'm doing a selling job on the importance of philosophy." She guessed she was confused as to what she really wanted to do. In his irritation he said to her, "Why don't you just get married?" This really surprised her. She said, "You know, he had always talked to me as if I'd do something more than just be a housewife, like mother. He said this seriously. He'd let my sister—the one who is two years younger—be kind of girlish. He didn't seem to have these plans for her."

I asked, "Does he sometimes seem somewhat contemptuous of women who are only housewives?" She thought maybe that was so. She wondered whether sometimes his male chauvinism were showing. Recently, while she was driving with him in the winter, they saw some girls outside in the cold wearing mini skirts. These are the kind of girls she doesn't like: cute, demure, pert girls in mini skirts. Dad said, "Look at those dumb girls out in the cold in mini skirts." This worried her. When she thought about it more, she felt this wasn't just an attitude about their wearing mini skirts, but seemed to be something about women in general.

She said, "Lately, father does tend to criticize me more. He says I don't respect our relatives." She referred to them as "our second generation fascists." He says she's ornery. He wants her to settle down and find something to do and not take things so seriously. Last summer, when T. wanted her to come and live with him, she went home and told Dad about it. He got angry and said he'd disinherit her if she did that.

She said, "I could understand his disinheriting me. It would be for my own good, but to put the cherry on the pudding, he said this would hurt mother." He confided that mother must be protected, because when the patient was one and a half years old mother had a nervous breakdown which had affected her for one year. "This was the first I'd ever heard of this." A few weeks later he told her that one of the reasons he was taking a strong line was that he had lived with a girl for two years before he met her mother. She said even the relatives think she's turning into a lost hippie type and going to pot. She was reminded of the last Thanksgiving dinner and the terrible argument she and a fascist uncle got into over her having been at a Washington peace rally. She shocked everyone during this argument by saying she no longer believed in the church. Father came to her defense when the uncle attacked; later, when her good grades came in, he showed them to the uncle. Even mother defended her. She said the uncle would never attack mother or argue with her because mother had this breakdown and has to be treated with kid gloves. She feels she couldn't be like mother, content with housework, children and clubs; she admires her for her skills, "She's very good at managing money. If it weren't for mother's skills we wouldn't be where we are today." After mother found out about her plan to live with T. last summer, mother wrote her a long letter that also bothered her. She advised her to try to get this man to marry her, saying that men will "otherwise just use you." She was surprised at this attitude of trapping a man, it really turned her off.

She then said that father and she try to think at times about what she should do and be. Dad once suggested that she consider the foreign service after college, and while dad had meant staff, her immediate fantasy was to be an ambassador. She said, "It's really me who blows up the expectations, not him." She is the one who somehow is making a big deal out of this philosophy thing as her goal. Father gets confused by her enthusiasm, and so does she.

I said, "It does sound as if tentative interest on your part is blown up by you as a career commitment. It must be important for you to do that. But your exploring philosophy—that sounds like a decision made in a different way than the way of choosing what a boyfriend is doing. This time, it seems you've looked more within a genuine interest." She said, "Yes, but I'm not sure how much that decision was due to reading *Portrait of the Artist* recently, and wanting to be like S.D., who read all that philosophy."

All right, maybe that's a good place to stop. What do you think of the information we got in these two treatment sessions? Who has any bright thoughts about it?

This girl reminds me of Julius Caesar who was 30 years old when he fell to the ground in tears and said, "By this age Alexander had conquered the world. What have I done? Relatively nothing." I've heard this from patients before: I'm 21, and I haven't done some grandiose thing. It's something like, "If I died now, 100 years from now the world wouldn't know I had lived."

In general, when I hear a story of this type I think rather well of that. I think the way you handled it left nothing to be desired. It was in good humor, and the setting was in an atmosphere of overall acceptance. On

the whole, these conscious ambitions, even though they are extraordi-
narily overgrown, are not as pathogenic as one thinks they might be.
This is not pathology. More often than not they are the direct successors
of life-enhancing early fantasies. I think you put your finger on something very important—but in the positive sense, to my mind, not the
negative.

Let me repeat and summarize what I have said earlier, because I believe the manner in which we respond to the voicing of ambition has
important repercussions, not only for the therapeutic relationship, but
for the further growth and development of the adolescent personality:

This girl has many positive qualities. She's really a bright girl even
though she's not brilliant. She has an attractive mind, and one has the
feeling of a background of some solid health, apart from her disturbances. I think that life will educate her that one cannot become an ambassador, or whatever other fantastic ideas she may have. But at this
particular moment, to seriously debunk her idea would be a mistake. It
is not so much what you say, but what you really feel about it that
counts. If you are deeply concerned that such overgrown ambition is a
terrible shortcoming in this personality, if you confuse this with unconscious grandiosity that can be a hindrance in certain people, then you
deprive her of a direct, forward moving ambition. I think you would do
the patient an injustice. If I have any ambition at all for our work here it is
to give you a sense at least of *the sophistication of how one listens to people.*

One has to have a feel for "Does it sound healthy or not? Does it sound
positive or not?" She may never become an ambassador. It may be crazy
for her to have such thoughts. But why shouldn't the girl want to be an
ambassador? What's so terrible about that? I have the impression that
these "grandiose fantasies" are probably the residuals of intimacy between her and her father, early in life, in which they were carried both by
a sense of likeness and by liking each other.

This became a really important nucleus for an inner strength rather
than an inner weakness, and it accounts for a good bit of what is so very
attractive about this girl. The therapist likes her. One can see that. It is
evidenced in the way in which you report the material. You respond to
her libidinally in the way in which one responds to an attractive person.
She must be an attractive person. Her mind is an attractive mind. When
she says, "Just to be on a staff—that doesn't send me. I want to be an
ambassador." She wants to have a brilliant mind, not just a bright mind.
Father says, "Come on now, you're good enough just being bright."
True, but I don't see anything so terrible about her wanting to be brilliant. This is not her sickness. This may give her a few bumps of disappointment in life. But I think its positive driving force betrays its genetic

derivation from a positive spinning out of fantasies about her future between father and herself. "Some time, maybe you will be an ambassador, and you will go back to the country I came from, but you will go as the ambassador to Poland," in the way parents and children will sometimes sit together and spin out fantasies. This is done in a setting of love, mutual understanding, fondness for one another and likeness, and the spirit of "you will fulfill some of my ambitions."

One does not protect people from all the bumps that life has to offer—people learn about those bumps and adjust. But this aspect of herself, as is so many times the case, is something positive. The skill of the therapist is not to accept something that is absolutely foolish. Then you must help to protect the person by toning these things down, while simultaneously accepting the positive aspects of it.

What I am trying to say is that for each of the grandiosities of early life there are two sides, as in a coin. It is a life-giving, self-esteem-supporting force which is forward moving—but with the wrong circumstances it is something that becomes a hindrance, a burden, something that from early life on one knew one could never live up to—and one feels bad about it. But if a person at this age still has the capacity for a fantasy life and thinks, "I want to become an ambassador," I would say, "Come now," but I'd say it with an accepting smile. This is the trait of the good psychotherapist—that one can accept the spirit behind it and at the same time say, "Come on now."

15

Idealizing Transference (Gratitude) and Its Role in Structure Building

T HE QUESTION IS: Under what circumstances and in what way is an old unrealistic fantasy from childhood helpful to the individual, driving him forward, leading to achievement, becoming part and parcel of his sustaining self-esteem, and under what other circumstances is it a grave hindrance, leading to inhibitions, to withdrawal from life, becoming a block? In general, and keeping the average in mind, the answer is not difficult to get. It depends on the gradualness of the integration of the early fantasy into the totality of the personality. The original fantasy may have been unrealistic, and undoubtedly it always is: the demand for baby worship later in life is obviously unrealistic. As an adult one cannot expect to be the center of attention in the way one can expect, and has the right to expect, when one is a newborn baby. Even early fantasies that can be verbalized, which as daydreams continue to exist and are to some extent helpful, are part and parcel of normal human equipment. They belong to the resilience of the human mental apparatus capable of reacting to disappointments with wish-fulfilling fantasies.

Although we are not very much aware of it, if we put our minds to it we can through self-observation easily see that when there have been blows to our self-esteem in daily life, we tend to spin out daydreams of successes that are quite unrealistic. So the gradualness of the integration allows a development in the grandiose sector of the personality in which the original fantasy is retained, but layered over. The original fantasy is somewhere still active, including the intense wishes that are connected with it, the intense exhibitionism, or the intense pleasure in oneself, but in addition there have been accretions to the personality that tame the original fantasy. We can use the fantasy as the driving fuel for our ambitions and actions, but let it change as we grow up. It is very different from not having in any way an access to old feelings of greatness. Then one is dependent on motivations from the surface only; great deeds are not achievable without a prerational source to one's achievements.

One has to be driven in some way by prerational—if you wish, infantile—motivations; yet, to be driven by them is not enough. In Freud's analogy of the rider on the horse, one has to have the capacity to use the intense power of the drive equipment of the child, including, in the self sphere, the wish to succeed, the wish to shine, the wish to do the impossible; at the same time this intense power has to be tamed. When the man is not on the horse he can move with comparative ease. He is not threatened by any explosions from this animal's strength, but he cannot go very far.

But why is such a person so inspired? The inspiration, for better or worse, is in the total conviction of the efficacy of the original grandiose fantasy, to which people in certain regressive moments subordinate themselves. The point I am trying to make is that the grandiosity, when it becomes gradually integrated, particularly when there is a gifted ego to support it, is a motivating force to successes, more or less great, depending on what other equipment there is present and the circumstances around it. It may also become a great hindrance in a person's life.

The skill of the therapist is to know, at any given moment, in which direction one has to steer one's reactions to the presenting grandiosity. The best thing is to see the positive aspects in the setting to which they belong. It should not be handled as something that one belittles or considers sinful. It has to be empathically accepted as appropriate to a certain phase of growing up; very frequently it is the nonfulfillment of phase-appropriate successes to which the patient has remained fixated. Then one can show that the unaltered grandiosity is in the way of the person at the present time, but it also can retain its life-giving, motivating power and lead to success. In the analysis of appropriately equipped individuals, this seems sometimes like an endless repetitive task, particularly when one has already intellectually grasped the specific interference or trauma that a person has suffered early in life in the area of his self-centered or object-directed grandiosity. I will remind you that these are traumata that occur not only in terms of the subject-bound grandiosity, but also in terms of the grandiosity with which the child imbues the surrounding figures to whom he wants to attach himself. These have to be individually investigated.

I worked through something of this with a patient this morning. One could clearly see how, as a child, this individual had admired his father greatly. His father was a skilled craftsman, an artisan of a lower grade, but at one time in this boy's life the father was enormously admired; in fact, the toolbox that the father had in the basement became the center of enormous fantasies. There may be screen memories underlying the tool-box, the admiration of the grown man's genitals, and so on, but I don't think one can handle it simply by explaining it on the basis of displace-ment. The consciously remembered admiration was not only for the tools, but also for the skill of the father. The great trauma for this boy was that both parents cooperated in demeaning the father vis-à-vis the boy. The boy was supposed to become something much bigger than the father. The father was an immigrant to this country. He and his wife wanted their son to become a professional person. But all his life he had the feeling of something lacking in him; he had to struggle against irra-tional grandiose ideals, which overstimulated him and which interfered greatly with his enjoyment of his actual successes. And the working-through process today dealt with an actual and considerable success that he had achieved recently, to which he reacted with a feeling of great disappointment. He could not enjoy it at all. What he really wanted was a success in which he had reached his father, not a success in which, in a sense, he was again the little darling of the mother, with the father being demeaned.

In the earliest phases of his life, and again in his adolescence, there were periods in which he had these successes—that is, he was the great man and the father was nothing. But that lack always remained in him, because he was what the father was too. And with the father being nothing, the stimulation from his own success was foreign and magical; it did not really belong to him.[1] He now tends to experience his successes as replicas of the time when he was already in the father's shoes. But he didn't want to be in the father's shoes. He wanted to look up to his father and admire him; in so doing he wanted to feel big and great. When now he is a success, to him it is again being the little boy, mother's darling, or the latency or preadolescent boy who supposedly is much bigger and better and more successful than the father, which is a sham and he knows it. He has a deep conflict about success. It was very important to work this through.

What I am trying to show you here is that the mere fact of the contin-ued existence of an old fantasy of grandiose achievement is in and of itself nothing. It is like the gasoline in a car. You can drive this way or that way, but whether the car will go depends on the machinery. Compara-tively unaltered grandiosity complexes from early life, which would be destructive to some people, are not destructive to other people. I think it

---

[1]The experience of a cohesive bipolar self with ambitions expressed through the tension arc of skills and talents in realizable goals was lacking in this instance.

depends on the degree of talent and how one can use one's enormous driving force. Some people are capable of handling it while others are not. I believe this is an interesting and worthwhile thing to think about, because we often think that success means happiness. There is no question that there are some people who have achieved enormous successes but who are not happy. They feel driven in an inescapable way throughout their lives to amass one enormous achievement after another, but they remain essentially unhappy. In these individuals there are probably early severe traumata, that leave them with the driving power of their earliest fixations on grandiose fantasies. They have talent to achieve success, which is demanded of them, but they remain rather unhappy personalities and are never pleased by success. The examples among geniuses are a dime a dozen I think. For example, Beethoven's life had one unhappy period after another, and yet he had enormous achievements.

I think many geniuses at the end of their lives would tell you they had the feeling that they did not live their lives actively, but were instead driven by what they believed to be their talent. I do not think it is their talent that drives them, but some kind of command that their talent can just barely perform; they are being pushed all the time and have very little free time or capacity to enjoy themselves. They are driven from one achievement to another.

Going back to something you said earlier, that this is different from the person who can't get in touch with the grandiose feeling, would you elaborate on that?

If an individual has been disappointed traumatically in periods of his life—when there is no echo to his grandiosity—any kind of interference with well-being is a blow to self-esteem, a blow to his grandiosity. I have used grandiosity for want of a better word. It includes what later become perfect beauty, a fine body, great achievement, brightness, moral perfection, a good feeling about oneself.

For example, any painful illness is experienced by the child clearly as a narcissistic blow, not as a reasonably suffered affliction that has a reason and that can be responded to. The child responds with anger to a stubbed toe, "How can they do this to me?" A bit of this narcissistic mode of reacting to illnesses is retained by many people in life. Let us assume that a child suffers a traumatic disappointment early in life at a time when under normal circumstances one should have confirmation of one's early unrealistic self-esteem. This may occur by reason of a mother's depression or a mother's incapacity to solve a problem for the child, such as a physical illness (though the actual fact of a physical illness is not likely to explain the story). The actual degree of lowering of self-esteem is enormously important for you to think through, even with severe illnesses.

In early life, when the child's self-esteem and self-experience include his parents or surrounding adults, the actual fact of the child's illness, even when severe, is not necessarily a trauma. It is only when there is parental rejection because of the physical illness that the drop in self-esteem becomes traumatic. The few cases that I have treated in which early physical illness played an important role in personality development led me clearly to conclude that it was not the illness per se, but the narcissistic blow of the child's illness to the parents, precipitating a drop in their own self-esteem and their rejection of the child, that was decisive.

This is something Freud spoke about a long time ago. I do not know if you know enough about the history of analysis to recognize which early deviant school is particularly involved in the last things I said. It is the Adlerian school (Freud, 1914, p. 99). Subject-bound inferiority became the nucleus for dynamic character formation—overcompensations, for example, overcoming of inferiority feelings due to organ inferiority, and so on. Karen Horney applied a variant of this to female psychology (1934). Freud did not pursue this particular line of thought.

There was a not very good but at one time enormously popular German novelist and biographer, Emil Ludwig, who wrote a number of best-selling biographies; some were not bad. Among the biographies was one of William II (Ludwig, 1928). Ludwig was a follower of Adler and explained the totality of the personality development of the Emperor Wilhelm on the basis of the fact that he had a birth injury. It was rather well-known that he had a withered arm, and on the basis of this nuclear organ inferiority, Emil Ludwig described his character. He said the Emperor could never rest and that the World War was the final outgrowth of this need to assert himself. His arm was withered, and he tried to prove that it was not.

I think that to read Freud's polemic statements vis-à-vis Adler is very instructive. Some of them deal with the history of the psychoanalytic movement. As I have already told you, he said it was not the withered arm, the organ inferiority, that later made the Emperor into such a striving, ambitious person, so easily depressed, disappointed and hurt when he did not get his way. He had to achieve one great overt success after another. This may indeed have been one of the many causes of war. But it was the rejection he received from his proud mother, who could not tolerate a deformed, imperfect child, and who therefore wanted nothing to do with him from the beginning, that Freud considered as the explanation for the Kaiser's personality.

To me, this makes eminent sense from my experience of patients in whom severe early injuries or diseases led, in the last analysis, not to the central feeling of incapacity, but to the central feeling of the impotence of the parents. It was because they were helpless that they rejected the child. They could not cure his imperfection and could not tolerate a crippled child.

The normal parental response to a crippled child is an overextension of affection toward the child. This is perfectly understandable psychobiologically, although sociologically it may lead to grave injustices. The mother gives everything she has to the crippled child, and it is frequently the other members of the family who suffer emotionally. Here they are, with their good bodies, wanting to have the mother's gleam and response to them, but the mother is taken up with the hunchbacked child or the limping child. It is very different when this is a momentary or transitory withdrawal of attention because of a temporary sickness in one of the children in the family. When there is a chronic withdrawal of love from the well children directed to the sick child, then the well children very frequently become terribly resentful. They will react with extensive personality changes and will be demanding, flaunting their achievements because of their contempt for that sick competitor who has taken the echo they need away from them.

Why is it necessarily psychobiologically sensible that the mother should overextend herself rather than reject? In the animal kingdom one might see a defective offspring rejected, not fed at all, and left to die. Is it not a reaction formation to that response that causes the parents to overextend themselves to the child?

I think that is an excellent question. I defined the difference, of course, when I said it is in one way a potentially good response, psychobiologically, but sociologically, as far as the family fabric and the other children are concerned, it is a disservice. The accent lies on *psycho* in the word psychobiological. In the highly differentiated way in which human beings react to one another, I believe this overreaction is much more broadly sustaining of humanness than rejection of the child and infanticide would be. There are all kinds of arguments here.

There is something about the human psychological makeup that cannot simply be compared to the behavior of animals. First of all, the human litter is small, usually one, whereas the rejection by an animal of a deformed member of a litter represents the rejection of only one out of many in this particular litter. This is very different from rejecting a child who has stimulated all the maternal attitudes in the mother. Secondly, there is a narcissistic involvement. Therefore, it is the normal outflow of protective narcissism that envelops the child, in the same way as it envelops a diseased organ of oneself later in life. In other words, the child and its defect are included in the self unit.

One comes to the very complex issues of how individual psychological attitudes must perhaps find and retain a place in the complexity of a technological society. Human behavior in large groups clearly deteriorates when sacrifices are no longer made for the runt of the litter. It is the end of an army when it leaves its wounded behind, even though, for the efficacy of the fighting force, this might be the better thing to do. It is the end of the army for two reasons. First of all, such abandonment is the result of disorganization. In other words, the human value in which one identifies with the wounded and helpless has been dropped. Secondly, and secondarily, people are empathically connected with those who are left behind. They know what is happening. They know that from now on they themselves will not be protected if something should happen to them. Thus, it becomes everybody for himself and it is the beginning of the end to organized cohesive group action.

When the three astronauts were in danger, there was concern throughout the world as to whether they would be rescued. Why? Because everybody can identify with the loneliness of the person who may not find his way back to earth but is allowed to suffocate somewhere in space. This is a replica of the earliest anxieties and fears of being away from home, lost, and not finding the mother again, mother earth, or whatever it may be. So it is important to save the astronauts even though it costs millions. Economically, it is irresponsible, but it would be totally destructive to civilization not to make the attempt to rescue them. It is not because these three men are so terribly important. Every day thousands die in Vietnam or in car accidents or in all the different ways life ends. These are not important, as far as group cohesiveness is concerned. But as far as the maintenance of a sense of responsibility is concerned, group cohesiveness to save them is important. If they cannot be saved, one has done what one could, but one cannot abandon them.

This is a long reply to the question of the psychobiological meaning of the human reaction to injured or defective young. In the human species this has become more complex—perhaps related to the smallness of the human litter.

Now what about the end of the case?

There isn't a great deal to be said about the last interview. I was a bit surprised that it was the last interview.

You mean, she said it was the last, and she does not want to come anymore?

Yes. Her mood had begun to pick up in the third hour. After she came back from this skiing trip and said she was going to switch from mathematics to philosophy, I noticed some shift in the depression. The following week she was just blooming. I had transferred out of Student Health, and I had my office in OPD. As we walked down the corridor I asked her if she had any trouble finding the clinic. She said, no, that she knows how to ask questions. She was putting me in my place, but in a nice way. Then she sat down in the chair with her legs hanging over the opposite arm of the chair. She said she had been feeling so good lately that she had come to tell me she really didn't have more to talk about. She related this to having decided to switch out of physics and math and into philosophy. Now she's taking courses she really enjoys and can genuinely do well in. She said this all went back to the ski trip where she had gotten a totally new perspective on her life. She had taken skiing lessons and discovered that by not caring whether she fell or not she was able to do very well. She returned with the idea that she could be a good skier if she wanted to. On the bus ride home she began to feel depressed again as she thought of returning to a group of physics courses she didn't enjoy. Then it hit her: Why continue it? Why not switch out? She said it was a revelation that she could do that. She had taken with her Joyce's *Portrait of the Artist* and read it on the way home with much enjoyment. And she said she could concentrate. She said she wasn't too concerned about picking a definite major, that she could decide that next fall.

I asked her if in this new curriculum she feels she still has to be the very best. Could she really read without anxiety? I reminded her of what she had told me about having to read all the books of Sartre. She said, yes, she really could, that somehow she feels more together. Her goals aren't as high. She reads and writes more easily in the last couple of weeks. And she isn't as lonely as before.

I thought maybe she went back to the old boyfriend. I was still a bit skeptical and said, "What about your boyfriend, T.?" I remembered that he had been on the ski trip.

She said she had seen him on the ski trip, but they just had dinner once. Then she had been feeling very sexually aroused, and she called him last weekend. They spent a very nice day together, walking. He told her about his personal problems, as usual, which depressed her. Nevertheless, she thought it would be good to sleep with him. She then decided, "No, I'd regret it later. Besides, I don't really want to continue the relationship." She said goodbye to him at the end of the day and felt very good about having done that. She knows there are plenty of girls at the university who sleep with the same fellow every night, and this makes her feel a bit out of it, having no one. But she feels better knowing it's her decision not to just sleep around. She says that a man shouldn't be such a big crutch for her. In fact, she finds herself talking to the girls in the dormitory more. But she does go out, and she told me about a recent date. She said she is even going to buy a few dresses for spring. She always wears slacks and a sweatshirt. A friend said, "Spring is coming, Tony, and we want to see your legs."

She said somehow she's able to hang loose now. She's not as concerned about the B.A. degree, if it doesn't lead to much—maybe grad school, maybe not. She just wants to take some brain-building courses, knowing she'll leave here with a better mind. Before she had this shift of attitude, the thought of a major meant specializing in only that— reading hundreds of books, and even talking like the people in the major she wanted to take. In philosophy she had the idea for a while that she had to change her speech in order to be more like the philosophy majors she saw walking around. She has dropped that idea.

I listened to the mood of all this and the kind of genuine self-confidence, the feeling of potency, and that she's into something she can handle. Then I had a sinking feeling. That's right, this should be the end of treatment, and I'm debating with myself if I should say anything. I really had a feeling of regret. She said she felt as if some scum had been removed from the surface of her mind. Friends had told her she was basically an all-right person, if she would only know it and stop confusing herself. Now she seems to know where she's at. She'd call me if any difficulties came up.

I said, "Well you have my number." At the door she thanked me for what I had told her. I said I didn't think I had told her anything in particular.

I said that therapy is often a self-discovery, and it seemed she had done just that.

That was all right. But never interfere with a patient's gratitude. I am serious about that. If you understand the gratitude, it can play an important role in acquiring psychic structure. In this particular case a firming of her personality occurred. Greater cohesiveness and increased self-acceptance were achieved as she related to an accepting idealized figure, the therapist. The traumatizing experience had been in her mid-adolescence, when the idealized father disappointed and abandoned her. But up to a certain point things had been going well. One could assume that the relationship to the father had been aim inhibited, and was a sustaining one for her. Seen through her eyes, father was an unusual person.

In adolescence there is one more testing of external objects. If this is permitted to become sexual, the end result is that value judgment, which should have been aim inhibited, becomes defective. The superego becomes sexually bribable. In this case, as the patient was allowed to idealize the therapist, a sustaining relationship permitted the patient to become focalized again. She was able to experience pleasure in her reading and had a positive feeling for the therapist. We have difficulty in being idealized, because *we need to fend off our own grandiosity* and so we often deprive the patient of his need to glorify us.

What about the whole matter of gifts?

First one has to accept the gift and then think about it afterward. The rule of abstinence is an old misunderstood rule. Those who follow the rule that no real gratification is permissible in therapy deprive therapy of the working-through of what ought to become a valuable insight. It is not crucial whether or not you accept gifts or whether, when patients ask you questions, you answer or not. It is a normal human reaction to normal behavior to react to what the gift or the question seems to be. By not accepting gifts or by not answering, the assumption is that neutrality has been preserved. But you have not acted neutrally. When one speaks of the therapist being neutral, one must not confuse neutrality with the absence of physical stimulation like noise or words. Silence, which is physically neutral, because there is no noise, is *psychologically not neutral*. If somebody asks you a question and you are silent, the patient experiences you as rude, not neutral.

I think neutrality must not be misunderstood as the absence of an emotion or a noise or a verbalization. Neutrality is very difficult to define. It is an attempt to respond appropriately within the setting that the patient can understand. It does not make any difference whether you accept the gift or not. It does not make any difference whether you answer the question or not. It depends on how you accept it or do not accept it, and how you answer or do not answer. One must make it an appropriate experience: You may prefer not to answer the question, but you explain why, and you explain that you understand the patient's reaction. If the patient has given inimically, this will come up in therapy. My own rule is, "When in doubt behave normally." Whether you reject a gift or answer a question is beside the point. When someone has finally broken through his coldness and is able to give, you do not refuse him. The real issue is the human attitude involved in what you do.

Let us now consider this patient's last interview. In some ways the development is very clear. What does she describe about herself? Who wants to formulate this?

In a way, she's letting herself act her age, in very general terms.

Yes, she acts her age, but what are the specifics about her acting her age? What are the positive things she stresses about herself? It seems to me they all have something in common. She does a variety of things—in her studies, in her attitude toward the boyfriend, in her attitude toward skiing, in her attitude toward reading. All these activities have something psychologically in common.

I meant that she wasn't overstriving, and therefore not reaching her goal.

That's one aspect. She said that about her classwork, and she said it about the skiing.

And about the boy, in a sense.

I don't see that quite so much, that she was overstriving. She came to the conclusion that it was better to drop him.

I got the flavor that she was mastering and being confident by not being that worried about it—by being able to let herself go in a controlled way, and not being so worried that something terrible would happen. The feeling that it was up to her to be in control.

I think you are close to what I feel, that she has a real sense of initiative. She is not being pushed around anymore. She has the initiative and she has choice.

It seems to me that the therapist has offered her the opportunity to separate herself in a significant way from the plans her father had about her and her own identification with him intellectually.

I think that is true. But the sense that she is of one piece now seems to me very strong. In fact, she even said so. In other words, she is of one piece, and one has the feeling that she's the center of real initiative now; she decides. She is still pushed by some needs—for instance, the need for the boyfriend; but she decides, no, this is not the most important thing. "The most important thing is me. Let's get rid of him now. This is no good." Her self-esteem is heightened. And with her sense of self-esteem and being of one piece, she also becomes a center for decisions, for choices, for plans and initiative. When she reads, she reads actively. When she drops one set of courses and takes another one, she makes a decision according to what is best for her. She is the center of activity now which is bound up, it seems to me, with this heightened self-esteem, with a greater cohesiveness of her self-experience.

She's riding the horse.
She decides to terminate therapy.

That's true. She's riding the horse, and she tells the horse which way to go. This is now a dynamic diagnosis. We can say this is what happened to her cohesiveness and her self-esteem. These are the results of her heightened self-esteem and, even more, of her cohesive self holding together in one piece. How did it happen? What brought it about? An accident? The result of psychotherapy? A little bit of each? What do you think?

I wonder if there weren't some stirrings of this which contributed to her coming into the clinic. She was moving from one mode of operating to another. It was the disequilibrium at that point which made her feel so uncomfortable. She was pushing herself to act in an old way, which didn't feel good anymore, and she could no longer force herself to do it.

When you think about it, according to her description—and I have no reason to doubt it, even though I know there may be some falsification of moods—this was not just a momentary bad feeling she had. She said her depression started when she was a senior in high school. I think what you have in mind is that her motivation to come for therapy was already part and parcel of a beginning of improvement. That may be so. I do not know what previous moves she may have made for help. It may be also that she felt particularly bad, that she was more depressed than before.

My feeling is that her improvement is more directly related to the psychotherapy. The question is how and why.

I have a feeling that what happened was that her therapist made no demands on her other than to allow herself to emerge and to present herself, rather than having to conform to any expectations of his, necessarily, as with her father. She somehow got that message that it was okay for her to come forth on her own and to throw off the cocoon of her father.

I think it was much simpler than that. I have the impression that, for whatever reasons, her therapist responded very positively toward her. You did not respond so much in words, but I think you were in tune with her. You liked her mind, you found her an attractive personality. Something positive was repeated in this encounter for her that enabled her to turn the tide, emotionally, whether this was done on the preconscious side or whether it was done with a degree of skill that one learns to apply intentionally, consciously, and yet naturally. You can do this without being unnatural at all, when you see the needs of the person. One always finds something to which to respond without being artificial about it.

I have the impression that this was a girl who had developed a good many fine qualities under the impact of and the interplay with her father, who admired her and with whom she felt very closely allied, but that a good many of the sustaining aspects of this relationship were lost to her when she got higher up in high school, where there was no more success. Her father apparently withdrew from her and wanted her to move away from him. When she finally got into the competitive atmosphere of the college here, it was even worse.

There was something about the acceptance you gave her, something about responding to her gifts, something about enjoying her—the way she looked, the way she talked, and particularly the way her mind worked—that allowed her to feel better about herself. This became, as it were, the opposite of a vicious cycle. Feeling a little better about herself, she achieved certain things, which made her feel even better. And having achieved certain things, she could suddenly get intellectual pleasure—expansiveness, philosophizing with father, and sharing ideas—which was repeated a little bit in the relationship to you. She went back again to the old balance, and she was suddenly in charge again. Being in charge of herself, she now lives according to what she needs, not according to what is being pushed. She doesn't need to struggle with physics and math, which is not her cup of tea; but she likes being in the humanities, and she likes to respond to this type of thought.

Isn't it also that she no longer needs to be father's son, as she described herself earlier, but through her therapist's listening and accepting her, she can also begin to see the reality of her mother's difficulties and early illness. She can also see that while father permitted the younger sister to be feminine, and so on, somehow this was barred from her, but with her therapist she regains this opportunity.

That may very well be true. At the end she did speak about some feminine attributes. She's going to buy some new dresses, and there is something forward looking in both directions. There is the sense of being a favorite of father's in the intellectual sphere, and yet being far enough away from him now so that she can blossom out and enjoy herself. Did you notice the switch? The switch is an enjoyment of herself. She wants to look pretty. It is not yet meant for anyone in particular. The need to call the boyfriend because she has to have somebody in bed declines as she feels more secure about herself, as an intellect, as a skier, and as a pretty girl. So she needs people less, and feels better. As such, she has initiative, and as such she'll probably be more attractive to other people too.

My impression, very clearly, is that her improvement is in response to the psychotherapy. You did everything fine, except the need to talk down her gratitude. If she feels pleased that here is an important person who has helped her, that has reinstated something from which she drew strength early in life, why interfere with it? In her mind you are assigned the role of the great, loving and admiring father, and you fill that role. And when she expresses gratitude, you accept it.

But what about the whole matter of testing out the relationship, the renewal and reshuffling of old feelings about father?

During the oedipal phase, what was external disappears, and internal sets of values and ideals take on firmness and power and become focalized. All this is loosened once more in adolescence and results in the final settling down of the basic personality. There is once more a testing of the external object. The scene is reenacted in which the adult is seduced. Where an aim-inhibited relationship is missing, a basic defect in the ability to control the drive results and acting-out occurs.

One can assume, in acting-out patients, that this has indeed happened earlier in their life, for example in camp experiences with adolescents. In a relationship with a level-headed counsellor, girls can idealistically improve the world, developing pioneer skills and spirit. These are all aim-inhibited. The heterosexual child in whose development actual seduction occurs is deprived of the depth of the love relationship. The refinement of the love relationship and an affectionate bond will be missing. Grown love relationships are multilayered. Gross sexual behavior or strongly negative behavior regarding sex will lead to deprivation of personality development and a failure in the refinement of the love relationship. In the case we have been discussing, father was not only a love object but an ideal. The father had to carry some idealizing of the mother who was ill, and the girl was deprived of something which should have become part and parcel of her self. In her father she found a man whom she could love and idealize. Although her goal structure will have a masculine cast, this is not deleterious. Not everybody has to grow with the same development: it is important to have values, but then content must not be schematic.

Can we assume that a seduction experience may have occurred in a patient characterized by acting-out, if the history, otherwise, would not explain the acting-out?

There are many forms of acting-out. With acting-out individuals you cannot conclude that there were specific kinds of adolescent or early experiences just on the basis of acting-out.

In adolescence, once more, but in a mitigated and much less deeply destructive way, traumata can occur, but you must not forget that there must be a certain sophistication to your perspective. We cannot simply think in terms of cause and effect, for then we usually do an injustice to the complexity of the psychological situations as they really are.

I have nothing against a comparatively simple type of formulation as we learn complex concepts. They may make things a bit more digestible. I have nothing against saying that if a camp director, for example, lets himself or herself become engaged in some kind of sexual relationship with a girl or boy who wants to idealize the relationship, this kind of situation may then become the cause, as it were, of the latest specific superego defect. This is correct, as far as it goes, but it is overly simplified. It may give a dynamic and structural explanation for the patient's later behavior. We will know later on that, when the patient has a task to perform, he can bribe his own conscience the way he formerly bribed, let us say, the camp director. "I'm so lovely and so lovable, I don't really have to do that, do I? I'm a very special person."

An idealized camp director will allow herself or himself to be idealized, but will not allow this idealization to degenerate into an actual love relationship. The leadership valence of this particular person, being loved and idealized, will give special power to the demands that this person makes. For love of the camp director one will be disciplined; one will get up at the first ring of the bell; one will turn off the light, even though one would still like to chatter. But if a gross sexualization takes place, then very soon the discipline will falter.

This behavior with the camp director, or similar situations at school or at home, may have contributed to a later weakness in the relationship of the ego to the superego, in the way the person can take discipline or tolerate tension. The difficulty lies in the following: Which of the many children in a camp is it who has the sexual relationship with that camp director? It does not occur with all the children. It is only with those who are already seductive toward the adult.

In other words, what specific earlier experience predisposed this particular child once more to test whether perhaps the new edition of parenthood will now not respond to his seduction? The pathogenic or pathological behavior of the idealized figure in adolescence, in most instances, simply adds to an already existing pathology. On the other hand, we might say that had the camp director not allowed himself to be seduced, then the tide might have been turned the other way—a degree of firmness would have been acquired. Perhaps this is the difference between a person who will later on have a successful form of psychotherapy and one who will never go into psychotherapy, but will keep acting out throughout life without ever thinking there is anything wrong. An awareness of pathology may be the best sign of health that may come from a camp experience that is positive, while a negative camp experience will result in a totally loose personality who will never consider herself sick and will never seek psychotherapy.

16

Acting-Out Differentiated From Action
Under the Dominance
of the Ego

W E TOUCHED LAST TIME on the subject of acting-out. Let us now approach the topic from a more general viewpoint. Acting-out probably plays a role in a high percentage of patients in the age group that
you treat. If there are questions, I would be interested in hearing them.
What kind of acting-out do you mostly encounter? How great are the
difficulties? How serious is the interference with therapy because of the
acting-out? How do you generally handle it? Do you handle it by explanations? Do you handle it by becoming a controlling external force sup-
plying ego or superego attitudes to the patient? Does it subside without
any particular need to do anything special as the therapeutic relationship
establishes itself? In general, is it something to be opposed? Is it just a
way of life? It seems to me this is an important issue, one of much greater
importance with adolescents and students than with adults.

I can perhaps briefly define for you what the term generally means,
but at the same time also admit that the term is used much more loosely
by most people than its original definition. It is a translation of a word
used by Freud. The common meaning of this word would be to "pretend
as if, or acting as if," but Freud didn't mean it in that sense. He talked
about this in a specific paper in which he compared remembering of the
past with the acting-out of the past in the analytic process (1914a, p.
150). It was an activity which was steered by unconscious forces, which
the patient did not understand, but which motivated him. It was clear
that the road had to go from acting-out to remembering, that acting-out
was undesirable and that remembering was desirable.

In other words, it corresponds to a slip of the tongue or to a dream. It is
a structure in which an unconscious motivation, an unconscious scene,

instead of being remembered, instead of the derivatives of it gradually entering memory and consciousness, is simply portrayed in a kind of communicative language that would be somewhat like a dumb show or an enactment.

The important thing in the classical definition of acting-out is that the motivation for what is done is strictly separated in the psyche. The simplest way of experimentally showing this would be through the analogy of the posthypnotic suggestion. The patient is first put into a trance, which means that he has a particular kind of relationship to the hypnotist. The hypnotist and his orders temporarily become, as it were, part and parcel of the endopsychic process of the patient. This is a very primitive type of relationship. The subject may be told, "You will wake up now, and ten minutes after waking up you will go to the umbrella that stands in this corner of the room, open the umbrella, and then you will close it. This is all you have to do. But you will not remember that I have ordered you to do that."

This example is very important for the following reason. About eight minutes after awakening, the patient becomes restless. He looks out the window and says, "It looks like clouds are coming. I wonder if it's going to rain. I've got to see if my umbrella is in good shape." He finds it in good shape and puts it away again. Everybody in the room knows that he did not look at the umbrella because he was concerned about the clouds gathering or needed to know whether his umbrella was working—that is, everybody except himself. He believes he went to the umbrella because he was suddenly concerned about the clouds gathering and whether his umbrella was working all right. And yet nobody in the room present during the time when the posthypnotic suggestion was given will be convinced. However, if a colleague comes in late and witnesses the behavior and is asked what he thinks about it, he may say, "Well it looks rainy and he's a little concerned about his umbrella." He would not have the slightest doubt of the explanation of the act.

And so it is with acting-out. Very frequently, when somebody acts out in the classical sense, it can only be known after the structural relationship between the activity and the motivational force becomes clear. If one sees such an individual without such knowledge, one is very likely led to believe that the motivation for these activities is reasonable. In other words, there is an integrative function in the ego that will not allow an act of this kind to take place without some regard to its meaningfulness and its rationality.

The point is that one cannot see, by looking at an activity, whether it is acting-out or an action. What is the difference? An action is truly motivated by the relationship between the ego and its environment. In other words, if a person truly sees that clouds are coming, and has had no posthypnotic suggestion, he may indeed wonder if his umbrella is in good shape, and he may look at it, even though such behavior would be a little odd. But if the person performs in this way exactly at the time of the command, everybody knows that all the reasons he gives for his behavior are secondary and are not the true motivation. They are only an explanation for a mode of behavior which is otherwise unintelliglble to the patient and which the patient could not tolerate, because one does not tolerate a rift of this type in one's personality. One tries to cover it over.

This is what I have often said about slips of the tongue—there is a momentary rift in the personality, although we are more used to this kind of rift than to other things. We know that slips of the tongue do occur, and we laugh at them, but we generally try to cover over. We try to supply motivation and say, "I know what I meant when I made the slip," and so on. When we see a person behave in a way that appears to be acting-out in the classical sense, the fact that the patient gives ego-syntonic explanations for his activity does not mean that the behavior is ego-syntonic.

How can you know whether it is acting-out or not? You do not know the traumatic situation that cries for its repetition, that pushes the ego to act in a certain way, so that the ego gives in to it. You obviously cannot know for sure, because you were not there when the posthypnotic suggestion was laid down by the patient's childhood experiences. You cannot understand the acting-out, even though it seems to be a reasonable activity, any more than you can the hysterical symptom. It is structured in the same way. It is amalgamation between an ego-syntonic secondary motivation and a push that goes far beyond that.

How can you tell the difference between acting-out and a hysterical symptom? There are ways and means of telling the difference. Among them is the stereotyped nature and the repetitiveness of the activity. For example, one hears that a girl has involved herself in a relationship with a man 25 or 30 years her senior—a married man—and she is dropped after a few months by this man. She then complains bitterly about what happened to her. One may say, "That kind of thing can happen." But when one hears that this same kind of thing has happened innumerable times, that every time she picks this type of man even though she may explain that her choice is a pure accident, one will surmise that this is not so, but that she is motivated to enact something over which she has no control. Something corresponding to the posthypnotic suggestion is acting in her which relates to the reenactment of an oedipal situation.

Classical acting-out, then, relates to an unconscious constellation, a repetition or an expression of something early in childhood that is now dramatized in the course of present life. One may ask why some individuals develop this kind of symptom and other individuals develop less dramatic symptoms. Why do some individuals reenact scenes by involving themselves in complex social situations, while other individuals develop paralyses, or characterological features, or psychosomatic illnesses? We are entering, here, into questions at the frontier of our science and not easily answered. In general one should remember that acting in a dumb show, acting on the stage, is probably an older form of communication than language, and that certain individuals—particularly hysterical ones—who use the body, for example, to communicate, to make scenes, are theatrical people, and apparently have a propensity toward expressing themselves in this particular way, while the compulsion neurotic does not. I would be unable to say whether there are inherited factors involved, whether such people live in environments in which scenes in the home are frequent and in which many of the pressures the parents exert on the child express their own needs and have to be resisted by the child's counter-activities, even early on. But I think all these factors are involved, even an inherited propensity for such behavior. Many actor-outers are hysterical personalities and tend to react toward rejection with hysterical symptomatology, with scenes, or with hysterical suicidal gestures, for example, rather than a true suicidal drive. So far, the central structural and dynamic relationships that underlie acting-out may be seen as a psychic split in depth—a horizontal split so that the top layer of the psyche behaves like a puppet moved by the bottom layer, without knowing why, but more or less rationalizing the behavior.

I am trying to explain a particular relationship between two different layers or areas of the mental apparatus of the psyche. The posthypnotic suggestion is its experimental replica. We assume that the residue of a childhood memory, attitude, wish or urge, relating to specific things that were repressed, may act upon the person's ego in the same way as the posthypnotic suggestion acts on the person's posthypnotic ego. In other words, it forces the ego to act; yet the ego pretends that it acts out of its own initiative. Freud made several jokes about this relationship, in an attempt to make an analogy. One was the story of the clown in the circus. He looks at what the big actors are doing, and then runs after them and does the same thing. He said the ego in such an instance behaves like the clown in the circus. The real actors are the childhood scenes, the childhood pressures, the unconscious motivations.

An even better example is the joke about the Sunday rider. It's the story about the man who only rides on Sunday (1933, p. 108). One Sunday he is proudly riding on his horse when he meets a friend of his who is on foot. The friend says, "Hey, where are you riding?" He says, "Don't ask me, ask the horse." In other words, he is not a real horseman. He only looks as if he were in charge of the situation, but in reality he just follows along where the horse is going.

In the old analogy of the rider and the horse—the id and the ego—in this relationship it is the unconscious urge that is in charge, while the rider only rationalizes. He says, "I want to go there because the horse is making us go there." And he hopes that when the horse finally gets hungry they will go back to the stable again, and they will, but he will act as if it was his intention.

I think you all understand the difference between an action initiated by the ego, adapted to reality, and following an autonomous ego goal, on the one hand, and a rationalizing ego that behaves like the clown in the circus or the Sunday rider, on the other. Of course, there are all kinds of relationships within this realm. There are even some individuals who can, having no choice because they are being pushed by an unconscious motivation, somehow harness these urges to some purpose.

I once knew a neurologist who had more tics than anybody I have ever known. He was filled with tics—so much so that I always said that, whenever there was something he wanted to do, he waited for the appropriate tic and then used the tic to do it.

What I am trying to say is that there are some individuals who are pushed by stereotyped unconscious motivations. The ego works as a distributing agency, as it were, and watches over these impulses, and then, if necessary, uses them for some particular rational or adaptive purpose.

So we have now talked about the relationship between what we call acting-out and a real action which is truly dominated by the ego and in tune with the ego's relationship as a mediator between the psychic needs and external possibilities. In extreme cases it is very clear. Obviously, somnambulistic walking into somebody's bedroom is clearly acting-out, or something akin to acting-out. The person does not know that it is the old childhood wish to interfere with parental intercourse, or something of that nature. He is simply pushed. However, let us say somebody is driven scientifically to investigate sexual behavior. He can rationalize it as scientific research; the question remains, where do you draw the line? As with the posthypnotic experiment, if you arrive on the scene after the posthypnotic order is given, you will be ignorant that it is in force. You must carefully investigate in order to find out how much of a certain behavior was indeed simply the ego's compliance and rationalizing and how much was truly an autonomous activity of the ego.

I have often said, and I continue to believe, that ego activities are not surface behavior, that a person's psyche and wishes and actions may have, and the important ones usually do have, depth. In other words, the deep layers of the psyche, including childhood experiences, reverberate and participate in a person's activities, particularly in the important ones. It by no means militates against the relevance or meaningfulness of a person's professional activity if you can show that the motivation for it arose in very important childhood settings. It by no means mitigates against the relevance of significant object choices in life, the choice of a mate, for example, if you can prove that it is the continuation of an important object choice of early life. There is a difference between choosing a mate according to the image of a beloved mother or sister or friend and acting-out a choice in which a particular relationship to a mother or sister or friend from early childhood is reenacted many times, for example, through marriages and divorces or through a variety of friendships. Where is the difference? Do you understand the problem? I want to be sure the problem is understood before trying to tackle the solution.

On the basis of a kind of rigid repetition, you may sometimes suspect that you are dealing with acting-out, but you cannot be sure. Behavioral characteristics are just not reliable. You have the feeling that it looks like acting-out—this person is just rationalizing, but you cannot be absolutely sure.

How can one differentiate the relationship of a childhood experience to present ego activities that are acting-out from the relationship of childhood experience to present ego activities that are action in depth, not acting-out? Is there an emotional and motivational force behind such action which harks back to early life? There are of course some activities that do not have deep reverberations. Perfectly adequate and important activities may really emanate from the surface of the psyche and respond to particular needs. I would imagine that abstract problem-solving activities in and of themselves are enacted in this particular way, although the devotion to a life of abstract problem-solving, sticking to it, choosing such a career, tells a different story. There may be very deep emotional forces behind such activity, for example, the identification with an admired, abstractly thinking father.

It is not difficult to understand that this discussion belongs to the higher mathematics of our field. The answer lies in the definition of the differential between the *tensions* that propel one from *early* life and the *activity* of the ego. For example, consider the child whose anxious interest in what the parents are doing in the bedroom is aroused. Great excitement is generated by the rhythmical noises, identification with both partners in the dimly seen activity, fear of some horrible mutilation going on or of somebody getting killed in the process. There is more excitement than the psyche can tolerate, and so the ego walls itself off; it forbids itself to be aware of this. This unaltered residue of the experience thus remains excluded from the ego, but it clamors for expression. In other words, there is a great difference between the ego that knows nothing of this particular childhood scene and the intensity of the childhood impulse to participate again, emotionally, and to interfere again. The anxiety about it all is walled off in the unconscious. The twain shall never meet, except for temporary sudden intrusions of the unaltered memory of the childhood scene into the present behavior of the adult. Then something happens. The ego makes emergency maneuvers to do something quickly about this intruding foreign motivation. This is very different from childhood impulses, participations, interests very gradually integrated into the psyche. For example, there can be intense love for a mother or sister that gradually becomes aim-inhibited, that is not countered by the fear, "If you love me, you will be killed by father," or whatever it may be. The individual instead feels, "You can love me, and you can love father too. It is true that there are conflicts, but you love me in a different way." In other words, there is a gradual aim-inhibited acceptance.

This does not mean that the old deep emotional and passionate roots are gone, but rather that they become gradually integrated into the psyche, so that they become feeders, as it were, of final ego activities with which they are in continuous contact. But as the psyche grows in depth, more and more sieves, as it were, more and more neutralizing forces, are interposed between the original childhood wish and the ego still under the influence of the old childhood needs and wishes.

To use an electrical analogy, it is as if a high-tension current suddenly interferes with a low-tension current resulting in a short circuit. This is in contrast with a high-tension current that goes through many transformers and finally ends up as the kind of current that is needed for the system that it activates. And so it is in a model of the mind, in transferences, or where there are progressive neutralizations; in both instances, drives and experiences from childhood push upward (Kohut and Seitz, 1963). Here, however, with gradual educational no's—"not this but that; you must change a little bit there"—one can finally come to the point where the old childhood wish, the old childhood experiences, the old childhood motivations nourish adult hopes. But the original unmodified incestuous love now leads into the aim-inhibited, or at least mature, adult object choice. This is very different, however, from the incestuous tie to the mother which is opposed by a strong counter-barrier. Here, the old original high-tension childhood sexuality and aggression are still active, breaking through only momentarily in the form of acting out, in the form of a symptom. But the symptom still betrays in some ways the old high-tension that intrudes here for a moment and is rationalized secondarily so that it is explained when it comes out, but it is not smoothly integrated.

I do not know if you can integrate this kind of explanation into clinical experiences. I think it is very helpful; it is not just an abstract kind of exercise. It can order one's outlook on a variety of clinical observations. Of course, it does not help you immediately in terms of determining, when you see some behavior, whether it is an acting-out or an action.

I am trying to think in terms of the type of pathology you are most likely to encounter. There are other types of disturbances in which activities of the patient dominate the symptomatic field, but which I would not put under the heading of this type of acting-out. This is what I am warning you about. Many things are called acting-out. Some call lack of impulse control acting-out, instead of identifying acting-out as a particular kind of structuralization of a symptom without moral or immoral meaning. There are other forms of activities that are often grouped under this heading, but are something very different from acting-out.

I would think that a great deal of the indiscriminate promiscuous behavior that one finds in young people, particularly when it has a joyless and compulsive quality, is of a totally different order of events. This is not motivated by an unconscious need to reconcretize a particular traumatic scene or interpersonal situation from childhood or a particular traumatic experience like the examples I gave earlier. It is a mode of activity that is much more closely related to the addictions. It is an attempt to find something, perhaps to counteract an otherwise noticeable depression, to find or to chase after some kind of pleasure. I think it is much more akin to the endless compulsive masturbatory activity of deprived children than to the hysterical scenes of hysterical patients. Here, it is not so much that a specific situation is reenacted many times, but rather a feeling of drivenness, an attempt to get something that is unobtainable. This is much more related to the area of low self-esteem, of feeling bad about oneself, or of feeling empty or unsupported. It is an attempt in some way to get something, perhaps orally satisfying, that some such individuals run after.

In such behavior, there is very frequently a superego question involved, although not primarily a superego defect. It is much more an ego defect. It is much more a frantic attempt by an ego to get something for reassurance, for feeling alive, for feeling that somebody touches the person, for feeling some warmth, for some activity that is basically directed against loneliness, against a feeling of unacceptability, of lowest

degrees of self-esteem. Such individuals not only feel low about themselves, but their ideal structure is very shaky. They not only often try to
get some warmth, touching, or contact-hunger satisfied in their promiscuous sexual activities, but they also very frequently enter into seemingly masochistic relationships. They feel themselves terribly humble, low
and deprived, and they throw themselves away on some idealized figures. At least they claim they are ideal figures. They themselves feel
empty and worthless, but they look up to the leaders. At the same time,
they debase themselves as they once felt debased in terms of the old
ideals of their parents. By this means, they gain contact.

*I don't understand why this doesn't meet the original definition of acting-out
in terms of stereotyped repetitious behavior, a component of which is out of the
awareness of the individual.*

The decisive thing is missing, that is, the motivational force is not
separated from the executive organ. The total personality is involved in a
much more regressive state. This is not a highly specific repressed type
of material that yearns for expression and then finds a particular circumscribed mode of action. What is involved here is a totally deprived personality that becomes addicted to a particular kind of environment. Such
a person could become addicted to drugs or to food, leading to obesity.
There could be addiction to a joyless, restless, learning activity. There is
no specific early constellation in which the self and the parents are
clearly separated from one another that is now reenacted in this compulsive way. This is, rather, a self and a dimly understood archaic environment which has not given the child earliest sustenance: the present
person, in toto, in depth, without any break in the personality, relates
now to the environment with the same need for reassurance and with
the same need for attention. It is the same need to have somebody
relating to it, to be held, to be fed, to have an ideal around to look up to
in the primitive way of a child who masturbates in a lonely corner when
the parents are gone again or do not pay attention to him. It is a different
structuralization of the personality in a more primitive relationship to
the environment.

In one way there is a similarity. This similarity is in a much reduced
capacity to tolerate internal tensions, to the degree that would allow the
formation of fantasies and word communication about fantasies. In both
instances this capacity is much reduced. The hysteric does not spin out
fantasies when he acts out but the fantasy is in the acting-out. It is the
trick of the therapy to change the acting-out into fantasies, and then
from the fantasies perhaps to lead, in the long run, to memories.

In other words, endopsychic constellations are being followed. In the instance of the much more archaic personality organization that I described in this addictive type of promiscuity, an external symptom does not tell you the meaning and the structure of the symptom. Compulsive behavior may be the symptom of a defense against hostile anal-sadistic smearing, but it may also be an attempt to deal with an ill-understood environment, as a primitive tribe does when going through rituals in order to get rain in a drought. They are both the same, but the structure is different.

To come back again to the second type of case that you were wondering about—in the second case, the primitiveness of the relationship to the environment is one of the reasons why delimited concepts in the forms of images and fantasies are not yet capable of taking up the pressure and absorbing the pressure. In earliest life there is not yet the differentiation between thought and action. As in observing, the child becomes the thing that he observes, so also in the impulse and wishes: direct fulfillment needs to be there right away.

So a great deal of work is needed before such individuals first develop enough tension tolerance to stop the activity. It rests, let us say, on the therapeutic relationship, because even the most extreme addictive searching will stop, sometimes very quickly, simply on the basis of the therapist now providing, in fact, what this particular girl had been searching for. By the therapist's interest, responsiveness, remembering from one time to another, all of a sudden a heretofore seemingly unstoppable behavior ends, not because there is any insight gain, but because the dynamic need for it is not as great anymore. Something wish-fulfilling has been supplied in the therapeutic situation which, hopefully, now includes some of the ideals that the child did not get because she lacked a relationship to the idealized grownups in her early life. Such children are deprived both in self-esteem and in idealism.

So here we have another mode of action which is often called acting-out, but which, strictly speaking, should not be called acting-out. But very frequently, if one calls everything acting-out, then it gets to the point where acting-out just means, "Don't be bad." This is nonsense. Children don't act out. They may destroy something, or they may be sassy, but they don't act out. They may be overstimulated, but acting-out, particularly with small children, is an inaccurate term.

Finally, there are a host of things that fall under the heading of impulse control or lack of impulse control. This is rarely seen in a pure form. But sometimes, particularly in terms of rage attacks, the inability to control the flooding of rage is probably best described as lacking impulse control.

But let me caution you again, one would have to examine the total personality to learn on what basis impulse control is lacking. Is it the secondary result of a schizophrenic crumbling in a personality which, up to now, has been very inhibited? Is there a sudden eruption into throwing things or threatening to run wild? Is this a total regression, including loss of impulse control? Is it simply a cultural phenomenon where what we would call "lacking impulse control" is considered appropriate? This has to be examined in detail. There is probably much more to be said about all of this, but I do not want to go into further details. I think this has to be discussed in terms of particular cases.

If you have the case of a person in whom a moral transgression plays a particular role, I think this will give us a fortunate example. On the basis of such things as plagiarism, cheating, or lying, one can examine the specific background that lies behind the symptom.

There are situations, particularly in younger people, young adults, in which there appears to be a psychotic state. It is a state that defies diagnosis but is usually described as being overburdened, overstimulated, an extreme degree of irritability. In other words, the psyche, under the pressure of enormous demands on it, temporarily disintegrates. A crazy temper tantrum gives the appearance of a permanently disintegrating personality, but it is not a permanent disintegration. It is, rather, the response of an overburdened, hyperstimulated, overirritated psyche, in which the simple removal from a situation of great stress and the calming presence of somebody who temporarily takes care of him put the person right again. In such individuals, there are paranoid features, but they are not paranoiacs. These paranoid features in terms of suspiciousness vis-à-vis the environment are nothing but an outgrowth of the thinness of the stimulus barrier.

In the Second World War, in the South Pacific jungle fighting, people were exposed for long periods to situations in which they were surrounded by a hostile environment. There was continuous anxiety that they were surrounded by an enemy that would shoot and kill them. They could tolerate this for a while, but at some point a number of people broke down.

You may encounter students from small towns who feel themselves in a strange environment in a big city confronted by all kinds of academic demands or by seductive situations. Everything is new, and they react with an overburdenedness, an overstimulation, a general diffuse suspiciousness. They appear to be terribly sick. They appear to be narcissistically regressed individuals on the verge of a paranoid breakdown, but no! If you reverse this by removing the intensity of the stimulation, then with your aid their stimulus barrier becomes firmer again. Then this general hypersensitivity toward the environment, the diffuseness of their rage attacks, and the disorganized responses to the environment subside. It is a traumatic state rather than a beginning schizophrenic disintegration.

The theme of acting-out and its relation to symptom formation, the difference between action and acting-out, represent crucial issues in your work with students. You have probably wondered, how can one explain the difference in the results of a real structural change achieved by years of psychoanalytic work as compared with the sudden and intense changes occurring as a result of therapy such as you practice in the Student Clinic. Both have their purpose, and both have their point, but the results are different. In analysis we hope to increase the realm in the particular area of the mind in which a person can in depth use forces that were formerly not at his disposal, so that he can now more broadly relate to his environment rather than simply abolishing symptoms by reinforcing repressive forces and by strong identification with a protective adult. It seems to me that the normal, healthy psyche should be able to choose activity which arises spontaneously in the ego itself and to discern between such activity and acting-out.

Let me use one more example, namely, the activity of the psychotherapist. This particular scheme, to my mind, lends itself especially well to studying oneself and others in our activity as psychotherapists. What I say here about action is also applicable for understanding—empathic understanding. This is our job. This is what we spend a lifetime doing. We not only want to do it, but we want to understand as much as possible about our own activities.

There are three ways in which one can understand other people empathically. The most significant and important activity is understanding in depth. In other words, when we listen to another person, when we listen to one of the adolescents who comes to the Student Clinic, we in some way relax our own personality. We are doing pretty much the replica of what in analysis we ask the patient to do. What we call even hovering attention is the replica of free association. This means that to some extent we are giving up the rigidity of the surface layers of our own personality. Our self diffuses, and we immerse ourselves in the other personality.

But we have to immerse ourselves, of course, under the domination of the ego. This is not a total giving up of one's personality. It is a temporary, controlled merging with another personality in the same way as in an artistic experience, let us say in the theater, when one immerses oneself in the tragedies of Shakespeare. The understanding comes by reason of the reverberations from our own early experiences to the experiences of the patient; they meet, as it were, halfway. It is from this recognition that one can understand another person psychologically, insofar as there are at least related experiences in ourselves. They do not have to be the same, but they have to be at least related. I wrote a paper about 15 years ago on introspection and empathy (Kohut, 1959); in that I tried to show that there is a whole hierarchy of lessened capacities for empathic behavior, depending on how different the observed is from the observer. One can still perhaps be empathic with a growing plant, but not with the running water. There may still be something about a plant striving toward the sun with which one can basically somehow be in empathy. There was the famous example of a poet, but he was a very sick poet—Keats—who claimed he could suffer with the billiard balls as they were hitting each other (Gittings, 1968, p. 152).

The point I am trying to make here is that in our most standard mode of comprehension of the psychological states of others—when we ask ourselves, "Is this guy acting out or is he acting?"—we do this first of all by somehow feeling ourselves into it. And we have a hard time. Only secondarily, after we have come to some kind of conclusion, will we then think, "Well, is this right?" This can only be a cue; it is not the total answer. We want our secondary processes to investigate afterward, but, as a preliminary first step of perception, we empathize.

The method that you all have asked about is equivalent to asking, "What are the three points by which one can recognize acting-out? Let's count it out again: it has to be this, it has to be that, does this or that fit?" This is perfectly legitimate. Here we do not think with the empathizing part of the psyche, but we think with an autonomous, in itself a split-off aspect of our personality, the thinking, secondary process. This is the kind of ego that we use all the time in most scientific activities—in almost all of them except for understanding depth psychology. For any kind of psychology that deals with the complexities of the human mind, the psychology of complex psychological states, we need the empathic side of the psyche in addition to the secondary process, the ego which follows criteria and clearly spells out characteristics. And very frequently, when our empathy fails us, when we cannot feel ourselves into an individual, we will then begin to scan the field, independent of empathy, and will ask ourselves if we can empathize with a person's behavior. Is this man driven by something he does not know about, or is there an urgency in him that I just do not understand? Then we will begin to think about it and reflect about it from the surface of the mind. This happens all the time. It certainly happens to me.

The analyst knows that when one is out of tune with the patient, one suddenly begins to think. One looks over the patient's last five dreams, and one thinks about how this analysis started or whether there is some thing related to his childhood. One actively reflects, then, in order to fit two and two together until one is again in tune. The ideal progress is first being empathically in tune, and secondarily elaborating on that.

The third method corresponds to acting-out, and sometimes is acting-out. It does not happen once or twice, but there are many times that I have had temporary moments of acting out with my patients. For example, I made remarks that I should not have made—I came late for their appointment—I was mistaken—something happened. And of course it is not good. I am not claiming that mistakes are good, but if they are handled in the appropriate way, then a virtue can be made out of the necessity. You may forget a patient's appointment and come fifteen minutes late, or something of that nature, because without your knowing it the patient had gotten under your skin by something he said to you. Now, you do a quick self-analysis. Not that you can do a self-analysis to any significant degree under emergency conditions of that kind, but little ones such as you do all the time. As a matter of fact, the older you get, and the more experienced you get, the more it is a symbolic kind of acting-out you do. You usually catch yourself before you act out. You begin to recognize the general symptoms of, "Now I'm going to act out," and you don't.

My favorite advice to students is, "Whenever you have the impulse to talk back, bite your tongue. Then you will have a little respite, and you can think about why you want to do it." The point is that you can then say, "I was angry at the patient. That is why I wanted to be late. That is why I nearly forgot his appointment. What was it yesterday?" You begin to see that the patient had suddenly gotten under your skin, and you see why. You can begin to work on the patient's problem, even though it started with a failure of your own—namely, a sudden intrusion of a countertransference activity, with the tension differential of which I am talking.

When I talk about tension differentials it is the high-tension activity I previously described leading to activity of the ego. There is a gradual transformation of the childhood scene, the childhood impulse, the childhood motivation, gradually integrated into the personality's purposes and goals. I am contrasting this with suddenly jumping in: the ego only attempts to use the next tic for the next purposeful action, as in my earlier illustration. This is how theoretical knowledge can be very useful in ordering one's knowledge of oneself.

Can an understanding of the difference between an action under the control of the ego and acting-out as springing from a highly charged, repressed childhood memory be used in understanding creativity?

The average kind of creativity, or even high-average creativity, is probably motivated from deep sources. The sculptor *has* to sculpt, the painter *has* to paint, and it has gradually become integrated from a smearing activity or from an aggressive activity into something extremely important. You know, my earlier example of the famous oral-sadistic chisel of Michelangelo—miles away from where his mother was, yearning for the breast, his anger at the breast, and the white marble from which he learned, within a male surrounding, to get rid of his oral-sadistic anger. All this may have led into forcing Michelangelo to produce something beautiful, something that recreated the mother whom at the same time he wanted to destroy. Some great art is on this level. Nevertheless, creativity arising from the surface only, unless it is a purely abstract field, such as mathematics or logical thinking, would tend in general to be shallower. But the really great artists, including Michelangelo, have something else, namely, they do not have a very good sieve.

In other words, the intense childhood tensions which rise to the surface are not so beautifully neutralized as in the average human being. They erupt with a volcanic, passionate and explosive force, and only by virtue of their unusual gifts are these artists capable of managing this force. In other words, there are individuals, high tension characters, who are capable of working well. The intensity, the passion, that goes into the work of some productions of genius is observable simply in the speed with which the action takes place—the number of hours, the incredible physical capacity that can be devoted to certain productions of a genius. Someone who watched Picasso do his bullfight series of 26 metal engravings timed Picasso while he was doing several. The average interval was something like two minutes for each engraving. And yet these engravings have great detail. One can observe the mood of the audience at the bullfight and how the bull behaves toward the matador from the way in which dots are put down! The observer who timed Picasso with a watch in his hand could not believe Picasso's speed, even though he saw it with his own eyes. There was a frenzy of activity.

Such frenzy of activity occurs in other fields as well: a whole complex of poems is suddenly created, apparently all at once. Even scientific work can be done with a kind of pressure of which the same person is not otherwise capable. I think we all have enough of a creative capacity to know a little bit about the experience. I have had periods in which I worked at speeds which I could not otherwise command.

Such bursts of creative activity need to be investigated, but they are not to be confused with the acting-out relationship. Creative activity does not occur across a repression barrier that suddenly gives way. It is simply that there is a comparatively thinly developed psychological buffering matrix, so that impulses from the depth erupt comparatively unchanged, and are then acted over, worked out and used by an enormously gifted ego. Of course, a gifted ego cannot be explained psychologically, by the relationships of early life.

I was wondering about the intuitive leaks in the therapist—I was wondering if that was acting-out.

The understanding of intuition is an interesting chapter in itself. As a matter of fact, I have worked on that too, particularly in delimiting it from empathy, with which it is too frequently confused. Empathy has absolutely nothing to do with intuition. I have always said that intuition relates to empathy in the way that a convex object does to a concave object. It simply sounds sort of similar but is not.

Empathy is a mode of perception in which the perceived is similar to the perceiver. You perceive another's mental state via the capacity of your psyche to relate to similarities or similar exprinces in yourself. You feel yourself into them. There are other modes of understanding, for instance, behavioral assessment or behavioral adding up. Either or both can be intuitive or non-intuitive. To my mind, intuitive means simply that an activity is performed with enormous expertness, very quickly, and predominantly preconsciously.

A good diagnostician or a good internist will enter a patient's room and in a flash say the patient suffers from a certain illness. How does he know? He himself scarcely knows how he arrived at the diagnosis. He has seen so many similar patients; in one moment he takes in that the fingernails are blue, that the breathing is of a certain kind, that the window is open, which means that although it is very cold he must have a need for air, and that there is a certain smell in the room that gives away the kind of medication the patient has received. He does not know all he adds up, but, because of his experience and perceptivity, he adds it up very quickly; later it may take him 20 or 30 minutes to figure it out, "How did I really know?" He could then perhaps dissolve the intuitive act into its rational factors.

Intuitive empathy can be achieved, but empathy must not be intuitive. It seems to me it is the essence of the science of psychoanalysis to have harnessed empathy to the slow and careful approach of science. We are not empathic in sudden intuitive flashes. The sudden, intuitive, empathic flashers are very frequently the beginners or the show-offs who do this as a kind of sport so that the young audience swoons over the great man. But it is perfectly true, you know, having had some 20 years of observing people under my belt now, I probably make diagnoses reasonably well, often very quickly, and frequently without immediately knowing how I did it. It is not magic. It is simply building up my experience in addition to a gift. Obviously, I chose this field because I have some gift for it, and so did you.

Such a diagnosis is intuitive only in the sense that it is done quickly, and many cues are picked up without conscious attention being paid to them. By the way, many complex activities are produced better preconsciously than consciously. But by *preconscious* we do not mean *unconscious*. We simply mean without focusing conscious attention on details. You pay a price for focusing on details. For every exact focusing on a detail you screen out a good deal of the rest of the field. However, if you diffuse the look at a broad field, then you may all at once take in a number of cues of which you are only dimly aware.

Occasionally I have to interview somebody and give a report, as when somebody applies to the Institute, and I have to consider whether he is going to make a good analyst or not. It is a consultation in which I have to give a broad assessment. I know that the older I have become, and the more experience I have accumulated in the field, the more I do something which is like stepping back from a complex painting and squinting my eyes. I do not want to see too much clear detail; I want rather to have the general flavor of the personality, a general hunch about how he works and what he does. After I have that, then secondarily I try to justify my hunch by the details of what I have seen. But I allow myself to arrive at a conclusion preconsciously and, if you wish, intuitively. It is not a magical intuition. It is simply that I trust my preconscious perception in facing the complex matter of a personality with so many assets and defects weighed against the complexities of a future career of an analyst to be started five, eight or ten years later. How can one figure that out? By adding two and two and making it four? It is almost impossible. But one gets a kind of feel by knowing the totality of the kind of demands that are made of an analyst, and seeing the kind of person this is, whether he will somehow be able to develop into an analyst. And if I have this feeling, after several hours of interviewing such a person, and gaining an understanding about what pushes him, then I say he may make a good analyst.

Returning to the subject of creativity, many young adults and late adolescents use creative activities for the important purpose of maintaining their psychic equilibrium, independent of the validity of their creativity. I think their creativity is frequently an important psychological mode of maintaining themselves. I would have my eyes and ears open to the creative activities they are engaged in and try to evaluate them. What do these creative activities contribute to their mental health? Are they creative activities that actually absorb some of their tensions or are they bizarre replacements? You know, to be alone and not make contact may have a totally different meaning in a person who is lost and lonely from that in one who is absorbed in modern poetry, has a sensitive perception of the world, and at least tries to use this perception.

There are many geniuses who clearly have a disturbed sense of self, as we can see from their disheveled appearance and the neglect of their clothes or bodily needs. Beethoven is an example, with his enormous need to perfect the work he was composing. It seems to me that the self-esteem regulation that relates to one's own body and one's own person is surrendered to one's work.

In other words, work becomes the true carrier of self-esteem, particularly in the perfecting of it. Once the work is done, it can be an enormous loss for the person to let it go. There is a peculiar jealousy toward the work taking on its own life and being admired by others. While the creator works on it, it really belongs to him, the creator. Another experience is the total loss of interest toward the work once it has been given up. Although some would say that work is specifically designed to undo the mortality of the finiteness of existence, I find it too narrow a concept. I think immortality and infiniteness of *existence* belong to the early blissful state that one strives to recreate in one form or another, so the immortality of *work* is very important.

There is no question that under certain circumstances work does become more important than the self. This occurs not because one loves it so much, but because the self is now in the work. That is the difference. It is not object love. This is where I am strongly in disagreement, particularly with Greenacre's theory of artistic creativity (1957, 1960). She believes this is a continuation of an early form of object love. I think she is wrong. I think it is an early form of object relationship, yes, but a narcissistic relationship to the object.[1] This is an extension of the self that is being perfected, but not something that is loved, from which one wants something back, and to which one enjoys giving his independent life. The relationship to one's children, which is important to study in your patients when you assess their relationship to their parents at the moment when they make themselves, perhaps for the first time, truly independent by going to a university away from home, becomes an enormously important area to assess in a sophisticated way. Parents, ideally, must be capable of shifting. They must be able to allow a narcissistic relationship and respond narcissistically to their children—include them into themselves and allow themselves to be included into the children's

---

[1]Kohut would later term this a selfobject relationship.

selves—so long as the children need it and it is phase-appropriate.[2] But they must be able to change their attitude, to curb their narcissism, as the child becomes independent. They must be capable, then, only of a faint echo of a narcissistic pleasure[3] in the independence and independent initiative of the child, which is a very distant kind of narcissistic enjoyment.

I think this is the use to which you can and should put these theories when you deal with actual clinical material, not point by point, but as a sort of ordering scheme in the back of your mind. The more unselfconsciously you do all this the better. But at first, as usual, it is like the old centipede that becomes aware of its feet, walking goes a little more slowly. The original increase of knowledge tends to be an interference, for good reasons. With any new acquisition of knowledge there is a setback in technical ability, which is temporary until the new theoretical knowledge has become truly integrated; then there is a more rapid advance.

---

[2]Mutuality of parent and child as selfobjects.

[3]An enhancement of self-esteem by reason of their pleasure in their offspring's capacity for independent initiative, mature narcissism (Kohut, 1966).

17

Plagiarism as Acting-Out

T HE FOLLOWING CASE is that of a student troubled by an episode in
which he has behaved in a manner foreign to his usual behavior. It
would appear that he "acted-out."

This is a 19-year-old first-year college student from an eastern city. He
gives his reason for coming to the clinic.

"It seems to me that my attitude toward studying at this university
will not lead to a long stay here, as indicated by a 10-page paper which I
plagiarized word for word from one book. I would like to speak to
someone here about my attitude, and try to ascertain for myself another
viewpoint on it."

He is six feet two, quite thin, with brown hair which comes down to
his shoulders and a beard. My first impression was that he was like the
picture of Jesus that we had in Sunday school—a gentle face. He is quite
serious and mature in many ways, but also very nervous; he alternates
between smoking and chewing gum. He pops his gum out and plays
with it, and then he smokes, and when he is through smoking, he pops
his gum back in again.

He said he came because he wanted to talk over what had happened
and what is happening, especially in his attitude about school. He
doesn't see the relevance of what he is studying. He said, "I got a D in
French, but that doesn't mean I don't know French. I've had five years
of it. But I learned to read and enjoy it, and not be concerned about all
the grammar, and that is what they are stressing here."

Last quarter he took social studies. He had a number of choices as to a
topic for a long paper. He chose Gandhi. He read all the original material—all the speeches Gandhi made, his autobiography—and then, based
on this reading, he made a formulation of what Gandhi was about. He
happened to read a book by a woman who had evaluated Gandhi, and,
to his annoyance, he discovered she had reached the same conclusions

279

he had reached. He was annoyed at being asked to do something that had already been worked over and he saw no value in doing this in college. He had his own ideas of what a university should do. His comment was, "In high school you're preparing for college, and you don't mind doing these exercises." He took the material, word for word, and with some rearrangement, handed in his paper. His plagiarism was discovered. He knew he would be caught, because this author had given some of the earlier lectures in this course; it would follow that the instructor would have read her book too.

The teacher was very puzzled, because he had received an A for the first quarter in her course and would have received the same this quarter if he had written his own paper. He talked to her about his disenchantment at being asked to do something that had already been done. She suggested that he speak to someone who had talked to a lot of students and that perhaps we might help him to understand his attitude and his behavior. After deliberating for several weeks, the teacher gave him an F for the course, but allowed him to continue the sequence so that next year he will only have to retake one quarter. He thought she was very considerate.

He could not explain his behavior. It has never happened to him before. He thinks part of it has to do with his doubts about being in the university at all. So much is happening, "There may not be a world in 20 more years, so what am I doing studying all these things?" He thought of dropping out, but the draft deters him and he doesn't want to go into the army.

I asked him what he would like to do if the army weren't a problem to him. He said, "I'd probably go to work for an organization that would do something about pollution. He is tentatively interested in Asian studies. In fact, he had started taking Chinese. He knew enough French; he had taken it for five years. So he started on Chinese, but he dropped it. Chinese was too much for him along with trying to get adjusted here. Another reason for his disenchantment is that, although he has friends here and has even dated some, his real commitment is to a girl at home, a senior in high school. She has been accepted to come to this university next year, and he thinks next year will be better. He has spent a lot of time writing, calling, and even going home for he misses her very much. In fact, last summer, knowing he was going to miss her, he went to Europe by himself for six weeks to prepare for being away from her.

He attended a very good private school in the east. The classes were very small and he had a lot of attention from the instructors with freedom to grow in his own way. This quarter he dropped humanities because he felt that what he studied in high school was being repeated here. He is only taking three courses.

He said things weren't always easy in high school. The first year he worried a great deal and didn't do well. It was only after he felt adjusted there that he began to be more active. By his senior year he became student vice-president. He was active in drama; it was in drama that he and his girlfriend became very friendly. In high school, he wasn't so worried because there was a goal—going to college. He chose this large campus because he knew it was one of the better schools in the country, and he was accepted.

He didn't make application elsewhere because he didn't want to have to make a decision about where he was going. He said he has an uncle and two cousins here. He had visited them and felt that, because of this tie, he wouldn't be in a strange city where he didn't know anyone. But now that he is here he doesn't have a goal and has doubts about many things.

He is the youngest of three boys. One brother is 25, the other 23. He mentioned only his mother on the application blank. His father died of cancer in 1960, when the patient was nine years old. He says very little about him and doesn't remember too much. "I wasn't close to him, but he was a good father." His father was the executive officer of a large research institute. Mother is some kind of managerial executive there now. The uncle here has contributed financially toward their care and is now paying for his education. This is father's brother, who took over the family business and is doing very well. The father, instead of going into the family business, went off on his own and had almost completed his Ph.D. when he died.

He describes his oldest brother as extremely bright. He went to an eastern school and studied physics, but, in May of his senior year, dropped out. The thought of working in a lab for the rest of his life was no longer acceptable to him. Instead he bought a truck and traveled around the country. Recently he began taking a course in bird watching, for he's interested in biology, and thinks he's going to settle down and go to school again.

The patient is very close to this oldest brother and it was he who introduced him to Asian studies. He's very interested in Confucius, and contemplates a lot. He said, "I'm very much like my brother. We both have brown hair, are tall, and have the same kind of build. I feel close to him." The 24-year-old brother is the opposite. An adopted child who came to live with the family at age one, he is short and dark, not good in school, but athletic. He was married right after he got out of high school and is doing well now. He was told that mother was expected not to have any more children after the first one, so they adopted the second child. He feels very lucky to have two older brothers because he can observe and learn from both of them. His academic interests derive from his older brother and his athletic interests from his second brother.

Toward the end of the hour he said, "I don't expect you to tell me why I did what I did, but what do you think?" I said his attitude toward academic work has been expressed by many students. The method he used to express it, in doing what he did, was his own; that's what he came to see us about. He said that was what he wanted to talk about.

I said I noticed that adjusting to a new experience took a lot of energy. He said, "I notice that too. I think a lot of what I'm feeling is getting used to this place. The grayness and the sub-zero weather is so different." At this point, he got up and came forward to shake my hand, which is unusual, and then he left. He's coming back next week.

You've seen him only once?

Twice.

What is your impression?

When you mentioned that the boy had plagiarized from a book his teacher had written, I was shocked at the obviousness. I expected something much more subtle, more obscure. But he was much more aware of what he was doing. Would you see this as a typical acting-out?

It sounds as if he was genuinely puzzled about what he did and why he acted in such a strange way. The way he presents it, it's clearly a symptomatic act that he does not understand.

Rather than acting-out, it's almost like a neurotic symptom.

That is the way in which he presents it—you know, I cannot say more about it at the moment. What else is there to be said about it?

His distress seemed to be that the work had already been done. He had gotten all this material together, and then found it had all been done already. Here he is, a boy who is the third of three brothers, and his comment that it's nice to have those brothers.

He's grateful to them.

Yes, but I wonder if that isn't one side of an opposing ambivalence, where the work has already been done by his brothers, and here it is again; perhaps this played into plagiarizing.

This student and his older brother seem to feel the same way, don't they? They seem to have a similar attitude toward their efforts and their life achievement. Am I right about that? The older one dropped his rather high-brow scientific career and became a truck driver. It seems to me that what your patient is doing is very similar.

I'm struck by the fact that the father died just this side of completing his Ph.D.

I don't think this is so terribly important, that it was just this side of completing the Ph.D. It may be. I understand your reasoning, but I have a hunch this is less important. What is important is that the father seems very clearly to be the person in whom the ambition for, as well as the goal of, a higher education and intellectual achievement was personified. It seems to me it is something in the personality of the father, the father's death, or the two together, which set up some kind of feeling in the oldest and youngest brothers. You see, the middle one is different; he is an adopted child with a different genetic endowment. He seems to have played a different role in the family. The oldest and the youngest are the two natural children of the father, chips off the old block, as it were, and this may have affected them. One was nine when the father died, and the other 15, an important moment in life for these boys. Father's death occurred when the younger boy was approaching puberty, and he had to live without the support and the leadership of an idealized father who stood for academic achievement. The older one was moving toward late adolescence and manhood when he lost his father. It is as if there was something lacking in the reliability of the goal structure which can be related to the sudden loss of their father. Did he die suddenly?

I think he was ill for about three months.

Anyway, this was not a man who had years of illness. What I am impressed about is not that this boy seems masochistic, unthinking, almost offering himself for defeat, which he does by copying this paper, but that his appearance shows a total lack of interest. Nothing has any relevance; what is the point of it all? Zest is lacking in everything. He picks as his hero a leader of passive resistance, and then acts out—if I may use that term—the passive resistance of his own convictions. "What's the point? Look at my father—he too disappeared. The ideals I have are meaningless. I might as well be a truck driver. I might as well hand in something that will be my undoing." And yet, not quite, you know, he looks for help. He wonders. He wants to understand. If there is more of a meaning to that, he would like to know.

He may very well be in search of somebody who takes over where the father left off and supports, gives new blood, new meaning, and new warmth to intellectual efforts and achievements. At one time, these were sustaining ideals to these boys, and yet they apparently were unable to follow through. It is interesting that he said he could work in high school, because it was in preparation for the real thing. But when the real thing comes up, it turns out to be nothing but busywork, and it is not meaningful anymore. He is doing exercises rather than the real thing. These are areas one would have to investigate further. We'll see what the second session will bring us. But at first sight that seems to be a good guess.

One question is whether this is a case of crypt-amnesia—that is, he read the monograph and forgot it? Or is it that he depreciates his own creative work?

I do not think that this student has a type of conflict over achievement, described by Kris (1934) as the need to depreciate his own work. He does not find a reference to some small part, similar to his own work, and attribute the importance to the reference rather than to his own creativity. In the analysis described by Kris this pattern related to the premature loss of his own father. You often find that this type of person longs for the omnipotent father figure, not the omnipotent self. Then, if such an individual happens to be gifted, he can proceed to be creative when he thinks he has discovered the omnipotent father figure.

Such people, in my opinion, have a clear idea of what is self and what is outside of self. I do not believe this patient belongs to this category because of the confusion predominating in his self-presentation. Is the student's exhibitionism involved in this incident? He read and discovered that somebody had done a better job than he could ever do, and this was a narcissistic blow; he then gave up completely. Was it a milder way of dropping out, as his brother had done? Let us proceed with the case.

He cancelled the next hour and went home for spring vacation, coming in the following week. He said he arranged, while at home, to see a pyschiatrist during the summer. He had known this psychiatrist because as a class leader in high school he had been included in a study by this psychiatrist. Also, while he was home, his mother encouraged him to remain in school. He talked with her about his brother's dropping out. His mother was overly upset about this. His brother went to a psychiatrist and convinced the psychiatrist that he was bisexual, but the patient assured his mother that he was not.

He himself has three heroes in his life—Gandhi, Jesus and Martin Luther King. He talked more about plagiarizing this article in a way that made the act more deliberate than the first time. He read the book; it presented all that he might have said. The deadline was approaching and so he thought, "Why bother?" He took sections of the book and rearranged them.

Then he talked about his general disenchantment with academic life, his resentment at people telling him how to be educated, his concern about being drafted into the army. He said he preferred his high school education in which, even if he had not learned so much, there was closer contact and more personal relations with the teachers. This was important.

In discussing his resentment at people telling him how to be educated—which he is greatly aware of here at the university—he said that his father had made the important decisions in the family. Then, when he died, except for the financial decisions which were made by the mother, the boys were allowed to make their own decisions.

In the third hour he was feeling better. It has been a good week. He was involved in the strike on campus but then decided to return to class. He said his brother is an activist, but he is not. He would like to work on pollution this summer. He wasn't going to work against the system, because he didn't think that would alter policy. He thought pollution was more important. He decided to stick it out in school. He thought he understood his rebellion against academic discipline, in view of having been his own boss since his father died. Then he talked about his periods of upsets, such as last quarter. He couldn't account for these times when he had a low level of energy and felt disgusted.

He then described his constant search for what we might call father figures. He gave more details about his father's academic career, and his memories of father when they went sailing. When the patient was at camp he was informed of his father's death by the camp director. He did not go home. There was no funeral. When he returned to the city his mother had moved, and so it was to a new home he returned. He said his father had once worked nearby and he had thought about going there to talk with some of the people to see if they remembered his father.

Father had studied here?

No, he had worked in one of the university related institutes.

As an employee of the university?

Yes. His father left the university before he got his Ph.D. He was working in Washington and then went back to work on his Ph.D., but he never completed the work.

**He volunteered that brother is a tougher man than he is, and that he
himself shares mother's interest in art and history. The oldest brother
had it harder, because he had no one above him to help him. Last year
when he went to Europe alone, he kept looking for people he knew
while he was traveling.**

The loss of the idealized father seems to be at play here. The plagiarism appears in the increasing evidence of resentment against the mother, i.e., the teacher and the woman author, as if to say, "I'm left with a
mother, but what I need is a father." This tendency exists in the older
brother as well as in himself. The father's ideals of academic achievement
still prevail in this family and help to sustain this family, even though he
did not finish his work before he died.

In the last few sessions, on the basis of this case and others, we have
discussed this very broad area of acting-out. These themes seem to be
invoked by this man and his brother, and by their early life with their
particular kind of loss. It seems to me that these boys turned away from
the mother, who perhaps demanded a much more structured life, more
purposive, more goal-directed. They turn away, as it were, with a contemptuous attitude about the negative value of her goals, enforcing at
the same time the seemingly positive values of drifting.

In other words, it is a homosexually tinged attitude toward such great
passive and yet omnipotent figures (Gandhi, Jesus, King), perhaps the
replica of the father, in some ways, while at the same time there is a
rejection of the demand of the maternal figure who did away with the
father, "Who didn't even call me, to be present at his death." Maybe,
down deep in the unconscious of this boy, there is the idea that the
mother did away with the father. At any rate, she survived, and the
father was gone when the boy returned.

That is as well as I can vaguely summarize this type of personality at
the moment, not just from the material of this particular case, but on the
basis of the material that I have heard so many times. I do not treat many
people in the age group that you are mainly in contact with, but I do see
many men who have remained essentially adolescent. There is a shift
from the attempt to regain a lost personified strong ideal to a religious-
like drifting attitude toward the world. This is a very common swing that
I notice in such people.

I was aware of all of this in a much more circumscribed way in the
course of an analysis, in which a patient wished to idealize me and I
rejected his idealization by being obtuse to his wish. The patient could
not accept the fact that I made an interpretation. It was premature, or he

found other objections. Then the next day this dreamy person came with little to say, talking about nature and an overall pantheism.

At such times I would ask myself, "What did I do yesterday that from a goal-directed devotion to your work here you have become this purpose-less dreamer who justifies it in this religious-like way?" I have reviewed my old cases, in which I was unaware of some of the things I know now. I have ended analyses with the patient drifting toward religious preoccu-pation, a clearly unsatisfactory result to me in the light of my present thinking. I know of individuals who after being treated by me, and by my insights, did drift into such an orientation. *They* were satisfied. I know of one such individual who is functioning very well but who clearly has channeled the incompletely analyzed, idealizing transference toward me into a very broadly religious attitude, and, within this back-ground, he now is functioning rather well. I have the impression that I would do better by this person now, not because I am against religion, but because I feel it was obligatory behavior, not a choice. It is something that has to be maintained all the time against reality. It falsifies this person's outlook on reality by a kind of pollyannaish attitude which, in the particular job that he has, is not the best attitude to have. One has to be more realistic to do a really good job in his line of work. He hires and fires employees, and one cannot be continuously playing pollyanna, with the idea that everybody is good. Everybody is not good.

We spent the whole session last time reviewing the theme of acting-out and its relation to symptom formation, the difference between action and acting-out. Even after knowing a little about this case, I cannot feel myself into this fellow. Somehow, there is still a good deal missing for me to make it click. We were discussing the action itself from two differ-ent sides. One aspect was stated very well—that of an angry, challeng-ing, belittling of the mother authority in terms of, "I really need and want a strong, idealized, helpful, supportive father; not having him, I have you," and so he sort of tosses his plagiarized paper in her face.

However, I do not consider this in opposition to our discussing the loss of the father. This loss has left him with a certain incompleteness in his own personality. He is looking for a part that should be in himself—his own ideals and goal structure, his own firm idealized internal leadership in the superego. He is still looking around on the outside for something of himself or something that should be himself. It seems that he attempts to make some tentative arrangement with these idealized figures of Gan-dhi, Christ, and Martin Luther King. Why he would have chosen this type of figure is a challenging question. What these people mean to him in his fantasies would be pure speculation.

It would be interesting to learn what is behind this choice of an ideal: the nonviolent, the nonaggressive, and yet enormously powerful father, whose very weakness, as it were, is also the source of his greatest strength. In other words, there was some such attempt to combine the various incompatible experiences and his yearning for such a man.

In some ways he is right, and in other ways he is wrong when he says the oldest brother was hit the hardest. He is right when he says he himself could at least use the oldest one as some kind of replica of, or substitute for, the father. He was nine, and the brother was 15. This was already near manhood. But a 15-year-old, in general, is not a good father substitute. He may be a reasonable one, but not a good one. A 15-year-old has so much work to do himself that he experiences the younger ones tagging behind him as a nuisance.

I often see this very poignantly in younger brothers and how they attempt to find some justification for being around the older ones and their peer group. They want to be messengers, anything, just to be allowed around. A character type develops around this particular situation. There is a pervasive disbelief, in some such youngsters, that they can ever be accepted for themselves. They can only be tolerated on the fringes of the group. If they can only find themselves a little job. They would so much like to be taken along—but the older ones begin to become involved in some experience, such as a sexual experience, clearly beyond the age of the younger boys.

I am talking about specific cases that I have in mind where such experiences played a tremendous role and led to a particular type of character formation. And so, I think, to lose a father at 15, traumatic though it is, with its specific influence in the final firming of the superego ideal, is to suffer a blow not as profound as that of the younger boy, who then has to grow up essentially without a reliable, ideal, strong father figure. I imagine the oldest one suffered something that is in degree perhaps less severe. He was not exposed as long to the overwhelming influence of the mother alone. We do not know enough about the personalities of the parents at this point to judge.

But there is a certain similarity, not only in the early life fate, but also in the character formation of both these boys. At decisive moments both of them have acted out in a particular way—at least it seems that way. We know a little more about the younger one. One would have to examine in greater detail what it meant to the older one. If somebody, on the basis of highest ideals, can lie in order to get out of the army, for example, it is likely to be in the particular way this brother lied. I would also suspect, as with the malingerer who intentionally lies yet at another level is not lying, so with this boy who says he is bisexual but is really not bisexual.

Such people, if investigated very carefully, will turn out, in some essentials, not to have lied at all, but actually to have used some unconscious truth in a peculiar way. Of course, we would have to investigate the details of the older brother's personality.

What is most striking, however, is a certain kind of similarity in both of these boys; there is an easy-rider kind of idealism or mentality. The older one became a truck driver. Is he throwing off the usual values of society and lifting himself into some kind of romantic drifter kind of existence? You find so many of these more or less poorly structured personalities living out a sort of poetic life that does away with all the usual bourgeois values, drifting through the world in a way that appears to have discarded circumscribed ideals. It seems hedonistic, but it is not really hedonistic. It is an absence of aggression. It is an absence of the usual fight.

It is a kind of fuzzy idealism that reminds me of the idealism that is not infrequently found in people who have lost idealized figures early in life, a kind of nature religion, nature philosophy of the Thoreau type, in which one relates fuzzily to the world in a nonfighting, noncompetitive way. Was the choice of the Gandhi-Christ-King personality an ideal? Was this kind of drifting toward traveling through the country, nomad-like, not belonging anywhere, such a choice?

What about his feeling that he got along better with mother? The older brother didn't. They were fighting all the time. He said, "I was lucky, because I got along with mother." This makes him different from the older brother.

Well, one would have to know what the fighting was about. The older brother, losing his father at the age of 15, and being alone with his mother, probably needed to defend himself against the seductiveness of a situation in which he was put into the father's shoes. His mother similarly, in all likelihood, had to defend herself. Very frequently, such fights are really attempts to escape from the incestuous dangers of such a situation.

As this case was presented, I had the feeling that this youth, in a sense, experienced an oedipal victory. You described the quality of drifting, and the transformation of the idealism, but I wonder if in your mind it is similar to the feeling one sometimes has of people who feel the world owes them a living; their behavior is justified and they ought to be allowed to get away with it. I heard that quality in part of the history, and I felt there was something in the possibility of later damage around oedipal issues and pre-oedipal issues, that he had superego defects.

First of all, this is not an oedipal situation. He was nine years old. This is significantly different from an oedipal situation. He was deep into latency. Age nine, you know, is the beginning of pre-adolescence. It is too late for the oedipal situation, but it is an interesting question to bring up. The fulfilling of a childhood wish prematurely puts a child in a difficult situation. It is easier to explain these things when one looks at age groups where memories are abundant and where less reconstruction is needed. The oedipal situation is, of course, repeated in early puberty.

Let us take the following case as an example, for I know this person quite well. This individual did not lose his father through death or illness, but he suffered a loss of the power of the father when he was about 13. The father became suddenly powerless, had to leave the scene where they were living, and went to another part of the country. He had to go into hiding for a while. The son was the only remaining male in the family. There were only his mother and sister present, and he suddenly became, at 13, the male figure in the house. The people who were after the father were now after him, and he had to try to handle this very difficult situation while the father remained in hiding for quite a long time.

This was not the only difficulty that the patient retained from this situation. The father did not want his son to become like him. He was a simple man, and the son was to become something much better. Therefore, he was pushing him away when the son wanted to become like the father. In addition, the father was always somewhat belittled by the mother, while the son was the apple of her eye. The father was short, and the son was a tall and lanky fellow. The son was good-looking, and the father not so good-looking. This is the way the son experienced it. I had the strong impression that this was not just fantasy, but that there was a good deal of truth to his feeling.

The nuclear memories around which we so frequently worked were those at about the age of 13, when the father suddenly broke down, disappeared, and the son carried the whole burden of keeping the family together. He did this beautifully, but at a tremendous cost to himself. While this was an enormous help to him, not being flooded by anxiety, not becoming panicky, it also tremendously deprived him of feeling really alive. He could never feel much of anything after that. This is something that had to be worked on for a long time.

This individual is now torn between two different difficulties. On the one hand, there is a deep conviction that he is something very special as the result of the oedipal victory. Although he was only 13 and only five feet six, he was the one who carried the day. He was stronger than the father. He was the omnipotent one. The father's omnipotence turned out to be nothing. He went away, he failed. But on the other hand, the son suffered a tremendous loss, for the father had been really strong and realistically protective. He could be the provider and he could really curb the child's impulses. The end result has been a tremendous yearning for greatness, for playing out unchecked exhibitionism and fantasies of grandiosity. At the same time, there was a fear of overstimulation that comes from such grandiosity. He became manic and intolerable. He yearned for an outside force that really would be the person that he played at being. He was too big for his breeches.

It becomes most beautiful to observe in the course of an analysis when this problem has been worked through over and over again. The individual yearns for fulfillment of the fantasy, as opposed to the wish, "Don't let me do that. Stick up for your rights and tell me you are the stronger and older one; and that these are just my fantasies, and I must not confuse them with reality." There is this great discomfort, and finally the wish that this idealized figure should become part of himself so that he can be the self-regulator of his own fate and emotions. Then the grandiose fantasies do not have to be totally suppressed, nor do they have to be lived out in the search for an externalized ideal figure. He then becomes an entity and can do it all for himself.

In treatment these things are most beautiful when they are almost worked through—when there are no longer violent swings between grandiosity or exhibition and the wish, "You put me down, and you stay strong, and let me idealize you. Don't expose me to that, as I was before, with all the anxiety that they will do away with me, because I'm just a child." You see, this is not real. This is only fantasy; in reality it won't lead anywhere. When all this has been worked out, the usual result is that such people's actual performance becomes much better. They do not have to worry so much anymore that it is fantasy. Their performance becomes realistic, and if they are gifted people they perform realistically well, but there are still swings back and forth.

I can illustrate this by a dream pair that I was told by a patient. The first dream was that the patient had on slacks and they were splitting all over. He was too big for his breeches. It must have been the fulfillment of the grandiosity, but I do not recall the manifest content of the dream. As is so frequently the case, when one analyzes the dream, not only does the patient forget it, but the analyst forgets the dream too. The work with it has been done, and the dream sinks into oblivion. In the second dream, he dreamed that he had gotten three gold fillings in his teeth. He suddenly noticed that these fillings had fallen out, and he was angry at the dentist for not putting in the fillings firmly enough. In other words, he reproached me that my work with him in analysis had not yet helped him to transform his infantile grandiosity firmly enough into adult realistic ambitions. It was the working-through process of something that he and I were already very familiar with.

But let us go on with your case.

With this hour I again had the impression of his height. He's very tall, and all through the hour he would pop gum in his mouth, and then take it out and play with it. This gave him the appearance of a little boy. He said he had his French mid-term this morning and he knows he passed it. He has a Western civilization paper due Monday, and then he can leave for home for the summer. When he goes home, he's definitely going to work for lobbying in the area of pollution. They always need people to do interviews and pass out things; he feels this is important to do. "If we don't do something there won't be any air left, and we'll have to go underground." He also said, "I've decided to come back to school here. I've decided the best thing for me is to stay here. I'm not saying this because of the draft. I realize that I need to gain more knowledge."

He has registered, and next year he's going to take many more interesting courses in Eastern studies, and he enumerated them. I asked him if he feels he has a choice. He said, "Yes, I only have a few required courses, and I can start on my major." I asked him how he became interested in this field, and he said that in high school he had a special course that was taught by a professor who was an expert on China. A few people were allowed to go to this special class to which students came from all over the city; there were only ten in all. They met once a week. This man was very interested in his subject and in students. The patient became very involved with him, and, with his encouragement, he used to go to a special library to read the translated Peking newspapers. He liked his high school and felt he received special benefits. He had some criticisms but they were not material because the goal was to get to the best college.

He talked about how conscientious he was in high school. He did all his work—in fact, he did his papers ahead of time. But in the winter quarter here he had trouble doing this and he began to be more resentful. He had written a paper in the history course, his own interpretations on China, but only received C-minus on it. He talked to the instructor about it and was told, "You wrote as if you were a Peking communist. It's all propaganda, and it's wrong." It was his feeling that the instructor had analyzed the situation and come up with another viewpoint, which could also be regarded as propaganda, as far as the Chinese are concerned. He felt it was unfair. He hates papers, because it seems you have to prove what you've already learned in classes.

I asked if this was going on with his other paper but he replied that this instructor knows a lot about her subject. He continued "Maybe I was lazy or too tired during the winter quarter." Then he became critical of the way school is taught. He knows a law student who recently took law board exams, who said they expected so little of him he felt he had wasted four years. "That shows you are not learning new things, or you learn so little." He has also talked to students at other colleges, and he found that they have to take many more required things than he has had to. Here, it is only the minimum. He said, "Next year it seems like I'm going to enjoy it. I knew this year was going to be hard."

We talked about the uncle who lives here and who is supporting him in school. I wondered if he were of any help to him. He said, "He's a fine person." But this man's position in life, as the older brother, left him the goal—"to make money." He is not a bit intellectual and that is why he can't be of much help to the patient with college. He has said father was the most intelligent in the family and the most promising. He smiled in a nostalgic way and said, "I wish he were alive so I could find out for myself."

He's now eager to get home and see what he can find to do of a voluntary nature. He'll find a few odd jobs, too, around his home, like cutting lawns, which he has done before. With this he can earn $300 to $400.

Then he said, "I'm glad I came. I have gotten an understanding of why I acted in this particular way." I asked what his understanding was, because I wasn't sure. He said, "I've gone to private schools all my life. The classes were small. Here at the university I needed attention that I wasn't getting. The teachers here are very knowledgeable, and they'll answer your questions, but you have to seek them out." That's new to him. He knew it was going to be different, and he'd have to be more on his own. He said that was why he went to Europe last summer on his own, to prepare himself, "and to see if I could manage on my own."

I said he had managed this year. He said, "Yes, and it doesn't feel so bad. I'll be leaving next week." I wished him a good summer. He said, "Thank you," and he got up and shook hands.

That was the happy ending to brief psychotherapy.

There are enormous swings in his performance, depending on whether he feels connected with somebody who takes an interest in him, and whom he admires, or whether he is drifting alone and feels lost in the shuffle. How quickly it changes—it is very striking, but by no means unusual. The relationship of the cohesiveness of the self experience and the cohesiveness of the idealized leadership figure as an organizer of ego function and ego activity is a very striking one in some individuals.

One would like to know what this boy's relationship was to his father shortly before he died. At that moment, was he the center of the father's attention? Was this why the loss was so traumatic? In the relationship with the father, was he learning, philosophizing, and researching in a budding form when he was about eight or so? Was that the point at which this relationship was interrupted, so that he was left floundering, unable to do it on his own, unless he had somebody to continue father's idealizing role? It may also be that he did it on his own, but felt insecure about his work.

I think this raises the very important question of the role of brief psychotherapy and how one can integrate such formulations to be of help to patients. I feel that in psychotherapy, when one finds such patterns, when one can empathize with the ebb and flow of the self-feeling, one can really help the patient to clarify the specific situations under which he works at his best capacity, and those in which he has this feeling of being lost. It is a very useful and helpful goal of brief psychotherapy for the patient to be able to regulate this himself. He can then arrange his life to put himself in situations which maximize his potential. I'm sure this is a much more limited goal than what you would hope to achieve in analysis but . . .

This is a perfectly legitimate statement. I have often felt the same way. One must not pitch one's hopes too high and think that such help will carry a person through thick and thin. The intensity of the fluctuations in self-esteem are enormous, even if one knows a great deal about these fluctuations and their causes. Even in an analysis, and with all the insights in the world, one is still prey to ups and downs. Nevertheless, as you said, having once met this experience, one can give the person some verbalized insight as to why he feels better.

I think I would say to such a person, "When you find somebody for whom you have a great deal of respect and who shows an interest in you, I'll bet that has something to do with what happened between you and your Dad. The old feeling of loss overtakes you sometimes, and then you flounder and can't work. But if you can find somebody who can help you to realize that, maybe that will help you." I would congratulate the patient on the insight he himself has acquired under those circumstances. I would say, "It seems to me you've put your finger on something very important in your life history and personality."

When this is done in a warm and human context, you then give him something he can hold onto and that he can search for. He can become a more conscious regulator of his own self-esteem, and secondarily of his own work capacity. This is the opposite of a vicious cycle. When he works better and achieves more, self-esteem rises; just as the other way around, once he began to drift, to be unproductive, and to cheat, he was upset enough so that he sought help. He had been used to getting a great deal of attention in a small private school, whereas here he was lost on the impersonal campus of a huge university.

You have probably had this insight for a long time, and you did not have to be told that it plays a role in the groups of students you see here. But still, to know more of how this all fits into the structure of the personality and the specific vulnerabilities of specific people makes it therapeutically more useful and gives you much more leverage than just to know it generally.

We don't really know what kind of relationship this youth had with his father. However, we may speculate. The parents didn't expect any more children; then they had this son and they always wanted to have at least two. We could say that he was expected with great pleasure.

That is an excellent thought. It may indeed have given them this great surprise, "My God, we were able to produce another child." It may have meant a lot to the father to produce another child.

I will give an example of another kind of delinquent behavior by which a patient got money he did not deserve. He ruined things and then made insurance claims. This always occurred in the context of the analyst's either leaving or not understanding. His behavior was a little related to the guiltless delinquent act. He "had it coming." But here you come to the difference in what you are stressing and what I tend to stress more. I think of it in its most striking form, delinquency without guilt and I-have-it-coming-to-me. This takes place not on the basis of past spoiling, but on the basis of past severe injustice. This man was clearly enormously deprived by an unempathic mother who couldn't admire the boy's body. Late in the analysis everything fell into place when the patient suddenly and finally supplied the material that the mother had been a drug addict, which we had not known for years in the analysis. We had only known that the mother was never dressed properly in the morning, she did not prepare breakfast for the boy, and so on. But she was actually upstairs taking drugs. (Do you know O'Neill's *Long Day's Journey Into Night*? I recommend it to all of you to read. It shows the influence of an addictive mother on the structure and cohesion of the family.)

But in this particular instance, this guiltless acting-out became an enraged grabbing of what by all rights should have been given to him empathically. When the analyst seemed to repeat the unempathic mother, then he grabbed, guiltlessly. It was only when this was understood in the context of analysis that his acting-out totally disappeared and instead a very interesting new symptom arose. He began to lie instead of stealing, but he lied in a very nice way. He lied in a way that recaptured his old wish to be paid attention to. He told cock-and-bull stories that drew attention from an admiring audience, and it became more and more a conscious joke. One day he told his analyst, "You know, I was in a john, and I urinated. There was a man next to me, and I could see him looking at me with the greatest astonishment. I looked down, and, by golly, my urine was pea-green." This was the style of his stories. You see, he was behaving like the cute little boy who wanted to be admired for his wit. This was on a much more acceptable and friendly level, and, in turn, it disappeared.

I wanted to show you the development of the same situation—how it becomes more and more integrated, acceptable, wise narcissism. The narcissism of a person who smashes his own house in order to make an insurance claim is obviously very sick. But his story about the green urine, and similar stories, it had a cuteness, and they began to be rather more fun than sick. There were fewer cock-and-bull stories, and there was more half-joking, and everybody knew he was just trying to be a cute fellow. This finally worked itself out into very creative productivity, which led to the publication of a substantial book on a very interesting topic.

Do you know Freud's paper called "The Exceptions"? (1916). This is a lovely paper, without any reference to the specific theory of narcissism. I think it was written before Freud made his first steps in the introduction of narcissism. It describes character types, particularly from literature, in which their callousness, their later severe acting-out, and their absolute self-righteousness about their imbalanced demands were made on the basis of an old severe injustice. This has nothing to do with prolonged and profound analyses but is available to much easier investigation.

When you find an individual who exhibits such self-righteous pomposity and a callousness toward the demands of others most frequently, he is one of two types. In one type, this is defensive and much harder to reach. It conceals a feeling of great uncertainty about the self and its acceptability. It often arises in relationship to two opposing attitudes toward the child. The mother, for example, shows off the child for her benefit, but does not allow him any real value for his own initiative. So he feels very depressed about himself and what he is when he acts independently. But having, as it were, the mother connected to him, he can allow himself to be boastful. The other type, as I said, is the exception—those who feel they have suffered a severe early injustice in life.

18

Self-Esteem and Ideals[1]

I N SUMMARIZING THE WORK we have been engaged in, I would like to begin
with a theoretical excursion. Self-esteem and ideals? What do we
know about these concepts? All of us know the fluctuations of our self-
esteem, whether as clinicians or in our daily lives. We feel good about
ourselves; we feel bad about ourselves; we feel good about the way
things are going and that heightens our self-esteem. We feel low because
somebody has not liked us, or somebody has not listened to us or has
turned away from us; we may feel low because we have not achieved
what we set out to do, and then our self-esteem drops.

In other words, self-esteem (we will come to *"ideals"* shortly) is something that is open to our observation. It is open to our observation
through empathy, which is the essence of all observations in our science,
whatever our science means. Whether it is psychoanalysis, which is my
particular narrower field, or depth psychology, to say it a little more
broadly, or any form of psychology or psychiatry that deals with the
inner experience of man, with the complexities of his inner life, the
phenomenon of self-esteem is open to both self-observation and introspection. It is particularly open in its fluctuations, because we always
observe things best when they fluctuate, not when they are stable. And
it is open to us as we observe others in this particular extension of
introspection, the vicarious introspection, thinking ourselves into others
and the way they experience feelings, which we call empathy.

So, too, with our ideals, that something higher than ourselves that we
prize very much: they also have their fluctuations. We seek for new
values and ideals. We are uncertain about the old ones which we have.
And we react to their being attacked, doubted or questioned, in the same

---

[1]This final seminar was presented as the second Charlotte Rosenbaum lecture to members of the Department of Psychiatry and to invited guests from the psychiatric community.

way that we react to our self-esteem, our self-organizations, being questioned and attacked. Fluctuations occur, then, in our ideals in the same
way that they occur in self-esteem. But, unless one already has some
theoretical prejudice, it would seem that self-esteem and ideals are rather divergent, disparate, dissimilar phenomena.

Just as phenomena in the outer world may be very disparate, and yet
take on some kind of relatedness to the scientist who examines what is
beneath them, there is also relatedness in many psychological processes.
Although self-esteem and ideals are tremendously different, one from
the other, through a theoretical investigation, an investigation beneath
the surface, we begin to see certain relationships between these two
outwardly so different phenomena.

Disparate phenomena become related if one knows more about them,
if one extends one's theoretical understanding of them. Let us take such
an obvious example as coal and diamonds, certainly very disparate phenomena. They look different. One is black, the other is clear. Each has a
totally different value. One is very expensive and the other is very cheap.
They have totally different functions and uses. And yet, if you ask an
organic chemist whether there is any similarity between coal and diamonds, he will say, "Of course. The underlying structure relates to the
carbon atom and to the carbon structure." Knowing this, we can then say
there is also some other relatedness between them. We can even attempt
to make diamonds out of coal, a step which has indeed recently been
achieved.

Something on that same order is the relatedness between theory and
the external introspective and empathic phenomena in depth psychology. We look at phenomena and we try to understand them under some
other valence than that given by our senses. The difference between
everyday observation and scientific observation is in the formation of
theory. It is not in the methodology of grading and measuring.

Theory, then, influences the mode in which we observe things. Disparate things will become similar, similar things will become disparate.
The leaf of the ginkgo tree looks like a leaf, but we know, when we study
the details of its genesis, that it is related more to the pine needle than to
the average leaf. Something of this order is also true for the phenomena
we are discussing. It is the difference between a helter-skelter collection
of plants and the creation of a botanical system. There has to be some
search for common derivation, for common deeper functions. Heinz
Hartmann, in his all too little known book, *The Basic Tenets of Psychoanalysis*, pointed out the difference between the study of phenomenology and
the creation of an underlying theory which makes the helter-skelter

collection of phenomenological data into a science of depth psychology.

Now, in order to carry on our particular line of thought, one asks how one chooses to investigate seemingly disparate phenomena to learn whether they have something in common. Does one begin with theory or does one begin with phenomena? Of course one begins with phenomena. Ours is an empirical science, and we take our cues for theoretical investigation from the examination of phenomena.

Indeed, when we begin to look at the phenomena that cluster around these terms *self-esteem* and *ideals*, we begin to see that there are certain likenesses. Let me start with the observable phenomenological side. Perhaps I can remind you that, apart from the deep inner motivations that always, so far as I can judge, spur any kind of prolonged research to which people devote their years and themselves, the trigger to my own interest in the phenomena of narcissism arose in the strange setting of organizational work. About five to eight years ago, I was probably at the peak of my involvement in organizational work in the national organization of analysts. Although in many ways I regret having devoted five intensive years to nonscientific pursuits, I think the experience has stood me in good stead and has taught me a great deal of value, which became an incentive in my work.

I was struck by the fact of the enormous dissension propensity even in a group so psychologically sophisticated and supposedly capable of controlling various drive tendencies. I began to wonder what it was that triggered all this dissension around fine points of theory or of organizational preference. There were legitimate differences of opinion, of course, but what happened? The intensity of the strife, the intensity of enmity, the emotional hardships, seemed totally out of keeping with what, I would say, was the rationalized explanation generally given for the dissension. When I observed somebody who had formerly been a friend of analysis and now had become critical, or had turned against the organization, I began to listen less to the theoretical reasons that were given from a great armamentarium of their bright thoughts. There are many bright people, and the brighter they are, the better their explanations, but these do not really explain very much.

I began to consider the point at which dissension arose. To which committee that an individual wanted to be appointed was he then not appointed? For which particular office was he defeated in an election? Did that perhaps precede his change of mind about the theoretical validity of the libido theory or something on that order? More times than not I could indeed find that something of this type had occurred. I do not say that good thoughts cannot come from irrational motives. Nor do I say that the criticism, let us say, of the libido theory, because it was triggered by someone's being defeated in an election, is therefore invalid. No. Obviously one still has to listen and to examine the lines of thought that are being presented. However, it is the very irrationality with which these battles are fought, the intensity of the feelings that goes far beyond what the theoretical difference would warrant, which illuminates what is occurring.

There is a special way in which people react to certain ambitions, to the ways in which they want to present themselves, particularly in groups. Why is this so? How is it different from being with just one other person? When an adult is in a group, particularly in a group of his professional peers, he is there in a slightly regressive situation. His self-esteem is really on the line. It echoes something from the distant past of the individual, when the beginning of his self-esteem was indeed dependent on supplies from the outside. Our exhibitionism, or the exhibitionism of our body, as it later becomes the exhibitionism of our mind, our performance, our goodness, and our morality had their beginnings in acceptance—the echo from the outside. In our slightly regressive position in a group, we want the nod and we resent it and feel desperate when we do not get it.

In certain group situations, something of this old feeling is poignantly revived, and under such circumstances we react regressively to disappointments. Our self-esteem sinks, we feel low, and we feel vengeful against those people who do not give us what we wanted and expected from them—praise, election to office, appointment to a committee, acceptance of our theories, or whatever it may be. So this particular rage or sensitivity has a certain phenomenological flavor. There is something highly specific that defies exact definition, that defies anyone's writing it up in the way one can, perhaps, write up sensory impressions. If properly evoked, all of us will recognize a psychological state; yet when asked to write it down in ironclad definitions, one always fails.

We rely so much in analysis or depth psychology on some common experience. The skill of communication in our field is not in ultimate detail and description. This seems strange and is regrettable, making it a little different from other sciences in that respect. The skill lies in the capacity to evoke similar recognition of basic experience in others.

Now, having pointed out something about the vulnerability of self-esteem, and therefore about the phenomenology of self-esteem, let me turn to ideals. Is there something similar in the way in which we experience our ideals, our values, to what I just said about our common self-esteem—namely, our ambition to get somewhere and to have our success confirmed by others? On first sight it seems very different. And yet, even without appealing to what undoubtedly many of you already know as the theoretical underpinning of this likeness, let me evoke once more your empathic recognition of a certain similarity. There is an absoluteness about our demands for self-esteem, and we only painfully learn (we never learn it completely or really well) that we must share it, that it is limited. As you know, even what we replace for the original self-esteem, even the height of replacement, which I refer to as wisdom, is only a new form of narcissism. There has really been no curbing, there has only been a shift to another and perhaps higher level. There is a pride in wisdom, acquired pride perhaps, but there is again something very narcissistic about being wise, too. In the direct experience of the vicissitudes of our ideals, there is something quite similar.

People are very touchy about ideals. Values may change in the course of a life, but there is always a degree of absoluteness about whatever nuclear value system one has at any given time, a degree of anger and rage when it is being attacked.

Let me give you a very timely example. As you know, there has been a great clash of value systems, of ideals, at the present time in our nations. There are the new ideals, characterized particularly by college youth, general human ideals that transcend the national ones. There are also strong nationalistic feelings, symbolized by the American flag and espoused, for example, by the construction workers, to use recent clashes on Wall Street as an example. It is easy enough for most of us who espouse a particular value system to say theirs is an old-fashioned, backward value system. And yet, we cannot make any progress in understanding the reaction of certain groups of the population unless we begin to be empathic with the absoluteness and position of a newly acquired value system. Who makes up the central group that now feels deeply offended when the American flag is turned upside down or burned? Who feels deeply offended when idealistic groups of people refuse to serve the country in the current war? Of course, a variety of people feel this way, but I am considering a group which I think is particularly important to understand, the construction workers. Who are they? They are usually people of lower-middle class who own their own homes in a comparatively cheap rental suburb. They are the sons or the grandsons of immigrants. They have known something about their fathers and grandfathers—namely, that they were new here, that they were insecure in their own standing and their own self-esteem. They have gradually come to the point where they have formed something solid about themselves.

One of the great buttressing forces of this newly found solidity is indeed that they are Americans, and the flag means something terribly important to them. The mere sight of people who dress in a different way from the way they have learned to dress, as it were, in this genera-tion—to have a hair-cut different from a style they have just learned to espouse as neat—to tear down that flag that they have just learned to put in the center of their value system—these threaten them deeply in the very core of their security. They react with the same kind of rage and destructiveness toward those who belittle, tear down this deep sense of inner value clustered around this particular value system, as we show when we have striven for a particular theoretical position that is not being examined or a particular administrative job with some prestige that is not given to us. I do not say that we should therefore consider all values as relative, and therefore values have no value, as it were. No. Values should be fought for and thought about, but they also need some understanding. Otherwise, there is no possibility of communication.

The narcissistic tensions between people play a role in group life—in the group life of the nation, and among nations—that corresponds to the drive conflicts, the structural conflicts in the individual neuroses (Kohut, 1966). The rage, the anger, the "rather die"—and really rather die—have deep roots. These roots are at the basis of individual development.

What I have said so far is that, phenomenologically disparate as self-esteem and ideals are, when they are looked upon with a little sophisti-cation, something seems to unite them. There is some relatedness and absoluteness. Values or ideals may change in a lifetime, yet, like fashions with which they have something in common, each time a value system is created it is absolute—the central one. If one were to say that some individuals have as a central value system the fact that values are rela-tive, or that values have to be scientifically examined, then that too is a value system. One cannot escape. This particular attitude of dispassion-ate judgment toward even the most prized possession of mankind has become your leading value at any given moment of your life. It may change in ten years, and you may have struggled through to another opinion, but then this central value system will be fought about just as strongly, and with just as much anger when it is attacked, as it would be now.

Now having established, or at least evoked, in you a sense of the similarity in something as disparate as values and self-esteem, let us examine their common root. As you know, psychoanalysis has one enor-mous theoretical tool—namely, it is a developmental psychology. We examine things not only as they are, but also as they were—their history, preferably to the point of their origin. Of course things change. They may start the same way, but they end up very differently. In develop-mental psychology this is called change of function. We know that the establishment of a common origin will perhaps tell us something about similar properties, about the possibilities for change over from one to another, and about similar reactivities, which otherwise would remain totally unintelligible.

With these concepts of ideals and self-esteem, we proceed in the traditional manner of psychoanalysis which, perhaps, I can, for most of you, quickly evoke by reminding you of that great contribution, despite its shortcomings, originally made by Sigmund Freud (1908) and Karl Abraham (1927). They wrote about certain character types in terms of a particular drive element. When I mention an anal character, a urethral character, a phallic personality, an oral personality, you will immediately know to what I refer. We can smile in benign fashion about the shortcomings of such beginnings.

We know there is more to personality formation than the simple drive dominance or drive orientation in a particular individual. Yet I would plead with you, at this moment, not to think of the shortcomings of these particular designations, but to realize what an enormous piece of progress was made by the discovery of such personality types. How is it that such strangely different features as parsimony, politeness, exactness, kindness, overkindness, orderliness—totally different phenomena—occur at the same time as clusters in particular people? The mere conception that there was something in the background of the drive developmental history of individuals that ended up creating certain clusters of such complexity as exactness, politeness, and cleanliness was a tremendous step forward. It is similar, it seems to me, to the kind of step taken to arrive at the fact that, although diamonds and coal are as different as diamonds and coal, yet there is something that they have in common.

Now how can we apply this to an understanding of self-esteem and ideals? Let me remind you that both self-esteem and what later becomes our system of ideals come from the same root. We assume that there is a prepsychological state. It is often referred to as primary narcissism, in which the psychobiological unit is at some time in balance, an approximation to perfect balance, yet with its disturbances and fluctuations, which always go hand in hand. I do not mention psychology here, because there is not even a rudiment of self-observation possible, and therefore no real capacity to think oneself empathically into this rudimentary self-observation. Whether this is during the fetal period, or quickly replaced during the neonatal period when the mother provides, or the external environment provides, this kind of balance, we do not know. But it is likely that here are indeed the roots of what later becomes differentiated into many qualities of perfection.

We also know that this original sense of balance cannot last. It cannot last because of the imperfection of the greatest of all instruments for the maintenance of narcissistic balance in all of us, whether we are babies or whether we are grown people—the imperfection of this greatest of all narcissism-balancing instruments—namely, empathy. The mother, being empathic and responsive to the needs of the child, cannot be perfectly empathic. She must fail sooner or later, she must delay, and the child will find something wrong. The original bliss, perfection, or balance is now gone. He tries to reestablish it in two totally different yet simultaneously established ways: by creating a perfection in himself, which is the future of all self-esteem, ambition, and striving for self-perfection; and by creating it on the outside, which is the future of all outside omnipotence, outside perfection, and finally, outside ideals.

We create this self-esteem by feeling perfect about our bodies, about our self, about our self-experience. But from the very beginning, this perfection of our self-esteem, this wish to exhibit and say, "Look, whatever I am, I am I," all this is aided and abetted by the empathic mother's responsiveness. There is a continuous flow from the responsiveness of the mother's gleam in her eye, her reactivity to the child's exhibitionism. We never totally rid ourselves of this need.[2] You may say, in theory, we should, and that we should create our own self-esteem. We do, up to a point. We are less dependent on others. Our best achievement is that, though we need it, we can wait. We think of past successes without becoming upset by the absence of an immediate response. But on the whole, we have eyes open and feelers out in all directions. With every word I speak, I look to see if you are listening to me. With every moment that you look at me, you want to see whether I am really talking to you or whether I am totally absorbed in my own thoughts. This is why a freely spoken paper or a talk in general is much easier to listen to than something that is being read. Someone who reads a paper is not with the audience. He is involved with himself. The audience strains and tries very hard to listen but, essentially, they feel left out; they do not feel involved. Secondarily, they think, "This guy is trying very hard. He has prepared something very carefully. He has done it for us. It really is worthwhile. I'll get something out of it," but basically they will be going to sleep. You laugh—you are not asleep. Well, so much about the self-esteem.

---

[2]One can see the beginnings, here, of Kohut's later conceptualization of the selfobject—its necessity in the creation of the self in infancy, the consolidation of the self in childhood, and the sustenance of the self throughout life.

The other, of course, is the omnipotent other—the omnipotent outside person, not yet experienced by the child as totally different from himself. It is the other who carries his omnipotence and carries him. Some of the great narcissistic fantasies—for example, the fantasy that one is able to fly—are related to the soaring of our intellect, the enjoyment of our expansiveness toward new thoughts, and exploration of new areas. This is one of the permanent contributions of early life, which depends on an omnipotent other who carries you empathically. In the history of the saints, Christopher, who carries the Christ child (the mother who carries the baby) is the symbol. If there is a disturbance in the omnipotent empathy of the other, it will be reflected in the later idealizations that we internalize. Freud's great early discovery about group psychology was that ideals bind the members of groups together. Individual members of a group identify with an idea, an ideal, or someone who is the personification of an ideal they have in common.

The pertinence of this understanding of the common root of self-esteem and ideals in your work with youth and young adults in the Student Mental Health Clinic lies in the fact that there is something in the second decade of life that repeats the first decade and its troubles before the permanent settlement of a comparatively stable personality takes place. The vicissitudes of the conflicts, the passions of the oedipal period, the jealousies, the competitions, the defeats, the victories of this period, are again repeated early in adolescence, early in puberty. During this period of change, under the impact of the newly established drive balance, under the impact of biological genital maturation, the old conflicts of the oedipal period are revived. And late adolescence I believe relates to the earliest period of the establishment of the self, the earliest period of the vicissitudes of self and ideal precursor formations—namely, the omnipotent, idealized objects—in the same way that early adolescence relates to the oedipal period.

It is clear why this would be so. This is a period of great new demands of the individual. Childhood will forever be past. School will soon be over. Independence will be reached. An enormous reshuffling, an enormous change in outlook, a totally new self-concept has to be established, and a whole new set of values corresponding to the new tasks has to be set up. Any severe and violent change, whether in personal development or in the development of a people, historically, economically, always creates insecurities, always creates tremendous imbalances. It is under the impact of this particular great change from adolescence to adulthood that many of the old insecurities concerning the self and the ideals are revived. This is normal, and up to a point it must be that way. Intense suffering during this period, intense psychopathology, has

something to do with the earliest insecurities, because the early establishment of reliance on omnipotent objects and their incorporation in the
form of reliable ideals has been disturbed.

The insecurities of late adolescence and early adulthood become the
trigger which revives deep fixation points around psychopathological
insecurities or potential insecurities of earliest life. It is under these
circumstances, then, that we see a revival of old insecurities, swings into
lowered self-esteem, simultaneously with an arrogant, absolutely certain
righteousness about who one is and what one is. The same occurs in the
realm of ideals—an absolute certainty about the ideals that are being
formed at that time, simultaneously with total questioning of whether
values still have any value at all.

Many of the well-known phenomena of adolescence through which
every generation goes, with different contents, modes of suffering, and
different kinds of creative solutions are familiar to everyone here. The
relationship between past and present, depth and surface, immature
and mature, archaic and developed, is of course the essence of our study
in psychopathology. As we examine much of the psychopathology
which we are studying and trying to understand, we can observe the
influence of past phases of development; these exert a disturbing influence upon mature function. If there is a fixation on masturbatory impulses present, a writer's cramp may ensue because writing becomes, as
it were, invaded by the old impulse to masturbate—or whatever the
simple hysterical symptom may resolve itself into. I am trying to show
something which, although it is occasionally mentioned, to my mind is
not mentioned with the emphasis it really deserves, namely, the positive
relationship between archaic and non-archaic, between immature and
mature.

The myth of rational man, like the myth of economic man, is something that is unfortunately hard to shake off. There is a narcissistic reason for this. We do not like to think of ourselves as being supported by
irrational and immature forces. Recently, in the development of psychoanalytic or depth psychological thought, this prejudice has taken on a
specific shape. It goes by the name of ego autonomy. It would suggest
that there is something on the surface of the personality that functions
all by itself. It is part and parcel of a healthy, properly balanced individual to be capable of using an autonomous ego, of working with the surface
of his mind.

You remember the analogy which Freud used when he introduced the
great reshuffling of his theory in the 1920s, the relationship of ego and
id, the structural model of the mind. It was the marvelous analogy of the
rider and the horse (Freud, 1933, p. 108). When he walks he is not likely

to be thrown. He can do all kinds of things but there are many things he cannot do when he is off the horse. He has to lead the horse along all the time, unless he lets the horse run wild, which he is not able to do. The autonomous ego keeps the horse in check. But there are certain things he cannot do. He cannot move very fast or jump over hurdles. He cannot, with any degree of triumphant pleasure, ride into new areas. What is needed is the rider *on* the horse who *controls* the horse. In other words, I think there is a difference between ego autonomy and ego dominance.

Ego dominance means that the enormous powers of the horse, the primitiveness, the vital forces are there. Its forces are being used, but tamed, for the purposes of the rider. He gives the horse free rein when he wants to, reins it in when he needs to go more slowly, and even gets off the horse when particular circumstances demand it. Freud knew this, although he never systematically studied it, for reasons that would be very interesting to investigate. He knew this when he made the often quoted statement that the firstborn son of a young mother receives from the mother's reaction the feeling of a conqueror, a feeling which will indeed lead into actual success. The small child who is the apple of the eye of a biologically well-functioning, responsive young mother, the firstborn son is infused with a feeling of utter self-confidence. It has to be tamed. It has to come under ego dominance through the vicissitudes of long development, about which we know a great deal. Nevertheless, deep down, although filtered through many disappointing experiences, something of it is retained.

I have stressed that narcissism is not bad, a thought that is opposed to the long established western value system of altruism under the Judeo-Christian influences of the last 2,000 years. We should learn to realize that some of our highest achievements and highest values are follow-up stages, under ego dominance, within the realm of the development of narcissism itself.

This leaves us with one final negative statement, namely, that pathological narcissism is obviously not to be desired. I even have a little objection there. At least, I want to consider it further. It is certainly a negative force in such clinical pictures as the schizophrenias, the depressions, and the less gross, common and analyzable ones in which we are all involved, namely, the so-called narcissistic personality disturbances, with their own fixations and their own hypersensitivities. We may say, on the face of it, that it should be overcome; it is bad narcissism; it interferes with our functions. But even here I have a slight doubt, for the following reasons.

Let us consider normality—I do not know what that is, really, but I assume that it evokes some imagery in all of us. There have been papers on normal cycles of groups who supposedly are in good shape. They like baseball. They like to have beer, but not too much. They like light literature, but not too much. They like their house, their wife, their children, and quite a bit. In other words, somewhere there is something normal that is to be striven for. These are not people in whom narcissism in its cruder or archaic forms is particularly an interference. And we would say, "Three cheers!" This is really something to be striven for.

In our work we are trying to help our patients and ourselves to overcome archaic narcissistic fixations and to move to a certain degree of normalcy. It does not have to be this funny kind we all smiled about. I do not want to demean this really. And yet, how does so much narcissistic fixation come about? No patient I have ever encountered is free of narcissistic problems. At least a third of our patients have this as the leading psychopathology, the central one, the nuclear one around which the tide has to be turned. People argue with me and say it must be two-thirds. Has this always been so, or is this something recent? Is it only that our attention has been sharpened so that we diagnose it more, or is it indeed increasing? I do not know the answer to that but I believe that it may be on the increase, and the question is, "Why?"

I think that normality and balance, though desirable, go against the grain of life in some way. Normality is not experimental. It is stable. It is set in its way. It no longer tries. It seems to me that everyone's psychopathology is an attempt to find some new balance. Nature works in an unplanned way, by millions and millions of failures, trying to find one positive result which survives. This is the essence of Darwinism supplied here now in the field of psychology.

Does this apply to the task of mankind? I think it does. As civilization progresses, think of the problems in its wake: overpopulation, the enormity of our aggressive capacities for destructiveness, the common clichés that are being complained about by anyone who wants to play Cassandra and to get his narcissistic gratification from predicting the doom of mankind tomorrow if not today. These complaints have a certain validity. Their validity is that certain ways in which the human organism or the human psyche could express itself in the past, and yet survive, will soon be incompatible with survival. One could kill with a spear and many people would survive; with hydrogen bombs no one would survive. One could move about restlessly and roam so long as there was place and space to roam in; but now there are fewer places and spaces.

In other words, the tremendous adaptive demand of mankind (contrary, I believe, to what most sociologically oriented people think) is not new social institutions. They are necessary too. The adaptive demand now is for a significant inner change, for the capacity to enjoy life—enjoyment being an indicator of successful living to some extent—to live with an increase of inner activities that gradually begin to replace other activities. Much of what we call culture is indeed just that. The enjoyment of people when they see a play by Sophocles or Shakespeare or when they listen to music is not action; it is an inner enjoyment. A genius has found a way of giving us a rich experience without our having to fight or to strive, without our having to move our bodies particularly. This is a mode of trying to come to some kind of a new balance in a future in which I think the inner life of man will have to be enriched and will have to replace a great deal.

This is the final thought with which I would like to leave you. I wonder whether some of the aspects of this increase of narcissistic psychopathology are not perhaps nature's way, by internal psychological attempts, wastefully, by millions and billions of failures perhaps, to find that kind of mutation toward inner life and toward the enrichment of inner life that is truly a solution which will allow us to survive. Thank you.

References

Abraham, K. (1949), Object loss and introjection in normal mourning and in abnormal states of mind, *Selected Papers of Karl Abraham*, pp. 442–443. London: Hogarth Press; New York: Basic Books, 1953.

_____ (1927), Contributions to the theory of the anal character, *Selected Papers of Karl Abraham*. London: Hogarth Press; New York: Basic Books, 1953.

Burlingham, D., and Robertson, J. (1966), "Nursery School for the Blind." Film produced by The Hampstead Child Therapy Clinic, London. (Distributor in the U.S.: NYU Film Library, 26 Washington Place, NY, NY 10003.)

Camus, A. (1946), *The Stranger*. New York: A. A. Knopf and Random House. Originally published in French 1942, *L'Etranger*, Libraire Gallimard.

Churchill, W. (1942), *My Early Life*. New York: Macmillan.

Coleridge, S. T. (1907), *Bibliographia Literaria*, Chapter 14, p. 6. Oxford: Clarendon Press.

Deutsch, H. (1942), Some forms of emotional disturbances and their relationship to schizophrenia. *Psychoanalytic Quarterly*, 11:301–321.

_____ (1965), *Neurosis and Character Types*, pp. 262–286. New York: International Universities Press.

Erikson, E. H. (1956), The problem of ego identity. *Journal of the American Psychoanalytic Association*, 4:56–121.

Ferenczi, S. (1950), On influencing the patient in psychoanalysis: *Further Contributions to the Theory and Technique of Psychoanalysis*. New York; Brunner/Mazel, 1980, pp. 235–237.

Freud, A. (1963), The concept of developmental lines, *Psychoanalytic Study of the Child*, 18:245–265.

_____ and Dann, V. (1951), An experiment in group upbringing. *The Psychoanalytic Study of the Child*, 6:127–168

_____ (1965), *Normality and Pathology in Childhood*. New York: International Universities Press.

Freud, S. (1900), The interpretation of dreams, *The Standard Edition of the Complete Psychological Works* (hereafter referred to as *S.E.*). Vol. IV:157.New York: Norton.

_____ (1905a), Three essays on the theory of sexuality, *S.E.*, Vol. VII:125–231. New York: Norton.

_____ (1905b), Jokes and their relationship to the unconscious, *S.E.*, Vol. VIII:229. New York: Norton.

_____ (1908), Character and anal erotism. *Collected Papers*, II:pp. 45–50. New York: Basic Books.

_____ (1910a), The psychoanalytic view of psychogenic disturbance of vision, *S.E.*, Vol. XI:209–218. New York: Norton.

_____ (1910b), Wild psychoanalysis, *S.E.*, Vol. XI:219–227. New York: Norton.

_____ (1911a), Psycho-analytical notes on an autobiographical account of a case of paranoia (Dementia Paranoides), *S.E.*, Vol. XII:3–82. New York: Norton.

_____ (1911b), Formulations on the two principles of mental functioning, *S.E.*, Vol. XII:213–226. New York: Norton.

_____ (1914a), Remembering, repeating and working through, *S.E.*, Vol. XII:147–171. New York: Norton.

_____ (1914b), History of the psychoanalytic movement, *S.E.*, Vol. XIV:7–66. New York: Norton.

_____ (1914c), On narcissism: An introduction, *S.E.*, Vol. XIV:67–102. New York: Norton.

_____ (1915a), Instincts and their vicissitudes, *S.E.*, Vol. XIV:117–140. New York: Norton.

_____ (1915b), Thoughts for the times on war and death, *S.E.*, Vol. XIV:273–300. New York: Norton.

_____ (1916), The "exceptions," *S.E.*, Vol. XIV:311–315. New York: Norton.

_____ (1920), Beyond the pleasure principle, *S.E.*, Vol. XVIII:3–64. New York: Norton.

_____ (1921), Group psychology and the analysis of the ego, *S.E.*, Vol. XVIII:69–143. New York: Norton.

_____ (1923), The ego and the id, *S.E.*, Vol. XIX:23–66. New York: Norton.

_____ (1926), Inhibitions, symptoms and anxiety, *S.E.*, Vol. XX:87–174. New York: Norton.

_____ (1933 [1932]a), New introductory lectures on psycho-analysis, *S.E.*, Vol. XXII. New York: Norton.

_____ (1933 [1932]b), Dissection of the psychical personality, *S.E.*, Vol. XXII:57–80. New York: Norton.

_____ (1933 [1932]c), Anxiety and instinctual life, *S.E.*, Vol. XXII:81–111. New York: Norton.

_____ (1937), Analysis terminable and interminable, *S.E.*, Vol. XXIII:216–253. New York: Norton.

Gittings, R. (1968), *John Keats*. Boston: Little, Brown, p. 152f.

Glover, E. (1956), The concept of dissociation in the early development of the mind, *International Journal of Psychoanalysis*, 24:7–13.

Greenacre, P. (1957), The childhood of the artist, *Psychoanalytic Study of the Child*, 12:47–72.

_____ (1960), Woman as artist, *Psychoanalytic Quarterly*, 29:208–227.

Greenson, R. R. (1967), *Technique and Practice of Psychoanalysis*. New York: New York University Press.

_____ (1965), The working alliance and the transference neurosis, *Psychoanalytic Quarterly*, 34:155–181.

Hartmann, H. (1958[1939]), *Ego Development and Adaptation*. New York: International Universities Press.

_____ (1972), *Der Grundlagen die Psychoanalyse*. Klett Verlag, Stuttgart.

Horney, K. (1934), The overvaluation of love: A study of a common present-day feminine type, *Psychoanalytic Quarterly*, 3:605–638.

Jones, E. (1957), *The Life and Work of Sigmund Freud*, Vol. 3:144–145, 246. New York: Basic Books, Inc.

Klein, M. (1932), *The Psychoanalysis of Children*. London: Hogarth Press.

_____ (1957), *Envy and Gratitude*. London: Tavistock Publication.

Kohut, H. (1959), Introspection, empathy and psychoanalysis. In P. Ornstein (ed.) *The Search for the Self*, Vol. I, Chapter 12. New York: International Universities Press, 1978.

_____ (1966), Forms and transformations of narcissism. In P. Ornstein (ed.) *The Search for the Self*, Vol. II, Chapter 32. New York: International Universities Press, 1978.

_____ (1968), The psychoanalytic treatment of narcissistic personality disorders, *The Psychoanalytic Study of the Child*, 23:86–113.

_____ (1970), Narcissism as a resistance and a driving force in psychoanalysis. In P. Ornstein (ed.), *The Search for the Self*, Vol. II:547–561. New York: International Universities Press, 1978.

_____ (1971a), Thoughts on narcissism and narcissistic rage. In P. Ornstein (ed.), *The Search for the Self*, Vol. II:615–658. New York: International Universities Press, 1978.

_____ (1971b), *The Analysis of the Self*. New York: International Universities Press.

_____ (1977), *The Restoration of the Self*. New York: International Universities Press.

_____ (1978), *The Search for the Self: Selected Writings of Heinz Kohut 1950–1958*, Vols. I & II, edited by P. Ornstein. New York: International Universities Press.

_____ (1984), *How Does Analysis Cure?* Chicago: University of Chicago Press.

_____ and Seitz, P. (1963), Concepts and theories of psychoanalysis. In J. W. Wepman and R. W. Heine (Eds.). *Concepts of Personality*. Chicago: Aldine.

_____ and Wolf, E. S. (1978). Disorders of the self and their treatment, *International Journal of Psycho-Analysis, 59*:413–425.

Kris, E. (1934), *Psychoanalytic Explorations in Art*. New York: International Universities Press, 1952.

Krystal, H. (1969), *Massive Psychic Trauma*. New York: International Universities Press.

Ludwig, E. (1928), *Wilhelm II*. New York and London: G. P. Putnam Sons.

O'Neill, E. (1956), *Long Day's Journey into Night*. New Haven: Yale University Press.

Reik, T. (1953), *The Haunting Melody: Psychoanalytic Experience in Life, Literature and Music*. New York: Farrar, Straus and Young.

Schreber, D. P. (1903). *Denkwürdigkeiten eines Nervenkranken [Memoirs of a nerve patient]*.

Spitz, R. A. (1945), Hospitalism: An inquiry into the genesis of psychiatric conditions in early childhood, *Psychoanalytic Study of the Child, 1*:53–74.

_____ (1946), Hospitalism: A follow-up report, *Psychoanalytic Study of the Child, 2*:113–117.

Tolstoi, L. (1915), *The Death of Ivan Ilich*. Translated by Constance Garnett. London: Heineman.

Winnicott, D. W. (1951), Transitional objects and transitional phenomena, *International Journal of Psycho-analysis, 34*:89–97.

_____ (1968), *Through Paediatrics to Psychoanalysis*, Chapter 18. London: Hogarth Press; New York: Basic Books.

Index

object, 126
self-, 47
separation and, 40
character disorders, narcissistic vs.
    borderline, 82–83
children:
    autonomy conflict in, 104
    decathexis in, 149
    developmental autonomy in, 157
    fantasies of, 48
    idealized superego in, 41–42
    mirroring relationship of mothers and,
        38–40
    mirror transference in, 64
    narcissistic aspects of oedipal phase in,
        35–36
    narcissistic character disorders in, 44
    narcissistic equilibrium of, 51–52, 62–63
    object cathexis for, 126
    during oedipal period, 148–49
    oral jealousy of, 230
    phallic narcissism of, 35
    self-cathexis in, 47
    sleep disturbances in, 125
    structure building in, 100–101
    toilet training of, 104
    traumata in, 52, 234–35
    traumatic separation from parents of, 40
    see also babies
Churchill, Winston, 7
cohesive self, 26–27, 32, 33
    disintegration of, 42–43
    fragmented self and, 44
Coleridge, S. T., 4
combined silence as merger, 67
cores, 213, 215
    eliteness and, 213
    of narcissistic neuroses, 83
    psychotic, 83
creative activity, 274–75, 276, 277
creative genius, effect of analysis on,
    164–65
crypt-amnesia, 284

Darwin, Charles, 9
death, fear of, 63
"Death of Ivan Ilich, The" (Tolstoy), 195
decathexis, 149
depression:
    in adolescents, 227–28
    parental, 232, 235–36
Deutsch, Helene, 97
developmental potential, 44
disequilibrium:
    degrees of, 69

impotence as, 141
narcissistic, 61
drives:
    hunger satiation, 62
    infantile object libidinal, 237
    mobilized infantile, 101
    sexual, 62

ego, 78
    acting-out vs. action and, 260–78
    autonomous functions of, 100
    autonomy vs. dominance in, 307
    childhood memories and, 263
    crude exhibitionism and, 164
    dominance, reassertion of, 156
    empathic extension and, 195
    freeing of, 100
    Freud on, 263–64, 306–7
    id and, 306–7
    structure of, 103
    superego vs., 99
    supportive, 217
ego identity, 222, 223–24, 225
empathy:
    in building self-esteem, 203–21
    of caretaking adults, 52
    instrumentarium of, 218
    intuitive, 275–76
    mode of perception, 275–78
    narcissistic roots of, 30
    verbal, 218
Erikson, E. H., 6, 222–25
"Exceptions, The" (Freud), 296
exhibitionism, 11–12, 35, 158, 231, 300

fantasies, 145
    ambition linked to, 244
    confusing, 184
    flying, 79
    grandiose, 78, 226, 242, 245–47, 291
    hysterical, 45–46
    infantile, 148
    merger, 28
    sexual, 162
fate neuroses, 76
Ferenczi, S., 195
fixations, 6, 7, 166–67
    latent, 166
    on masturbatory impulses, 306
    oral sadistic, 13
    potential, 166
    regression linked to, 167–68
"Forms and Transformations of Narcis-
    sism" (Kohut), 61*n*
fragmented self, 33